BATTLING WESTERN IMPERIALISM

BATTLING
WESTERN IMPERIALISM

MAO, STALIN, AND THE
UNITED STATES

Michael M. Sheng

PRINCETON UNIVERSITY PRESS   PRINCETON, NEW JERSEY

Copyright © 1997 by Princeton University Press
Published by Princeton University Press, 41 William Street,
Princeton, New Jersey 08540
In the United Kingdom: Princeton University Press,
Chichester, West Sussex
All Rights Reserved

Library of Congress Cataloging-in-Publication Data
Sheng, Michael M., 1950–
Battling Western imperialism : Mao,
Stalin, and the United States / Michael M. Sheng.
p.   cm.   Includes bibliographical references and index.
ISBN 0-691-01635-6 (cloth : alk. paper)
1. China—Foreign relations—Soviet Union.   2. Soviet Union—
Foreign relations—China.   3. China—Foreign relations—United States.
4. United States—Foreign relations—China.   5. Mao, Tse-tung,
1893–1976—Contributions in international relations.
6. Chung-kuo kung ch' an tang—history.   I. Title.
DS740.5.S65S562   1997
327.51047—dc21   97-10035   CIP

This book has been composed in Times Roman

Princeton University Press books are printed
on acid-free paper, and meet the guidelines
for permanence and durability of the Committee
on Production Guidelines for Book Longevity
of the Council on Library Resources

http://pup.princeton.edu

Printed in the United States of America

1 3 5 7 9 10 8 6 4 2

TO MY CHILDREN

———————— Julie and Michael Jr. ————————

WITH LOVE

Contents

Acknowledgments

THIS STUDY could not have gone this far without help from many. Since it is based on my doctoral dissertation at York University, my first and foremost thanks goes to Professor Jerome Chen. A helpful supervisor and caring friend, Jerome is the most wonderful mentor any graduate student could ever hope for. Before my doctoral program, my master's degree program at the University of New Brunswick laid the first building blocks for this study, and Fredericton is the first place I lived outside China. Although I have lived in many other places in North America since then, Fredericton remains in my heart and mind the second hometown. I wish to express my gratitude to Dr. Larry Shyu, my thesis supervisor, and Dr. Peter Kent, then the Director of Graduate Programs, now the Dean of Arts. Their assistance and friendship carried me through the first two years of my overseas intellectual and career pursuit. A special thanks goes to Ms. Linda Baier, whose companionship covered my entire graduate school years, and whose careful proofreading made my writing process successful.

This study, however, goes far beyond my doctoral dissertation. In the process of further research and rewriting, many colleagues and friends offered me invaluable advice, insights, encouragement, and other forms of assistance. I am indebted to Professor John L. Gaddis, who read the entire manuscript and encouraged me to submit it to Princeton University Press. As a reader for the Press, Dr. Steven Levine's comments were particularly valuable and thought-provoking. Professor Warren Cohen read a number of my articles, which were stepping stones to this end product, and encouraged my continued enquiry by involving me in scholarly discussion in the form of various conferences and workshops. Dr. Chen Jian, a respected colleague whose friendship can be traced back to the early 1980s when we taught history together at the Tibetan National College, has been very generous in sharing his thoughts and materials with me. Drs. Steven Goldstein, Michael Hunt, Douglas Macdonald, Daniel Teodoru, Odd Arne Westad, and many others, have read either the whole, or a part, of my manuscript in different stages, and their comments, criticism, and encouragement are deeply cherished. I am, of course, the only one who is responsible for the opinions expressed in this book.

I owe a great deal to my friends and fellow scholars in Beijing, whose insights and various assistance given in the form of interviews, casual and formal discussions, and correspondence are invaluable to my studies. Special thanks go to Jin Chongjie, Li Ping, Niu Jun, Tao Wenzhao, Xu Yan, Yang Kuisong, and Zhang Baijia; others prefer to remain anonymous.

My children, Julie and Michael, Jr., weren't with me physically all the time during the past years when I was laboring on this project; their smiles and laughter, nonetheless, were always with me, providing an enormous amount of strength and courage. This book is dedicated to them.

BATTLING WESTERN IMPERIALISM

Introduction

THIS STUDY deals with the Chinese Communist Party (CCP)'s relations with the United States and the Soviet Union in the fifteen years prior to the proclamation of the People's Republic of China (PRC) in October 1949. Our story starts from Mao Zedong's rise to power within the Party in 1935; when the story ends, Mao had become the paramount leader of the new Republic, and was about to go to Moscow to forge a military alliance with Joseph Stalin's Soviet Union. The subsequent two decades of history in the Asian-Pacific region were earmarked with the Korean War, the Vietnam War, and the cold war antagonism of hostile confrontations between the United States and Mao's PRC. The period under discussion was a formative and crucial one in CCP history in which the Party not only transformed itself from a group of defeated "bandits," as the Guomindang (GMD) put it, to the ultimate ruler of China, but also prepared itself for handling the outside world with an established outlook of international politics and patterns of behavior in the diplomatic arena. Suffice it to say, a fine understanding of the origins of CCP foreign policy before 1949 is essential to the study of the PRC's foreign policy as well as the Beijing-Moscow-Washington relations in the decades to follow.

To understand the CCP's foreign relations, one faces the issue of the role of ideology in the foreign policy process. Some scholars are of the opinion that "the Chinese Communists acted not according to some ideology or vision of world order, but simply in response to the limits and opportunities of the situation they found themselves in."[1] Others assert that compared with national interest and security concerns, ideology "played a secondary role" in shaping Mao's decisions, and that the Marxist-Leninist language of the CCP was more rhetorical than meaningful in realpolitik. Since both Mao and Stalin were driven by "pure nationalism and naked power" of their own, they were more antagonists than comrades. This line of interpretation ultimately leads to the "lost chance" argument which assumes that Washington's uneven-handed China policy pushed the CCP to form a reluctant alliance with Moscow, and the United States thus lost a chance to strike a favorable balance in postwar Asia.[2]

Apparently, the "lost chance" argument is associated with neorealism, which was influential in the academic discourse of international politics in the 1970s and 1980s. This neorealism, in E. P. Thompson's view, abolishes the role of "agents" in the making of history, and what is left is a "totalizing anti-historical structure" in which men and women are the objects, not the makers, of their circumstances, and the dominant structures are not social classes, but modern states. According to a key neorealist principle, in the autonomy of the political sphere, the emphasis is on power, national interest, and the historically effective agency of the state, while the attributes of individual actors' subjective perceptions played no significant role in constituting and reproducing the "system" or "structure."[3]

A fundamental question emerges here: whether or not all Chinese leaders of various political-ideological persuasions shared one single idea about what China's "national interest" was and how to bring it about. Was there a sociopolitical program of Chinese nationalism which was universally accepted by the one-quarter of the human race who claimed to be Chinese? The answer of the "nationalism theory" seems to be affirmative and its notion of Chinese nationalism comes close to what Professor John Fairbank termed "cultural nationalism," which stresses "a strong sense of identity and onetime cultural superiority."[4]

I recognize that although the Chinese ethnic identity and the collective memory of the past were important sources of nationalism, nationalism is not just a sense of identity and shared past, which had existed in China long before the birth of modern nationalism in Europe. If there is a well-defined Chinese nationalism, what are the essential contents of it? Scholars who have attended this question had a hard time finding a list of ideals, myths, symbols, heroes, and values which were "basic to orientations toward the nation-state" of China. Even the famous Great Wall has hardly become a symbol of China's greatness for its own people, while the westerners seem to be more enthusiastic about it than the Chinese. This suggests that although China has a long history of great civilization, its modern nationalism remains "nascent and amorphous," and it was somehow "shanghaied."[5] The question this begs is: How can such an amorphous "nationalism" with only a sense of ethnic identity and past glory possibly serve as an explanatory framework for China's recent diplomatic history to interpret different political parties' foreign policies?[6]

Even if a well-defined modern Chinese nationalism had existed, it would still have been inadequate in explaining the CCP's foreign policy. For as its specificity is understood, nationalism locates the source of individual identity within a "people" which is always seen as "fundamentally homogeneous" and only "superficially" divided by the lines of status, class, locality, and so on.[7] Nationalism, therefore, is blind to the sociopolitical and religious-ideological divisions within a nation, assuming that all the members of the nation share a common identity and loyalty. China's reality before 1949, however, was that the nation was deeply divided since the collapse of the ancient dynastic system in 1911, and the GMD's nation-building effort, constantly under attack by the Japanese from without and the CCP from within, was essentially a failure. The image of a "holistic" China with its people sharing one identity and being loyal to one "state" is only a myth. The Communists were the first ones to deny the "homogeneity" of the people and to promote class struggle within the nation even long after they gained national power.[8]

In fact, the "holistic image" of China was originally created and "sedulously propagated" by China's ruling class, which insisted that China was an integrated society and culture, distinct and persistent in its own ways. Initially conveyed by Jesuits centuries ago, the West has come to accept this myth even to this day.[9] Behind this mythical "harmonious" facade, however, the articulate and politically active Chinese failed to reach a consensus on a general program for China's nation-building and modernization: the CCP was on the left; the GMD on the right. True enough, they all shared the Chinese identity and cultural pride, but when it boils down to what the ideal for China was and how to bring it about, they represented two opposing ideologies which in turn provided two conflicting sociopolitical programs at home and two foreign policies compatible to their respective domestic agenda. They were locked in a life-and-death struggle from beginning to end, attempting to physically annihilate each other to prevent their enemy's "ideas" from being fulfilled. Like many other self-styled revolutionaries before and after them, the Communists pitched against the establishments of China's nation-state under the GMD; therefore, they would naturally denounce "nationalism," which held the national authority sacred. Instead, they espoused a "higher moral authority," namely, international communism, which transcended the boundaries of any nation-state. Given the Chinese "all under Heaven" psyche of cultural universalism, one should keep in mind that "international communism" did not sound as "evil" in China as it did, and does, in the capitalist and nationalist West.

If the GMD espoused "narrow bourgeois nationalism," it was what Mao called "proletarian internationalism" that molded the minds and souls of the Mao generation of partisans. Their patriotism (*aiguo zhuyi*), a term chosen to differentiate themselves from "bourgeois nationalists," was highly conditional: China as a nation would deserve love and devotion only when it was totally transformed according to their ideas, for "all that which lay in the past [of China] was wrong and evil."[10] On the eve of his conversion to communism, Mao was convinced that "the decadence of the state, the sufferings of humanity, and the darkness of society have all reached an extreme," and he desired no less than a "complete transformation, like matter that takes form after destruction." His revolutionary outlook soon led him to embrace internationalism, and to identify Lenin's Russia, not China, as "the number one civilized country in the world."[11] It is abundantly clear that Mao and his comrades were attracted to a pro-Soviet position principally because of their spiritual-ideological conversion. In contrast, Sun Yat-sen and his successor, Jiang Jieshi, befriended Moscow early in the 1920s and again in 1937–40 only because they wanted Moscow's military aid; and they flatly rejected the Soviet sociopolitical system from beginning to end. The opposing belief systems of the CCP and the GMD made the former born to be pro-Soviet, and the latter pro-West.[12]

The core of Mao's "proletarian internationalism" lay in the doctrine of "class struggle." As Schram points out, Mao displayed no interest in Marx's writings such as *The 18 Brumaire of Louis Bonaparte*, but was deeply intrigued by *The Communist Manifesto*, from which the essential message for Mao was "*Jieji douzheng, jieji douzheng, jieji douzheng*" (Class struggle, class struggle, class struggle)![13] Following Lenin's idea that socialism "is the ideology of struggle of the proletarian class" against its class enemy, Mao consistently saw the struggle between the rulers and the ruled, the oppressors and the oppressed, and the haves and the have-nots as the locomotive of historical progression from one stage to the next until the communist society came into being. If Marxism is a systematic complex of thoughts, Mao's understanding of it was more simplistic than comprehensive. To him, Marxism-Leninism was a "philosophy of struggle." The simplistic nature of Maoism with a distinct accent on class struggle doctrine made Mao inherently a radical, and he claimed shortly before his death that class struggle would continue for ten thousand years, although he had almost destroyed the CCP by waging class struggle within the Party. To rectify the Cultural Revolution of Mao's making, his successors had to announce an end to "class struggle." Since this "struggle outlook" was so essentially characteristic of Mao's ideology, I term the hard core of Maoism "class struggle ideology," or "class struggle outlook," with realization of possible simplification of the complicity of Maoism as a system of its own.

Based on this radical outlook, the Mao generation viewed a "nation" as divided into different social classes, and a "state" as a class instrument, either to maintain the "evil" capitalism or to advance human society toward communism via a socialist stage in which "proletarian dictatorship" was the essence of the nation-state. As Chen Duxiu, one of the principal founders of the CCP, put it in 1920:

> I recognize the existence of only two "nations," the "nation" of the capitalists and the "nation" of the workers. At present the "nation" of the workers exists only in the Soviet Union. Everywhere else we have the "nation" of the capitalists.[14]

For the Mao generation, China as a "nation" ruled by the "state" of reactionary landlords and bourgeoisie did not deserve their devotion and loyalty. Rather, the CCP's revolution, with Soviet political advice and material assistance, aimed at the ultimate demise of the Chinese state under their class enemies. Thus, to uphold "Chinese nationalism" would not do the CCP any good in claiming legitimacy. A "higher" or "greater" moral value than modern nationalism had to be in place. Communism, to the CCP, not only represented the interest of the majority underdogs in the world, but also reflected the universal value of human society in the future. Because the Party symbolized the self-acclaimed higher moral value, it received the "mandate" to rule the "nation" and the "state."[15] Within the context of the traditional Chinese conceptual world, it is easy to understand that the CCP's ideological commitment to international communism was not only a preferred system of belief to those individuals, it also played a significant role in the Party's quest for national power. To offer an antithesis to neorealist theory which excludes ideology from realpolitik, I argue that the CCP ideology, as an essential component of this particular political culture, is the "soft core" of the power structure.[16]

Since they perceived every "nation" to be divided into two categories of "revolutionary classes" and "reactionary classes," and every state was dominated by one or the other category, Mao and his colleagues believed that the class nature of a state could foretell the government's attitude toward, and thus its relationship with, the CCP. As the state of the proletariat, the Soviet Union was naturally the comrade-state of the Party, while western capitalist states were the enemies; and the Chinese ruling classes were only the "running dog" of the western states.[17] This led the CCP to regard its own revolution in China as an integral part of the Moscow-led "world proletarian revolution," and an intimate but secret relationship between Moscow and the CCP persisted and prevailed despite all the twists and turns in the international politics in those years. Contrary to the hitherto prevalent western assumption that the Mao-Stalin relationship was characterized by "bitter memories and betrayal," recent historical evidence reveals that Mao was Stalin's chosen man in 1934–35, and he followed Moscow's instruction step by step almost religiously throughout the pre-1949 period. The Soviet political-institutional, psychological-spiritual, and military-strategic support was vital to the CCP's success, and Mao was grateful and obedient to Stalin.

On the other side of the coin, Mao's internationalism led him and his colleagues to identify the United States as the principal "foreign master" of the GMD and the main opponent of the world revolution. Only by following Moscow's "antifascist international united front," did Mao start to deal with the Americans on a "bedfellow" basis during World War II. This study will show that Mao's occasional flirtations with the United States were purely tactical in nature, and that at no time did Mao contemplate the possibility of forging a genuine long-term alignment with Washington at Moscow's expense. In fact, when the final defeat of Germany and Japan was in sight, Mao keenly anticipated the coming of the cold war between the Soviet Union and the United States, just as the CCP-GMD anti-Japanese united front would be replaced by a fierce confrontation after the Japanese were gone. Mao chose to identify the CCP-GMD postwar struggle as the reflection of the Soviet-American global conflict. Thus, his class struggle outlook led him to form a two-camp vision on the postwar international politics even before the end of the Pacific War. His worry of a possible U.S. intervention in China on behalf of the GMD further intensified his urge for a closer strategic and tactical coordination with Stalin in the postwar world politics.

This is, however, not to suggest that the CCP leaders of Mao's generation were tactless doctrinarians whose policy was determined by a few cut-and-dried ideological principles. On the contrary, as committed to the long-term revolutionary goal as they were, Mao and his comrades were at the same time flexible tacticians who were ready to make compromises and take detours to reach their ultimate goal, if the situation necessitated such undertakings. They not only found the united front doctrine in Leninist tenets to legitimize their tactical maneuvers, but also learned how to perfect it in practice through their domestic experience in dealing with the GMD and foreign experience in dealing with the Americans. The united front doctrine can be seen as an integral part of Maoist ideology, which thereby became dualistic in nature.[18]

Moreover, due to the fact that the Party's united front with the GMD and other military and political forces in China remained to be the single most important policy issue throughout the CCP's entire pre-1949 history, the doctrine itself became highly institutionalized. There was a specialized crew of cadres under the leadership of Zhou Enlai to carry out various united front operations, such as gathering intelligence on, penetrating into, promoting friendship with, or inciting defection within, the targeted organizations. Later, a United Front Department was established as a part of the Party Center's apparatus, which exists to this day. If Zhou was the principal functionary, Mao was the guardian providing direction and guidelines for the Party's united front policy. Stalin, too, often offered the CCP his advice on how to deal with the GMD and other political forces in China.[19]

Once they perfected and institutionalized the united front doctrine through their domestic experience, Mao and his colleagues extended its usage to the Party's diplomatic operations to deal with the United States, Japan, and other western capitalist nations. Although from the class struggle proposition, all imperialist nations were ultimately the enemies of the CCP, the Party should not refuse to unite itself with certain nations against others at a given time. As Mao stated:

> We deal with imperialism in the same way [as we deal with different GMD factions]. The Communist Party opposes all imperialism, but we make a distinction between Japanese imperialism . . . and British and U.S. imperialism. . . . Our tactics are guided by one and the same principle: to make use of contradictions, win over the many, oppose the few, and crush our enemies one by one.[20]

Mao's words demonstrated the spiritual unity between not only the Party's long-term revolutionary commitment and short-term tactical flexibility, but also the domestic united front operation and diplomacy in dealing with different "imperialist nations." After the arrival of the American Dixie Mission in Yan'an in August 1944, the Party issued a secret document entitled "The Directive on Diplomatic Work," which spelled out clearly that "the tactical principles of the domestic united front should be generally applicable to the international united front work."[21] In fact, in the CCP's vocabulary, *tongzhan* (united front) was synonymous with *waijiao* (diplomacy). For instance, in a Party Center's telegram dated 12 August 1936, a united front action aimed at winning over some GMD factions in the northwest was called *"waijiao,"* and on another occasion, Zhou Enlai told his diplomatic crew that "generally speaking, diplomacy is a form of united front operation."[22]

Interestingly but not surprisingly, the CCP's practitioners in the domestic united front operation were often the same ones who were involved in foreign affairs. For instance, Wang Bingnan, one of the old united front practitioners during the Xi'an Incident in 1936, was also the one who frequented the U.S. Embassy in Chongqing in the early 1940s. In 1947 he was appointed the head of the Foreign Affairs Group (*Waishizu*). So too, when the Party wanted someone to go to Hunan in 1949 to persuade the GMD governor to defect, Zhou Enlai sent Qiao Guanhua, a leading CCP diplomat and later the Foreign Minister of the PRC, to carry out this typical united front operation.[23]

While I consider highly the role of ideology in the CCP's foreign policy, I do not argue for "ideological determinism." Instead, I argue that it was the combined effect of the class struggle outlook and the united front doctrine that shaped the CCP's diplomacy. The former gave the Communists political identity as revolutionaries committed to their long-term goals, while the latter legitimized and guided their tactical maneuvers with short-term flexibility. When Mao and his colleagues were acting flexibly at a given time to achieve a set of short-term objectives, they did not abandon their long-term revolutionary commitment which was defined by their class struggle outlook. Moreover, the class struggle outlook not only dictated the CCP's selection and treatment of enemies, but also set the limits of the Party's tactical moves and the manner in which the united front operations were carried out.

The coexistence of, and a relative balance between, the two sides of the dualistic Maoist policy structure was vital to the very survival and success of the Party. It is easier to understand the importance of the CCP's tactical flexibility than to comprehend the role of the CCP leadership's class-struggle outlook in its foreign decision making, and the former seemed like a search for a pragmatic and rationalized solution to a particular situation. In order to understand the role of ideology in the CCP's foreign policy, a highly metaphysical undertaking, it is helpful to borrow the "identification theory" from psychoanalytical scholars, particularly Erik Erikson. According to the Eriksonian theory, in order to survive and function in a society every human being needs a psychological self, the "ego identity," which is anchored in one's sociogenetic evolution. An individual's sense of well-being depends on an increased sense of identity; otherwise, personality breakdown will ensue. For Erikson, an ideology is a synthesis of historical identifications with a general mode of behavior or culture, and it is identical to the "ego identity." A threat, therefore, to one's established ideology is a threat to one's identity, and the person will have to protect and enhance his/her identity through defending and enhancing his/her ideology. Moreover, identification is necessarily a group process even if the group only involves a parent and a child. Therefore, individuals in a group will together synthesize, protect, or enhance a shared identity/ideology.[24]

The conversion of Mao and his generation to the class struggle ideology, a set of concepts with which they interpreted history and perceived reality, was a result of "sociogenetic evolution" of each of those individuals. Once this evolution was completed, they acquired their personal and group identities and became who they were. "Marxist Ideology" was no longer a "theory," it became intimately personal to them as their ego identification. If there was a consistency in Mao's thinking and behavior throughout his entire political career, it was his application of class struggle theory to explaining and rationalizing a particular situation and a policy change. For instance, in the late 1930s and early 1940s, China's domestic and international situation was changing rapidly; so was the CCP's policy. In every occasion of such change, Mao tried to explain and rationalize it within the framework of changing class relations among "national bourgeoisie," "grand bourgeoisie," "petty bourgeoisie," and their political representation in the GMD. One can well argue that Mao's analysis was often self-contradictory and theoretically bizarre; the point is that it was not so much about the relevance of Mao's theory as his persistence in applying his class struggle outlook even at the expense of logical coherence. If one's behavior is a way of self-expression, Mao's persistence in applying class struggle doctrine was a stubborn effort to safeguard and reinforce his ego identification. The class struggle outlook became characteristically who Mao was.

The Communists were a tiny minority of rebels, striving against the "norms" of the establishment of a nation-state. Just as any pioneering martyrs against a dominant religion/ideology in a given society, they were constantly pursued and persecuted, and they had to be prepared to sacrifice themselves for their belief. Thus, they tended to have an extraordinary tendency toward what Erikson called "totalism," that was to "make a total orientation out of a given state of partial knowledge."[25] Mao's theory of class analysis might seem to be simplistic or extremist in an academic sense, but this was nonetheless a psychological necessity to safeguard his and the group's ego identity. In other words, their need for psychological well-being was compounded with the extraordinary circumstances to compel them to hold their belief religiously. If Marxism was the Communists' religion, class struggle theory was the doctrine of Maoist denomination.

To be firm in one's belief, however, is not enough to keep one's sense of successful identification, which also depends upon the sense of "gratification" in the process of interacting with the outside world. If one's action is a cognitive self-expression, the results of the action will have a strong impact on one's psychological being: successful results will generate a sense of self-fulfillment, or "gratification," while negative results will generate a sense of self-questioning, if not self-negation, which leads to an identity crisis and possible personality breakdown.

Whenever Mao and his comrades suffered a defeat, they would naturally feel the lack of gratification, and this would trigger anxiety, a sign of an identity crisis. When the crisis persisted, many individuals would experience a personality breakdown, and then leave the Party and abandon their existing identity/ideology. But Mao and his colleagues went the other way: they defended the fundamentals of their ideology/identity, but altered some details within the existing framework to make it more flexible and feasible in the given situation. The result was that they toughened their ideological commitment, and at the same time learned how to adapt to the reality. In this way, the CCP's ideology is also linked with, rather than separate from or in opposition to, its tactical maneuver in the struggle for power; the latter was for the fulfilment of the former. Had the Communists' pursuit of the latter resulted in the abandonment of the former, it would have been self-defeating, and they would have not been who they were.

This identification theory explains a dualistic pattern that emerged in the Party's policy process. This pattern combined, to borrow CCP terminologies, the firmness of revolutionary principles (*geming de yuanzexing*) and the flexibility of tactics (*zhanshu de linghuoxing*). Mao himself once referred to his double-sided identity. In his last years, with much philosophical self-reflection, he told Edgar Snow that he had both the "tiger spirit" (*huqi*) and the "monkey spirit" (*houqi*) in him. By "tiger spirit," he meant one's courage to pursue his ultimate goal righteously according to his fundamental belief regardless of how formidable the obstacles might be; and the "monkey spirit" meant one's ability to alter his course flexibly to accommodate the limits of the realities at a given time. "Monkey spirit" in Chinese has a negative connotation as being "cowardly," and as an egotistic man, Mao was inclined to assert his "tiger spirit" as far as he could. At the same time, he could be very flexible just like a monkey, if he saw it necessary. I call this double-sided identity the Maoist dualism.

The two sides of the Maoist dualism were, more often than not, in conflict, as the CCP tried to balance its policy at a given time. It was very difficult for Mao and his colleagues to find a happy medium at which point the Party's policy was neither "leftist" nor "rightist." The former meant too much emphasis was placed on the revolutionary principle to achieve a short-term gain through making temporary concession; the latter meant too much weight was on the short-term flexibility to safeguard the Party's identity and ultimate goal. In real historical terms, Mao's class-struggle ideology had two agents which Mao considered essential to realize the ultimate goal. The first was the Party-controlled armed forces, and the second was the Party-controlled rural base areas. Any policy that would lead to the weakening of the Party's independent control over the two "treasures," as Mao put it, was of a "rightist deviation." Mao knew that the GMD and the Americans intended to disarm the CCP and incorporate its base areas into the GMD state—he would never let this happen. And yet, he had to form a united front with the GMD and the Americans at some points in time, which entailed a modification of his class struggle program in building up the armed force and the base areas.

How much modification was necessary, and what was the limit of compromise in a given time? This the CCP alone could not control, for it had to be played out in the contest with the GMD and the Americans who were forced to make concessions to the CCP from time to time as well. In the process, Mao and his colleagues were gradually becoming real experts in juggling the two considerations of the class-struggle program and the united front with the bedfellows. But the battle was always an uphill one, and whenever the Party suffered a setback, tension built up within the leadership, which was what Maoist historians called "line struggle" against either the "leftist" or the "rightist" deviations. The Maoist historians interpreted the whole CCP history as one of "two-line struggle" between Mao's correct line and the others' erroneous lines. This led some western scholars to believe that there were two groups of people in the CCP: one stood for the revolutionary cause against the GMD, and the other for the united front with the GMD; and the latter was associated with Moscow, while the former resisted Stalin.

In contrast to this outmoded "line-struggle" interpretation, I propose a "cultural mode" which interprets the CCP internal policy debate as a way of communication among individuals in time of crisis, a way of expression of individuals' anxiety triggered by the failure in their search for a happy medium to gratify their sense of shared ideology/identity. At no point in the entire CCP history before the death of Mao was there a breakaway from the class-struggle ideology as a result of such a debate. Some within the Party might be identified as "leftist" or "rightist" deviationists, but they were always criticized, or self-criticized of being influenced by the bourgeoisie or petty bourgeoisie, for the proletariat would never make such mistakes, so went the CCP logic. This pattern of behavior made clear that Mao and his comrades never abandoned their ideology and never tried to resynthesize a new one. Instead, they made every effort to "purify" and enhance their ideology/identity so that it would be gratified in the coming struggle. This was the CCP's collective behavior. The process in which the Communists engaged themselves in the struggle against the "leftist" or "rightist" tendencies was so intense, frequent, and unique that we shall view it as the culture of the CCP, the way of life for the Mao generation. The "anti-leftist deviation" struggle ensured the Party's adaptability and flexibility, while the "anti-rightist" struggle maintained the CCP's long-term revolutionary commitment characteristic of its very identity/ideology.

Given the CCP definition, being "leftist" is being less tactful or having too much revolutionary zeal to be patient; while being "rightist" is being less committed to the revolution or uncertain about one's communist identity. If the CCP's pursuit of short-term gains resulted in the abandonment of its long-term revolutionary goals and the Party's communist identity, not only was it self-defeating, it was also a betrayal of the "Marxist truth" that the Communists held so religiously as the very essence of who they were. Thus, it is not difficult to understand why Mao and his comrades treated "rightist deviation" much more harshly than they did the "leftist error." Mao in fact identified the "rightists" as "counterrevolutionaries" in the infamous "Anti-rightist Movement" in the 1950s. "*Ning-zuo bu-you*" (rather being "leftist" than "rightist"), therefore, became a common tendency among the Party's rank and file. This suggests that the Party had an inherent inclination to protect its long-term revolutionary direction and its ideology/identity at the expense of tactical flexibility. Mao contributed to the making of this political culture, which in turn came to confine him and his colleagues as its prisoners. The kind of radicalism characteristic to this culture eventually led to the CCP's self-destruction during the Cultural Revolution.[26]

This CCP political culture, however, seems to have a positive defining and constraining effect on the CCP's policy-making process before 1949, when opposition to Mao's "leftist" radicalism from Stalin and other CCP leaders was effective and Mao was cautious and amenable enough. The combination of CCP's *yuanzexing* (nature of principle) and *linghuoxing* (nature of flexibility) was demonstrated in Mao's dealings with the "Dixie Mission." When Mao was shaking hands with the Americans in the mission in the summer of 1944, he had two objectives to gain: U.S. military aid to strengthen his armed forces and U.S. recognition of the CCP government in the base areas. In other words, by pursuing the united front with the Americans, Mao intended to enhance his class-struggle program. He also knew that the Americans, no matter how liberal they might be, disliked communism; therefore, the CCP's name itself might damage his chance of success. Mao told John Service that they were thinking of changing the Party's name. When Hurley, however, made it clear that the United States would only recognize Jiang's government, and the CCP's armed forces should be reorganized into the national military system under the GMD, Mao knew his effort of wooing the Americans failed, and quickly turned the united front with the Americans into the united front against the U.S. As early as February 1945, Mao started to use the hyphenated term, *Mei-Jiang* (U.S.-Jiang), to identify the enemy camp, and warned the Party of the possibility of U.S. intervention in China on behalf of the GMD against the CCP in the postwar era. Before long, Mao further concluded that the postwar world would be divided into two camps: the U.S. and the GMD on one side, the USSR and the CCP on the other. Stalin shared this two-camp vision with Mao, and Soviet assistance was vital and instrumental to the CCP's victory in the civil war.[27]

This example is illustrative of my major arguments: (1) Mao's class-struggle outlook, of which the vital historical agents were the CCP armed forces

and base areas, played an essential role in the policy process, not only in identifying the Party's enemies and friends, but also in safeguarding the Party's
political identity and ultimate revolutionary commitment. (2) The CCP ideol-
ogy/identity demanded, rather than rejected, the coexistence with the united
front doctrine, which rendered the Party the mechanism to adapt to reality
flexibly so that the sense of gratification would enhance the Party's identity
and the ultimate goal could be gradually approached. (3) In the process of
making tactical maneuvers, the very class-struggle ideology of the CCP did
not recede into the background; instead, it set the limits for compromise, and
dictated the manner in which the maneuver would be carried out so that taking a temporary detour would not make the Party lose its long-term revolutionary direction.

I believe that by claiming that the Communists were free from ideology and
merely responding to the situation imposed by the U.S. and the USSR, neorealist scholars repeat an old pattern in western sinology known as "western
initiative, Chinese response." This perspective has been attacked by many who
call for a "China-centered" perspective of Chinese history.[28] I would like to
push the argument further by calling for a "CCP perspective" in studying the
history of the CCP, since I contend that there is neither a "holistic China," nor
a "holistic Chinese perspective." I believe the CCP's behavior can be better
understood if we put ourselves into their shoes. To do so one first needs sufficient CCP materials to reconstitute the CCP "shoes." A large corpus of CCP
materials has become available, including inner-party documents such as
directives, resolutions of the Party Center, and telegrams between Mao and
Stalin, various memoirs, biographies, and chronologies of important CCP personalities such as Mao, Zhou, Ruo Ronghuan, Xiao Jingquang, etc., and historical writings by, and interviews with, researchers in China who have privileged access to the Central Archives of the CCP. To a large extent, this corpus
of new materials itself represents the flesh and blood reality and calls for a
more lively historical approach than the deadening ahistorical "structure" of
neorealism.

CHAPTER I

The Roots of Mao's Pro-Soviet Policy before 1937

IN a historical perspective, the Sino-Soviet Pact of 1950 should be seen as the end result of a long process from the very beginning of the CCP's history. If the Mao generation's spiritual conversion to Marxism-Leninism made them a part of the Comintern early in the 1920s, the following decades of their life-and-death struggle for power reinforced their political-ideological identity as communist internationalists. Their loyalty toward the Moscow-led proletarian world revolution was continuously rewarded by Moscow's material or immaterial supports. Suffice it to say that the intellectual-psychological, political-institutional, and military-strategic ties between the CCP and Moscow were so extensive and strong that Mao repeatedly stated throughout the pre-1949 period, publicly and privately, that the "Chinese people's interest" (read the CCP interest) was inseparable from the Soviet interest.

This history of CCP-Moscow relations was, however, obscured and distorted by Mao himself in the post-Stalin era for his own contemporary reasons. In numerous occasions after Stalin's death Mao purposely discredited Stalin's contribution to the CCP cause, thereby creating a myth that Stalin was always wrong in his China policy, and Mao was always correct and he resisted Stalin and saved the CCP revolution single-handedly.[1] The myth of Mao's own making has been influential in the western scholarship in the field.[2] It is time to use new historical evidence to straighten out the basic facts; first of all, whether or not Mao was in conflict with Moscow before 1935, the year in which he rose to power in the Party.

CCP-MOSCOW RELATIONS BEFORE 1935

Mao told P. F. Yudin, the Soviet Ambassador to China, in 1956 that Stalin committed a "grave mistake" in 1926 by ordering the CCP to "subordinate itself to the GMD," thereby "undermining the CCP's independent work to mobilize the masses." Then, Mao charged that Stalin ignored the Central Committee of the CCP, and treated Wang Ming or Li Lisan as the "only mouthpiece" of the CCP. Mao himself, on the other hand, was accused of being a "rightist opportunist and narrow-minded empiricist."[3] What one sees here is an ambitious Mao attempting to seize the leadership of the world communist movement after the death of Stalin; his memories were selective and distorted, purposely or not. To use "history" for political purposes was not something new to Mao, nor was he the "inventor" of it. His memories about Stalin's policy in 1926 contradicted the historical evidence.

In fact, Mao was very much a part of the adventure under the Comintern-CCP leadership; these men, despite their courage and conviction, had not found the charted route to power. They were experimenting in dangerous revolution collectively, although they would blame each other after suffering a defeat. The most intricate and fundamental dilemma for the Moscow-CCP leadership in 1921–27 was how to maintain the united front with the GMD, and at the same time wage a class struggle to build the CCP's strength so that it could eventually take over power from the GMD. After the CCP adopted the Comintern policy of a united front with the GMD in 1923, the party membership increased dramatically, and CCP influence penetrated into every GMD political and military establishment as well as the mass movements in the cities and countryside. This, however, also made it inevitable that the GMD's animosity toward the CCP was increasing, especially in the spring of 1925, when Sun died and the May Thirtieth Movement radicalized China's mass movement. The Comintern-CCP leadership reached the conclusion that the GMD was internally divided into three groups: the left, the center, and the right. Accordingly, the CCP should join hands with the left-wingers, win over the middle-of-the-roaders, and defeat the right-wingers. This policy, however, did not prevent more and more GMD members from turning toward the right. Shortly after the "West Hill Clique" split from the GMD Central Committee, Jiang, who was regarded by the CCP as a left-winger, turned on the Communists.[4]

This crisis triggered immense anxiety within the Comintern-CCP leadership, and opinions divided. According to the Maoist history, Mao advocated a radical policy to take over control of the GMD Central Committee into CCP hands. Mao said that because the CCP members and the left-wingers still formed the majority of the Second Congress of the GMD in January 1926, they could elect themselves into power to check Jiang. The Chen Duxiu-Borodin leadership, however, promised Jiang that the CCP would take no more than one-third of the seats in the Central Committee, but Jiang was not appeased. Two months later he staged the "March Twentieth coup" against the CCP. Mao argued again that the CCP should split with Jiang immediately, for the CCP together with the "left-wingers" still controlled superior military forces and Jiang could have been defeated. The Chen-Borodin leadership again ruled out Mao's policy proposal.[5] Mao later claimed to be "always correct," and his fellow comrades were "always wrong."

The new evidence, however, reveals that the CCP-Comintern leadership did consider the option of using force against Jiang, as the CCP Center's letter of 9 June 1926 indicated. The CCP leadership calculated that among the four armies under the Guangzhou coalition the combined strength of the Second and Third Armies could not compete with the First Army under Jiang's control. If the CCP had allied itself with the Fourth Army, which was led by generals trained in the Baoding Military Academy, to defeat Jiang, the result could have been worse, because the "Baoding Clique" was more reactionary than Jiang. Furthermore, the CCP leadership realized the infighting in the south would strengthen the hands of northern warlords. If the South was to be defeated by the North, the CCP would have a more difficult time to survive. Thus, the only option was to continue the united front with Jiang for now, while building the strength of "left-wingers" and increasing the CCP's control over the mass movements.[6] After the decision had been made, Mao actively carried it out, and it worked well for about one year up to April 1927. In this year, the so-called left-wing GMD headed by Wang Jingwei took control of the party apparatus and a part of the GMD armed forces loyal to the Wuhan Government. At the same time, the peasants' movement in Hunan also developed dramatically. Had Mao's radical policy prevailed early in 1926, he would have lost his chance to write his famous report on Hunan's peasant movement, and the CCP could have been crushed by Jiang then and there. If the Comintern failed to provide the CCP with a winning policy under the circumstances, Mao's policy proposal could have been more disastrous.

The so-called "rural strategy," which has been attributed to Mao, had in fact originated in Moscow, and Mao only followed the Comintern's policy to organize and arm the peasantry.[7] As early as 1924, Borodin, discouraged by Sun's conservatism, proposed that the CCP go to the countryside to disarm landlords, to organize peasants, and to confiscate large estates to redistribute land to the landless.[8] In late 1926, Stalin urged the CCP to radicalize the peasant movement, and to discard "the fear that the aggravation of the class struggle in the countryside will weaken the united anti-imperialist front."[9] Mao's "Report on Hunan's Peasant Movement" in early 1927 became well known only because the Comintern-CCP leadership supported it. Because it was Stalin's policy to radicalize China's peasant movements, *Xiangdao*, the CCP Centre's official organ, published Mao's report in March with an introduction by Qu Qiubei, a Moscow-trained young revolutionary and then the chief of the CCP; in May and June, both the Russian and English versions of the *Communist International* carried Mao's article as well. In the same period, Bukharin, then the head of the ECCI, praised Mao's report highly at a Comintern meeting.[10] Without Moscow's support, Mao's popularity within the movement would not have been nearly as high.

If the CCP revolutionaries had thought of "armed struggle" in terms of workers' and peasants' insurrections, Stalin was the first one who called upon the CCP to form a Party-controlled professional army. On 1 June 1927, he personally instructed the CCP not only to take over the leadership of the GMD by packing "a large number of new peasant and working-class leaders" into the GMD Central Committee in Wuhan, but also to "mobilize about 20,000 Communists and about 50,000 revolutionary workers and peasants . . . to form several new army corps . . . and organize your own reliable army before it is too late."[11] This was, however, easier said than done. In July, Wang Jingwei and his armed forces turned on the Russian advisors and the CCP, and the first united front thus ended disastrously. Stalin's directive, however, dictated the CCP's new strategy in 1927–35, and this policy was officially adopted by the CCP in an emergency meeting on 7 August 1927. Mao was then named by the presiding Comintern agent to direct the fall insurrection in Hunan.[12] Mao was very much a part of the collective experimentation of the Comintern-CCP leadership. Together they made progress; together they made mistakes as well.

This is also true in the development of the CCP's military strategy in which Mao was far from being "always correct." In reality, in the so-called first and second "leftist-opportunist" period, Mao was as eager as everyone else to win an instant victory, and he actively led his troops to attack major cities, a fundamental feature of the "leftist opportunism." For instance, after the 7 August 1927 meeting, the CCP Center instructed that the insurrection in Hunan should take place in the southern rural part first, and then spread all over to include Changsha. But when Mao was in charge of the provincial committee meeting on 18 August, the meeting decided to take on Changsha first. Only after the Changsha campaign failed did Mao decide to retreat to the remote border area in Jiangxi. Even so, Mao still remained over-optimistic about national victory in the near future. In October 1928, Mao claimed that due to the divisions and wars among domestic and international reactionaries, the small-sized base areas of the CCP would grow, and "[we] are approaching nationwide victory daily."[13] This statement was typical of "leftist adventurism."

In the summer of 1930 when the so-called Li Lisan line was at its peak, Mao was active in carrying out Li's plan to "strive for victory in one or several provinces" as the first step toward nationwide takeover. He led the First Army Corps to attack Ji'an, and then, Nanchang. Only when the troops came close to their targets and he discovered that the enemy forces there were too strong to crack, did Mao change the original plan. Nonetheless, he soon miscalculated that his Red Army had a better chance to win in his home province. He ordered his men to march from Jiangxi back to Hunan to launch the second Changsha campaign. On 10 September, however, Mao's troops suffered a great loss in the attempt to seize Changsha, and he was forced to call off the campaign the next day. One week later, Moscow ended Li's "leftist adventurism" by removing him from the party chief post. At the same time, Mao was elected as an alternative member of the politburo. Due to inefficient communication, however, this news didn't reach Mao until the end of the year. Mao continued to pursue the "adventurist" policy in the following two months.

For instance, after taking Ji'an, Mao reported to the Center that the Ji'an battle was only the beginning of the struggle for victory in the whole of Jiangxi province, and, within a week, his troops would be attacking Nanchang again. At the time, Jiang was gathering his troops to crush Mao's Jiangxi base.

On 25 October, the CCP Center, which was criticized by Maoist historians for committing the "third leftist deviation," issued a directive to instruct Mao that the first priority at the moment was not to seize Changsha or Nanchang, but to defend the home base. This eventually ended Mao's "leftist" military policy. It did not, however, curb his impulsiveness which led him to envision a quick final victory. Early in December 1930, Mao claimed that the current international situation favored a "final battle of class warfare against imperialism," and the domestic situation favored a "final battle of class warfare against Jiang Jieshi."[14] For these reasons, Mao was criticized at the Ningdu meeting of 17 April 1931, and its resolution pointed out that his military policy followed the Li Lisan line until after the second Changsha campaign. Mao admitted his error.[15] His "leftism" in fact reflected a general mood of the CCP and the Comintern at the time. Jiang's bloody purge had made them vengeful and they were impatient to endure a long and bitter struggle in the rural areas.

However, Mao's narcissistic personality continued to lead him to argue that had the Party followed his policy, a failure could have been avoided. At the Zunyi conference in January 1935, Qing Bangxian, then the Party chief, stated that the Red Army's defeat in 1933–34 in Jiangxi was due to the overwhelming strength of the GMD. Mao disagreed, and he contended that it was due to the incorrect strategy of the Qing-Braun leadership which abandoned guerrilla strategy. In reality, after pacifying the rebellions of the GMD local factions, Jiang gathered massive forces to attack the CCP using the blockhouse strategy. Facing the new situation, Mao too doubted the efficacy of guerrilla warfare. He proposed on 20 November 1933 that the Red Army abandon the Jiangxi area and thrust into the Zhejiang-Jiangsu-Anhui region to wage mobile warfare in Jiang's home base.[16] Mao's idea was too bold and its result too unpredictable for the CCP Center, which refused to adopt it. The Qing-Braun leadership decided to defend the soviet area in Jiangxi at any cost. The defeat of the CCP was predictable. The Qing-Braun strategy failed; nonetheless, this should not be taken as proof that Mao's could have succeeded. One could well argue that the CCP armed forces would have been totally wiped out, had they marched into Jiang's home base.

Nor was Mao demoted by the Comintern and the "returned students" for his failure to follow Moscow's strategy. The opposite is true: Mao was Moscow's chosen man. The story started on 21 July 1932, when the Shanghai Center criticized the Central Bureau in Jiangxi headed by Zhou Enlai of not being aggressive enough in military operations. Zhou thus left the rear base to join Mao, Zhu De, and Wang Jiaxiang at the front. In September, the four men at the front disagreed with the other members of the Central Bureau who remained in the rear. The former wanted to give the troops a seven-day respite since they had fought three successive battles in the past month, while the latter wanted them to fight a battle in Yongfeng where enemy troops had gathered. The difference between the two sides was purely technical, if not trivial; there was no "two-line struggle" whatsoever. The four men at the front proposed on 25 September that a meeting of all members of the Central Bureau be held. When all the members met in Ningdu in the first week of October, Mao's argument apparently became unpopular, and he was criticized for being "rightist." Some proposed that Mao leave the military command, and Zhou, who was presiding over the meeting, suggested two alternatives: either Mao be the commander while Zhou served as overseer; or Zhou take command, with Mao acting as assistant. Mao rejected the first alternative. The meeting accepted the second one, but Mao asked for a "sick leave" to stay at the rear, and the meeting granted his request. The Shanghai Center endorsed the meeting on 6 October.[17]

This was how Mao left his military command. His egotistic personality led him to clash with his colleagues, and the Maoist story of Mao's demotion due to his opposition to Moscow's policy line is a lie. The truth is that when Mao was in difficulty with his colleagues at home, Moscow came to his aid. In the Fifth Plenum in January 1934, which was regarded as the peak of the Wang Ming line by Maoist historians, Mao's position in the Party was upgraded from an alternate to a full member of the politburo.[18] This was largely due to the Comintern's intervention on Mao's behalf. In March 1933, the ECCI telegraphed the CCP Center and stated that the way in which Mao was treated "must be gentle and comradelike, and Mao should be allowed to undertake a leading position." The Center subsequently relayed this directive to the rank and file.[19]

Throughout 1934–35, Mao's name frequently appeared in the Comintern's publication and the reports of the CCP's delegation in Moscow headed by Wang Ming. In these documents, Mao was praised as "the leader of the Chinese soviet movement," and the "preeminent young politician and military strategist of the Chinese Soviet Republic." Moscow even published a volume of his selected works, probably the first of its kind. In October 1934, Mao's work on guerrilla warfare was printed by the CCP's Central Military Committee as its instruction to the rank and file.[20] At the Seventh Congress of the Comintern in 1935, Mao was praised as an "outstanding and valiant standard-bearer" of the communist movement, the same praise as Dimitrov received. In Moscow's exhibition hall of CCP history, the only personal portrayals of CCP leaders were Mao and Zhu De. In *Pravda* of 13 December 1935, and the *Communist International*, nos. 33–34, 1935, Mao was praised highly as the "legendary leader of the Chinese people" and the "first one who recognized and openly exposed the Chen Duxiu capitulationism."[21] It was this kind of unprecedented support and endorsement from Moscow that paved the way for Mao's rise to power at Zunyi.

Mao's victory at Zunyi was also attributable to the support of the key members of the "returned students" who understood that the Comintern favored Mao. In November 1934, the CCP delegation in Moscow headed by Wang

Ming informed the Party Center that the Comintern considered Mao an experienced leader.[22] It was not a coincidence that shortly after the Moscow message, two key members of the "returned students," namely, Zhang Wentian and Wang Jiaxiang, became closer to Mao and more receptive to his opinion. It was after Zhang and Wang had leaned toward Mao that Zhou Enlai came to Mao's side, followed by Zhu De. Thus, Mao gained the support of the majority in the Politburo, and he became increasingly vocal in criticizing the military conduct of Qing and Braun. On 12 December 1934, an emergency meeting, presided over by Zhou Enlai, was convened to discuss military strategy. Qing and Braun insisted on following the previous decision to head toward the central Hunan area. Mao contended that the new base area should be on the border of Hunan and Guizhou. Zhang and Wang voted for Mao first, and then Zhou swung to Mao's side. Thus, for the first time, Mao overrode the Qing-Braun decision. A week later, a Politburo meeting further confirmed Mao's strategy.[23] It became clear that Mao had gained the upper hand in the Politburo with the support of the "returned students." This was not due to his "correct" strategy because Mao's idea to head toward Guizhou was soon proven "wrong" and abandoned.[24]

Suffice it to say that before the Zunyi conference, Mao was not in conflict with Moscow and he had no reason to stage an anti-Moscow "coup" at Zunyi. In fact, Mao was supported by the Comintern and the key members of the so-called "returned students," and his loyalty to the Moscow-led world revolution remained intact. This becomes more evident when a fact, which has long been kept secret, comes to light: Mao was responsible for the restoration of radio communication between the CCP and Moscow.[25]

THE CCP-MOSCOW RADIO COMMUNICATION SYSTEM

CCP-Moscow radio communication was disrupted in Shanghai in August 1934 by the GMD secret service. After Mao's rise at Zunyi, he took the restoration of CCP-Moscow radio communication as one of the priorities on the Party's agenda. Due to Mao's persistent effort, the CCP-Moscow radio communications were restored in the summer of 1936, and Mao took the system under his close personal control throughout the pre-1949 era.[26]

Under Mao's direct supervision, CCP-Moscow radio communication was frequent, especially in times of urgency. For instance, in the early morning of 12 December 1936, Jiang Jieshi was kidnapped in Xi'an by generals Zhang Xueliang and Yang Hucheng. The CCP Center transmitted the information to Moscow immediately. Before the day ended, three more telegrams were dispatched to the ECCI.[27] From that date until early 1937, Moscow continuously dispatched instructions to the CCP to direct the Party's policy in dealing with the Xi'an Incident and its aftermath.[28] If the radio transmitting system was not entirely reliable during the Xi'an Incident, it was greatly improved after Zhou Enlai's trip to Moscow in 1939–40. On 27 August 1939, Zhou left Yan'an for Moscow via Xinjiang. While receiving medical treatment for his right arm, Zhou acted as the CCP's emissary to the Comintern. He wrote a comprehensive report of 55,000 words to the ECCI, and Stalin took the lead in the discussion of Moscow's China policy which resulted in a resolution of the ECCI. When Zhou departed from Moscow on 25 February 1940, he was given a set of radio transmitting equipment and two sets of codes to take home.[29]

Ren Bishi, one of the five Standing Committee members of the Politburo and one of the "returned students," came back from Moscow on the same plane with Zhou. Ren immediately set out to establish a special department under the Party Center to manage radio communications with Moscow. To hide its top-secret mission, this new department was disguised as the "Agriculture Department," commonly known within the Party's highest circle as the "Agriculture Committee" (nongwei). By the end of 1940, repeated tests proved the new radio transmitting system reliable and efficient. Ren turned out to be one of Mao's trusted lieutenants, and Mao personally dominated this "Agriculture Committee." He used this secret agency frequently as well. Before the eruption of the German-Soviet war in June 1941, Mao was sending Moscow messages once or twice a week. The messages tended to be quite long; some were as long as several thousand words.[30]

Under normal circumstances, Moscow's telegrams would be translated by Shi Zhe, Mao's Russian translator, but when the message was classified as top secret, it would be translated by Ren Bishi himself. Without exception, all telegrams from Moscow would go to Mao immediately and Mao had the full authority to decide who should read them. According to Shi Zhe, Moscow's telegrams were not printed for circulation among the Politburo members; they were for Mao's eyes only. Mao would occasionally make oral reference to some of Moscow's telegrams at the Politburo meetings, if he considered them important. All the files of the "Agriculture Committee" were kept in Mao's personal residence, and no one else had access to them. In late December 1946, when the CCP was preparing for evacuation from Yan'an, Mao personally supervised Shi Zhe to burn all the files related to CCP-Moscow communications since 1940.[31] Mao knew well that should these files fall into GMD hands, not only would Stalin have been embarrassed by his secret involvement in Chinese affairs through the hands of the CCP, but also the Communists' political reputation among their countrymen would have been endangered by revelations which seemed to prove the GMD's charge that the CCP was a Soviet proxy.

The active communications between Mao and Stalin through radio transmitting systems provided an institutionalized mechanism essential to CCP-Moscow relations. Both Mao and Stalin not only had the desire to consult one another, but they also had the means to do so. Mao was responsive and amenable to Moscow's advice, while the voice from the "remote place" (*yuanfang*, a codified name for the Comintern or Stalin) was, at least after 1941, more suggestive than instructive, giving Mao enough leeway to make concrete and final policy. In the long run, this enabled Stalin to function as a participant in the CCP's policy making, as a tutor in the CCP's search for a happy medium between two extremes of the "right" and the "left," and as a balancing factor when Mao leaned too far "left." In the short run, in 1936–37, CCP-Moscow radio communications to a large extent determined the CCP's strategic planning.

MOSCOW'S ROLE IN THE CCP'S STRATEGIC PLANNING, 1935–1936

If Mao's internationalism, which resulted in his loyalty to Moscow, was initially a matter of ideological conviction, it was greatly enhanced and cemented in his struggle for survival in a dangerous environment, in which he came to perceive that the CCP's very existence was dependent on Soviet assistance. Stalin's willingness and persistent effort to provide such assistance further gratified and confirmed Mao's ideology/identity as a part of the Moscow-led world revolution. In fact, Mao's entire strategic planning in 1935–37 revolved around one scheme: how to reach out to the USSR or People's Republic of Mongolia (PRM) so that Soviet aid could be obtained. Mao was desperate in trying to bring the surviving CCP forces physically close to the USSR or Outer Mongolia so that the Party could rebuild its strength under the protection of the Soviet umbrella. This was the core of Mao's northwest strategy, which, however, originated from Moscow.

As early as March 1933 the ECCI indicated to the CCP that Sichuan and Shaanxi would be a better base area from where the CCP could expand toward Xinjiang.[32] In late 1933 and early 1934, the Soviet military went into Xinjiang and helped Sheng Shichai, the Xinjiang warlord, defeat other local warlords' forces in Yili and Gansu. With the Soviet influence in China's northwest enhanced and the CCP forces in southern China doomed, Moscow became more interested in having the CCP establish a new base area in the northwest.[33] At the same time, the ECCI was thinking of establishing a CCP Northwest Bureau which would include the Soviet authorities in the Central Asian region. The Soviets even thought to build a secret cadre training school and an arsenal large enough to arm 50,000 CCP troops in Central Asia. On Moscow's list of military aid to the CCP were airplanes and heavy artillery.[34] In spring 1935, a joint committee, which included the Soviet Defense Ministry, Soviet military intelligence, and the Comintern, studied the feasibility of CCP future expansion in China's northwest, and the committee reached a positive conclusion. In August 1935, Stalin told Lin Yuying, who was about to be sent back to transmit Moscow's instructions to the CCP, that he was clearly in favor of the idea that the CCP main forces should expand in China's northwest.[35]

Apparently, Stalin's preferred strategy in the Far East was to facilitate the CCP armed quest for national power, since a CCP-controlled China would serve Soviet interests the best. Only when China's reality proved that the CCP was still too weak to take charge, and a GMD-Japan joint force would inflict great danger to Soviet security interest in the Far East, did Stalin retreat to a second alternative to have the CCP form a temporary alliance with the GMD to prevent the Japanese from attacking the USSR.[36] It was equally clear in Mao's mind that the Soviet and CCP interests were one and the same, and Stalin would certainly support the CCP to the best of his ability as the circumstances would allow.

It is not surprising that Mao's planning turned out to be exactly along the Moscow line of strategic thinking. Since his rise to power early in 1935, Mao's main task had been to lead the CCP forces to escape their pursuers' fatal grip, and to find a new base area to survive and grow. On 29 April, the Politburo issued a directive, designating the western Sichuan as the future base area.[37] Mao, however, soon changed his mind. On 16 June, he suggested that the CCP forces choose the border area of Sichuan-Shaanxi-Gansu for the new base, while Zhang Guotao still insisted on heading toward western Sichuan. Mao's main argument was that his choice of location was close to the USSR, and the CCP could launch an expedition at a later date to reach Xinjiang.[38]

In the summer of 1935, Mao's desire to find a future base area under the Soviet umbrella was growing stronger. He repeatedly stressed that China's northwest was "the weakest link on the chain of the Chinese ruling class and foreign imperialism," and geographically close to the USSR. A CCP base area in the northwest would enable the Party to obtain the USSR's political and material assistance. He further reasoned that the CCP was defeated by the blockhouse strategy of the GMD in Jiangxi only because the CCP forces had no heavy artillery or airplanes. If the CCP could establish a base near the USSR, the Party could "obtain Soviet political and material support, including airplanes and heavy artillery. . . . [the Party] can also send a branch to Xinjiang to build airports and arsenals."[39] It was natural for Mao, a man who had barely survived the bombardment by the enemy's heavy artillery and air raids, to have the inspiration that one day he would possess such powerful weapons as well. If the GMD got its modern weapons from the U.S. and Germany, the Soviet Union was the only place for Mao to acquire powerful and efficient killing machines.

Mao's desire to reach the Soviet Union became stronger after Zhang took more than half of the CCP armed forces away. Mao was devastated; he no longer believed that it was feasible to establish a new base area in China's northwest. Instead, he intended to retreat into the territory of the USSR or the PRM. On 12 September, Mao said at the Ejie conference that the strategic goal of the Red Army was to use guerrilla methods to reach the border of the USSR via northeastern Gansu and Shaanbei, and to seek refuge in the Soviet-controlled area. After rebuilding the Red Army with Soviet assistance, Mao said, "we can march back into the vast area in Gansu and Shaanxi with much stronger forces." That was the only way to preserve the few hundred remaining cadres and a few thousand soldiers. Otherwise, Mao asserted, the CCP would have to fight guerrilla warfare forever, or be caught by the enemy "like a turtle in a pot." To add momentum to his argument, Mao raised his voice and stressed: "We are not an independent communist party. We are a branch of the Communist International. Our Chinese revolution is a part of the world revolution. We shall march to the Soviet border, create a base area, and then, expand eastward."[40] It is worth noting that in the early 1930s when the Japanese occupied Manchuria, the CCP forces there retreated into the Soviet territory where they were reorganized into a Soviet military system and were brought back to Manchuria in 1945. Thus, it is not surprising that Mao desired to seek refuge in Soviet territory when the CCP was facing a fatal blow. Mao and his colleagues, as we will see later, were preparing again in the early 1940s for retreating into the USSR and integrating into the Soviet military system. It seems that it was the USSR, the "fatherland of Socialism," not China under "reactionary bourgeoisie," that inspired a sense of security and patriotism in the hearts of the Chinese rebels.

Mao, however, soon realized that his "fatherland" was too far away for his remaining troops to reach; a halfway station was desirable. By sheer accident, the CCP found out that a small CCP base existed in Shaanbei. Thus, Mao and his comrades decided to go to Shaanbei first. If Mao's loyalty to Moscow was rooted in his spiritual conviction at first, the availability of a refuge in the "fatherland" must have an awesome grip on the psyche of a man facing ultimate danger. Now, Mao's faith in internationalism was not only ideology-inspired, but also survival-driven as well. Ideology and the reality of a life-and-death struggle thus converged in Mao's policy perspective.

In November 1935, Lin Yuying brought Mao the news that Stalin endorsed the northwest strategy.[41] It is not difficult to imagine the excitement Stalin's message generated in the hearts and minds of the Communists. In his speech on 30 November 1935, Mao told his audience that the new task of the Red Army was to expand the base area in the five northern provinces so that it could join together with the territory of the USSR and the PRM.[42] Mao, however, was realistic enough to know that it was impossible for the few thousand remaining men to control the vast area of Shaanxi, Shanxi, Suiyuan, Gansu, and Ningxia. In fact, Mao's reference to the five provinces not only was a morale-boosting technique, but it also reflected a lack of precise decision as to where the CCP should go to reach the USSR.

At the time, the CCP forces were in Shaanbei, an area geographically cut off from Outer Mongolia and Xinjiang by the Yellow River loop. The CCP had two alternatives: to head toward the west to Gansu and Ningxia first, and then expand toward Xinjiang; or to head toward the east to invade Shanxi, and then turn toward the north to reach Suiyuan, today's Inner Mongolia. Zhang Wentian and others were in favor of the "west-bound" strategy, while Mao favored the "east-bound" plan.[43] The Eastern Expedition started on 20 February 1936. At the time, the Japanese had started to penetrate into Chahar and Suiyuan, approaching Outer Mongolia. Against the background of the upcoming "Anti-Comintern Pact," the Japanese action convinced Mao that war between the USSR and Japan was imminent. In this international war, the CCP would fight shoulder to shoulder with the USSR and Outer Mongolia. As Mao put it, the CCP should "combine the Chinese Red Army with the Soviet Red Army on the basis of opposing the common enemy of Japanese imperialism."[44] With the CCP participating in the Soviet-Japanese war, Mao hoped, Soviet technological and material aid would strengthen the CCP's military forces; and the CCP could turn the international war into a domestic revolution in the future to seize national power.

Mao was so enthusiastic about this prospect and so serious about obtaining Soviet aid that he sent Deng Fa to the USSR in late April. With Deng was a list of requested Soviet aid in terms of both strategic coordination and material assistance from Moscow. Mao asked Moscow to provide: (1) a plan for bilateral military coordination against the Japanese; (2) equipment for radio communications between the military command systems of both sides; (3) Soviet cooperation with the CCP Red Army's effort to establish a base area in Suiyuan; (4) immediate Soviet supplies of rifles, ammunition, light and heavy machine guns, antiaircraft artillery, infantry cannons, modern bridging equipment and technology (to cross the Yellow River); and, (5) Soviet special advisors on military technology, planning, and education.[45] Envisioning massive Soviet aid forthcoming, Mao became even more ambitious and grave. On 1 April 1936, he issued an order to change the name of the CCP forces into "Anti-Japanese Vanguard Army," of which the first task was to recruit 50,000 troops in the following seven months so that the Army's operation would cover the entire area of the five provinces in North China.[46]

Mao's east-bound strategy, however, was frustrated by Jiang who sent the Central Army into Shanxi and defeated the CCP. On 5 May, Mao was forced to call off the Eastern Expedition. This setback, however, did not frustrate Mao's will to reach the USSR; he issued another order to launch the Western Expedition on 18 May. In the new order, Mao reiterated that the aim of the military action was to "reach out to Outer Mongolia and the Soviet Union."[47] Instead of a North China base, Mao intended this time to create a Chinese Defense Government in the northwest, centered in Gansu and Ningxia, where Soviet military aid could reach them. This northwest strategy was also initiated by the Comintern in several messages which reached Mao by the end of May.[48]

Two new developments prompted Mao's idea of the northwest defense government. First, Moscow had just signed a mutual defense treaty with Ulan Bator, which indicated an ever stronger Soviet intention to separate Outer Mongolia from China permanently. This was bad news for the GMD government in Nanjing, but good news for Mao. On 25 May, Mao told his colleagues that "Outer Mongolia has signed a military alliance treaty with the USSR, and the Comintern expects our Red Army to approach Outer Mongolia and Xinjiang."[49] Mao envisioned that once the Northwest Defense Government was established in the near future, it would sign a mutual defense treaty with both Moscow and Ulan Bator.[50] In this way, the CCP-controlled northwest could integrate with Soviet-controlled Outer Mongolia and Xingjiang to creat a vast buffer zone for Soviet security, which would be a safe haven for the CCP as well. Second, in April and May, the CCP had successfully made a secret alliance with the local GMD forces under Generals Zhang Xueliang and Yang Hucheng who were attracted by the CCP's promise of massive Soviet aid. With the combined forces of the CCP and the Zhang-Yang camp, Mao was confident that his northwest scheme would work. He was keenly aware, however, that the key to success lay in the forthcoming Soviet political and military assistance. In June 1936, when the CCP-Moscow radio communication channel was resumed, Mao's first telegram to Moscow was to report in detail his northwest strategy. In his second cable, Mao reiterated that the "important precondition for the northwest strategy is the assistance from the International."[51]

Mao's planning was also outlined in his telegrams to Peng Dehuai on 29 June and 1 July.[52] In these cables, Mao again pointed out that the key to the northwest strategy was to "open up a path to reach the USSR" so that Soviet military aid could flow into the hands of the Communists. Mao knew that it was not only the vital condition for rebuilding the CCP armed forces, but it was also the key to winning over the Zhang-Yang regional forces to form the coalition of the Northwest Defense Government.[53] The fact which could not escape any contemporary's observation was that without the promise of Soviet assistance, the regional forces would not be interested in allying themselves with the CCP. As the memories of the contemporary players in China's politics would testify, Jiang's power got a start in the middle of the 1920s only because Sun Yet-sen allied with the USSR which became the patron of Jiang's Huangpu Military Academy. In exchange, the GMD accepted the CCP as a partner. Ten years later, by the same token, the Zhang-Yang forces in the northwest could see the possibility of allying themselves with the CCP as a way to gain Soviet military support, with which they could later replay recent history to conquer the whole nation. Mao knew the history well and tried to play it to his own advantage. In Mao's mind, Soviet military assistance, or the promise of it, had a political dimension, which served the CCP as a critical precondition for the establishment of a united front with the regional forces in the northwest. As early as 6 April 1936, Mao cabled Zhang Xueliang regarding the upcoming Zhou-Zhang meeting at Yan'an. Mao proposed five issues for discussion, one of which was "to unite with the Soviet Union," and Mao suggested that Zhang send representatives to Moscow as well.[54] Mao used the CCP's Soviet connection to lure Zhang into a coalition, and it worked very well. Mao must have realized that without the Soviet connection, the CCP would have been one more "bandit force" in China's remote area. The CCP's Soviet connection, or its political identification as a member of the Comintern, had an important role to play in China's realpolitik.

Regarding the concrete steps to open up a path to reach the USSR, Mao had two alternative routes: one would go north through Ningxia and central Suiyuan to reach the PRM; the other toward the west through Lanzhou to reach Xinjiang. Mao left both options open, but took the northern route as the priority for the moment, because he hoped that Moscow would send military equipment from the PRM to meet the CCP half way. If the "brothers" in Outer Mongolia would send troops to deliver Soviet weapons, Mao told Peng, the CCP forces should head north as soon as possible. Mao wanted the CCP forces to cross the Yellow River during the summer of 1936 if possible; should it fail, the troops would have to wait until winter when the River was frozen. In any case, Mao told Peng, in July and August the Red Army first of all had to defeat the pro-GMD Muslim forces in Ningxia and Gansu in order to consolidate the CCP's control over this area.[55]

On 25 August, Mao cabled Moscow to report his plan, and to ask for the assurance that the Soviet Union would provide military aid from Outer Mongolia. On 11 and 27 September, the ECCI telegraphed Mao that his plan was approved and that the Soviet aid would arrive after the CCP occupied Ningxia. On 2 October, Mao again telegraphed Moscow, and this time he provided a long list of what the CCP wanted from the Soviets, which included airplanes and heavy artillery. At the same time, he asked the Soviets to send their military aid to Ningxia.[56] Apparently, Mao's expectation far exceeded what Moscow had in mind. Stalin intended to support the CCP in the northeast, but not openly, for he realized by then that his overt assistance to the CCP in the northwest would push the GMD government into Tokyo's embrace, and a conflict with a possible Chinese-Japanese alliance was what Stalin wanted to avoid at any cost. On 18 October, Moscow informed Mao that instead of being directly involved, Moscow would hire a "foreign company" to purchase and deliver the aid, which would be about 550 to 600 tons of materials, but airplanes and heavy artillery would not be included. They would send the materials toward Ningxia, but would not exceed 100 kilometers from the border of Outer Mongolia.[57]

This must have been disappointing news for Mao, who, nevertheless, started to carry out the Ningxia campaign as outlined in his 14 October order.[58] On 24 October, a section of CCP military crossed the Yellow River; on the same day, Mao cabled Moscow again, not only to report the unfolding military action, but to again ask the Soviets to send the materials further toward Ningxia. However, the CCP's Ningxia campaign did not go as Mao expected, and the GMD forces were much too strong. By the end of October, the CCP was defeated. On 30 October, Mao reported the military situation to Moscow. Three days later, the ECCI cabled Mao and instructed him to call off the Ningxia campaign. Moscow listed three reasons: first, it was impossible for the CCP to overcome the severe conditions during the winter; second, should the CCP receive the materials, they could be attacked on their way back by the Japanese air force; third, should the Japanese learn of this operation, it could cause a serious confrontation between Japan and the USSR. Moscow, however, promised Mao to increase efforts to deliver much needed military aid from Hami, Xinjiang, and the amount of material would be more than 1,000 tons.[59]

Accordingly, Mao outlined a new plan on 8 November. He called off the hopeless Ningxia campaign, and ordered the Fourth Front Army of 21,000 men to reorganize into the Western Route Army (*xilujun*), whose task was to reach Hami in one year.[60] Mao reported his plan to Moscow the same day. Within a week, Mao cabled the ECCI twice, appealing for an emergency cash delivery, for the CCP troops were desperately in need of food and winter clothing. Mao cried out in his 9 November cable that more soldiers would die of starvation and hypothermia daily, should the Soviet aid fail to arrive quickly. Moscow responded immediately on 12 November, promising a cash shipment of 550,000 U.S. dollars, of which $150,000 would be delivered via Madam Song Qingling in Shanghai. This shipment reached Mao early in December.[61]

At the same time, the Soviets were actively piling up military aid in the Central Asian region, and Stalin promised to deliver a shipment including 90 tanks and 90 heavy artillery pieces from Xinjiang. Together, 50 Soviet-trained Chinese military experts would be sent back with these weapons. The CCP's Western Route Army, however, failed to reach Xinjiang, and it was wiped out by the Muslim forces in the northwest early in 1937. To compensate for this failed undertaking, Moscow increased its cash flow. On 2 March 1937, the ECCI informed Mao that a cash shipment of $800,000 (U.S. dollars) would be delivered, and another shipment of the same amount would follow.[62]

Stalin's generous assistance to Mao saved the CCP from total destruction, and Mao and his colleagues had good reasons to repeat publicly and privately that without Soviet assistance there would have been no chance for the Chinese revolution to succeed. More important, the Soviet aid, or the promise of it, yielded an unexpected political result at the end of 1936, which served the CCP well, and a new era in modern Chinese history was thus started. This was the Xi'an Incident. Having been entangled in the Mao-Moscow northwest scheme, Zhang Xueliang and Yang Hucheng had high expectations for Soviet military aid. When the scheme failed, and Jiang came to Xi'an to force them either to fight the CCP or to move into another area where Jiang's forces prevailed, the two generals had no choice but to kidnap Jiang on 12 December 1936. Moscow intervened to promote a peaceful solution to the incident, and Jiang was released with the understanding that he would stop the civil war against the CCP, and unite with the CCP against Japan. The rest of the story is well known: during the anti-Japanese war, the CCP strengthened its military muscle, and when the war ended, it was ready to contest the GMD for national power.

In short, Mao and his colleagues had more than ideological reasons to maintain their commitment to international communism led by Moscow. Their ideology rendered them a unique perspective to read into, and to interact with, the circumstances; and in turn, their interaction with the circumstances further confirmed and enhanced their ideology/identity, which led them to identify Soviet interests as the same as their own. Since Mao and his comrades perceived that the very survival and future development of the CCP was dependent on Soviet material and political-psychological support, it is no wonder that they acted as loyal and obedient subordinates of Moscow. If Mao's rise to power at Zunyi was to a large extent due to Moscow's intervention and promotion on his behalf, he did not disappoint Stalin. In the two years after Zunyi, he, driven by both his faith and survival instinct, tried his best to integrate the CCP's cause of action and the Moscow-led world revolution not only on the conceptual level, but also on the operational level. Mao in fact followed Moscow's instructions almost religiously, and he disregarded China's national boundaries completely. Mao truly deserved the title of "International Communist."

CHAPTER II

CCP-Moscow Relations during the
Anti-Japanese War, 1937–1945

ON 24 January 1937, about a month and a half after the Xi'an Incident, a CCP politburo standing committee meeting was held to discuss the Party's policy of the united front with the GMD. Speaking softly, Mao was "making self-criticism" while puffing on a cigarette. He said, "Our mistake was that when we wrote the [Wayaobao] resolution in December 1935, we mentioned the task of resistance to Japan, but we failed to give up the slogan of 'opposing Jiang.' In May [1936], we were still in the slow process of changing [the anti-Jiang policy]. The thorough change of that policy took place only after the receipt of the Comintern directive [of 15 August]. During the Xi'an Incident, we proposed in our circular telegram that Jiang be brought to a public trial. This was also wrong."[1] Everyone else in the smoke-filled room was, of course, in agreement with Mao. Mao's self-criticism was in response to two telegrams from Moscow on 19 and 20 January, in which the ECCI sharply criticized the CCP leadership for being too radical in its policy toward the GMD. Mao seemed very receptive, if not obedient, to Moscow's messages.

Less than twenty years later, however, Mao began to complain that Stalin did not believe in the CCP's strength, and supported Wang Ming's "defeatist program," which was "against the Communist Party's independent policy, the strengthening of the CCP's armed forces and revolutionary bases, and wanted to prevent all the strata of the Chinese society from rallying around the CCP."[2] In other words, Mao charged in 1956 that Stalin's China policy during the anti-Japanese war was wrong, and his own policy was correct; he, and only he, saved the CCP from being ruined by Stalin and his proxy. Mao's later contention has had a notable effect on western scholarship in the field.[3]

Which image of Mao is closer to historical fact? The obedient one or the defiant one? The new evidence seems to point at the former, and the latter is Mao's self-portrait in a later day. In fact, due to his megalomaniac personality, Mao was often too emotionally impulsive and politically radical to be strategically cautious and tactful; he often exaggerated the "people's strength" (read the CCP strength), and was unwilling to make temporary concessions with the GMD. It was Stalin who pulled Mao back from his radical and potentially ruinous grandioseness, and Mao heeded Stalin's advice closely, if not religiously. Stalin was thus instrumental to a well-balanced CCP policy, and Mao's respect for, and obedience to, Stalin saved the CCP in numerous critical moments when Mao's impulsiveness and radical policy could have doomed the communist cause then and there. In this view, one can very well make an argument that after Stalin's death Mao's grandiosity and megalomania were set loose, and his personality cult ruined the CCP in the process of the Great Leap Forward, and the Great Proletarian Cultural Revolution.[4] A brief revisit of history is in order.

MOSCOW'S LEADING ROLE IN THE
TRANSITION TOWARD THE UNITED FRONT

In line with the Comintern's radicalism of the "third period," Mao and his comrades before 1935 did not consider the issue of a united front even with certain anti-Jiang groups within the GMD. Moscow's radicalism was reflected in a directive to the CCP on 8 February 1929, which stated that China's bourgeoisie and its government had turned themselves into a counterrevolutionary camp, and together with various warlords, they were only "the ready tools" of different imperialist powers. Thus, the Chinese revolution could be carried out only by the soviet government of proletarian-peasant dictatorship.[5] This mood continued to prevail within the Party until the end of 1935. When Mao addressed the rank and file on 30 November 1935, he still lumped Jiang together with Zhang Xueliang and Yan Xishan, calling them "Chinese traitors" and the main enemies of the CCP.[6] This, however, was soon to change.

In 1935, Japanese expansion from Manchuria toward China proper stirred up a rising anti-Japanese nationalist sentiment among the general population of China, and pressure on the Nanjing government to take forceful means to resist the Japanese aggression mounted. While the United States was still in an isolationist mood, Moscow was eager to check Japan's further expansion which, combined with the Hitler menace from the west, threatened Moscow with the frightening prospect of a two-front war. Thus, the Japanese threat created a common interest between Moscow and Nanjing. In October 1935, Kong Xiangxi, Jiang's brother-in-law and the Finance Minister, met with Dimitri Bogomolov, the Soviet Ambassador to China, to express Jiang's readiness to resist Japan militarily and the desire to obtain military aid from the USSR. Moscow's response to Nanjing's overture was both positive and cautious. As much as he desired Nanjing's anti-Japanese position, Stalin remained distrustful of Jiang. He instructed Bogomolov to find the "true purpose" of the GMD, and to watch out for the possibility that Jiang was using a potential Sino-Soviet rapprochement as a bargaining chip to strike a deal with Tokyo.[7]

Jiang was fundamentally distrustful of Stalin, too. To Jiang, the Japanese threat was an external concern, like skin disease; while the CCP posed a threat from within, like heart disease. Jiang feared that the possible Nanjing-Moscow rapprochement might facilitate the CCP's cause at home. Therefore, he instructed Chen Lifu, who was encouraged by Bogomolov to meet Stalin in

Moscow secretly, to tell the Kremlin that the spirit of the agreement between Sun Yat-sen and Joffe in 1923 should be the foundation of the new Moscow-Nanjing understanding. What Jiang really meant was that Moscow should support his effort to resist Japan, and at the same time declare the unsuitability of the soviet system in China. More concretely, Jiang wanted Stalin to instruct the CCP to subject itself to the authority of the GMD-dominated Nanjing regime.[8]

Distrustful of Jiang's intention and skeptical of Nanjing's willingness and ability to fight the Japanese in the event of a future Soviet-Japanese war, Stalin rejected Jiang's proposition and refused to even meet with Chen, who was soon recalled by Jiang.[9] Nonetheless, the Japanese threat was too real for both Moscow and Nanjing to ignore; and yet, the mutual suspicion between Stalin and Jiang was too deep-seated to be discarded completely. Consequently, both sides continued to play a double game, leaving all options open. On Moscow's part, the ECCI directed both the CCP delegation led by Wang Ming and Mao's Center at home to start negotiations secretly with Nanjing's representatives, and at the same time, to continue the military effort to establish an anti-Jiang coalition in China's northwest. Instructed by Moscow, Mao played a double game with Jiang as well. He personally directed the secret negotiations with Nanjing through different channels in 1936, but Mao's primary focus remained on the creation of a new base under the Soviet umbrella.

The united front between the CCP and the Zhang-Yang forces in the northwest was based on an anti-Jiang and anti-Japanese spirit with the understanding that Moscow supported the scheme. As long as Moscow continued to support the CCP's effort to create a "defense government" in the northwest in opposition to the Nanjing regime, Mao had every reason to believe that Stalin would welcome any action which would undermine Jiang's power. Thus, when the provincial military leaders in Guangdong and Guangxi staged an uprising against Jiang early in June 1936, Mao was excited by the development and firmly supported the uprising which, to Mao's dismay, was soon defeated by Jiang. During the event, *Pravda* published an article on 24 June to condemn the anti-Jiang uprising of a pro-Japanese plot sponsored by Tokyo. This indicated that Stalin was apparently concerned with the prospect that the fragmentation of China would facilitate Japan's aggression. Before this uprising, moreover, the ECCI had instructed the CCP to relinquish the slogan of "resist Japan and oppose Jiang." Yet, neither Stalin nor the ECCI explained to the CCP how to reconcile a friendly policy toward Jiang and the effort to create an anti-Jiang coalition in the northwest. Consequently, both Wang Ming and Mao took the ECCI directive and the *Pravda* article only as a propaganda tactic. Wang proposed changing the old slogan into a new one: "resist Japan and oppose the villain" (*kang-Ri tao-zei*). Jiang's name was removed only to be replaced by *zei*, a bandit, a thief, an evil man. In opposition to the *Pravda* article, Wang further asserted that the anti-Jiang uprising was not a plot of Tokyo, and the "man who is provoking a new civil war is Jiang Jieshi," not the generals in the south. He even stated that the CCP should make use of the warlords to defeat "Jiang *zei*." Mao was totally in agreement with Wang.[10]

This discrepancy between Moscow and the CCP forced the ECCI to formulate a clearer policy with regard to CCP-GMD relations. On 23 July, having received Mao's reports and the Wayaobao Resolutions through the newly resumed radio communication, the ECCI held a meeting, which eventually resulted in the ECCI directive of 15 August. At the meeting Dimitrov praised the CCP's achievement in expanding the Red Army and the soviet area, but he explicitly stated that the CCP's current priority was not to further expand its military force but to form a national united front which would include Jiang's Nanjing regime.[11]

Moscow's new line marked the beginning of the stage of "compelling Jiang to resist Japan." Mao followed Moscow's signal quickly.[12] After having received the news about the ECCI meeting of 23 July, the CCP politburo held a meeting on 10 August. At the meeting, Zhou Enlai stated that the old slogan of "opposing Jiang and resisting Japan" was no longer suitable and Jiang should be included in the anti-Japanese united front. Mao expressed his total agreement with Zhou. When the ECCI's 15 August directive arrived, Moscow's new policy became more concrete: the ECCI instructed Mao to take the initiative to contact Jiang, and to announce openly that the CCP was ready to send a delegation to negotiate with Jiang to establish a defense government in which the CCP would be a subordinate and would obey the central government's order. Mao followed the ECCI instruction closely. The CCP sent an open letter to the GMD on 25 August, appealing for a GMD-CCP united front against Japan. On 1 September, Mao issued an inner-party document on the policy of "compelling Jiang to resist Japan," and the language of it was almost verbatim from the ECCI's directive of 15 August. One week later, Mao personally wrote to Shao Lizi, Jiang's political adviser, to call for a reunion of the GMD and the CCP.[13]

To include Jiang in a national united front remained wishful thinking of the Moscow-CCP leadership, for Jiang was unwilling to accept the CCP as a partner before it was disarmed and its base area incorporated. In other words, Jiang intended to dismantle Mao's class-struggle program once and for all before he would consider a second united front with the CCP. Neither Stalin nor Mao would trust Jiang enough to disarm themselves, especially after they had experienced what Jiang did to them in 1927. The ECCI directive of 15 August made it clear that "the establishment of an anti-Japanese national united front should never be meant to reduce the soviet power, or to integrate the Red Army and the CCP into the anti-Japanese [national] armies and a certain Chinese political coalition, respectively." It explicitly argued for the maintenance of the CCP's absolute political and organizational independence, and vigorous expansion of the strength of the Party and the Red Army. Ironically, it was not Moscow but Mao who appeared to be on the "rightist track" after he received the message after the ECCI meeting of 23 July. Mao, eager to follow Moscow's changing direction, proposed to the ECCI that in order to enlarge the anti-Japanese united front the CCP should allow as many people as possible to join the Party and the Red Army no matter what their family backgrounds were. Mao even argued that Zhang Xueliang should be allowed to join the Communist Party. This was too "rightist" for Moscow's taste, and the ECCI sharply criticized Mao's proposal. Moscow demanded that the CCP make every effort to "maintain the class purity of the Party, the Red Army, and the soviet government." After having been criticized, Mao did not show any sign of defiance; instead, the Party Center held special meetings to conduct a round of self-criticism, which led to the Center's "Announcement of Self-Criticism" issued to the rank and file on 22 September 1936.[14]

Evidently, the ECCI's new policy was a dualistic one, which insisted on uniting with Jiang and maintaining the CCP's military and political independence at the same time. The problem was that Jiang was still determined to have the CCP disarmed first. Under the circumstances, both Moscow and Mao understood that Jiang would accept the CCP's terms for a coalition only when he was cornered, and to corner him one must win over many other anti-Jiang factions within the GMD. "The more we can win over the warlords outside of the Nanjing orbit to resist Japan," Mao wrote in the directive of 1 September, "the more we are likely to realize the policy [of compelling Jiang to resist Japan]."[15] Thus, the CCP and Moscow continued a "two-track" policy: to negotiate with Jiang for a peaceful settlement to end the civil war, and at the same time, to make every effort to establish an anti-Jiang coalition in the northwest.

From Mao's perspective, the two sides of the CCP-Moscow dual policy toward Jiang were mutually complementary. Mao's logic was expressed in his telegram to Moscow on 25 August 1936. He argued that the Shaanbei region did not produce enough food to enable the Red Army to survive, and the CCP force could expand southward or eastward, which would inevitably clash with the GMD again. The better alternative was to expand westward to occupy Ningxia. In doing so, the CCP could not only avoid civil war with Jiang, but also open up a path to reach the USSR. With Soviet military aid, the CCP in the northwest could attract various anti-Jiang forces within the GMD, and this could eventually force Jiang to come to terms with the CCP. In this way, Mao's class-struggle program in the northwest would serve the purpose of "compelling Jiang to resist Japan." Moscow was receptive to Mao's reasoning, and the northwest scheme continued until the Xi'an Incident.

MOSCOW AND THE XI'AN INCIDENT

Frustrated by the defeat of the northwest strategy and forced by Jiang to renew their warfare against their secret ally, Generals Zhang and Yang detained Jiang in Xi'an on 12 December 1936. They immediately informed the CCP and invited Zhou Enlai to Xi'an to help manage the situation. By kidnapping Jiang, Zhang and Yang apparently intended to form a Soviet-supported northwest defense government. Mao was in agreement with Zhang and Yang, and he told them on 13 December that their "righteous action" had the CCP's full support. A joint military plan to engage Nanjing's armies was also laid out.[16]

In the telegrams to the ECCI on 12 and 13 December, Mao reported his strategy: to eliminate Jiang once and for all, to divide and defeat the Nanjing regime, and to make Xi'an a new national center. Mao was quite optimistic about his plan. In his telegram to Zhang on 14 December, Mao said that "if we can win a few battles, the military situation will soon be in our favor."[17] Nevertheless, Moscow's policy was changing rapidly in the first few days following Jiang's kidnapping. First of all, Stalin had to avoid diplomatic embarrassment for secretly supporting anti-government activities in China's northwest. The Nanjing government was convinced that Moscow had played a decisive role in the Xi'an Incident, and it instructed China's ambassador in Moscow to tell Litvinov on 13 December that China knew that the incident was the result of Soviet secret involvement in China's northwest. Nanjing also told the Soviet embassy in China that if Jiang was endangered, China would hold the CCP and the USSR responsible, and China would be forced to ally with Japan against the USSR.[18] Partially for whitewashing Moscow's involvement in the northwest scheme, on 14 December *Pravda* strongly accused the Xi'an mutiny of being a "pro-Japanese scheme" instigated by Wang Jingwei, the pro-Tokyo leader of the GMD.

Mao understood that Moscow's propaganda against the Xi'an event was only a diplomatic necessity, which did not reflect Moscow's true policy. A few months earlier, *Pravda* made the same accusation against the southern anti-Jiang uprising, but Moscow continued to support Mao's northwest scheme after that. When Zhang was disturbed by Moscow's propaganda accusing him of being "pro-Japanese," Mao telegraphed Zhang to offer some comfort. Mao said that "[we] guess Moscow should render its sympathy to the event, if they know that it is not purely a military mutiny, but action based on people's support. However, the USSR government might not support us openly because it has to deal with current international diplomacy."[19] Thus, although the CCP learned Moscow's public reaction toward the Xi'an event right away, Mao continued to pursue his plan to eliminate Jiang and to turn Xi'an into the national center. On 15 December, the CCP sent a cable to Nanjing to demand that Jiang be dismissed from office and brought to trial.[20] Mao's hard-line approach to the event was apparent.

The next day, however, Mao had to do a complete turnaround. Having finally made up its mind, Moscow sent instructions to Mao on 16 December. Drafted by Dimitrov, the ECCI's telegram stated that "no matter what Zhang's intention is," his action of kidnapping Jiang "only promotes Japan's invasion in China." This appears to be a response to Mao's previous telegrams which tried to explain to Moscow that Zhang's action was propelled by the "good intention" to form a pro-Soviet solidarity in the northwest. In its own way, Moscow accepted Mao's defense of Zhang's intention, but made it clear that the consequence of Zhang's action was detrimental. Since the event had occurred, the ECCI instructed the CCP to secure a peaceful resolution. To direct the CCP's negotiation with Jiang for his own release, Moscow laid down four conditions: first, to reform the Nanjing government by incorporating representatives of the anti-Japanese movement; second, to guarantee people's democratic rights; third, to terminate the policy of a civil war against the Red Army and to cooperate with the CCP in resistance to Japan; finally, to cooperate with countries which were sympathetic to the Chinese people's resistance to Japanese imperialism. The ECCI pointedly stated that the CCP should avoid using the clause of "unite with the Soviet Union."[21]

One has to admit that Moscow's new policy was much more realistic and advantageous than Mao's approach of eliminating Jiang. If Jiang were executed, the Nanjing forces would certainly attack the Xi'an forces. On the same day the ECCI telegram was dispatched, Nanjing formed two army corps under the slogan of "crusade against rebels," and five divisions occupied Tongguan, the strategic gate to Xi'an from the east. In addition, the Zhang-Yang forces were not reliable; on 16 December, as soon as the Nanjing forces approached, one division of Yang's Northwest Army defected.[22] It was quite obvious that the CCP-Zhang-Yang alliance would not win the civil war against the Nanjing forces. Zhou Enlai in Xi'an sensed this gloomy prospect and sent Mao a cable on 17 December which predicted that it was impossible to defeat the Nanjing armies; therefore, the CCP should give up its policy of physically eliminating Jiang. Instead, Zhou suggested, Xi'an should guarantee Jiang's safety provided Nanjing did not push further militarily.[23] On the part of Moscow, if a civil war were to erupt and the USSR were to take sides with the Xi'an alliance, the Chinese government in Nanjing would surely ally itself with Tokyo; and Moscow would be condemned and isolated by the international community because of its behavior. Once the ECCI clarified its position, Mao followed the new policy line closely.[24]

It was certainly much easier for Moscow to formulate the new policy than it was for Mao to carry it out. First of all, Mao had to persuade Zhang and Yang that the best and most realistic policy was to release Jiang with conditions attached. To do this, Mao needed a few days. Had Mao passed on Moscow's telegram of 16 December to Zhang and Yang, one day after Mao himself officially announced his policy of eliminating Jiang, the result would have been disastrous. Zhang and Yang not only would have felt that Moscow betrayed them, but they would also have looked down upon Mao as Moscow's puppet. Mao, therefore, did not inform Xi'an of the Moscow message until 20 December.[25] On 21 December, Mao cabled Pan Hannian, the CCP representative in Nanjing, and instructed him to propose four conditions to the Nanjing government for Jiang's release. Mao's conditions were copied from the ECCI directive almost word for word.[26]

After Jiang was released and he in turn detained Zhang Xueliang, the tension between Nanjing and Xi'an mounted again. Mao's policy was to divide Nanjing and to force Jiang into line (*fenhua Nanjing, bi-Jiang jiufan*).[27] From Moscow's point of view, however, Mao's policy was too "leftist." On 19 and 20 January the ECCI sent two telegrams to Mao. In the first cable, Moscow sharply criticized the CCP's policy and stated that the Party's previous policy to eliminate Jiang and overthrow the Nanjing Government had been a mistake. Now, the ECCI continued, the Party had not yet thoroughly corrected this mistake, and in fact, was still pursuing a policy of dividing the GMD, rather than cooperating with it. Moreover, the Party's cooperation with the Xi'an generals had turned out to be an anti-Nanjing coalition. "All of these," the ECCI concluded, "actually helped to increase the pro-Japanese clique's power." The ECCI's directive instructed the CCP that the Party's main task was to stop civil war, and strive for resistance to Japan in cooperation with Nanjing. The Party's cooperation with the Xi'an generals and other regional powers should be subordinate to this main policy line, not in opposition to it.[28]

Mao immediately convened a politburo meeting at which he made his "self-criticism" described in the outset of this chapter. He also, of course, followed Stalin's advice step by step. As it happened, Moscow's assessment of the situation was proven correct: Jiang did not continue the war against the CCP and the Zhang-Yang forces. Peace became reality in February, and the GMD was to convene its national plenum soon to adopt a new policy for the new era as well. On 5 February and 5 March, the ECCI sent Mao additional telegrams to instruct the CCP how to deal with the upcoming GMD Third Plenum. Moscow was more explicit this time and told Mao that the CCP should recognize Nanjing as the national government, and based on this recognition, it should adjust the relations between the CCP's regional government and Jiang's Nanjing government. In other words, the CCP should subordinate its local control to Jiang's national government. Moscow also suggested that Sun Yat-sen's Three People's Principles should be adopted as a common program of the national united front, and class struggle should be downplayed.[29]

The ECCI's instructions were fully accepted and implemented by Mao. On 21 January, Mao telegraphed Pan Hannian that "in order to avoid civil war and realize national resistance in cooperation [with the GMD], we should not oppose Jiang's policy in principle. [We] should persuade the Xi'an generals to subordinate themselves to Nanjing's policy of domestic unity, and on the other hand, advise Jiang to show leniency toward Zhang and Yang in order to comfort them." On 29 January, Mao cabled Pan again that "in order to support Mr. Jiang's policy of bringing a peaceful solution to the northwestern situation, to stop civil war forever, and to cooperate in resisting the intrusion of outsiders, we decided to give up our former demand for the Red Army's deployment in southern Shaanxi." The CCP armed forces would withdraw from that region before Nanjing's army moved in. On 10 February, following the ECCI's directive of 5 February, the Party Center telegraphed the GMD Third Plenum to pledge that the CCP would, among other things, relinquish the policy of armed insurrection aimed at overthrowing the GMD government, and cease confiscating landlords' land. The CCP's local administration and military force would also subordinate themselves to Nanjing's leadership.[30]

Stalin wanted Mao to form a united front with Jiang, but he did not advise him to do so at the expense of the Red Army and the soviet region. In fact, in the same ECCI telegram of 19 January it was unequivocally stated: "Under any circumstances, the more important matter is to maintain the unity of the Party and the Red Army, because they are the guarantee of overcoming any difficulty." Moscow also instructed Mao that if the Nanjing troops attacked any CCP area, "your task then is self-defense."[31] Evidently, from both Moscow's and Mao's point of view, the Party's dual policy served a dual purpose: to establish a united front with the GMD, while striving for the preservation and expansion of the Red Army and the CCP base area, the essence of Mao's class-struggle program.

To serve this dual purpose, Mao followed Moscow's line to establish a policy of hard bargaining with the GMD. The results of negotiations between Zhou and Jiang and the CCP's policy in dealing with Jiang's terms were duly reported to the Comintern on 17 and 26 June.[32] We do not know the content of the ECCI's reply, but we do know that the ECCI advised the CCP that in the future national war against Japan the Red Army should be concentrated on one front in order to secure the Party's control over the Army.[33] This, however, was unacceptable to Jiang, and negotiations failed to reach an agreement even after the war with Japan erupted on 7 July. On 20 July, Mao telegraphed Zhou: "The Japanese attack has already become an established fact, and the realization of the war of resistance to Japan is possible. We have decided to adopt a policy that if Jiang does not compromise, we shall discontinue negotiation."[34] Mao deemed that Jiang had to accept the status quo because the war with Japan had already begun, and Jiang needed Moscow's help. Mao was right.

On 13 August, the Japanese helped to break the deadlock by attacking Shanghai, the home base of Jiang. On 22 August, one day after the Sino-Soviet nonaggression pact was signed, Jiang announced the acceptance of the CCP and its armed forces as a part of the national defense. The CCP's insistence on its independent control of the armed forces and the base area finally succeeded. In the entire process, an old pattern repeated itself again and again: while Mao was radical and reluctant to compromise with Jiang, Stalin intervened with a moderate and reconciling approach, which balanced Mao's radicalism decisively. Mao's willingness to obey Stalin proved to be the key to a balanced winning strategy, which was not a result of Mao's "correct line" against the Wang Ming-Stalin "erroneous line," as Mao claimed ungracefully after the death of Stalin. In fact, the opposite is true.

THE DEBATE OVER CCP MILITARY STRATEGY

Nor was there a fundamental difference between Mao and Wang Ming-Stalin over the CCP's military strategy, as Maoist history later claimed.[35] In fact, both Stalin and Mao were gravely concerned, up to 1942, about the possibility of Jiang's about-face to a pro-Japanese and anti-Soviet position, especially when the United States, Jiang's ultimate "foreign master," was continuously negotiating with Tokyo to promote a so-called "Far Eastern Munich." To prevent such a possible GMD turnaround, Moscow instructed the CCP to play a double game just as it did before. On 10 August, the ECCI held a special meeting to discuss its China policy. Dimitrov cautioned that the united front with the GMD would probably bring grave danger to the Chinese comrades: "I am referring to Jiang Jieshi's plot and his encirclement [of the CCP]," Dimitrov warned. He said that "the most important task at present is to bring the Chinese working masses under the influence of the CCP, not the GMD or other political groups," so that the CCP could rely upon not only its armed forces but also the support of the working class.[36] It is untrue and ungraceful for Mao to accuse Stalin in the 1950s of wanting to sacrifice the CCP's independent control over its military and base areas, and to prevent the people from rallying behind the CCP.

Regarding military conduct on a day-to-day basis, Mao's policy was not so much determined by his long-term revolutionary vision, but by his deep suspicion of the GMD and his calculation of the situation in the battlefield. Mao's policy was thus very changeable from day to day, if not moment to moment, depending upon the changes of his feelings about the CCP-GMD relations and his evaluation of the military situation. If there were a "two-line struggle," it was constantly going on in Mao's own mind. In the search for a balancing point, he constantly switched back and forth between the "leftist" position and the "rightist" one. In fact, before Wang Ming returned from Moscow, Mao himself had already experienced such turnabouts many times.

In early July, when anti-Japanese sentiment was on the rise, Mao was ready to send all the CCP forces to North China to fight the Japanese in cooperation with the GMD.[37] However, at the end of July, the news from the battlefield in north China was gloomy. Mao was alarmed by the Japanese military might; the initial euphoria was over. On 31 July, Mao had second thoughts, and he cabled his military lieutenants that the quick movement of the CCP troops toward North China should be for propaganda purposes only. In reality, Mao stated, the troops should not move hastily. They could "move 50 *li*

[25 km] each day, and pause one day after every three days." At the same time, Mao continued, the Red Army should "ask for [military] supplies from Nanjing."[38] Mao's strategy of dispersed guerrilla warfare started to emerge; its main goal was to preserve the CCP's military forces by avoiding costly fighting with the Japanese so that the CCP could fight the GMD later.

The very next day, Mao dispatched three telegrams in a row to Zhou Enlai and others who were invited by Jiang to discuss the defense issue in Nanjing. Mao reiterated his independent dispersed guerrilla strategy, and cautioned that the departure of the Red Army should be slow, and the Red Army's tactical maneuvers should not be controlled by Jiang. On 4 August, Mao cabled his comrades again, stressing that "to mobilize and arm the people in a self-defensive war is the key to the victory of the Red Army."[39] Mao was not concerned with the victory of the "Chinese nation," which was represented by Jiang's regime. In Mao's mind, a Chinese national victory over Japan under the GMD's leadership would only serve bourgeois interests, and turn China into an "American colony," which was no better than a Japanese one, if not worse. Only with the victory of the Red Army could China be saved by the CCP.

Mao's military conservatism in the face of a national war effort against Japan, however, was not entirely acceptable to his colleagues. On 4 August, Zhou Enlai, Zhu De, Qing Bangxian, Lin Boqu, Peng Dehuai, and Ren Bishi cabled Mao twice to debate Mao's new military strategy. They disagreed with Mao's proposal of sending out only one-third of the Red Army, and insisted that all three divisions should go to the front quickly and decisively. Their reasoning was two-fold: first, it would enable the Party to earn a "better political reputation" among the people; second, the Red Army would be in a better position to remain unseparated and carry on independent military operations, as Moscow had instructed. They were not against Mao's guerrilla strategy, but insisted that mobile warfare should also be carried on when the situation was suitable. On the other hand, they shared Mao's caution and stated that the principles of "saving troops (*jieyue bingli*), carefully using troops (*jingshen shiyong*), and not engaging [them] in too costly battles (*buda yingzhang*)" should be observed.[40]

Mao was ready to reconcile with his colleagues, for he understood the importance of showing the GMD as well as the people that the CCP was committed to the anti-Japanese patriotic cause. Had the CCP followed Mao's partisan military conservatism, the political damage to the Party could have been fatal. Mao knew this well, and he cabled his colleagues on 5 August to make more moderate proposals: (1) the Red Army's basic strategy should be "independent guerrilla-mobile warfare," and (2) the main forces of the three divisions should be sent out, provided the GMD recognized the CCP's right to use these troops according to the situation as the commanders saw fit.[41]

Having modified his previous proposals, Mao felt it necessary to caution his colleagues that they should not forget that Jiang was a warlord and it was

Jiang who demanded that the entire Red Army be moved to the front. Mao further argued that northern Shaanxi was the only reliable base area of the CCP where Jiang had ten divisions. Should the CCP's troops be annihilated in North China, Jiang could take over the CCP's home base with ease.[42] In the following two weeks, however, Mao seemed to be concerned with the necessity for the CCP to demonstrate its willingness to fight the Japanese. On 17 August, the GMD asked the CCP to deploy its troops in northeastern Shanxi. Mao immediately cabled the GMD, expressing the CCP's acceptance of the GMD plan. At the same time, he ordered the three CCP divisions to get ready to go to the front.[43]

However, on 18 August, the very next day, Mao changed his mind again. He sent three telegrams to Zhou Enlai, asserting that "the GMD's plot is now obvious and its scheme is [threefold]: (1) to send all the Red Army to the front; (2) to make the Red Army deploy separately in order to force it to obey GMD orders; (3) having subdued the Red Army, Jiang would then be able to decide the fate of the Party and its home base as well." Based on that judgment, Mao went back to his 4 August position.[44]

Mao's capriciousness would certainly stir up again the debate between himself and his colleagues on the issues which seemed to have been settled early in that month. The debate resumed at the Luochuan Conference in 22–24 August. At first, Mao insisted on his formula of "independent guerrilla warfare," and added one more condition: guerrilla warfare in the mountainous area. Mao's purpose was to "preserve and expand the Red Army," and to create base areas for the Red Army. Only then, Mao told the conference, could cooperation with the GMD army have a foundation. Mao's logic was pure and simple: without the strength of the armed forces and base area, they would have nothing left to bargain with the GMD.[45] On the other hand, Zhou Enlai and others advocated "mobile-guerrilla warfare" in cooperation with the GMD.[46]

Since all the arguments had been discussed and opinions reconciled before, a compromise formula similar to that of 5 August was reached. Mao was elected Chairman of the newly established Military Committee of the CCP, with Zhu De and Zhou Enlai as the Vice-Chairmen. On 24 August, Zhou cabled the GMD on behalf of the CCP Center that the 115th Division had departed for the area designated by the GMD on 22 August, and the other two divisions would follow. On 30 and 31 August Mao twice instructed Zhou to go to Shanxi to discuss the Red Army's (now the Eighth Route Army [ERA]'s) cooperation with Yan Xishan.[47] Apparently, Mao had reconciled with his colleagues' arguments.

Nonetheless, the different emphases of the two sides would persist. For the survival and future expansion of the Red Army, Mao was inclined toward dispersed guerrilla warfare. On the other hand, to facilitate the national effort of resistance, to prevent a possible GMD turnabout to ally with Japan, and to gain political influence and credit for the CCP, Mao's colleagues were dis-

posed to commit the Red Army in concentrated mobile warfare in cooperation with the GMD. These considerations were not mutually exclusive, but
complementary in the minds of both Mao and his colleagues. When Mao felt
the CCP troops had a good chance to win in a given situation, he was willing
to let his lieutenants engage in major operations in cooperation with the GMD;
otherwise, he would fall back on his military conservatism. His mood and policy kept switching constantly.

From late August to late September, the military situation in North China
was not promising for the Chinese. In mid-September, the Japanese occupied
northeast Shanxi, and were heading toward Taiyuan, the provincial seat. On
16 September, Zhu De and others cabled Mao to suggest that the Red Army
defend northeastern Shanxi in cooperation with Yan Xishan in order to keep
the resistance in North China alive. Mao did not want to sacrifice the Red
Army in the battle against the Japanese. He cabled Zhu De on 17 September
to cancel the previous plan for the Red Army's deployment in northeastern
Shanxi. Mao proposed that only one CCP division should go to northwestern
Shanxi, while the other two be deployed in mountainous southeastern and
western Shanxi. In his cable of 21 September, Mao further pointed out that
Taiyuan and all of North China would sooner or later fall into Japanese hands.
Therefore, the CCP's troops should be dispersed in a "truly independent guer-
rilla warfare in the mountainous area, not mobile warfare," and that the Red
Army's task should focus on creating base areas and mobilizing the masses.[48]

But, Mao was well aware that a negotiated truce between Nanjing and
Tokyo was possible. This would mean a joint attack on the Communists by
both the GMD and the Japanese. Therefore, it was vital for the CCP to maintain the united front with the GMD and to keep the national resistance alive.
For that purpose, Mao had to modify his military conservatism and let the Red
Army engage in combat against the Japanese more actively and visibly, and
in cooperation with the GMD. On 24 September, Zhou cabled Mao to suggest the plan for the battle later known as the Pingxingguan Campaign. It was
typical conventional warfare with concentrated forces, but Mao approved it.[49]
On 25 September, when the battle in Pingxingguan was unfolding, Mao felt
uneasy about his approval of the campaign and he telegraphed Zhou and others twice to emphasize that the only correct direction was guerrilla warfare,
and that the Communists should now be concerned about how to carry on
guerrilla warfare after the Japanese occupation of the entire North China
region. Therefore, Mao suggested that at present all CCP troops should be
sheltered from, not exposed to, enemy attack.[50]

On 26 September, the very next day, Mao received Lin Biao's report of the
favorable result of the Pingxingguan Battle, the first CCP victory against the
Japanese. Mao's idea of exclusive guerrilla warfare in the mountainous area
thus changed again. On 29 September, he cabled Zhou and others to suggest
that under advantageous circumstances the Red Army could be concentrated

in combat, that the 115th Division could attack the Japanese rear in cooperation with two to three GMD divisions. He estimated that if this attack by the Chinese divisions on the Japanese rear was successful, a promising situation in Shanxi might ensue.[51] On 6 October, Mao further suggested that two CCP divisions under Lin Biao and He Long should actively participate in Yan Xishan's northern Shanxi campaign, and that Nanjing should send three or four additional divisions to reinforce this campaign.[52] Obviously, this was not independent and dispersed guerrilla warfare at all. Under the influence of Mao's directive of 6 October, the CCP North China Military Sub-committee dispatched its directive of 8 October, calling for active participation in the coming Xinkou Campaign.[53]

Mao's shift to approve the CCP forces' more active and visible role in the resistance was derived not only from the encouraging result of the Pingxingguan Campaign, but also from his concern over a possible Nanjing-Tokyo negotiated truce. In mid-October, the CCP sensed the impending danger of a compromise between the GMD and the Japanese. Due to the Japanese military success in both North China and the Shanghai area, plus the "international seduction" (read encouragement from the U.S., Britain, and Germany), Zhou Enlai told Mao on 19 October that China's resistance to Japan was facing a "new crisis," and that "clamor for peace and compromise with Japan" was on the rise. To prevent Nanjing from "surrendering to Japan," Zhou proposed, among other things, that the CCP take direct and active military action against the Japanese in North China in cooperation with the GMD. Mao replied that he was in "full agreement" with Zhou. With Mao's full support, Zhou sent Mao telegrams on 12, 18, and 19 October, proposing plans regarding the unfolding Xinkou Campaign. All these plans were for mobile or positional warfare, yet Mao offered his full approval.[54]

In November, Taiyuan was occupied by the Japanese. This marked the end of conventional warfare in North China. Even the GMD remaining forces had to go underground to wage guerrilla warfare against the Japanese. Mao's guerrilla strategy thus became the only alternative for the CCP as well. In the latter half of 1940, when the Communists saw the danger of a GMD-Japanese compromise in what was called the "Far Eastern Munich" again, Peng Dehuai took the lead to stage the "Hundred Regiments Campaign." Mao might not have been enthusiastic about the campaign, but he certainly understood the necessity of it; and therefore, he allowed Peng to pursue it for several months. Only in 1942, after the Japanese had stepped up their pressure on the CCP areas and the Communists suffered heavy losses, did Mao cable Peng again to suggest a more conservative military policy.[55]

Evidence suggests that the "two-line" theory, which holds that Mao stood for a "correct strategy" of independent dispersed guerrilla warfare while his opponents, supported by Moscow, were for conventional warfare in cooperation with the GMD, is only a myth, if not political nonsense, promoted by Mao himself for his contemporary agenda. The fact was that Mao and his colleagues shared a two-sided policy, and Mao often appeared to be in constant self-adjustment to maintain a relative balance. When Stalin was not involved directly, the willingness of Mao's colleagues to debate with him, thanks to the still relatively democratic atmosphere within the Party leadership, provided a balancing mechanism to Mao's often too radical orientation. Had Mao already acquired the kind of dictatorship he enjoyed in his later years, and had Zhou and others been as intimidated by Mao as they were later on, the CCP would have been doomed during the anti-Japanese war.

MOSCOW'S SUPPORT FOR THE CCP'S DUAL POLICY: 1937–1941

In the last months of 1937, Moscow was alarmed by international developments: Tokyo was to join hands with Germany and Italy, and the GMD was negotiating with Japan under the mediation of Oskar Trautmann, the German Ambassador to China. Stalin knew that Jiang was partially using the possibility of a peaceful settlement with Japan as a threat to force the USSR to participate directly in the war against Japan. In order to keep the GMD in the war against Japan, Stalin explained patiently to Jiang why the USSR could not take part in the war directly at the moment. At the same time, he promised Jiang that Moscow would help him to establish a mechanized modern army of 300,000 troops.[56] Stalin also knew that Jiang had always looked at the CCP's attitude to the GMD as a barometer of Moscow's policy. Thus, the last thing Stalin wanted at the time was a radical CCP policy to scare off Jiang from a pro-Soviet policy.

In line with Stalin's thinking, the ECCI held a meeting on 10 October to define its China policy. In its resolution, the ECCI made it clear that the "anti-Japanese cause is above anything." The CCP should subordinate itself to the national anti-Japanese united front, and the Party's action should be approved by the GMD which was the leading force in the united front. Since the CCP strength was still weak, it was not the time to argue for "proletarian leadership" within the united front; nor should the Party propose radical political reform against the existing GMD regime.[57] To emphasize this policy line, Stalin and Dimitrov received Wang Ming before his departure for Yan'an. Stalin encouraged the CCP to take more aggressive action in participating, in cooperation with the GMD, in the resistance to Japan. He told Wang that the CCP's current task was resistance to Japan, and the past struggle with the GMD should not be brought to the surface. When Wang asked about the Party's long-term struggle for future national power against the GMD, Stalin said that "in the future, wherever your army reaches, the political power there will be yours."[58] Stalin drove the point home that the CCP should uphold the anti-Japanese national united front for the time being, building the Party-controlled military force quietly for the future struggle against the GMD.

The ECCI also made it clear that it endorsed Mao's leadership within the Party; Wang under no circumstances should challenge Mao's position as leader. At the time, Zhang Wentian was still the Secretary General of the Party, but he was regarded as unsuitable for the position. It was speculated that when Wang came home, he might take over Zhang's position. Nonetheless, Dimitrov put it explicitly to Wang that he should not take up this position even if the comrades at home recommended him. As a Beijing leading scholar on the CCP-Comintern relations points out, at the time, Wang Ming's mentor, Pavell Mif, had already been purged, and Moscow no longer had any particular affection for Wang. Mao was the chosen man for the position.[59]

Although Mao might have been inclined to a more radical attitude by emphasizing the "proletarian leadership" in the united front, he understood Stalin's advice perfectly. In 9–14 December 1937, the politburo held a meeting in which Wang was the main speaker. Wang in effect criticized Mao's radical approach in stressing the struggle for leadership with the GMD; Mao did not even defend himself. Instead, he voted to endorse Wang's report at the December Conference. He also agreed to let Wang draft the resolution of the Conference. It was because Wang was too busy to take care of it, not because of Mao's opposition, that the resolution did not come into being.[60] If Mao had relinquished his guerrilla strategy and let his generals in North China fight a conventional war alongside the GMD, one has no reason to believe that he was forced by Wang-Moscow to adopt a policy which amounted to nothing more than a "public relations campaign" toward the GMD.[61]

Mao in fact fully understood the necessity of wooing the GMD to keep the anti-Japanese united front going. During the entire year of 1938, Mao's activities in courting the GMD surpassed Wang Ming in many ways. For instance, in February he told an American reporter that GMD-CCP cooperation would be permanent. The Communists and the Nationalists would not only fight the Japanese together, but would also reconstruct the country together after the war. Of course, Mao would never tell any American reporter what Stalin had told him about the future armed struggle against the GMD. Instead, he tried hard to demonstrate the CCP's whole-hearted support of the GMD government. On 12 March, Mao appeared very sincere at a mass gathering in Yan'an, stating that "at this gathering, we shall especially extend our greetings to our national leader and the commander of the war of resistance—Generalissimo Jiang—because he leads the whole country to struggle with determination and tirelessness. He mobilizes and conducts the great war of resistance."[62] In his report to the Party's Sixth Plenum, which was to be published, Mao stressed the necessity of a lasting national united front under the leadership of the GMD and Generalissimo Jiang. On 29 September, Mao wrote Jiang personally, and the CCP Plenum sent Jiang a telegram on 5 November. Both were remarkably humble in tone.[63] Mao even proposed that the Communists enter the GMD as individuals just as they had done in the 1920s. Mao's proposal was delivered by Zhou Enlai to Jiang in person on 4 October.[64] Stalin must have been contented with Mao's performance.

Mao, however, did not mean what he said in public.[65] In his closing speech at the Sixth Plenum on 6 November, which was not to be published, Mao told the Party that China had no parliamentary system to enable the Communists to wage a legal struggle for power. The only way to seize power, therefore, depended on the Party's armed struggle. He reiterated that "political power grows out of the barrel of a gun . . . Having guns, we can create party organizations . . . create cadres, create schools, create culture, create mass movements." Mao also quoted from Stalin that the characteristic and the great merit of the Chinese revolution was that it was an armed revolution.[66] Mao must have been greatly inspired by Stalin's remark that future power would be in the hands of the CCP wherever its military forces prevailed.

The real problem between Mao and Wang Ming was the former's fear that the latter might challenge his position in the Party. Wang enjoyed enormous prestige within the Party when he came back from Moscow after being received by Stalin. He, nonetheless, was not "prudent" in a Chinese way. Not only did he criticize the resolution of the Luochuang Conference, drafted by Mao and adopted by the entire politburo, he also issued statements or directives in the name of the Party Center or Mao without Mao's consent. When he was in Wuhan, he proposed that *Jiefang* (Liberation), the CCP organ, be moved there and placed under his supervision. Because of Wang's previous association with the Comintern, which gave him enormous prestige in the Party, Mao tolerated Wang for a few months. In March 1938, Mao decided to act by winning Moscow to his side first. Ren Bishi was chosen to go to Moscow, and his task was twofold: to report to the ECCI the CCP's dual policy in dealing with the GMD, and to explain what was happening within the Party leadership with regard to Wang's behavior.[67]

Based on Ren's report, the ECCI's resolution of 11 June 1938 confirmed Mao's dual policy. It explicitly stated that "the anti-Japanese united front does not and should not violate the participating parties' political and organizational independence," and the CCP should use all its capacity to develop guerrilla bases behind enemy lines. Dimitrov received both Ren and Wang Jiaxiang, who arrived earlier and was about to return to China. Dimitrov criticized Wang Ming's behavior, and instructed Wang Jiaxiang to tell the comrades at home that the ECCI wanted the CCP to strengthen its internal unity under the leadership of Mao, who was "the leader created in the real struggle." On 6 July, *Pravda* unprecedentedly printed Mao's portrait. When Wang Jiaxiang got home, bringing Moscow's messages with him, Mao's position in the Party reached an all-time high. He immediately decided to convene the Sixth Plenum, which lasted from 29 September to early November. During this period, Mao's dual policy toward the GMD was fully adopted and his authority became undisputable.[68]

The GMD, however, was no fool, and GMD-CCP tension increased. If the year 1938 was one of peaceful relations between the GMD and the CCP, the following years witnessed a series of military clashes between them. A measured civil war actually existed within the war of resistance against Japan. A major clash was inevitable. To prevent the CCP from further expansion, Jiang not only stationed massive troops in the northwest, he also ordered the CCP New Fourth Army in the Yangzi valley to move to the area north of the Yellow River. In the fall of 1940, when pressure from the GMD mounted, Mao concluded that Jiang was going to ally himself with Japan, and to resume his anti-CCP and anti-Soviet policy. The CCP, therefore, should be prepared for a final split with Jiang. He cabled Zhou Enlai on 2 November, and ordered an emergency measure to disperse and hide the Communists working in the GMD-controlled zone. He told Zhou that "we have five hundred thousand troops and enjoy the people's support all over China. . . . We cannot allow ourselves to be blocked, and we must [launch an offensive] to march to the rear of the [GMD] anti-Communist troops." The next day, Mao telegraphed Zhou again and said that the central task of the Party at present was to oppose Jiang's attempt to surrender and to prepare for civil war.[69]

On the same day, Mao told Peng Dehuai that Jiang would surrender to Japan and unite with the Japanese to attack the Communists. Mao proposed two plans for consideration. The first plan was to launch a political offensive to expose the GMD's pro-Japanese move and to mobilize the people to oppose it. Militarily the CCP would maintain a defensive position, and wait until "the whole nation realized Jiang's plot of surrender to Japan." Then a military offensive could start. Mao believed that this plan might be advantageous politically, but disadvantageous militarily. Therefore, he was inclined to a second plan, according to which the CCP would take the initiative to attack the GMD politically as well as militarily. A detailed military plan was thus sent to Peng for consideration. On 4 November, Mao sent a cable to the Comintern, proposing a "counteroffensive for self-defense in order to defeat the GMD troops and their blockade." A concrete military plan was also sent to Moscow for approval.[70]

Moscow was at the time concerned with a possible German-Japanese attack due to the formation of the Axis in September 1940. Stalin expected a united China to keep the Japanese fully occupied within Chinese borders. Moscow disagreed with Mao's assessment that Jiang was going to surrender to Japan. Therefore, the Comintern rejected Mao's plan immediately. In the face of Moscow's opposition, Mao backed down. In late December, Mao told the Party that the danger of GMD surrender to Japan had been checked, and that "left deviation" was the main danger to the Party at present. Mao also stated that even Jiang Jieshi needed to relax the tension between the two parties.[71] Just after Mao "made a self-criticism" in the face of Moscow's opposition, the "New Fourth Army Incident" occurred early in January 1941. Mao jumped the gun again to conclude that Jiang had already taken on a totally opposite position, and the Party's conciliatory attitude to Jiang should be terminated immediately. The whole Party should prepare for a full-scale counteroffensive, politically and militarily.[72]

Once again, Moscow disapproved of Mao's policy. On 4 January 1941, Dimitrov cabled Mao, stating that "we believe that the total split [with the GMD] is not inevitable, and you shall not rest your policy on the split. In contrast, you should rely on the people who advocate the maintenance of the united front, and our Communists and the Army should do everything to avoid the spread of civil war."[73] It was clear to Mao that Moscow did not want to see a civil war between the CCP and the GMD, and he once again backed down. He said to Zhou in a telegram of 20 January 1941: "GMD-CCP relations as such have no benefit to us, and to the revolution." But, the Comintern and the Soviet Union "are not in agreement with what we think. Back and forth [in negotiating with the GMD] for three months like this, [the issue] is still unresolved. Therefore, we shall launch a fierce political offensive at present, but remain on the defensive militarily. Nonetheless, we should actively prepare for an [military] offensive, in case we can transform our position into a forceful offensive four to six months later."[74]

But, Moscow did not allow Mao to take any military offensive against the GMD in the near future either. On 20 January and 5 February 1941, Dimitrov cabled Mao twice, reiterating the importance of maintaining the united front with the GMD. Moscow insisted that the CCP maintain the national united front and make use of the contradiction between Jiang and the Japanese. On 9 February, Mao received Stalin's advice: as a revolutionary army, the more active the CCP troops were in waging war against Japan, the more vigorously they would expand as a result. Mao also learned that Stalin had delivered a message to Jiang that Moscow did not want to hear any news about the GMD-CCP conflict.[75] It so happened that Jiang did not intend to ally with Japan, nor did he want a full-scale civil war with the CCP. Moscow's estimation was again proven "correct." Later, even Maoist history would have to acknowledge that the CCP's policy of "political offensive and military defensive" in dealing with the NFA Incident was "correct," but Mao was unduly credited for this, and his radical military planning for civil war has been kept in the dark.

The peace with the GMD which followed the NFA Incident enabled Mao to build the CCP's military force. He realized Jiang was also avoiding costly military operations against the Japanese in order to save strength for the future civil war; thus, the CCP must do the same. He cabled Peng on 18 May:

> We [the CCP] should attack the Japanese, "but the attack must not be too fierce. [If we] do not attack [Japan], the GMD will not forgive [us]; the middle-of- the-road forces will also complain. However, if our attack is too fierce, we will face danger. The Japanese will turn round to [attack us] in revenge, and the GMD will sit there and profit from it, or even attack our border region.[76]

In the directive of the Military Committee of 7 November 1941, Mao made clear that in the coming period the Party's military strategy should aim at "killing-time" (*moshijian*); should use "protracted dispersed guerrilla warfare. . . . to play with the enemy, to save and build up our strength (including armed strength and that of the masses), to wait for an opportune time."[77]

Soon after this, the Pacific War erupted, and both Mao and Jiang could leave Japan's final defeat to the Americans. Mao's strategy of dispersed guerrilla warfare behind enemy lines thus made perfect sense, not in terms of consuming the enemy's strength, but in terms of expanding the CCP territory and armed forces. This was accomplished often at the expense of the GMD. When the Japanese Ichigo campaign wiped out the GMD in Central China in 1944, the CCP poured into the vacuum left behind by the Japanese. Yet, throughout the period of 1941–1945, Mao kept the CCP-GMD negotiations alive. In the summer of 1942, he intended to meet with Jiang directly in order to prevent major military conflict with the GMD.[78] At the same time, the CCP's "political offensive" against the GMD became increasingly fierce and effective, as the political, economic, and social problems in the GMD-controlled area were mounting. In retrospect, Mao's "leftist" tendency in the NFA Incident was probably the last such occurrence during the war, and so was Moscow's direct interference. Shortly after the incident, the German-Soviet war kept Stalin occupied, and the Stalin-Mao secret radio communications became less frequent. This, however, did not indicate any significant change in their relations. Mao remained loyal to Moscow, and responsive to Stalin's advice, although sometimes unwillingly.[79]

MAO-STALIN RELATIONS: 1941–1945

Shortly after Hitler's attack on the Soviet Union, the ECCI cabled Mao on 9 July 1941, just as it did to all other communist parties around the world, calling for all-out support of the Soviet antifascist cause. Mao convened a politburo meeting on 13 July, and everyone at the meeting was fully in agreement with the ECCI directive.[80] However, there was some difference within the Party as to how to assist the USSR. Although all members in the CCP leadership, including Mao, shared the fear that the Japanese would attack the USSR soon, Mao wanted to wait and see, while preparing the Party for such a scenario. On 6 July, he cabled Zhou that "the military situation in the Soviet Union seems to be stabilized, and Japan appears to aim at Britain and the U.S., not the USSR." Mao's sense about the possible Japanese move turned out to be correct. Based on this appraisal, Mao called for caution in taking any drastic military action against the Japanese prematurely.[81] Mao appeared to be concerned that the CCP's active military action against the Japanese would not only put its armed forces in danger, but also provoke the Japanese to attack the USSR.

At the time, some members in the Party leadership seemed to be impatient. They tended to believe that the Japanese attack on the USSR was imminent; they wanted to launch an all-out attack on the Japanese to protect their "socialist fatherland" even at the expense of the CCP's base areas behind enemy lines.[82] Mao, on the other hand, seemed to be more prudent than emotional. On 2 July, Mao, together with Zhu De and others, telegraphed Peng Dehuai that if the Japanese attacked the USSR, "our army should be prepared to fight in cooperation with the Soviet army. At present, we shall prepare for dealing with this situation, while waiting for the opportunity [of cooperating with the Red Army] to come. When it comes, we can operate immediately." Nonetheless, Mao cautioned his comrades that due to the poor equipment of the CCP forces, their cooperation with the Soviet Red Army "should be strategic and long-term cooperation, not one-time and tactical cooperation." Mao cabled Zhou on 15 July to reiterate that "we are determined to do our utmost under the present conditions to help the Soviet Red Army achieve victory." Due to the tremendous imbalance between the Japanese military capacity and that of the CCP, Mao stated, "our military ability to cooperate [with the Red Army] will not be very strong. If we do not consider any limit and make every sacrifice, we would be beaten down and could not maintain our base areas. It would not do anybody any good." The CCP's policy, Mao continued, "should be of a widespread and protracted guerrilla warfare against the Japanese in the base areas, not a policy of 'gambling everything on one throw of the dice.'"[83]

On 18 July, in response to Liu Shaoqi's suggestion of an all-out offensive against the Japanese in case of a Soviet-Japanese war, Mao explained that an all-out attack was the ideal plan in the long run; at present, however, "a large-scale campaign is not yet suitable." That was because, Mao reasoned, Jiang was not about to waste his armed forces in fighting the Japanese. If the CCP did what the GMD refused to do, Jiang would benefit from it, but it would not benefit the CCP, nor the USSR. Mao sounded very convincing to his comrades at home. On 21 July, a politburo meeting endorsed Mao's policy. They believed that the GMD was forcing the CCP to move to the area north of the Yellow River, and Jiang was waiting for the USSR to be further trapped by the Germans on the western front so that Moscow would not be able to interfere on the CCP's behalf. At the same time, they also believed, the U.S. was still plotting a "Far Eastern Munich" to make a Tokyo-Washington-GMD alliance against the USSR. Therefore, the maintenance of the CCP's base areas behind enemy lines would serve the CCP-USSR long-term interest.[84]

Moscow, however, was very nervous about a possible Japanese attack. On 3 September 1941, Moscow cabled the CCP again to propose that if the Japanese attacked the USSR, the CCP armed forces should go to Outer Mongolia to receive Soviet military equipment and to engage the Japanese in southern Manchuria. In response to Moscow's proposal, Mao drafted a reply which was approved by the Party Center's meeting on 7 September. We do not know the exact content of Mao's reply; but we do know that the politburo held another meeting the next day and it was decided that some troops and cadres should be sent to southern Manchuria.[85] On 7 October, Dimitrov cabled the CCP with fifteen questions about the military situation in China. He sounded particularly demanding in asking what the CCP would do in the case of a Soviet-Japanese war. Mao's answer to Dimitrov is unknown at this point. One thing is clear, however, Mao's attitude was amenable and responsive.[86]

Stalin might not have been pleased by Mao's lack of enthusiasm when Moscow was feeling the heat of a possible Japanese attack. However, it would be wrong to assume that Stalin had demanded the CCP's immediate action when the Soviet-Japanese war was only a possibility. The fact that the seemingly imminent Japanese attack on the USSR never took place indicates that Mao's "wait-and-see" attitude was prudent, and Stalin had no reason to be resentful. There is no evidence to suggest that Moscow was unhappy with the CCP's reply to Dimitrov's inquiry of 7 October, nor should Stalin have been concerned with the "nationalistic" tendency of the CCP, because Mao had continuously demonstrated his "internationalistic" nature in this policy thinking, in which the well-being of the Soviet state occupied a central position.

In fact, Mao's immediate concern in the scenario of a Soviet-Japanese war was that the GMD would take advantage of a weakened Soviet Union and attack the CCP. Thus, he told Lui on 30 July that two positive developments were vital to the CCP: (1) the Soviet Union would defeat the German offensive, which would deter Japan from attacking the USSR; and (2) Britain and the U.S. would stand with the USSR, which would deter Jiang from attacking the CCP.[87] Clearly, Mao viewed the USSR's well-being as essential to the CCP. He was thus willing to do anything possible to enhance the Soviet interest, which he always identified as the same as the "Chinese interest" (read CCP interest) privately and sometimes publicly as well.[88]

Zhou Enlai was of the same mind as Mao. In his telegram to Mao on 26 June 1941, he reasoned that if the Soviet Union defeated Nazi Germany, the U.S. and Britain might not make further concessions to Japan, and the situation would become more favorable to the CCP. If the USSR was to be attacked from both sides by the Germans and the Japanese, the Anglo-American supported GMD would take advantage of the situation to mount pressure on the CCP.[89] To prepare for the worst, the CCP actually planned to retreat into the Soviet Union or Outer Mongolia. Zhou proposed on 7 July that the Communists should start learning natural science, Russian language, and modern military technology, so that they could improve their ability to receive and utilize new military equipment provided by the Soviets when the CCP retreated into the USSR or the PRM, fighting shoulder-to-shoulder with their Soviet comrades. The Party Center discussed Zhou's proposal, and Mao fully endorsed it. He informed Zhou that the Center had decided to embark on military preparations for the worst possible situation, starting with learning the

Russian language, natural science, and training cadres of Manchurian origin. Presumably, according to previous Moscow messages, Manchuria would be assigned to the CCP in case of a Soviet-Japanese war.[90]

After Japan's attack on Pearl Harbor, Mao's phobia about "Eastern Munich" was not entirely over, and he instructed the CCP military to take the opportunity to rest and rebuild its strength. He made clear in his directive of 28 December 1941 that the CCP's conservative military policy against the Japanese was under condition of the absence of a Soviet-Japanese war. In the event of Japan attacking the USSR, or the USSR attacking Japan, Mao said, the rejuvenated CCP forces could fight together with the Soviet Red Army with full vigor.[91] From February to August 1942, the CCP saw no dramatic improvement in the relations between the Anglo-American camp and the USSR; therefore, Mao and his comrades were constantly concerned with the possibility of Japan attacking the USSR, in which case, as they were convinced, Jiang would attack the CCP.[92] This CCP nightmare was finally over when Churchill met Stalin on 12–15 August, and the relations between the USSR and the Anglo-American forces improved. This development led Mao to conclude that Jiang would not cooperate with Japan and attack the CCP because his "foreign masters" had improved their relations with the USSR. Moreover, after the Japanese controlled Burma, Jiang had to rely on the Soviet route to obtain military aid. Thus, the GMD was forced to abandon its anti-Soviet policy, and the CCP was once again safe.[93] Evidently, Mao continued to view Soviet well-being as the key to the well-being of the CCP. His assumption about world politics revolved about the standing of the USSR. The "proletarian internationalism" convinced Mao and his comrades that revolutionary bonds tied the CCP to the USSR, as did the "bourgeois reactionary nature" bond the GMD with the Anglo-American camp. In other words, Mao's two-camp concept of the postwar world, rooted in his ideology, was taking shape long before the war ended. How could it be possible that Mao took the German-Soviet war as an opportunity to "emancipate" the CCP from Soviet influence?

The dissolution of the Comintern was not a "windfall" to Mao, but to Jiang.[94] Mao was in fact nervous to see that the GMD press launched an "anti-CCP offensive" by arguing that the CCP, as a branch of the Comintern, should also dissolve itself after the Comintern voted itself out of existence. Mao and his comrades considered the GMD propaganda campaign as a signal of the coming of the "third anti-CCP high tide." Zhou Enlai cabled Mao on 26 and 30 May 1943 to warn that a GMD political and military offensive was likely.[95] Stalin, however, soon came to Mao's assistance; Soviet diplomats in China frequently made their concern over a possible CCP-GMD conflict known to their U.S. counterparts; *Pravda* carried articles attacking the "die-hards" in the GMD.[96] This indicates that the Comintern's dissolution was actually for western consumption, not a real indication of any significant change in the

relations between Moscow and communist parties elsewhere. What changed was that Stalin now replaced Dimitrov to use the secret radio system to keep in touch with Mao directly, and he adopted "Filipov" as his pseudonym.[97] Mao thus had direct access to Stalin, which made him unique among all communist leaders around the world.

The Comintern's dissolution did add momentum to Mao's Rectification Movement, which called for the combination of "Marxist truth" with Chinese reality, and opposition to "doctrinairism." Behind the high-sounding words, Mao's critical spearhead was nonetheless directed toward Wang Ming and others, including Zhou Enlai, who opposed his "correct line" in the past. The method of the Rectification was to have the Party's leading members study some designated writings of Marx, Lenin, and Stalin, and review the Party's history along Mao's line. By doing so, Mao intended to and succeeded in establishing his unchallenged personal authority within the Party; the building of the Mao cult started. This was done, however, not at the expense of Stalin's godlike status in the hearts and minds of the CCP members. In contrast, one of the most emphasized "Marxist classics" designated by Mao as a "must read" was the so-called "Eighteen Items," which included the six points of the conclusion of *A Brief History of the Communist Party of the Soviet Union* and Stalin's "On Bolshevization, Twelve Items." On 7 June 1942, Mao directed the General Study Committee to pass a decision to organize leading members of the CCP into ten study groups in which Mao himself was the head of the first group. The first thing on the study agenda was the "Eighteen Items," on which individuals' study notes were to be inspected and examinations to be held. On 21 and 23 November 1942, Mao gave a lengthy talk at a high-ranking cadres' meeting, and his topic was how to apply Stalin's "twelve items" to Bolshevize the CCP. At the end of his talk, he said the "twelve items" were the "Bible of our Party, and we shall study them devotedly."[98]

This demonstrated that Mao had little intention of damaging Stalin's prestige in order to establish his own. He understood that his purposes could best be served if he built his own authority on the basis of the Party members' reverence for Stalin, who, from all the indications mentioned above, enjoyed a tremendous amount of prestige and power to influence the CCP's policy and leadership structure. Had Stalin been displeased with Mao, he would have made Mao's position in the Party, to say the least, very troublesome. Only after Stalin's death and Mao became ambitious enough to claim the leadership of the world communist movement, did he need to discredit Stalin to a limited extent. In the 1940s, however, when Mao's aim was to achieve recognition of his unchallenged power within the CCP, he would have been a fool to challenge Stalin, who after all endorsed his leadership versus Wang Ming, as we have documented.

After being criticized of being a "rightist deviationist" for his policy in the early period of the anti-Japanese war, Wang Ming appealed directly to

Moscow via Vladimirov's radio station in Yan'an in October 1943.[99] Dimitrov cabled Mao on 22 December 1943, expressing Moscow's concerns over two issues in a subtle yet direct way: First, Moscow believed that the CCP had scaled down its anti-Japanese military activities and the policy of a united front with the GMD was not adhered to closely, and that was "politically erroneous." Second, Dimitrov said that it was also politically erroneous to launch a campaign against Zhou Enlai and Wang Ming, who were charged because they adhered to the Comintern's policy at the outset of the anti-Japanese war. Dimitrov also expressed his concern that some Party members harbored an "unhealthy feeling toward the USSR."[100]

As megalomaniac as he was, Mao would not be pleased by this cable, and he must have been resentful of Wang Ming's attempt to get Moscow involved in the CCP internal conflict. On the other hand, Mao could easily detect in the same message the nonchallenging nature to his consolidated power and the "goodwill" of Comrade Stalin toward him. Mao must have noticed that while Wang Ming brought the issue to Moscow's attention via Vladimirov's radio station, and Dimitrov's telegram was sent to him directly, Vladimirov did not know of it until a few days later. Instead of presenting himself as a superior, Dimitrov purposely acted as Mao's "personal friend," and told Mao about his personal care of Mao's son who was studying in Moscow. Mao must have also noted that Stalin avoided interfering in this matter, although after the dissolution of the Comintern it was Stalin, not Dimitrov, who was on the other end of the CCP-Moscow radio channel. All Dimitrov did on Wang Ming's behalf was to plead to Mao that Wang and Zhou should not be driven out of the Party, and their talent should be utilized for the common cause.[101]

Mao seemed to be eager to demonstrate to Moscow his loyalty and humbleness. He had been meeting Vladimirov, the other one in Yan'an who had access to Stalin's ear, regularly and frequently. On 4 January 1944, shortly after the Dimitrov cable, Mao invited Vladimirov to spend an evening with him and he expressed his respect for the Soviet Union, Stalin, and his colleagues who had been educated in Moscow. "He spoke of the Soviet Union's significance for the existence of the Special Area, the importance of the united anti-Japanese front, and the political role which the former Comintern played for the CCP. . . . He thought at length over the telegram, which excited him, and he took its apprehensions and concerns close to heart. He understood Comrade Dimitrov's profound and sincere desire to help the CCP leadership and he appreciated his assistance, which had always been wise." Two days later, all the Soviets in Yan'an were invited for dinner with Mao. On 8 January, Mao visited Vladimirov again and had a long talk with him. Mao seemed "worried and his eyelids were red. . . . He looked extremely tired, as if he had not had a moment's sleep that night." Mao repeatedly expressed his adherence to the united front policy and his sincere desire for the unity of the Party. In addition to the telegram he sent to Moscow on 2 January, Mao wrote another one, and asked Vladimirov to dispatch it immediately. He said Dimitrov's concern was the same as his, because they had the same thoughts.[102]

Mao would have convinced Stalin to trust him by not only words but also deeds. Shortly after receiving Dimitrov's cable, Mao received Guo Zhongrong, the GMD's liaison officer, and told him that the CCP's policy of "upholding Jiang to resist Japan" and "upholding Jiang to reconstruct the nation" would "never change" even after the defeat of Japan. On 18 January 1944, he drafted a directive to urge every CCP unit not to provoke any conflict with the GMD troops, so that "the peace between the CCP and the GMD can be preserved and the final victory over the Japanese can be won." On 4 February, he ordered the CCP press to avoid "stinging" the GMD. At the same time, Lin Boqu and Zhou Enlai should go to Chongqing to resume talks with the GMD.[103] As for Wang Ming, Mao treated him leniently. When the "Resolution on Several Issues in the Party's Past" was being drafted, Mao sent it three times to Wang for comments, and visited him in person. Wang accepted the resolution and made a statement of self-criticism on 20 April 1944. At the Seventh National Congress of the CCP in 1945, Mao let Wang be elected a member of the Central Committee.[104] If Dimitrov was influenced by Wang Ming's report and thus criticized Mao, Mao's words and deeds in response to Dimitrov's telegram would have made Stalin at ease, had he been uneasy with Mao.

In short, new historical evidence indicates that Mao and his comrades were internationalists loyal to the Moscow-led world revolution. In addition to their initial spiritual-ideological conversion to Marxism-Leninism, the Chinese communists had extensive political and military reasons to keep their identity as Moscow's loyalists who considered Soviet support vital to their physical survival and future growth. Contrary to the Maoist myth created after Stalin's death, Mao was consistent in clearing the CCP's decision with Moscow and following Stalin's advice religiously, even when it went against Chinese national interests or the immediate interests of the CCP. Mao often hid his ego away, willingly or not, rationalizing Moscow's changing positions and readjusting his own accordingly. At the same time, Stalin respected Mao and supported his leadership; he demonstrated his willingness and persistent effort to assist the CCP's cause. If there was a personality conflict between Stalin and Mao, two egotistic and suspicious men, they both worked to avoid or minimize such conflict, and to achieve maximum unity within the world revolutionary movement. The CCP-Moscow solidarity also manifested itself in their common struggle against the capitalist West in general and the United States in particular.

CHAPTER III

From Enemies to Friends

CCP POLICY TOWARD THE UNITED STATES

BEFORE PEARL HARBOR

America is actually the most murderous of hangmen.
—*Mao Zedong in 1923*

Countries such as America, Great Britain, France . . . we
consider them our friends and invite their cooperation.
—*Mao Zedong in 1936*

No matter if it is Germany, Italy, Japan, or if
it is Britain, the U.S., or France. They are all imperialist
countries, taking part in the war directly or indirectly,
for only one aim which is to carve up the world
and to rob the people of the world.
—*Mao Zedong in 1939*

WHY DID Mao's attitude toward the United States switch so drastically before Japan's attack on Pearl Harbor? The answer can be found in the CCP's ideology, its relations with Moscow, and its domestic politics. When the CCP was founded in the early 1920s under the Comintern's direction, it was born anti-imperialist in general and anti-American in particular. If the Leninist theory of obtaining national power through violent revolution and class warfare shaped the CCP's domestic program, Lenin's theory of imperialism laid the foundation of CCP perception of world affairs. Moreover, the CCP's anti-imperialist ideology intensely interacted with its domestic politics, for it persisted in viewing the West as the master of reactionary classes in China, a "semi-colonial" nation.

Nonetheless, when Moscow adopted an "antifascist united front" policy in 1935 in order to offset the Berlin-Rome-Tokyo threat, Mao promptly followed suit. Parallel with the domestic united front, Mao used Americans such as Edgar Snow as a channel to call for an antifascist united front with the U.S. and England. Just as the CCP's deep-seated suspicion against Jiang made it certain that the second CCP-GMD marriage of convenience was only a temporary tactical move, the CCP's anti-Americanism ensured that Mao's united front with Washington was only a facade behind which his hostility toward the "imperialist robbers" remained acute.

The changing attitude of Mao toward the U.S. strikes the point home: the Party's class-struggle outlook and its perception of world politics intertwined with its domestic struggle to determine its U.S. policy before Pearl Harbor. The Maoist ideology not only determined the CCP's selection of the U.S. as a fundamental enemy, but also prescribed the way in which the CCP dealt with the Americans within the framework of the united front.[1]

THE CCP'S ANIMOSITY TOWARD THE U.S. BEFORE 1935

The CCP's perception of the United States was based on its anti-imperialist ideology, which in turn determined how its leaders viewed U.S. foreign policy in general and U.S. China policy in particular. As a branch of the Comintern, with extensive communications with Moscow, the CCP's foreign policy was greatly influenced by the Soviet perspective from the very beginning. When the Party was established in July 1921, it issued no manifesto to pronounce its political position on domestic and international politics. But, in the following year, the Comintern convened the Congress of the Toilers of the Far East as a counteraction to the Washington Conference. In accordance with Moscow's new line, the CCP formulated its first manifesto at the Second National Congress in July 1922. The Communists believed the Washington Conference was a meeting of imperialist "robbers" to redivide the spoils and reestablish the balance of power in the Pacific region after the Versailles Conference of 1919. Therefore, the Manifesto went on, the western imperialist powers achieved a certain degree of unity which would bring China to bear the "cooperative exploitation" of various western powers. "This will completely overthrow Chinese economic independence and will compel 400 million Chinese people to enter into slavery under the new international trust." Because of its economic development, the Communists insisted, the U.S. had become the No. 1 imperialist power, which played a major role in the new order after the First World War.[2] The CCP's animosity toward the U.S. was not merely rhetorical, it actually dictated the Party's policy. For instance, the CCP leadership was initially opposed to the Comintern's policy of forging a united front with the GMD, and one of the reasons for its opposition was its conviction that Sun Yat-sen's GMD was pro-American.[3]

Also along the line of Leninist theory of imperialism, the CCP leaders were further convinced that the conflict of interest between the Japanese and the Americans in China was particularly important in shaping Chinese domestic politics. The United States failed to reconcile its interests in China with those of Japan at the Versailles Conference, and that was part of the reason for the U.S. to resist the League of Nations. But, the imperialistic U.S. tried hard to use its economic superiority to export more capital to China in order to compete with Japan and England, and to dominate China's economy. Washington's "open door" policy was designed to breach Anglo-Japanese hegemony in China, and to put its own foot in the door, so went the CCP argument. The Party also believed that China was only one among many colonies and semi-colonies to the British, but to both the Japanese and the Americans, China was the only major market left, which possessed so great a potential that neither the U.S. nor Japan would dare to miss their opportunities. Thus, the Japanese-American conflict in China would necessarily be fierce, and its consequence on Chinese politics overbearing.[4]

In perceiving the nature of the U.S. involvement in China, the CCP came to the conclusion that in order to advance their own interests, Washington and Tokyo were supporting different Chinese "running dogs." The CCP believed that the U.S. was the master behind the Zhili Clique headed by Wu Peifu and Zao Kun, while Japan was behind the Fengtian Clique. When the Wu-Zao force defeated Zhang Zuoling's force, the CCP thought that the Beijing Government was "drifting gradually into the hands of pro-American bureaucrats." In the summer of 1923, the Zhili Clique seized control of the Beijing Government and bribed the members of the Chinese Parliament. The CCP reacted to this event forcefully by issuing an official statement on 1 August, which implied that Zao Kun's action was backed by the U.S. and some pro-American elements such as Feng Yuxiang and the Diplomatic Clique.[5] Mao wrote an article to condemn the United States as "the most murderous of hangmen."[6]

However, during the period of the "great revolution" in 1925–27, the CCP's anti-imperialist focus was on the British and the Japanese, simply because of their direct involvement in a series of events which stirred up great resentment among the Chinese population. In 1926 the CCP thought that the British would probably intervene directly to stop the Northern Expedition; it thus suggested that the GMD-CCP coalition make diplomatic efforts to win over Japan and the United States in order to isolate Britain.[7] This is arguably the CCP's first attempt to apply united front tactics in dealing with imperialist powers by making use of contradictions among them.

Nonetheless, developments in the spring of 1927 soon rendered CCP united front policy, both at home and abroad, irrelevant. After Jiang Jieshi's coup of 12 April, the GMD became the formidable foe of the CCP, whose perception of the U.S. was accordingly conditioned by its assumption of GMD-U.S. relations. In September 1928, when the conflict among various factions of the GMD was unfolding, the Communists came to the conclusion that the U.S. was the chief backer of Jiang Jieshi and his Central Government in Nanjing, while the British supported Li Zhongren's Guangxi Clique in the South and the Japanese sustained other warlords in the North. On 18 September 1928, the CCP Central Committee issued Circular No. 3 which stated that because the Americans lacked a particular sphere of influence in China, they were pursuing the "open door" policy by supporting the Nanjing Government, at odds with the Japanese and British backing of local warlords in the North and

South. Consequently, the fight between Jiang's central government and various local warlords was inevitable.[8] One month later, Mao expressed the same opinion.[9] From that time onward, the CCP firmly believed that the U.S. and the GMD were natural allies, although there might exist some conflicts between them to be exploited. This became a central assumption dictating the CCP's policy thinking regarding the United States for years to come.

In the late 1920s and early 1930s, the Communists recognized the disunity among foreign powers as well as various GMD factions; but they did not intend to make use of these contradictions, because they had abandoned the united front policy altogether after 1927. The above-mentioned circular stated that the Party must clear up any illusion among the masses toward the GMD, and make the class division sharper and more intense. The CCP should resolutely oppose any bourgeois factions no matter what kind of policy they adopted. The Party thought that reformist groups of the bourgeoisie could be even more deceptive to the masses; and therefore, more dangerous.[10] Likewise, the CCP's anti-imperialist stance against foreign powers should be intensified, and no compromise should be made with any one of them. Since Jiang and his regime in Nanjing was the No. 1 enemy of the CCP, and the U.S. was the master behind this regime, the Communists' anti-Americanism was greatly fueled.

To a large extent, the CCP's anti-Americanism was dictated by Moscow's "monolithic imperialist" view at the time. In a letter in response to the above-mentioned CCP circular, the Comintern criticized the CCP's formula that "the policies of the British and the Japanese are entirely opposed to the policies of the United States." The letter stated that

> American policy toward China, like British and Japanese policy, is imperialistic. The difference lies only in the means of application. The American "Open Door" policy is not designed to remove China from a colonial status. It is a liberal hypocrisy designed to cover up imperialist aggression. . . . The heart of American policy is to obtain economic control and to make the Chinese Government financially and diplomatically dependent upon the United States—unlike England and Japan who use force to consolidate their position in China.[11]

Moscow's warning of American "liberal hypocrisy" as being more deceptive and dangerous than Anglo-Japanese forceful aggression influenced Mao and his comrades, who, in the years to come, regarded the U.S. policy with deep suspicion. After the Mukden Incident of 1931, Washington pursued a "non-recognition" policy toward the Japanese de facto occupation of Manchuria. But, the CCP propagated the idea that the United States was a leader of the capitalist world after the First World War, and that the U.S. was plotting to invade the Soviet Union with the help of Japanese aggression. The Communists even charged that Washington was sending the U.S. fleet to the Far East in 1932 in order to strengthen the anti-Soviet international forces, and that President Hoover, loyal representative of Wall Street, would send Secretary

Stimson to Tokyo to plan the attack on the USSR.[12] Apparently, the CCP was, at least at this point in time, rather ignorant about the United States and its foreign policy, and its hypersensitivity to a possible U.S. invasion on the Asian mainland was by and large ideologically driven with little factual foundation. Moreover, this CCP perception of world politics was in line with the Comintern's radicalism of the "Third Period." If these were characteristics in the CCP's foreign policy thinking before 1935, they would manifest themselves again and again in the years to come.

MAKING FRIENDS WITH THE UNITED STATES: 1936–1939

This Moscow-CCP radicalism was, however, to change in 1935. To face the menace from the rising German-Italian-Japanese powers, Stalin pursued a collective security system with the Anglo-American powers. In accordance with Stalin's diplomacy, the Comintern decided on a policy of an antifascist world united front, which not only turned the CCP's domestic policy around, but also led Mao to court the United States. To express the CCP's willingness to form a united front with the U.S., Mao told Edgar Snow in the summer of 1936 that "except for Japan and those countries which help Japanese imperialism," the United States and other western democracies "can be organized into antiwar, antiaggression, antifascist world alliances."[13]

However, Mao's willingness to court the U.S. in the face of a Japanese invasion was overshadowed by his deep concern over a hostile GMD whose strength might gain a boost by possible U.S. assistance. Mao was keenly aware that if any U.S. aid would come to China, it would definitely fall into Jiang's hands. A strengthened GMD regime would be a vital threat to the very existence of the CCP. At the time, the CCP was busy itself in creating a Soviet-sponsored northwest government in opposition to the Nanjing regime, and any American aid to Jiang would counterbalance the Soviet aid to the coalition in the northwest. Thus, Mao was extremely concerned about possible U.S. aid to China, even in the name of resistance to Japan. He told Snow, "In the past, Nanjing has received much help from America, England and other countries. Most of these funds and supplies have been used in civil war . . . it has cost the Chinese people about $80,000 for every Red soldier killed." Mao made his point clear: only when the Nanjing Government ceased civil war and united with the CCP to fight the Japanese, would America's aid be "of real benefit to the Chinese nation."[14] To the Communists, if an American-boosted GMD could defeat Japan, it could easily wipe out the CCP as well. This plain logic in the minds of the Communists made them extremely suspicious of, and hostile to, U.S. aid to China, even when they were calling for an anti-Japanese united front with Washington. This became a pattern in CCP policy thinking, which would assert itself again and again throughout the pre-1949 period.

No matter how dubious they were in regard to the possible aid from the West to China's resistance against Japan, the Communists hoped that the United States would somehow facilitate China's effort against Japan at least for the time being. Even this modest hope of the CCP, however, was frustrated by Washington's Asian policy. After the undeclared Sino-Japanese war erupted in July 1937, America continued to supply Japan with the materials necessary to sustain Japan's war effort. The West also encouraged a peaceful settlement between the GMD and Japan, which would, if reached, put the CCP in a worst possible scenario to face attacks from both the GMD and the Japanese. There was no real ground for the Communists to play one off against the other among the various imperialist powers. Even when Mao appealed for Anglo-American support in China's resistance to Japan in August 1937, he pointedly stressed the imperialist nature of the Anglo-American camp. He warned that acceptance of aid from the U.S. and Britain should be conditional, and that on no account should China's territory and sovereignty be infringed.[15] In the Communists' minds, American aid was always aimed at damaging China's territorial integrity and sovereign rights. This assumption would manifest itself repeatedly in the CCP's policy thinking in the years to come.

In September 1937, when the Sino-Japanese war was intensifying in both North China and the Shanghai area, and the CCP-Moscow leadership was concerned with a possible peace solution between Nanjing and Tokyo, Mao and his comrades realized that "Britain is preoccupied with the conflict in Western Europe, while the U.S. clings to isolationism. . . . All of these are detrimental to China's resistance to Japan," because Anglo-American inaction would make the GMD more inactive in resisting Japan, and a GMD-Tokyo compromise was likely. After all, Jiang was only a servant of Anglo-American power. So the Communists appealed for support directly from the people in the U.S. and Britain. They asserted that "not only can people give us various forms of assistance directly, but they can also push their governments to fight Japan. . . . This is an important part of our foreign policy."[16] The division between "bad government" and "good people" in the U.S. and other capitalist countries served as a foundation for Mao's "people's diplomacy," which would continue to play a significant role in the CCP's foreign policy toward the West in the future.

Throughout 1938, however, while Stalin was still pursuing a collective security system with western democracies, Mao and his colleagues continued their effort to court the Anglo-American forces in hopes that Washington and London would prevent Jiang from making a deal with Tokyo. This hope, however, was diminishing quickly, while Stalin was turning toward the direction of making a deal with Hitler. Mao's frustration and hostility toward the U.S. was to burst out soon.

BATTLING THE BOURGEOISIE AT HOME AND ABROAD: 1939–1941

After his collective security with the western democracies failed, Stalin began to change his foreign policy in the spring of 1939. He told the Eighteenth Congress of the Communist Party of the Soviet Union (CPSU) on 10 March that Britain, the U.S., and France had blundered into a new economic depression since 1937. As a result, Stalin asserted, the struggle among capitalist countries for markets and raw materials was intensifying. A new imperialist war had started. By a policy of nonintervention or appeasement, the western powers were conniving at aggression, Stalin said. He stressed the inevitability of war and revolution that would follow.[17] In effect, Stalin eliminated any distinction between the western democracies and Nazi Germany, preparing for his next move to sign the Soviet-German pact five months later.

Mao had already felt a dangerous prospect that the western democracies would compromise with the fascist powers, and thus, Jiang would likely "surrender" to Japan.[18] Mao's anxiety over the possibility of a Jiang-Tokyo compromise within the framework of the "Far Eastern Munich" was greatly facilitated by an ECCI directive at the end of May. In line with Stalin's speech, the ECCI instructed the CCP that the danger of a new "Munich plot" in the Far East between the Anglo-American powers and Japan was imminent, and the GMD would be more inclined to surrender to Japan. The GMD's increased anti-CCP activities should be seen as the preparation for surrendering to the Japanese. The CCP's priority at the moment was thus to oppose the GMD's compromise with Tokyo, the ECCI said. Mao was so alarmed by the Moscow message that he saw an immediate possibility of a GMD military attack on the CCP's base areas. He immediately convened a meeting on 31 May 1939, at which he emphasized the "self-defense" principle against any GMD military adventure.[19]

Because Mao and his comrades understood that the GMD's anti-CCP activities were encouraged by the London-Washington "Far Eastern Munich" plot, their hostility toward the Anglo-American powers mounted in 1939–1941, when the GMD-CCP relations were deteriorating. On 1 June 1939, one day after the receipt of the ECCI directive on the "Far Eastern Munich," plot, Mao wrote an article on the anniversary of the British Committee of Assistance to China. In the article, after expressing the CCP's gratitude to the British people who stood together with the Chinese people against aggression, Mao stated that the best way for the British people to assist China was to pressure the London government to push for a more active anti-Japanese policy.[20] Frustrated by the "bad bourgeois governments" in London and Washington, Mao again placed more emphasis on the "people's diplomacy."

Mao believed that because an imperialist war was inevitable, the western democracies intended to divert the "fascist flood" toward the east to attack the

USSR, and the Munich-type of appeasement policy was a device to that end. Should this "Anglo-American plot" succeed, the CCP was to suffer first, because Jiang, encouraged by Washington and London, would ally with Japan to eliminate the CCP before they launch an offensive against the USSR, so Mao predicted. To avoid this dangerous development, Mao designated the theme of "opposing [Jiang's] surrender" as the centerpiece of the Party's policy, which dominated the CCP political agenda until the eruption of the German-Soviet war in June 1941.[21]

It was, therefore, little surprise that immediately after the announcement of the Soviet-German pact and the outbreak of the European war in August–September 1939, Mao came to endorse Moscow's new foreign policy. In Mao's eyes, the world was now bipolarized: on one side, all capitalist countries were directly or indirectly involved in the imperialist war; and on the other side, the Soviet Union stood firm for peace, while preparing for the defense of the socialist fatherland and possible revolution in the belligerent countries. As for the United States, still in the mood of isolationism, Mao asserted that "American imperialists are now avoiding taking part in the war under the pretence of neutrality in order to grab the leading position in the capitalist world later."

Clearly, the CCP had resumed its previous world vision of "monolithic imperialism," and the united front policy toward the western democracies was abandoned. Mao concluded that the Party's policy was to arouse the people in the belligerent countries, to turn the imperialist war into a revolutionary civil war, and to expose the ulterior motives of U.S. policy, a policy nominally neutral but actually encouraging the war. The Communists also believed that the U.S. reactionary ruling class of monopoly capitalists was taking advantage of international hostility to intensify a repressive domestic policy and an anti-Communist movement, which signaled a move toward fascism. "We should oppose the political fascistization of the U.S. and its involvement in the war," Mao stated.[22] Mao did not know, or cared little, about what was happening in the United States under FDR's New Deal. His understanding of the U.S. appeared ideologically driven; his priority was to legitimize and rationalize Moscow's policy.

From this point on until June 1941, the CCP experienced a deep dilemma in its policy thinking. For the anti-Japanese cause, American-Japanese contradictions should be exploited, and the CCP should cooperate with or use the U.S. But since the Communists perceived that Japan and the United States belonged to the same imperialist camp in opposition to the Soviet Union, China should not enter into any formal alliance with the U.S. This policy was reinforced by U.S.-Japanese diplomacy before Pearl Harbor, which the CCP believed was a part of the "Far Eastern Munich" plot. But, the international situation took a rapid turn in 1940, which posed more questions to the CCP than it could solve within the framework of the bipolarized world order.

Frustrated by fruitless dealings with Tokyo, both Washington and London became more active in supporting the GMD National Government in 1940. The British reopened the China-Burma road to allow outside aid to flow into the GMD-controlled area, while the Americans promised loans to the GMD government. The CCP was alarmed by these developments and they identified them as the motivating factors for the GMD's increased anti-Soviet and anti-Communist activities after April 1940. In the Communists' eyes, it was only because of the isolationist mood in the U.S. that Jiang was forced to adopt a pro-Soviet policy to gain diplomatic and material support from the USSR. As a result of this pro-Soviet policy, Jiang took a moderate attitude toward the CCP as well. But after the Soviet-German pact, the USSR moved to sign a nonaggression agreement with Japan. On the other hand, Japan joined the Axis and American-Japanese hostility was impending. The CCP believed that Jiang's pro-Soviet policy would soon change, for the GMD would turn back to its traditional pro-Anglo-American policy, and both Washington and London were anti-Soviet, especially after the German-Soviet pact. This also meant the GMD's hostility toward the CCP would intensify as well.

On 10 September 1940, Mao predicted three possible developments in China's politics in relation to the world situation. First, Mao believed, Jiang would very much like to see American participation in the war. Since the U.S. entry into the war would mean active American support for the GMD, the Japanese-American war would strengthen Jiang's force to maintain its power at home. However, if the U.S. did not enter the war soon, Jiang might be forced to continue his previous pro-Soviet policy. This second prospect would work to the CCP's advantage, but would not be a desirable choice for Jiang, Mao reasoned. The third prospect was that after the Japanese occupation of Chongqing, a part of the GMD would surrender to, and cooperate with, the Japanese. This would make the country more chaotic; but it would also destroy the GMD. Mao believed that only a portion of the Jiang force would choose to surrender.[23] Apparently, it was the first possibility, that is, the U.S. entry into the war and the U.S. full-scale assistance to the GMD, that seemed most worrisome to Mao. On 20 October 1940, the Party Center dispatched a secret directive: "The Anglo-American Powers Are Seducing China to Join Their Warring Camp." Along the line of the Comintern directive of May 1939, the CCP document stated that from April to September, the GMD's anti-Soviet and anti-CCP activities had increased. "That is a concrete step by the GMD pro-Anglo-American clique to prepare for giving up its independent resistance to Japan and joining the Anglo-American alliance."[24] Mao was very nervous about the possibility of an Anglo-American-GMD alliance defeating Japan, since the alliance would then easily wipe the CCP out of existence.

On 25 October, Mao cabled Zhou Enlai twice to analyze the world situation and its possible impact on China. He thought that the GMD had two alternative moves in the near future: first, Jiang was hoping for a quick outbreak of the Japanese-American war, so that the GMD could rely upon the Anglo-

American camp. This was what Mao called the "Anglo-American line," or the "de Gaulle line." If the Americans were not ready for the war, Mao continued, Jiang could become Petain, the head of the Vichy Government. The "Petain line" implied Jiang's surrender to Japan. At present, he said, Jiang had not yet made up his mind, and was wavering between the two lines. Consequently, the GMD had not decided to break with the Soviet Union and resume a full-scale anti-CCP policy, although in order to pave the way for joining the Anglo-American camp, the GMD had already launched an anti-Soviet and anti-CCP "high tide." Then, Mao went on to say:

> The darkest scenario is that Japan's attack on Singapore become protracted without success, and the U.S. Navy controls Singapore; and the Germans also fail to occupy Britain. [Under such circumstances,] the danger of the Chinese pro-Anglo-American clique's attempt to give up independent war [of resistance] and join the Anglo-American alliance will increase. The danger of the majority of the middle-of-the-roaders lining up behind Jiang will also increase. Another scenario should also be considered: if the U.S. Navy concentrates its force and defeats the Japanese Navy, and Japan surrenders to the U.S. and the Japanese Army withdraws from China. [Then,] the United States will arm China's pro-Anglo-American clique financially and militarily, and China will become an American colony instead of a Japanese one, and the GMD-CCP cooperation will be replaced by a large-scale civil war. Nothing else can be more gloomy than that.[25]

Mao's words enunciated a fundamental CCP perception: American imperialism was more dangerous than the Japanese in the long run. By using force to invade China, Japan alienated many Chinese to whom the CCP became an attractive alternative. But if the Americans were able to defeat Japan, they would be taken as China's liberators, and the middle-of-the-roaders would lean toward Jiang because of his Anglo-American background. The U.S. financial and military aid to the GMD would further endanger the very survival of the CCP. For that reason, the CCP was strongly opposed to the "de Gaulle line," that is, Jiang's attempt to join the Anglo-American alliance. Wittingly or not, when Moscow was on good terms with Berlin and Tokyo, Mao came to identify the CCP long-term interest with that of Japan and Germany. Mao, however, also feared the "Petain line," because if the GMD got together with the Japanese, it would be a vital blow to the CCP. Thus, the ideal situation for the CCP was a protracted and "independent" war with Japan, in which the CCP could build up its political and military strength. No wonder Mao would later express thanks to the Japanese for their invasion of China, without which the CCP's victory in the postwar era would have been impossible.

This illustrates how Mao's "proletarian internationalism" influenced the way in which he perceived world politics and defined China's national interest. For Mao and his colleagues, the interest of China was the same as that of the CCP, which was, in turn, identical to that of the USSR. From this perspective, it would be better for China to suffer from a prolonged war with Japan than to defeat Japan quickly in an alliance with the Anglo-American forces. In their minds, the ruling party's class nature would determine the nation's fate. As Zhou Enlai said at the politburo meeting on 4 August 1939 that although Jiang was a realist who would be forced to compromise in certain situations, his "basic class instinct will never change," and his "class standing" determined his threefold attribute: compromising to the Japanese, dependent on the Anglo-American powers, and persistent in anti-communism. "That is the true dialectic of Jiang," Zhou concluded.[26] It was, therefore, obvious to the CCP that Jiang's victory over Japan would turn China into a U.S. colony. This reasoning morally justified Mao's preference for protracted suffering of the Chinese nation under the Japanese to a quick victory over Japan by the U.S.-Jiang alliance. Due to his identification of China's national interest with that of the CCP and that of the USSR, Mao actually perceived a GMD-Anglo-American victory over Japan as being more dangerous and less preferable. With this perspective, the triumphant march of the Axis didn't seem to be a bad thing to Mao. In the face of an all-out war between China and Japan, had Mao's thinking been made public, he would have been regarded, rightly or wrongly, as a "Chinese traitor" and a "Soviet running dog" by many of his countrymen.

The situation at home and abroad in the fall of 1940, however, was so subtle and complicated that Mao could not really grasp it, and his analysis and prediction were rather tentative. In his directive of 1 November 1940, he thought that if the American-Japanese war would erupt soon and the U.S. victory would come about quickly, Jiang would likely join the Anglo-American camp. But the American-Japanese war would not break out very soon, and the Americans would be unable to defeat the Japanese within two years. In this case, Mao felt, if Japan would make some concessions to Jiang, "Jiang would be willing to surrender to Japan, and it is most likely that he would do so."[27]

If Mao was confused by whether Jiang would become Petain or de Gaulle, he was quite certain that in either scenario "the serious struggle between the CCP and the GMD would become inevitable," because the GMD's pro-Soviet policy would come to an end in either case. He realized that "whether Jiang would surrender to Japan or to the Anglo-Americans, he would attack our Party vigorously.... Therefore, we should determine our policy quickly."[28] Mao's policy turned out to be a radical one. He not only drew up an "explosive declaration" (*zhadan xuanyan*) to publicly announce the final CCP-GMD split, but also planned to attack the GMD's rear by sending 150,000 CCP troops to fight what he called the "revolutionary national war in the form of civil war."[29] This was too radical a step to be taken lightly, and Mao appeared rather uncertain. In his telegrams to Zhou Enlai and Peng Dehuai on 2 and 3 November, respectively, he was hesitant to take any immediate action, and he suggested that the publication of the "explosive declaration" be delayed and a gentler attitude be adopted to deal with Jiang for the moment.[30] He needed time to consult with Moscow.

On 4 November, Mao telegraphed the Comintern to report on the situation and his own analysis and plans. He stated that "we prepare to launch a self-defensive counterattack, breaking down his [Jiang's] armies and blockade. . . . [We] expect a thorough victory in smashing his offensive, thereby stopping him from surrendering; this will make the situation turn for the better.[31] Although the exact content of Moscow's reply is still unknown, the major themes conveyed in Moscow's instruction can be conjectured through a reading into Mao's various telegrams in the subsequent days. First of all, Moscow apparently disapproved of Mao's judgement that the CCP-GMD split was inevitable, and that a military offensive against the GMD was advantageous. Instead, Moscow insisted that the CCP-GMD united front be continued and the Communists' attitude toward Jiang be more friendly than belligerent. As a result of Mao's compliance with Moscow's instruction, the CCP's policy toward the GMD changed significantly in Mao's various telegrams on 6 November. If Mao had lumped together Jiang and the so-called pro-Japanese clique headed by He Yingqin, and his attack on the latter was only a matter of "*qinjunce*" (to undermine the king by attacking his close associates), Mao now started to advise not to criticize Jiang but "*aihu* Jiang," that is, "love and protect" Jiang from the influence of the "hidden pro-Japanese clique." The planned "revolutionary national war" was, of course, called off.[32] Moscow's advice saved the CCP-GMD anti-Japanese united front at least in form.

Second, Moscow disagreed with Mao's analysis that Jiang's pro-Japanese or pro-American moves would be equally detrimental; and therefore, the GMD's attempt to join the Anglo-American camp should be opposed. Following Moscow's instructions, Mao changed his position. He telegraphed Zhou Enlai on 6 November: "Jiang's joining the Anglo-American camp would be advantageous and harmless [to us], while his joining the German-Italian-Japanese camp would be harmful and disadvantageous. [Therefore], we should no longer emphasize our opposition to [Jiang's] joining the Anglo-American camp." Mao went on to say: "Currently, not only should the forces of the Chinese people, the CCP, and the Soviet Union join together, we should also make diplomatic contact with the United States and Britain, in hopes that it will be [useful] in checking the [GMD's] tendency to surrender [to Japan], and to oppose the pro-German-Japanese clique's activities."[33] This was how the CCP started to resume the united front policy to exploit the contradictions between the U.S. and Japan, and the U.S. and the GMD. Moscow was instrumental in the CCP's "diplomacy" with both the GMD and the U.S. It appears that Stalin, though having signed the German-Soviet pact, and about to sign a treaty with Tokyo, was nonetheless concerned more with the danger from the aggressive Axis powers than from the Anglo-American camp. A victorious Japan would impose grave insecurity on the Soviet eastern frontier, and thus needed to be prevented at any cost. In other words, Stalin did not take the German-Soviet and Soviet-Japanese pacts at face value, as Mao appeared to. Mao, still an ide-ology-driven revolutionary, had much to learn from his comrade Stalin before he could become a more sophisticated statesman in world politics.

Coached by Moscow, the CCP's first united front action with the U.S. took place when Zhou Enlai met with L. Currie in Chongqing on 14 February 1941. According to the CCP records, Currie told Zhou that the U.S. supported Chi-nese unity and the war of resistance, that the U.S. did not want to see the spread of civil war, and that the U.S. advocated government reform toward democracy and efficiency. Currie also asked Zhou if Jiang would surrender to Japan, and, if so, what the CCP's policy would be. Zhou offered some infor-mation designed to "expose" Jiang, stressing that if Jiang did not change his anti-Communist policy, a civil war was possible, the war of resistance would fail, and the Japanese would head toward the south to fight the Anglo-Ameri-can force there.[34] Here Zhou's intention to use the Americans to check the GMD could not be more obvious.

Nonetheless, the intention to use the Americans in accordance with the united front doctrine did not make the Communists less suspicious of the "American imperialists" and their "evil intention" in China. On 3 March, Zhou told Mao that Currie wanted the GMD government to distance itself from the USSR, but not to split with the CCP to cause a civil war, because the Ameri-cans wanted the Chinese to fight the Japanese. According to Zhou, the inten-tion of Currie's visit was threefold. First, Washington wanted to investigate China's economic situation to explore possibilities for U.S. capital investment, which Zhou deemed a form of economic imperialist exploitation of China. Second, the U.S. wanted to gauge China's political and military strength in order to explore the possibility of establishing U.S. air bases in China, a form of military imperialism. Finally, the Americans had the evil intention to occupy Hainan Island as an American concession after the war, which was an imperialist violation of China's territorial integrity. Zhou also informed Mao that the GMD went along with the U.S. demands in principle, asking for loans in exchange.[35] In the CCP's eyes, as we have repeatedly demonstrated, U.S. assistance to China was always motivated by its intention to "colonize" China.

Moreover, in the back of Mao's mind, the prospect of a U.S.-Jiang alliance dominating China after Japan's defeat was too frightening to put aside. In March 1941, Mao learned that Jiang's government was negotiating with the British authorities in Burma, which he saw as a sign that Jiang was one step further toward joining forces with the Anglo-American powers. Mao's attitude toward this development was dubious. Having been coached by Moscow, he thought that if Jiang became a part of the Anglo-American coalition, the GMD would not surrender to Japan, and the Japanese would likely head toward the south to confront the Anglo-American forces, which would also result in the decline of the GMD's anti-CCP activities at home. Thus, the CCP should not openly oppose the GMD's joining the Anglo-American camp. Nonetheless, Mao was still very nervous about the long-term impact of the U.S.-Jiang alliance, and he emphasized that in principle the CCP must oppose any "imperialist war." The CCP's foreign policy would not oppose the Anglo-American assistance to China's resistance to Japan, Mao claimed, but the Party was opposed to China's entry into the Anglo-American camp.[36] Plainly, Mao's policy on whether or not China should formally ally with the U.S. against Japan was not based on the calculation of Chinese national interest. Rather, it was determined by Moscow's foreign policy and the CCP's partisan long-term objective to seize national power.

Before Mao could be really concerned with the long-term consequence of a GMD-U.S. alliance, however, things changed again. On 20 May 1941, Moscow informed the CCP that Washington was negotiating a peace settlement in the Far East with Japan. This message made Zhou Enlai conclude that the GMD government was likely to follow Washington's footsteps to compromise with Japan. He claimed that "the GMD tendency toward relying on the U.S. and surrendering to Japan will increasingly manifest itself. It is a tendency worthy of attention in the near future."[37] Mao, upon receipt of Moscow's message, resumed his assumption that in the long run Jiang becoming either a de Gaulle or a Petain would be equally detrimental to the CCP. He wrote an inner-party directive: "Japan, the United States, and Jiang Jieshi are plotting a new Munich in the Far East against the CCP and the Soviet Union. . . . We must expose their plot and fight against it."[38] This showed vividly how the Communists' ideology and their partisan interest came to define their perception of international relations and China's best interest. By putting the U.S., Japan, and the GMD in one category, the CCP intended to keep China's war effort against Japan "independent," that is, isolated from possible international assistance so that there would not be a victorious U.S.-GMD power in postwar China to threaten the Party's existence.

The CCP's opposition to the U.S. entry into the war was indeed consistent and firm, and it did not change until the outbreak of the German-Soviet war. After Mao's directive on the "Far Eastern Munich," *Jiefang ribao* published a series of editorials and articles in late May and the early half of June to attack the "warmongers" in the U.S. On 27 May, President Roosevelt spoke to a national radio audience, and declared an unlimited national emergency, which indicated the likelihood of U.S. entry into the war. While the GMD warmly welcomed Roosevelt's move, the CCP condemned it, asserting that the U.S. ruling class was preparing to "drive the American people into the slaughterhouse of imperialist war to generate great war profits for some sixty richest families in America."[39]

On the other hand, when Moscow signed the Soviet-Japanese pact in April 1941 and recognized the puppet state of Manchuguo in exchange for Japan's recognition of the People's Republic of Mongolia, the CCP came to rationalize and endorse the deal which was so obviously against China's national interests. One month before the deal was done, Mao felt very encouraged by the prospect of a Soviet-Japanese friendship (*Ri-Su qingshan*). He cabled Zhou on 17 March that Japan was pursuing a Soviet-Japanese treaty, and the U.S. and Britain intended to stop it. Washington and London, therefore, instructed the GMD to court the CCP. Jiang was also in fear of a Soviet-Japanese friendship, and he wanted to improve relations with the CCP so that Moscow would be less willing to strike a deal with Tokyo at the expense of the GMD.[40] In Mao's mind, Moscow's every policy move would generate a GMD-London-Washington reaction toward the CCP, a client of the USSR in China, and the CCP-Moscow relations were as intimate as the GMD-Washington-London ones. One wonders whether Mao's perception of the GMD as a "running dog" of Anglo-American imperialism was a mirror image of, and a psychological-moral justification for, his perhaps subconscious self-image as a faithful client of the Soviet Union.

Since Mao knew that Jiang understood the nature of the CCP-Moscow affiliation, his instinctive reaction toward the Moscow-Tokyo treaty on 13 April 1941 was to put the CCP military on alert to prepare for a possible GMD assault on Yan'an.[41] Nonetheless, Mao's overall assessment of the impact of the Soviet-Japanese treaty was positive. First, Mao believed that by signing such a treaty with Japan, the USSR freed herself from the danger of a war in the Far East; thus, Moscow carried more weight to influence world politics and China's domestic development. The Anglo-American plot of pitting the Axis against the USSR was now totally bankrupt, Mao declared. Second, Mao believed that Jiang had thought that the USSR was dependent on him to prevent a Soviet-Japanese war, and thus, Jiang dared to ignore Moscow's will to launch "anti-CCP high tides." If making a deal with Tokyo was Jiang's leverage against the USSR before, this would not work for Jiang anymore. Thus, Mao concluded, the Soviet-Japanese treaty had a positive effect on the development in China, and it would deter Jiang from "surrendering to Japan and attacking the CCP." On 14 April, one day after he put the CCP military on alert, Mao sensed that the perceived GMD attack was less likely.[42] Mao was further of the opinion that having suffered military defeat by the Germans, Britain now moved to improve its relations with the USSR, and the U.S. would follow suit. Accordingly, the GMD would also court the Soviet Union and improve relations with the CCP as well. The CCP, Mao declared, should take advantage of the situation to push Jiang to meet the CCP's terms.[43]

Mao's optimism, however, was soon shattered by the aforementioned Moscow message of May on the so-called "Far Eastern Munich." It is not difficult to imagine Mao's angry reaction toward the United States and Britain, for he believed that a compromise and coalition among Japan, the U.S., and the GMD would turn Tokyo against the USSR and the GMD against the CCP. Paranoid and somewhat confused, Mao even came to identify the CCP's interests with that of Germany. In April, Mao believed that the German victory over Britain made the Anglo-American powers move closer to the USSR; but, he changed his mind on this after the receipt of the Moscow message on the "Far Eastern Munich." Mao now came to believe that due to the German victory London and Washington were eager to reach a compromise with Japan so that they could concentrate on dealing with Hitler first. Consequently, Mao stated on 25 May that "although the 'Western Munich' plot has been defeated by the Soviet policy for now, the 'Eastern Munich' danger is increasing daily. A round of negotiations is taking place between Tokyo and Washington to plot a Japanese-American-Chinese compromise against the CCP, the USSR, and Germany." Paranoid by this perceived danger of "Eastern Munich," Mao's attitude toward the GMD changed as well. Instead of "pushing Jiang" forcefully, Mao now put on a friendly face; on 26 May he cabled Wei Lihuang, a GMD general close to Jiang, that "China can be saved only when the GMD-CCP unity under the leadership of Generalissimo is strengthened, and a pro-Soviet diplomacy followed, and the war of resistance continued. The United States is unreliable, and the plot of pursuing a Japanese-American-Chinese compromise should be firmly rejected."[44] The CCP so identified with the interests of the USSR and Germany, that on 20 June it even praised the German-Turkish pact as a victory of Soviet diplomacy.[45]

The German attack on the USSR, however, changed everything completely overnight. On 25 June, a *Jiefang ribao* editorial called for an antifascist international united front again, and Roosevelt's image in CCP propaganda changed from a "warmonger" to an "enlightened bourgeois politician."[46] On 6 July, Mao telegraphed Zhou Enlai to propose a clear-cut, if not simplistic, line in dividing friends and enemies: "No matter they are imperialist powers or not, if they are antifascist, they are good; if they assist fascists, they are bad. To use this line of division, there will be no mistake."[47] Mao must have been delighted that the situation had finally become less confusing and he would no longer make erroneous judgments and flip back and forth in order to keep up with Stalin's changing positions.

The new historical evidence smashes the icon of an "always correct" Mao, who turned out to be, one might say, a rather muddle-headed strategic thinker, poorly informed, with little real understanding of world politics. More to the point is the fact that up to this period of time Mao had not had any firsthand experience in international politics and had been in isolation from the real world. Poorly informed, with the major source of information fed by Moscow, Mao's worldview and foreign policy thinking could not but be ideologically driven and Moscow-inspired. From a psychoanalytical perspective, according to the Eriksonian theory of identification, it was mentally healthy and comforting for Mao to make a total orientation out of a given state of partial knowledge. This "totalism" tendency explains Mao's constant changing position as an effort to reinforce his established ideology/identity via rationalization of the ever-changing reality along the line that was familiar and manageable to him so that his mental stability would be sustained, and a possible personality breakdown avoided. Had Mao been curious about the "objective truth" of the United States and the Soviet Union in a professorial way, he would not have been the Mao we have come to know. Single-mindedness, or simple-minded-ness, is sometimes the precondition for one to keep functioning normally, especially in a state of confusion and turmoil.

CHAPTER IV

Courting the Americans

THE CCP'S UNITED FRONT POLICY TOWARD THE U.S., 1942–1945

There is no such thing as America not intervening
in China! You are here, as China's greatest ally.
The fact of your presence is tremendous.
—*Mao Zedong, 1945*

The Comintern had no place in the Far East.
— *Mao Zedong, 1944*

DID Mao really mean it when he uttered these words to the Americans in the "Dixie Mission"?[1] According to new evidence, it is clear that at no point in time did Mao intend to form an alliance with the United States against the Soviet Union. Mao's occasional flirtation with the U.S. was intended, with specific purposes, to mislead the Americans within the united front framework. Shortly after the arrival of the "Dixie Mission" in Yan'an, a CCP inner-party directive, drafted by Zhou and approved by Mao, stated unequivocally that the Party's united front policy in dealing with domestic political establishments was by and large applicable to dealing with the Americans.[2] What was, then, Mao's real intention in courting the Americans, and how did Mao pursue his diplomacy with the U.S. during the Second World War?

ENLISTING THE AMERICANS TO CURB THE GMD, 1942–1943

After the eruption of the German-Soviet war and the Pacific war, the United States became a paramount force influencing not only China's war effort with Japan but also its internal politics and its future in the postwar era. At the same time, the Soviet influence in the Far East receded, and it did not come back until 1945. This was the background against which the CCP decided to use the united front doctrine to play with the Americans. Although Mao and his comrades turned themselves around completely from an anti-American to a pro-American position overnight when Germany suddenly attacked the USSR, they were still suspicious of the U.S. imperialist nature and their concept of world politics revolved about Moscow's diplomatic standing.

In Mao's mind, it was apparent that the eruption of the German-Soviet war made Germany's enemy, the Anglo-American camp, a friend of the Soviet-CCP camp. But, whether or not London and Washington would go along with Moscow remained to be seen. Mao was delighted when Winston Churchill signed an alliance treaty with Stalin on 12 July 1941. The CCP had been in fear that after the German-Soviet pact the USSR was relatively isolated and the Soviet influence diminished in the Far East. At the same time, the American influence was on the rise in the region and an American-GMD alignment could be a fatal threat to the CCP's survival. Now, with the establishment of the Anglo-Soviet alliance, Moscow's role in world politics was enhanced and the dominating American influence in the Far East could be counterbalanced. On the same day that the Anglo-Soviet alliance was announced, Mao predicted that the United States would possibly follow the trend set forth by Stalin and Churchill, and enter the war against Japan. Three days later, he optimistically told Zhou Enlai that "the Anglo-Soviet treaty will become the key to world politics. The U.S. has to follow this line, and it can no longer dominate the whole situation [in the Far East]."[3]

Mao must have felt that his prediction was correct when he learned that Roosevelt and Churchill signed the "Atlantic Charter" in August 1941. At the politburo meeting on 18 August, Mao said that the Atlantic Charter indicated that the U.S. had determined to take part in the antifascist war, and this was beneficial to the USSR and China. Roosevelt and Churchill were firm on the total defeat of Germany, Mao observed, but they still left a space for making compromise with Japan. Thus, Japan could still possibly attack the USSR, due to the Anglo-American appeasement. Thus, it was still a possibility that the GMD would attack the CCP in the case of a Soviet-Japanese war.[4]

On 8 December 1941, Mao was excited by the news about Pearl Harbor. He called a politburo meeting immediately, and he stated that the danger of a Soviet-Japanese war was now over, and the GMD's attack on the CCP base areas was less likely.[5] Nevertheless, after he saw Japan's initial victory over the Anglo-American forces in the Pacific region, Mao became increasingly nervous about the possibility of an impending war between Japan and the USSR. He was very disgusted with the Anglo-American performance in the Pacific theater at the time. And yet, both London and Washington were reluctant to open up the second front in western Europe. In Mao's mind, the Anglo-American powers were indeed hypocritical: they would not establish the second front in western Europe until the USSR defeated Hitler; only then, they would join in to "beat up the dead tiger," Mao said.[6]

Mao's attitude toward the Anglo-Americans soon changed. On 26 May, Stalin signed a Soviet-British treaty which declared that the Anglo-Soviet wartime cooperation would continue in the postwar era. This was followed by a similar Soviet-American treaty on 11 June. The improvement of Moscow's relations with the western democracies changed Mao's perception of the situation at home. Now he came to believe that the danger of a GMD attack was over, and the GMD had to negotiate with the CCP. Mao even envisioned a "long-term cooperation with the GMD in the postwar era" just like a Soviet-Anglo-American postwar cooperation was possible. On 7 July, the CCP publicly announced that the Party recognized that "Generalissimo Jiang is not only the leader of the war of resistance, but also the leader of China's postwar reconstruction," and the CCP would cooperate with the GMD during and after the war "on every issue." In his telegram to Liu Shaoqi on 31 July, Mao stated that because the U.S. and Britain did not want to see a civil war in China, the GMD's attitude to the CCP improved. Mao was further encouraged by the news that Churchill met with Stalin on 12–15 August to discuss the matter of the second front in western Europe. Mao thus came to the conclusion on 18 August that the situation in China would soon improve, and Jiang would pursue a policy of "befriending the USSR, uniting with the CCP."[7] If Mao's assumption of CCP-Moscow versus GMD-Washington as two opposing camps determined by their class nature was initially an "ideological" conviction, it had become far more than a matter of "philosophy"; it served as a fundamental guideline dictating the way in which Mao perceived the realpolitik situation and made his policy accordingly.

Since Moscow had formed a united front with Washington and London, the CCP would certainly follow suit. Mao could also see the possibility of using Washington's influence to check Jiang's anti-CCP activities, for he knew that ultimately the U.S. wanted Japan to be defeated. If the Americans could help to lift the GMD's military pressure on the CCP's base areas to a certain degree, it would allow the CCP forces to consolidate and grow. In the first half of 1942, the Soviets were hard put in their struggle with Nazi Germany and their capacity to influence China's politics declined quickly. Therefore, to enlist the British and Americans to check the GMD was not only possible but necessary. Since Washington wanted the CCP to fight the Japanese, Mao reasoned, it was possible that the Americans would even give the CCP a portion of U.S. military aid to China. Toward these ends, the CCP's united front activities with the British and Americans became increasingly active, even though Mao and his colleagues were still suspicious of their bedfellows in every way.

In May 1942, Zhou Enlai met Edgar Snow to express the CCP's hope that an American military delegation and international news reporters would visit Yan'an. He also asked Snow to take a letter and some materials, which propagated the Communists' achievements in fighting the Japanese, to L. Currie. For the first time, Zhou's letter specifically requested that the CCP receive a portion of American China aid.[8] On 31 July 1942, Mao told Liu Shaoqi that the Americans did not agree with the GMD's policy of a civil war against the CCP, as a united front in China was needed to fight the Japanese. Mao wished that the U.S. government would intervene outright to stop a perceived attack by the GMD on the CCP.[9] After the dissolution of the Comintern in 1943, the CCP was again nervous about a possible GMD attack, and Mao again thought to enlist the Americans to check the GMD. He telegraphed Dong Biwu, the CCP representative in Chongqing, instructing him to spread the news about the GMD's anti-CCP move. He emphasized that the British and the Americans in particular should be informed. The Communists in Chongqing were instructed to translate into English various CCP propaganda materials and send them to the American Embassy. They even gave the Americans Mao's public statement on the dissolution of the Comintern, in which Mao stressed the independence of the CCP from the USSR in order to minimize the CCP-Moscow ties the West might perceive.[10]

Mao knew that if he wanted to woo the Americans, he had to demonstrate that the CCP had little to do with Moscow. In light of various reports written by American officers in China, such as John Service and John Davis, Mao had good reasons to believe that his policy of enlisting the Americans to curb Jiang was rather successful. On 13 July 1943, Mao told Peng Dehuai that "our propaganda campaign has got positive result. Not only foreign reporters asked Zhang Daofan [a GMD official] tough questions on 7 July, the ambassadors of Britain, the U.S., and the Soviet Union also warned Jiang that if he started a civil war, international aid would stop coming in." Mao was so encouraged and optimistic that he said if domestic peace could be preserved for one more year, the CCP would be in an "extremely advantageous position."[11]

To use the Americans to disadvantage the GMD, Zhou himself frequented the U.S. Embassy in Chongqing in the same period. He told the Americans that the GMD was withholding offensive action against the Japanese in order to conserve its strength for a civil war against the Communists, and that the CCP's military strength had become stronger than that of the GMD in North China. He suggested that the U.S. Government take steps to insure that its lend-lease supplies to the GMD would not be hoarded for a civil war. Zhou even went on to say that U.S. propaganda in China should emphasize the theme of "democracy against fascism. . . . It should imply to the Kuomintang [GMD] our [the U.S.'s] knowledge of and concern over the situation in China"; that the U.S. should recognize the Communist army "as a participant in the war against fascism"; that the U.S. might "intervene to the end that the Kuomintang blockade be discontinued"; and that Communist armies might "receive a proportionate share of American supplies sent to China."[12] The purposes of the CCP's united front with the U.S. were thus made clear to the Americans in China who seemed quite receptive to the CCP's arguments. Meanwhile, the Communists also created a liberal democratic image of themselves for American consumption. It was so successful that John Davis reported in 1943 that foreign observers agreed that the Communists were really agrarian democrats.[13] John Service was convinced that "the Communist political program is simple democracy. This is much more American than Russian in form and spirit."[14] By concealing the Party's true identity and its relations with Moscow, the CCP managed to confuse and deceive the Americans to its advantage.

The Communists' efforts to enlist the U.S. to curb the GMD were not at all wasted. In the summer of 1943, after receiving Stilwell's telegram reporting the GMD's military action against the CCP, George Marshall immediately expressed U.S. concern over China's domestic situation to Song Ziwen [T. V. Soong], China's Ambassador to Washington. Stilwell himself went to see Jiang, demanding the withdrawal of Hu Zongnan's troops from engagement in an anti-Communist blockade.[15] When FDR sent Wallace to China in 1944, the vice president let the GMD leader know again that Washington was dissatisfied by the GMD's military blockade against the CCP Shaanbei base area, while the GMD was passive and ineffective in fighting the Japanese. Of course, Washington did not know anything about Mao's "killing-time" strategy, and the materials which Mao had sent to the U.S. embassy to propagate the CCP's anti-Japanese military actions appeared to be working. Wallace told Jiang that the U.S. government believed the CCP was doing nothing other than demanding some political reform. If the Jiang government would adopt some of the CCP reformist proposals, Yan'an would cooperate with the Central Government. Jiang disagreed, and he maintained that if the CCP was to be tolerated now, it would seize the national power, and sovietize China on behalf of Moscow. Wallace then claimed that Jiang's perception of the CCP as a party controlled by the USSR was unsound, and the policy based on this harmful. Then, he relayed FDR's message to Jiang: the GMD and the CCP shall not continue to struggle against each other, they shall unite together to fight the Japanese. If the two parties could not negotiate directly with each other, and a third party was needed, the president would like to be the mediator.[16] Niu Jun, an outstanding historian of post-Mao China, is right to say that the CCP's effort to enlist the Americans to check on the GMD's anti-CCP action was "the most successful diplomatic action of the Party during wartime."[17]

MAO HANDLES THE "DIXIE MISSION," 1944

If we recall that Mao in 1943 hoped that with the Americans enlisted in the effort to check on the GMD, the CCP would be in an "extremely advantageous position" in one year's time, Mao's wish seemed to come true in 1944. He got additional help from the Japanese as well. After the Japanese "Ichigo" campaign wiped out the GMD troops from central China, the Communists swiftly poured in to fill the vacuum left behind by the Japanese. While the GMD's reputation at home and abroad was at an all-time low, the CCP's united front activities of courting the Americans reached a peak. The arrival of the Dixie Mission in Yan'an on 22 July not only indicated a major victory of the CCP over the GMD, it also provided the CCP with an opportunity to interact and influence the Americans directly. It so happened that Mao and his comrades performed well along the line of the united front to make use of the Americans to advance its revolutionary program at home.

Zhou Enlai started to invite the Americans to visit Yan'an in 1942, and this invitation was repeated to the U.S. foreign service in Chongqing several times thereafter.[18] Zhou's effort apparently made an impact on U.S. diplomats. They repeatedly proposed to Washington that an American mission be sent to Yan'an, not just for a visit, but to establish official, or at least semiofficial contact with the Communists. Their reason was three fold. First, the CCP held access to Inner Mongolia, Manchuria, and Japanese North China bases. The CCP's strategic importance "would be enhanced by the entry of Russia into the war against Japan." Second, in a future civil war the CCP was more likely to win not only because it "will be in a position to move into the vacuum created by the Japanese withdrawal," but the CCP had the sympathy among the liberals, intellectuals, and students. Third, in a civil war the CCP would give up its struggle for a "democratic nationalistic state" in order to obtain Soviet support, thus becoming just another Soviet satellite. Then, the U.S. would find itself entangled in a fight with Russia on the GMD side. Or a Russo-Chinese Communist bloc would dominate China and the rest of Asia.[19]

Based on these conceptions, the U.S. foreign service in China suggested that (1) "We should avoid committing ourselves unalterably to Jiang," and "firm coordinated American pressure" and "stern bargaining" should be adopted in dealing with him. The U.S. should be ready to "support a strong new coalition offering cooperation mutually more beneficial to China and the United States."[20] (2) "A consulate general be established in Chinese Communist territory and that a military observers' mission also be sent to that area."[21] President Roosevelt seemed to like these suggestions. He cabled Jiang personally on 9 February 1944, suggesting that "an American observers' mission be immediately dispatched" to the CCP area.[22] Jiang politely rejected Roosevelt's request. Stilwell and C. E. Gauss, the U.S. Ambassador to China, proposed again that Roosevelt urge Jiang's assent on this issue and the President agreed.[23] When Henry Wallace visited China, the President sent him a message to advise him to press Jiang to permit the dispatch of the Dixie Mission. Jiang eventually gave in.[24]

Before the Dixie Mission, a group of Chinese and western journalists had obtained permission to go to Yan'an. The CCP viewed this as the first step to breach the GMD's political blockade, and the Party leadership was fully mobilized to make use of this opportunity to stage a united front operation to win over public opinion at home and abroad. On 22 May, Zhou Enlai told an inner-party audience that the Party's initiation for a GMD-CCP negotiation, the defeat of the GMD in the "Ichigo" campaign, plus the arrival of the journalists at Yan'an, all indicated the GMD's weakness and the CCP's increased international influence. The aim of receiving the group of journalists, Zhou stated, was to "win over [their sympathy], and spread out [the CCP's glory]." Zhou then clarified that the "CCP glory" referred to the Party's success and ability in fighting against the Japanese and reconstructing the economy.[25] In other words, the CCP wanted to use the media to let the nation and the world know that the CCP promised an alternative to the GMD as the leader of China.

Mao directly involved himself in this united front operation targeted at the journalists who arrived at Yan'an on 9 June. In the next three days, Mao was with the visitors all the time. In his welcome speech, Mao focused on China's lack of democracy, which, according to him, hindered the Allies' effort to defeat Japan. He treated the journalists with a banquet, and then accompanied them to see a play.[26] On 14 June, the journalists witnessed a mass rally in Yan'an, celebrating the anniversary of the United Nations and calling for decisive action to defeat the Japanese. On the same day, Mao wrote an editorial for *Liberation Daily*, which emphasized that the military situation in China was critical, and the GMD troops had lost their fighting power, and "they disintegrate as soon as they encounter the enemy." Mao concluded, the GMD must undertake overall political reform before the military crisis could come to an end.[27] On 22 June, Ye Jianying, the CCP's chief of staff, made a lengthy speech to the visitors on the topic of the CCP's military achievement against the Japanese. He vowed that the CCP, up to March 1944, had tied down five-sixths of all the Japanese troops in mainland China. Ye's talk was written beforehand and revised by Mao who added that the GMD secretly encouraged a part of its armed force to defect to serve the Japanese so that when Japan was defeated, those puppet troops could switch sides to serve the GMD again by capturing the main cities and railroads on behalf of the central government.[28] Mao's intention was to use the journalists to undermine the GMD's credibility and to promote the CCP's prestige.

What the CCP told the journalists was, however, not the real situation necessarily. For instance, on 21 July, one day before Ye's self-aggrandizing talk, Lin Ping asked for permission to undertake more aggressive actions in Japanese-occupied Hong Kong and Macao. The permission, however, was denied by Zhou, who stated that the CCP should not undertake such actions to expose its force; otherwise, the Japanese would seek revenge against the CCP.[29] This indicated that Mao's "killing-time" policy was still in effect while the CCP was propagating the Party's vigor and achievement in fighting the Japanese.

After the arrival of the Dixie Mission in Yan'an, the CCP's united front operation was concentrated on wooing its members, and the success of the operation was reflected in the reports written by U.S. officers in the field. David Barrett felt that almost none of the Americans' demands were left unmet by the Communists, whose cooperation was total.[30] John Service reported back from Yan'an that his impressions of the CCP area were extremely favorable, and he considered the base area the most advanced and progressive place in China.[31] The Communists, however, did not tell the Americans their real thoughts about the United States and their ulterior motives for befriending the once-demonized Yankees. The Party's secrets were only revealed in the inner-party documents, such as a report on 16 August written by the Southern China Bureau led by Zhou.

The report first of all stated that judging from the arrival of the U.S. mission and the forthcoming British mission to Yan'an, western powers could not but take the CCP into consideration in their postwar planning. Then, the report compared the U.S. and British policies in the Far East. It contended that the British planned to "recover and consolidate the colonies of the British Empire"; and therefore, London would not like to see an independent and strong China under the CCP emerging in Asia, nor the growing influence of the Soviet Union in the region. Thus, even though London might be dissatisfied with the GMD government, it would be certainly hostile to the CCP. For the same reason, London did not want to defeat the Japanese so that Japan's presence in Manchuria and North China would effectively counterbalance the Soviet influence and the emergence of a "new China."[32]

In contrast, the report went on, the Roosevelt administration desired the total defeat of Japan, which could be done only by landing on the Chinese mainland. Thus, Washington needed to use the CCP, as it wanted Soviet participation in the Pacific war as well. In this regard, the report stated, FDR was "progressive; but, he is after all a representative of the bourgeoisie, and thus, his China policy cannot but include certain contradictions. He is on the one hand dissatisfied by Jiang's fascist tendency and the passivism in fighting the Japanese; he nonetheless continues to support Jiang politically, militarily, and financially." The report concluded that the U.S. today intended to join hands with the CCP and try to force the GMD to do the same; but it was only because Washington wanted Japan's total defeat. The U.S. did not wish the CCP's "new democracy" to prevail nationwide; instead, it would like to see a reformed Jiang regime to confront the CCP. "The U.S. will never give up its domination over Chinese politics and economy, nor will it reduce its power to influence China's central government." The report claimed that if the Jiang regime could not serve the interests of the United States, Washington had the ability to prop up a government which would see to its needs. The report thus asserted: "If we want to become the center of China's politics, [we] have to go through the process in which [our] 'new democracy' must struggle against [U.S.] 'old democracy.' "[33] Again, the ideological input in the CCP's perception of world politics and its alliance policy is obvious here.

Then, the report turned to address Moscow's China policy. It stated that although "the Soviet Union is the most reliable friend of China's national democratic revolution," the question of whether or not the USSR would enter into the Pacific war remained to be seen. The Americans in Chongqing were very sure that after the end of the European war, the USSR would take part in the anti-Japanese war. But the Soviet diplomats avoided any commitment, or denied the possibility. Given such an attitude of the Soviets in Chongqing, Zhou suggested that the CCP should not openly talk about the Soviet partici-pation in the anti-Japanese war, because Soviet entry would "mean the victory of China's new democratic revolution, and that is what Jiang and the Anglo-American conservatives do not want to see." Zhou's point was clear: if the CCP publicly displayed its craving for Soviet participation in the Pacific war, the Anglo-American camp would be alarmed by the possibility of a Moscow-supported CCP victory in China, and act against the CCP accordingly.[34] This was the last thing Zhou wanted to see because at the time the CCP was to use the united front technique to court the Americans.

Two days after this report by Zhou and his bureau, the Party Center issued a directive on diplomacy on 18 August, which stated that "if the united front policy we have carried out in the past eight years at home ensured consider-able development for us, the international united front will ensure even greater growth for us." It went on to say that within the U.S. and Britain, just like in China, there were divisions between the progressive force, the middle-of-the-road force, and the die-hard reactionary force. "Thus, the principles of the domestic united front are generally applicable in the international united front."[35] The CCP perceived that Soviet cooperation with the Anglo-American powers during the war would likely continue in the postwar era. Consequently, the postwar government in China would likely be a coalition of the CCP and the GMD. The CCP envisioned a coalition government of "the people's dem-ocratic dictatorship"—a form of government between the Soviet system (pro-letarian dictatorship) and the Anglo-American one (bourgeois democracy)—as a result of compromise.[36] However, the immediate purposes of the CCP's united front with the Americans were (1) to use the Americans to press the GMD toward political reform which would allow the CCP to share national power, (2) to obtain a significant share of U.S. military aid to China, and (3) to facilitate the CCP's southward strategic expansion.

To carry out this threefold program, Mao personally engaged in wooing the Americans. On 23 August, he offered Service a lengthy interview. He said that the CCP at present only expected Washington "to use its influence to force the Kuomintang [GMD] to carry out such a proposal [of government reform]," but if the GMD refused, "then there must be a second stage of American policy," in which the CCP expected official American recognition and military assistance. In order to court the Americans, Mao went out of his way to identify the Com-munists' political identity with that of the Americans. He stated: "We Chinese consider you Americans the ideal of democracy. . . . We do not expect Russian help. . . . The policies of the CCP are merely liberal. . . . Even the most conser-vative American businessman can find nothing in our program to take excep-tion to." Mao even suggested that the Party had thought about dropping the word "Communist" from its name.[37] Apparently, Service was quite convinced by Mao, who knew exactly how the Americans were frustrated by the GMD's performance and hopeful for the CCP as a liberal alternative.

The CCP must have been encouraged by the British military assistance to Tito's Yugoslavian Communists. To have the Americans do the same, on 15 September, a "qualified figure in Yan'an" publicly remarked that China's current situation was characterized, on the one hand, by the GMD's inability and unwillingness to resist Japan and, on the other hand, by the CCP's decisive role in defeating Japan. The Yan'an spokesman declared that if the CCP would not receive western military assistance, "the Allied war effort against Japan would not only last longer but be costlier."[38] A week later, the Party Center held a meeting to discuss how to play the American factor. After the meeting, Zhou wrote a letter to Stilwell in which he raised four points: (1) the crisis in China was caused by the GMD's political fascism and military defeatism, and therefore, the Jiang regime should be replaced by a coalition; (2) in contrast to the GMD, the CCP was fighting the Japanese victoriously, so the CCP forces should be recognized and supplied with military materials; (3) a civil war was still possible, and the GMD military blockade against the Border Region should be removed; and (4) the CCP should attain "at least one half of the total U.S. ammunition and goods for China under lend-lease."[39]

Mao knew that the United States was pressing the GMD for political reform and military activism against the Japanese, and he tried to get the Americans to increase their pressure on Jiang. On 19 July 1944, Mao cabled Li Xiannian that the present negotiations with the GMD would not produce any positive results, and that Jiang would not yield any ground unless (1) he suffered further political and military setbacks, and (2) the Americans brought more pressure to bear on him.[40] One month later, Mao told John Service:

> The United States has handled Chiang very badly. They have let him get away with blackmail. . . . With Chiang you can be friendly only on your own terms. He must give in to constant, strong and unified pressure. Never relax your objectives; keep hammering at him. . . . There is no longer any reason to cultivate, baby or placate Chiang. The United States can tell Chiang what he should do.[41]

Obviously, at this stage, the Communists welcomed American political intervention in Chinese domestic politics because they saw the benefit of playing the American factor against the GMD.

The success of Mao's campaign of courting the Americans is reflected by some U.S. officials' policy suggestions. Based on both military consideration and their confidence in the CCP's ideological and political identities, Barrett and Service called for immediate military assistance to the Communist Army. Barrett suggested on 14 August 1944 that "if the Communists are willing to fight and have the people on their side, it would appear that they are worthy of the support of the United States. I believe that a small amount of aid in the way of ammunition, automatic weapons, pack artillery, and signal equipment would bring immediate results."[42] General Stilwell and the War Department shared the same idea.[43] But, as later developments would prove, the more the Communists were encouraged to hope for a share of U.S. military aid, the more frustrated and angry they would become when they finally learned that it was only an illusion.

By courting the Americans, not only did the Communists have high expectations for U.S. military aid, they also hoped the Americans would support their strategic expansion toward the South. This strategy, first formulated at the Yangjialin Meeting in Yan'an on 1 September, consisted of two major courses of action. First, some units of the ERA were sent to the Wulin Mountain area, together with the guerrilla forces in South China, to open up a new base area. On 10 November, some 5,000 troops left Yan'an, heading toward the South. In June 1945, a second reinforcement of 6,000 troops was sent out toward the South, and a third one was also in preparation. Second, some branches of the NFA were sent to the Jiangsu-Zhejiang-Anhui border area and the southeast coast.[44]

The goal of this southward strategy was twofold: to create a stronghold in South China in preparation for the final contest with the GMD; and to meet the American landing forces in order to obtain military aid. But the Communists stressed the latter part to the Americans to justify their expansion under the name of the United Nations' war effort. On 31 August, one day before the Yangjialin Meeting, General Chen Yi, the commander of the NFA, discussed this matter with Service and convinced him that

> this section of Southwest [southeast?] China may be of great importance to the war against Japan because it must be the site of an American landing. If the GMD cannot hold it, the Communists can. They could easily send officers and old cadres into the old bases from their present operating areas in the Yangtze Valley.

Chen further claimed that the action had already been delayed,

> because they [the Communists] want to avoid more trouble with the Kuomintang. . . . Now, however, the situation may be changing. The possible near collapse of the Kuomintang in these areas, and the importance of the areas to the United Nations' war effort must be considered.[45]

However, Mao's telegram to General Wang Zheng disclosed the true purpose of this "down-south strategy." He estimated that the war with Japan would last for another year and a half. Within this period, the strategic goal of the CCP was to establish a CCP stronghold in South China, "so that when the GMD launches civil war, [the southern base] can pin down the GMD on one [additional] front."[46] The CCP, however, would never tell the Americans its true strategic intention.

In private, the Communists had always maintained a sharp vigilance as far as cooperation with American troops was concerned. At the end of 1944, Mao instructed Zhou to chair a meeting to discuss with Zhu De, Ye Jianying, and others, the conditions in which the CCP-U.S. cooperation should take place. The conditions they laid down were (1) U.S. troops must obey the CCP's policy and law; (2) GMD troops should not follow the Americans into the CCP areas; (3) before the arrival of U.S. troops, an agreement to this effect should be reached; and (4) U.S. armaments for twenty brigades should be delivered to the CCP.[47] Apparently, the CCP was concerned with the possibility of what Mao later called the "Scobie model." In Greece, General Scobie of Britain led the march into the communist-controlled areas, and the Greek reactionary forces followed behind. Would that happen in China? Zhou Enlai voiced this concern in his telegraph to Lin Ping. Zhou cautioned that as soon as the U.S. army landed, the Communists would encounter complicated and difficult situations. They should be prepared for anything and everything that might happen.[48] The CCP's worry about American intervention in China on behalf of the GMD would intensify in the spring of 1945.

MAO HANDLES PATRICK HURLEY

In the summer of 1944, while the CCP was in the midst of a campaign to woo the Americans, Patrick Hurley arrived in China. Mao intended to use Hurley's mediation to advance the CCP's interest at the expense of the GMD. On 19 July Mao acknowledged that the CCP failed in negotiations to force the GMD to recognize the CCP's de facto control over its base areas and its military forces; all Jiang would recognize as legitimate were the CCP's Shaanbei base and ten thousand troops. When the CCP's strife for legitimacy was frustrated, the Americans came to help. Mao noted that the western journalists who came to Yan'an would boost the CCP's international image, and their reports would "benefit us [the CCP]." More encouragingly, Mao knew that FDR was pushing Jiang to allow an American "military mission" (Mao's words) to come to Yan'an.[49] If the United States would recognize and cooperate with the CCP, Mao did not need the GMD recognition anymore. He wanted to use Hurley to promote a coalition government which would dismantle and replace the GMD's "one-party dictatorship."

The CCP was aware that the Americans were frustrated by the GMD's military defeat, and they were seeking political reform in China. On 4 July Ambassador Gauss suggested that Jiang "call all factions (including the Communists) and himself into a military council or high command" for joint responsibility and military effectiveness. Later, President Roosevelt and Secretary Hull cabled Guass that his suggestion of a coalition council "is practical and timely and deserving of careful consideration." Washington wanted to see "a strong but representative and tolerant government" in China.[50] Since American democracy would deliver a vital blow to the GMD political system and legitimize the CCP, Mao quickly came to embrace the coalition idea. On

12 August, he ordered the CCP negotiators in Chongqing to stop negotiating for GMD recognition; he said the critical problem was the GMD "one-party dictatorship."[51] Mao delineated his new program of coalition to Service on 23 August. He said that the GMD government should call a provisional assembly in which the GMD could take half of the total seats, while the CCP and other parties took the other half. Jiang could be the provisional president, but the assembly should have the full authority to reform the government and make new laws. It then would supervise a general election to form a permanent assembly and pass a constitution. Mao also told Service that given the GMD current situation, Jiang had to "look at the face of the United States before he would do anything," and the U.S. China policy should push the GMD to reform.[52]

If Mao was testing the possible U.S. reaction toward his new political agenda, he was satisfied by Service's response. Service told Mao that the United States would like to help establish a coalition government in China. Mao was so delighted that he said at the Seventh Plenum on 1 September 1944 that it was time to "stage a diplomatic offensive" to make use of the Americans to undermine the GMD government. The Coalition thus became the catchword of the Party's political program.[53] On 4 September, Mao cabled the CCP representatives in Chongqing: "It is time for us to propose to the GMD and the international community a plan for government reform." Mao then laid out the details of the plan as he told Service. Mao calculated that Jiang would surely reject the plan; but, the GMD local authorities, various small parties, and the progressives in the Allied governments would endorse it. Following Mao's instructions, the CCP representatives in Chongqing officially announced Mao's plan for a coalition.[54]

It is a historical irony that while the CCP was still negotiating for the GMD's recognition of its legitimacy in July 1944, the Americans came to inspire Mao with the coalition agenda, and Mao's domestic policy was thus further radicalized. The U.S. intended to promote its political system and ideal elsewhere in the world, but the result was not always what was initially expected.

Mao understood that if the GMD would agree with this power-sharing scheme, which he doubted, a coalition would mean the end of GMD monopoly of national government, thus a political victory for Yan'an; but if the GMD rejected the coalition, it would not only offend the third parties and regional anti-Jiang forces at home, but Washington and London would also be dissatisfied. In either case, the CCP was going to win. It was against this background that Patrick Hurley arrived in China on 6 September.

Ignorant of Chinese politics and ambitious, Hurley did what Mao expected him to do and he assumed himself a mission impossible: to mediate the CCP-GMD conflict. On 17 October, Hurley met with Lin Boqu and Dong Biwu, the CCP representatives in Chongqing, for the first time. After the meeting, Lin and Dong sent a report to Yan'an: Hurley stated that the CCP was a well-organized and well-trained strong military force; it would play an important part in determining China's destiny; and it deserved legal representation in the national government as well as in the military high command. Hurley also reportedly said that China's existing government was not democratic; nonetheless, Jiang was the nationally recognized leader of resistance against Japan. In response to the report, Mao stated that the U.S. current China policy was twofold: to uphold Jiang's leadership, and to incorporate the CCP into a democratic government. He reasoned: "Jiang fears that we'll directly criticize him, and the U.S. also fears that we'll reject Jiang. Therefore, under the condition that we recognize Jiang's [existing position], [we] can make a deal [with Hurley] which will benefit us."[55] What Mao meant was that to give the CCP's nominal recognition of Jiang's leadership, Hurley could be persuaded to go along with Mao's coalition agenda.

Hurley, on the other hand, seemed utterly naive, and just couldn't understand why it would be so difficult for the two Chinese parties to form a coalition against the Japanese. They were all Chinese, were they not? In his second and third meetings with Lin and Dong on 18 and 24 October, Hurley outlined his plan: he would participate in the negotiations currently taking place in Chongqing; when a preliminary agreement was reached, he would get Jiang's consent to go to Yan'an to lay the foundation for the Mao-Jiang direct talk; and then, a joint declaration would be issued, and the two parties' union would be in place. To win the CCP's trust of his impartiality, he told the CCP representatives that he rejected Jiang's plan of 21 October. He didn't tell the CCP the details of Jiang's plan, but implied that it was unfair and that it intended to weaken or eradicate them. He also said that he had told Jiang that democratization should be carried out immediately, and political prisoners should be released, too. There was no reason to wait any longer.[56]

Mao must have been delighted to hear Hurley's innocently naive statements. On 6 November, one day before Hurley's arrival in Yan'an, Mao summoned a special meeting which decided a basic policy in dealing with Hurley. Mao and his colleagues believed that the Americans had two weak spots: they were eager to have Communist cooperation to fight the Japanese, and they wanted to consolidate Jiang's position as the nation's leader. Therefore, if the CCP could criticize the GMD government without pointing a finger directly at Jiang, it would be able to push the Americans to increase pressure on Jiang to force him to go along with the coalition line. Mao said that Jiang's intention to send Hurley to Yan'an was to trade a small promise for a life-saving benefit; Hurley underestimated the problems involved. But, when Hurley came, Mao said, "We'll have a warming party for him anyway. Zhou Enlai will introduce us to him, and then, we'll have an evening party and music for him."[57] Mao seemed jubilant and hopeful that Hurley would be on his side.

Hurley arrived at Yan'an airport on 7 November; the next day, he handed over to Mao a draft agreement drawn up by the GMD. In this draft, the focus was on the submission of CCP military forces to Chongqing's authority and the reorganization of the CCP forces by Jiang's regime. Only when these conditions were met, would the National Government recognize the legal status of the CCP. Mao was furious and fiercely attacked the corruption of the GMD government and the inability of the GMD military in fighting the Japanese. Hurley could not deny what Mao had to say about the GMD, and consequently, had to accept Mao's argument: the GMD government lacked credibility to make demands to incorporate the CCP military forces as subordinates, and the CCP deserved an equal partnership. Was this not what a coalition was all about? Notably, Mao did not criticize Jiang in person; instead, he agreed to uphold Jiang's supreme position in the coalition, as the U.S. so desired. Hurley seemed happy to let the Communists offer a counterdraft, and Mao proposed a five-point agreement to Hurley on 9 November, of which the essential points were the reform of existing government, the establishment of a coalition and a joint military committee, and the legal status of the CCP and all anti-Japanese parties. Since in his mind the opposition between the CCP and the GMD had no significant difference from that between the Republicans and Democrats at home, Hurley could not see any reason to reject Mao's demand for an equal partnership in a democratic coalition. He said to Mao that he thought Mao's draft was alright, and he would make every effort to persuade Jiang to accept it. The confused man from Oklahoma cheerfully put his name on the CCP draft beside Mao's signature on 10 November.[58]

While Hurley was innocently optimistic about his "achievement" in the mediation, the CCP leaders were not. The night before Hurley's departure for Chongqing, Mao and Zhou addressed a special plenum of the Party. Mao said that the CCP draft "thoroughly defeats Jiang's attempt to sabotage the liberated areas, and leads to the destruction of the GMD one-party dictatorship, wins the CCP legal status, and benefits small parties and the people in general." Zhou Enlai keenly pointed out the mistaken assumption which Hurley held when he signed the CCP draft. Zhou said that Jiang's reform by offering a few CCP positions in the government was one thing, and the CCP's program of a coalition was another; but Hurley was mixing apples and oranges.[59] Hurley's mistake, however, provided the CCP an opportunity to play the U.S. off against the GMD, and Zhou was happy to be on board with Hurley for Chongqing to negotiate with Jiang on the base of the CCP draft.

Back in Chongqing and surrounded by Jiang and his men, Hurley soon changed his mind to endorse the GMD's position. On 21 November, Hurley met Zhou twice and tried to persuade him to accept the GMD position. Zhou, apparently outraged by Hurley's flip, pointed out that to let a few CCP members take part in the existing government in Chongqing would not change the GMD's "one-party dictatorship," and the CCP would have no real power at all.[60] When Mao learned about this development, he commented that the GMD position was "One-party rule remains intact; a few guests are invited [to join the government]; our [the CCP] military is trapped."[61] He would not let Jiang or Hurley do that.

On 22 November, with Hurley present, Zhou met with Jiang. He insisted that the principle of a coalition was the only basis for further negotiations. At the same time, he privately worked out another CCP draft, the essence of which was to reform the existing power structure in Chongqing into a coalition government and a joint military committee; and then, the CCP's troops would be reorganized into a national army. In short, the CCP wanted to dismantle the GMD's monopoly of power first, and talk about the reorganization of the CCP's military forces later. If Zhou in Chongqing remained diplomatically flexible, Mao in Yan'an was increasingly impatient. On 23 November, Mao stated that the Party should insist on the Yan'an draft, and should launch a political offensive to criticize Jiang's rejection of it. He mapped out two alternatives: to continue the coalition program, or to establish a separate government in the CCP-controlled area. First of all, Mao said, the CCP should make every effort to expand its armed force nationwide. On 26 November, he cabled Zhou to propose that the Yan'an draft, which Hurley signed, and the GMD's rejection of it, be leaked to the press. On 1 December, Mao telegraphed Zhou again: since the GMD had rejected the coalition proposal, negotiations should be terminated and Zhou should return to Yan'an. On 2 and 4 December, Zhou met Hurley twice, and the latter urged the CCP to take part in the existing government in Chongqing. If the CCP could be more amenable to the GMD's position, Hurley promised, the U.S. would deliver military aid and training to the CCP. But, from the Communists' point of view, if their troops were to be placed under the command of the GMD, U.S. aid and training would mean nothing to them. Zhou left Chongqing for Yan'an on 7 December, and Hurley sent David Barrett to go with him, hoping that Mao might be persuaded to continue the dialogue.[62] Mao, however, had made up his mind that Hurley was pro-Jiang; therefore, he was no longer useful to push a coalition program, which Jiang would never accept anyway.

At this point in time, however, Mao still believed, or rather hoped, that the FDR administration was progressive, and the U.S. military personnel in China formerly under "Vinegar Joe" Stilwell was progressive, too. Referring to "bourgeois personalities" such as FDR and some U.S. officers in China, what Mao meant by being "progressive" was their advocacy of "uniting with the USSR and the CCP," just as Sun Yat-sen's policy in 1924. Thus, it was possible for the CCP to make use of this "contradiction" to exploit the differences between Hurley, a "reactionary," and U.S. "progressive" officers in China to the advantage of the CCP. On 7 December, Zhou reported to the Party's plenum his mission to Chongqing. The plenum then decided to discontinue negotiations with the GMD, to publish the Yan'an draft, and to form a separate government in the base areas under the name of the "Association of Liberated

Areas."[63] The next day, Zhou telegraphed Hurley to inform him of the Party's decision. At the same time, Mao gave Barrett an animated talk. As for Mao, his outrage and fury at Hurley's betrayal was juxtaposed with a moving expression of his willingness to cooperate with the Americans who supported a U.S.-CCP military cooperation. He said:

> If the United States abandons us, we shall be very, very sorry, but it will make no difference in our good feeling toward you [the American military men in China]. We will accept your help with gratitude any time, now and in the future. We would serve with all our hearts under an American general, with no strings or conditions attached. That is how we feel toward you. If you land on the shores of China, we will be there to meet you, and to place ourselves under your command.[64]

Mao did not really mean what he said. On 25 January 1945, when Hurley proposed that an American officer be appointed as the Commander-in-Chief of the CCP troops, Mao rejected it angrily: "[It] is a policy of placing Chinese troops, especially our Party's troops, under foreign command, turning them into a colonial army. We shall never agree to that."[65] It should be noted that this comment was made privately in an inner-party document. In December 1944, Yan'an was not prepared to dissolve ties with the U.S. publicly yet. On 9 December, two days after Mao decided to split with Jiang and Hurley openly, he changed his mind, and put the proposal for a separate government on hold. He said that the Party should think about it more cautiously in terms of possible repercussions: Would the U.S. stop military aid to the CCP, which, Mao believed, was forthcoming? Would Jiang take the opportunity to remove his existing recognition of the CCP military units? Would the middle-of-the-road parties disagree with it? Mao decided that the CCP needed more time to think about it, while continuing the coalition agenda.[66] Thus, keeping ties to Hurley would be beneficial to the CCP.

On 11 December, Hurley cabled Mao that he was strongly against the publication of the Yan'an draft, and that the GMD was willing to continue to negotiate. On the same day, Barrett told Wang Ruofei, the CCP representative in Chongqing, how furious Hurley was when he knew that Yan'an had decided to publish the Yan'an draft that bore his signature. Barrett also advised Wang that it would be unwise for the CCP to embarrass Hurley, and that Jiang would denounce the CCP for splitting the nation during the anti-Japanese war, if Yan'an was to establish a separate government. Wang cabled Yan'an immediately to report Barrett's advice.[67] The next day, Mao and Zhou instructed Wang to tell the Americans that "we have not the slightest intention to split with the United States," and all Yan'an asked for was that the Americans should not force the Communists to take a few official posts in the Chongqing government at the expense of democratic principles. Wang was specifically instructed to pass on the message to Barrett and John Davis.[68]

In his speech to a Party Center meeting on the same day, Mao proposed that the preparation for a separate government be postponed. Zhou agreed with Mao, offering two reasons: first, the slogan of a coalition was more advantageous politically than a separate government, especially when the nation was still at war with Japan; and second, if more of Jiang's forces were to be wiped out by the Japanese in the near future, the CCP might become the power center in the coalition.[69] The CCP placed much hope on the Japanese operation in the south to further weaken the GMD, and Mao was not disappointed in this regard. Early in December, a GMD strategic position in Guizhou province fell under a Japanese attack, and Chongqing's fall and the total collapse of the GMD was thus predicted by many at home and abroad. Anticipating a fatal defeat of the GMD, Yan'an decided to continue the coalition agenda instead of establishing a separate government. Therefore, Hurley's mediation between Yan'an and Chongqing was needed to keep the charade going. The CCP hoped that after the Japanese crushed the GMD, the U.S. would have no choice but to recognize CCP supremacy in China.[70]

Consequently, Zhou wrote Hurley on 16 December to promise that the CCP would not publish the Yan'an draft for now, and that it was willing to continue negotiating with the GMD under Hurley's mediation. On the same day, Mao also wrote Hurley that he was in agreement with President Roosevelt that Chinese forces should join hands with the United States to defeat Japan, and he wished that the ambassador would relay his opinion, together with many thanks, to the President. The U.S. ambassador was encouraged and sent Yan'an a cable on 21 December to invite Zhou to Chongqing again. But Mao was not really interested in negotiation at this point. He cabled Hurley the following day, stating that since the GMD didn't show its willingness to negotiate on the basis of the Yan'an draft, there was no reason to send Zhou to Chongqing. But Mao proposed that Hurley send Barrett to Yan'an again.[71] This time Mao had something else in mind.

While Hurley was increasingly leaning toward a pro-Jiang position, the U.S. military establishment was concerned about the possible total collapse of the GMD and what to do about it. On 14 December, Stimson, the U.S. Secretary of War, wrote in his diaries: "If we can't get rid of Chiang Kai-shek, we can't get in touch with the only live body of military men there in China at present, [*sic*] namely, the Communists."[72] At the same time and with the same logic, General Robert McClure, the chief of staff in the U.S. headquarters in China, proposed a plan for a CCP-U.S. joint operation in which an American airborne unit of 4,000 to 5,000 technicians would be involved.[73] From 15 to 17 December, accompanied by Barrett, Willis Bird, the head of the Office of Strategic Services (OSS) in China, brought Yan'an a plan which suggested that the U.S. would provide complete equipment for up to 25,000 guerrillas and at least 100,000 Woolworth one-shot pistols for the "people's militia."[74] This is what was in Mao's mind when he refused to send Zhou to negotiate with Jiang but invited Barrett to Yan'an again. On 27 December, when Barrett came to Yan'an, Mao was not disappointed at all. This time the American military establishment in China proposed a plan for a CCP-U.S. joint operation in Shandong which would involve American divisions of 28,000 troops.[75]

Yan'an thought there was a gap between the pro-Jiang Hurley group and the U.S. military establishment, and Mao was determined to exploit this "contradiction" to his advantage. After General Stilwell was recalled, General Wedemeyer was appointed as his successor. The CCP thought of Wedemeyer as being of the same persuasion as his predecessor; and therefore, on 9 January 1945, Mao tried to have him pass on a message to President Roosevelt: Mao and Zhou wanted to visit the White House.[76] In the Communists' minds, Roosevelt was their last hope. They believed that Roosevelt's policy of "uniting with the USSR, the CCP, and pressing Jiang" had been violated by Hurley. For Yan'an, a direct meeting with the U.S. President would not only greatly enhance its political prestige at home and abroad, making the issue of GMD recognition irrelevant, it would also make the "enlightened" Democratic Roosevelt repudiate the "reactionary" Republican Hurley. But, to its dismay, Yan'an's attempt failed quickly because Wedemeyer turned its message over to Hurley, who in turn began to purge those "China hands" in Chongqing.[77] The CCP now realized that Hurley's policy was the policy of the U.S. government; and therefore, its animosity against "American imperialism" rose quickly, and friends turned into enemies again.

FROM FRIENDS TO ENEMIES

If the process in which the CCP-U.S. relations turned from enemies to friends before Pearl Harbor was torturous and dragging, the reverse course in the first half of 1945 was rather summary. Since the U.S.-CCP cooperation was a "marriage of convenience," the quick "divorce" was nothing of a surprise. Hurley frustrated Mao's two basic goals in courting the Americans: to use the Americans' idea of a democratic representative coalition to dismantle the GMD's political institutions, and to obtain U.S. military aid to boost the CCP military strength. Thus, the U.S.-CCP cooperation on the CCP terms became impossible, and Mao was so irritated by the Americans that he decided to take direct actions against the GMD "one-party dictatorship" with support from the people in the GMD-controlled area, the Democratic League and other small parties, and GMD local authorities. If the CCP's effort to woo the U.S. was the "united front from above," it now turned to the "united front from below," that was to mobilize Jiang's domestic opponents. On 7 January, Hurley proposed that renewed GMD-CCP negotiations be held in Yan'an under his personal mediation. In response, Mao cabled Hurley on 11 January, proposing that instead of a bipartisan meeting a multiparty conference should be called to discuss concrete measures toward a coalition.[78] Zhou Enlai went to Chongqing briefly, but he was not interested in making a deal with the GMD under Hurley's mediation. He left Chongqing for Yan'an on 16 February 1945.[79]

The CCP's hard-line approach to the GMD and the Hurley mission was in part encouraged by Moscow. On 3 February, one day before the Yalta summit, Stalin informed Mao of the upcoming event and promised to send him further information about the result of the summit in a few days. Moscow's message also gave Mao enough information to conclude that the Soviet Red Army would come back to the Far East in the near future. Mao immediately sent a cable to Zhou in Chongqing, suggesting that the CCP-GMD talks under Hurley's mediation be terminated. He reasoned that the Soviets' coming back to the Far East would certainly increase the weight the CCP carried in China's politics. Consequently, the *Mei-Jiang* (U.S.-Jiang), a hyphenated term to be used by the CCP in years to come, were becoming more eager than ever to settle on a deal with the CCP before the Soviets reappeared on the scene. Feeling much stronger than before, Mao decided not to reach a deal with the U.S. and Jiang hastily; he suggested that Zhou come back to Yan'an immediately.[80] Although Mao held a "wait-and-see" approach for now in order to take full advantage of the increasing Soviet influence in the Far East after Yalta, his use of *Mei-Jiang* as a terminology in his telegram indicated that he had made up his mind that even FDR, a "progressive," was not to change the bourgeois reactionary nature of the Washington government, which would continue to support the Jiang regime in China anyway. With the prospect of strong Soviet support in the near future, Mao's unyielding attitude toward the *Mei-Jiang* was toughened.

Frustrated by the CCP's hard-line position, Hurley became increasingly short-tempered and undiplomatically direct to the Communists. On 18 February, Zhou cabled Hurley to propose that the Chinese delegation to the United Nations Conference in San Francisco be comprised of representatives from the GMD, the CCP, and the Democratic League in equal number. Hurley immediately slammed the door on the CCP, and told Zhou in a stern and unequivocal voice:

> The President and Generalissimo of the National Government of China . . . will be recognized as the representative of China at the conference and the President alone . . . will select the staff which will accompany him. . . . The Communist Party of China is not a nation. . . . It is one of the political parties of China. The only difference from the ordinary political party is that it is armed. I am further of the opinion that recognition by the conference of any armed political party in China other than the National Government would destroy the possibility of unification of China. I urge that Mao Tse-tung [Zedong] . . . and you . . . consider only the methods by which you can unite with, be included in, and cooperate under the National Government of China.[81]

This led Mao to conclude that U.S. policy had changed from "uniting with the CCP and pressuring Jiang" to "supporting Jiang, dragging the CCP along, [in order to] beat the Japanese [*fu-Jiang, la-Gong, da-riben*]." Only the Soviet Union was truly supporting the democratic movement and the establishment of a coalition. On 3 February, the same day when Stalin's aforementioned message was received, the Party Center warned that the main danger in the Party was "the rightist deviation," which referred to any hopes for a compromise with the GMD under U.S. mediation. Whenever the Party called for an antirightist move, it indicated the turn toward a more radical policy. This time Yan'an called upon all Communists to be prepared for harsh struggle and bloodshed against *Mei-Jiang*.[82] On 12 February, Mao told his comrades that the CCP must attack the U.S. Government policy of supporting Jiang and opposing the Communists: "Do not be afraid of their [the Americans] anger, and their loud accusations."[83]

Nonetheless, in February and March Yan'an had not decided to split with the U.S. completely. The Soviets were to come back, but not in the immediate future; the Americans were more likely to land in China first. Moreover, the CCP still saw the possibility to take advantage of the "contradiction" within the U.S. ruling circle. After Hurley left China for Washington in February, the foreign service officers in Chongqing got together and collectively drafted a lengthy telegram to the State Department on 28 February, appealing for a reevaluation of the U.S. China policy. They were of the opinion that "the President inform the Generalissimo in definite terms that military necessity requires that we supply and cooperate with the Communists. . . ." They also disagreed with the policy of unconditional support for the GMD.[84] The CCP must have been further encouraged when President Roosevelt wrote Mao on 10 March that "I am confident that the cooperation of the Chinese and American people will greatly contribute to the achievement of victory and lasting peace."[85] Three days later, John Service was sent to Yan'an again, and Mao had a lengthy conversation with him on 1 April. Capitalizing on a then widely held western belief that the CCP was a group of indigenous agrarian reformers rather than authentic communists, Mao told Service that

> the peasants are China. . . . The problems of the Chinese farmers are, therefore, basic to China's future. . . . The Kuomintang [GMD] has no contact with the agrarian masses of the population. It is the party of the military and landlord groups. . . . The Chinese Communist Party . . . is the party of the Chinese peasant. . . . Just as the Chinese farmer cannot be ignored in China's future, neither can the Communist Party.[86]

However, Mao's effort to make use of the contradiction within the U.S. government proved to be futile. Hurley won the support of the White House, and removed the officers in opposition to him from China. To celebrate his triumph, Hurley gave a press conference on 2 April, reiterating that the U.S.

would recognize and support the Central Government only. He said that "the military strength of the armed political parties and the warlords has been over-estimated in the United States." On the other hand, Hurley announced that "the Chinese military establishment, the American military establishment, the Chinese National Government, and the American Embassy at Chungking [Chongqing] are now all one team."[87] In other words, Hurley contended that there was no loophole in official Sino-American relations to be taken advantage of by Yan'an, and Washington would not work with the CCP, bypassing the Chinese Government. That was enough for Mao.

Immediately after Hurley's press conference, Yan'an started to attack "American imperialism" openly. The *Liberation Daily* of 9 April commented on the U.S. policy in its "backyard" in a Leninist hostile fashion:

Latin America has been a place where the imperialist powers scrambled for supremacy. . . . The United States is the only powerful neighbor in the area which has been actively seeking control over this rich piece of land since the U.S. had developed into the imperialist stage from the [liberal] capitalist stage.

The article gave a detailed description of how the U.S. monopolized the Latin American economy in terms of raw materials and markets. It also charged that the Americans were currently seeking military control of the whole continent. All of this, the Communists believed, "is actually the further development of the Monroe Doctrine."[88] The underlying message of this article was clear: the behavior of American imperialists in Asia would be a mirror image of its policy in Latin America, should it control the area after the war.

The death of FDR in April further concerned the CCP that the United States was turning toward a reactionary direction. The CCP leaders already smelled a rat when Truman, instead of Wallace, was chosen as FDR's vice president at the Democratic convention in 1944. In a report written by Zhou Enlai's Southern Bureau in August 1944, it was stated that Truman's nomination was FDR's concession to the right-wingers in the Democratic Party, who were "conservatives, Catholics, harboring deep anti-Soviet and anti-communist bias. They have considerable strength in U.S. politics." The report concluded that the U.S. government would turn to the right. This danger could be averted only under two conditions: the Soviets would soon participate in the war against Japan, or the CCP would grow strong enough to have more say in Far Eastern affairs.[89]

With FDR deceased, Mao and his comrades were visibly nervous about the consequences of a "right-winger" in charge of the White House. They soon found enough "evidence" to convince themselves that the whole U.S. domestic politics was turning toward a reactionary direction. In June 1945, John Service and five other people were arrested on charges of conspiring to commit espionage. This was the so-called Amerasia Case.[90] The Communists saw the six as "friendly Americans sympathetic to China's cause of resistance and democracy." To the CCP, the arrest of these people was clear evidence of the victory of "American reactionaries" over the "enlightened bourgeoisie."[91]

The Communists believed that reactionary trends in U.S. domestic politics explained the American imperialistic policy in China. Mao on 2 June reformulated the CCP's perception of U.S. China policy as "uniting with Jiang to resist Japan, [while] confronting the Soviet Union and opposing the CCP" (*lian-Jiang kangri, ju-Su fan-Gong*). He foresaw that the U.S. was attempting to gain hegemony in the Far East, which would compete with the growing Soviet strength in the area. Consequently, Mao predicted, U.S. hostility toward the CCP would increase. Mao's perception of U.S. hostility against the CCP was immediately translated into the Party's daily policy conduct. On the same day, Zhou telegraphed Lin Ping, the CCP leader in South China, that the U.S. policy of all-out support for Jiang had been established, and the GMD was actively preparing for a civil war; therefore, the CCP should be watching for the U.S.-GMD secret agents' cooperation in sabotaging the Communists militarily. Zhou reiterated the same theme on the 16th and 17th of the same month.[92]

If Mao had hoped for military cooperation with the American landing forces in order to gain U.S. military aid a few months ago, he was now increasingly concerned with the possibility of U.S. intervention on behalf of the GMD in the last stage of the Pacific war. On 8 May, he warned that the Party should consider the danger of a "Scobie in China" more seriously, although the Communists should not be scared by it, for the Soviet Union was stronger than ever, and so was the CCP.[93] On 17 June, Mao issued an inner-party directive to make the Party fully prepared for a civil war launched by *Mei-Jiang* in the near future. He said that although the Soviet-British-American unity was an established fact, the United States, "as the home base of capitalism," had a policy of "resisting the USSR and opposing the CCP," for it intended to establish U.S. hegemony in Asia. The British General Scobie was suppressing Greek communists, Mao claimed, and this was the "signal of ideological confrontation in the postwar era." He also believed it was proof that "the 'Scobie danger' will necessarily occur in China"; therefore, the CCP should expand its armed forces and liberated areas rigorously.[94] In his conclusion at the Seventh National Congress, Mao sounded the alarm again that the Party should watch out for the danger of an American intervention of the Scobie type. China could become America's semicolony under a GMD regime in the postwar era, which, Mao said, would be a source of long-term trouble for the CCP.[95] Apparently, with the anti-Japanese war drawing to a close, the CCP's old fear of an American dominated postwar China, explicitly expressed in Mao's telegrams of 25 October 1940, came to the surface again and became a predominant concern in the CCP's policy thinking.

As his anti-Americanism resurfaced, Mao was progressively militant in verbal attacks on U.S. imperialism. He told a visitor on 4 July that "with these few rusty guns, I could fight the Japanese, I can fight the Americans, too. The first step, I want to drive Hurley out, then we shall see."[96] Mao did launch a propaganda offensive against Hurley in particular, and U.S. imperialism in general. In the middle of July, Mao wrote three articles to attack the Americans.[97] In these articles, he did nothing less than depict a political and ideological confrontation between the U.S. and the USSR in the immediate future, and announced the CCP's "lean-to-one-side" policy. Ideology and the unfolding reality, as Mao saw it, again merged in his perspective, leading him to form a two-camp vision in the postwar era even before the war ended.

CHAPTER V

Postwar Alignment

CCP-MOSCOW VERSUS GMD-WASHINGTON IN MANCHURIA, AUGUST–DECEMBER 1945

The central problem in the [postwar] world is the struggle
between the United States and the Soviet Union.
The reflection of this struggle in China is the struggle
between Jiang and the CCP.
—*Mao Zedong, November 1945*

IF Mao predicted on 15 June 1945 that the Pacific war against Japan would last another year and a half, the dramatic change in international politics two months later came much sooner than Mao expected.[1] Stalin ordered the Red Army to rush into Manchuria and North Korea before the burning ash in Hiroshima and Nagasaki cooled down. American-occupied Japan and South Korea versus the Soviet-occupied Manchuria and North Korea set the stage for the cold war in Asia, and Manchuria had a crucial role in the Chinese civil war between the CCP and the GMD. Mao quickly adjusted himself to the new reality and came up with a two-camp formula to sum up his cold war world vision in the postwar era in which a clear-cut alignment between the CCP and Moscow versus the GMD and Washington was at the heart of his postwar strategic thinking.[2] It was this belief in "class association" in international politics that made Mao adjust and readjust the CCP's policy, willingly or not, in accordance with Stalin's changing position.[3]

MAO'S INITIAL ADJUSTMENT TO STALIN'S POSTWAR POLICY

The making of Mao's two-camp vision can be traced back to 1944, when the Allied forces were pushing the Germans back and a victory was almost in sight. Although the CCP was wooing the Americans at the time, they were alarmed by the emerging rift between the USSR and the western allies on the postwar European settlement in general and the Polish issue in particular. In the perception of Mao and his comrades, had the Anglo-American forces marched into Poland, the "reactionary government-in-exile" in London would have been brought back and an "old Poland" under landlords and capitalists would be restored. They thus felt fortunate that the Soviet Red Army was liberating Poland, which brought about an "upsurge of the new democratic movement in liberated Eastern Europe." During the Warsaw uprising in August 1944, the Red Army stayed put while the Germans were slaughtering the Polish insurrectionaries. When the West condemned the Soviet behavior, the CCP blamed the London-based Polish government-in-exile for "harboring an evil motivation . . . gambling with thousands of lives of Polish patriots." When the Lublin government was put in place, the CCP hailed it as representing the "unanimous demand of the Polish people," and the landmark of "a new stage in the democratic movement in East Europe." Mao and his comrades went on to claim that the Red Army took on all the German forces in Europe before the Normandy landing; thereafter, the Soviets were still handling four-fifths of Hitler's army. Thus, as the "real emancipator of Europe" and the "protector of human civilization," the USSR should have more say in the postwar settlement; otherwise, "there will be no stable and lasting peace in Europe."[4]

The CCP's comments on the Polish issue were not just a public display of loyalty to Moscow; rather, they reflected an old nightmare of the Party leaders: when the Anglo-American forces came to China to fight the Japanese, they would back up the GMD against the CCP, just as they supported the Polish government-in-exile. When General Scobie of Britain intervened in Greece against the Greek Communists, Mao concluded that the Americans would likely do the same when they came to China. This CCP nightmare seemed to come true at the end of the anti-Japanese war. At the time, most of the GMD troops were in the remote areas of southwest China, while the CCP troops were near cities and railways in north, central, and east China. If the Communists had taken over Japanese arms and strategic positions in these areas, the Nationalists would have been out of the game sooner. On 11 August, Jiang Jieshi ordered the Communists to remain where they were, pending further orders, and not to accept Japanese surrender. The next day, Hurley suggested to the Secretary of State that the CCP capture of Japanese arms would make civil war inevitable and the U.S. should warn the Japanese against laying down their arms to anyone but the forces of the National Government. He also urged Wedemeyer to assist Jiang in regaining control in north China. On 15 August, General Douglas MacArthur issued General Order No. 1, instructing the Japanese troops in China to surrender to the National Army only. On 23 August, He Yingqin, the Commander-in-Chief of the National Army, ordered the Japanese not only to hold their arms and position but to retake positions lost to the Communists.[5]

With the Americans backing the GMD, the CCP naturally placed high hopes on Soviet support of their cause. It was equally clear in Mao's mind that when the Soviets came to China, they would do just that. Mao's perception of the postwar alliance with the GMD-U.S. on one side and the CCP-USSR on the other was not really off the mark. In fact, it was shared by Washington's policy makers at the time. For instance, Harriman told FDR in 1944 that "it must be assumed that the Soviets will back the Communists in the North and turn over to them the administration of the Chinese territory liberated by the Red Army. Then the situation will be progressively difficult for Chiang [Jiang]." FDR was receptive to this observation, and he told Hurley to advise Jiang that he should solve his problem with the CCP before the Russians came back to the Far East. "I cannot tell you more at this time," said FDR to Hurley, "but he [Jiang] will have to take my word for it. You can emphasize the word 'Russians' to him."[6]

Neither Jiang nor Mao actually needed to be reminded by FDR on the nature of CCP-Moscow relations; they knew much better on that matter than any American politician. With the war ended abruptly, both the CCP and the GMD rushed to prepare for a civil war, and they all expected help from Moscow and Washington, respectively. Mao made his approach toward the postwar situation apparent on the day when the second A-bomb exploded. On 9 August 1945, *Liberation Daily* carried an article describing the deadly power of the bomb as a "revolution in war technology." Mao was annoyed by the article and he called in his propagandists. He lectured them that they should not have "exaggerated the power and role of the atomic bomb."[7] Within one year, Mao was to tell Anna Louise Strong that atomic bombs, together with "American imperialists," were all but "paper tigers." What Mao really wanted to say was that people's zeal and boldness to fight U.S. imperialists shouldn't be discouraged by the fear of the destructive power of the bomb; and the defeat of Japan was not due to the bombs, but the entry of the Soviet Red Army into the war. On 13 August, he reiterated that the "political implication" of Soviet entry into the war was "historical" and "beyond any measurement." Yet, "the U.S. and Jiang Jieshi's propaganda try to diminish the Red Army's political influence by exaggerating the two bombs. This cannot be done."[8]

At the same time, Mao was very excited by the Soviet entry into the war, which, as the CCP had believed, meant the "victory of new democracy in China," just as had happened in Eastern Europe. He told a party meeting on 9 August that it was "thoroughly joyful" (*tongkuai*) to fight shoulder to shoulder with the Soviet Red Army. In fact, he was expecting a type of "direct assistance" from the USSR and to turn China into a "new democracy" just like the "New Poland." Mao was also worried about the Americans who would support the GMD. He said that the Red Army's presence in the Far East would change U.S. China policy somehow: "It is, however, absolutely certain that the U.S. will stand with Jiang. Thus, it will be a long-term problem for us to deal with *Mei-Jiang*. With Japan's collapse, the danger of a civil war is mounting."[9] Facing the U.S.-backed GMD, Mao expected Soviet support; and he acted swiftly. On 10 August, he cabled his lieutenants in the south: "The USSR has taken part in the war, and Japan has surrendered. A civil war is pending. Considering your circumstances, you cannot seize major cities; nonetheless, you should take advantage of the situation to expand your territory, to seize weapons, to strive for small cities. You should mobilize the masses to prepare for a civil war."[10] In the minds of the CCP leaders, it was in the south, the traditional Anglo-American sphere of influence, where American intervention on behalf of the GMD was most likely.

In the north, where the Russians were in control and the CCP's forces were strong, Mao's plan was more ambitious. On 12 August, Mao ordered his lieutenants in North China to make every effort to destroy the GMD forces in Inner Mongolia, and then, to march northward to meet the Outer Mongolian forces and the Red Army. The same day, he also ordered General Wan Yi's Manchurian troops to march into the northeast to meet the Soviets there. On 19 August, he again cabled his lieutenants in North China that in a week he would dispatch 1,200 cadres to go to Manchuria, together with the military forces under Lin Feng.[11] Outside Mongolia and Manchuria, Mao ordered to end the guerrilla strategy and regroup all the CCP armed forces into regiments, brigades, and divisions to expand territory, and to seize all the major cities and railways in north and central China, such as Beijing, Tianjin, Taiyuan, Nanjing, and Shanghai.[12] Mao's ambitious plan was apparently encouraged by his assumption that Stalin would enact a kind of "Polish solution" in the northern half of China.

Mao was not alone in this regard. Jiang was deeply concerned that Stalin would turn the northern half of the country into a Far Eastern Poland. For Stalin, the key to fulfilling the Yalta protocol was to have the Chinese government sign a bilateral treaty. The Sino-Soviet negotiations started early in July, and soon went into a deadlock over the issue of Outer Mongolia. Song Ziwen, the U.S.-educated chief Chinese delegate, cabled Jiang on 4 July, asking whether or not he should terminate negotiations if Stalin insisted on the independence of Outer Mongolia. On 6 July, Jiang told Song that the issue was negotiable if Stalin would agree on three conditions, one of which was the GMD government's complete control over the CCP's military and administrative command. The next day, Jiang sent Song two more cables to reiterate this proposition.[13] Jiang was ready to give up Outer Mongolia should Stalin agree to curtail the CCP. Jiang realized that should Stalin intend to support a "friendly regime" in Manchuria, Mongolia, and North China, as he did in Poland, he would not need to send personnel from Moscow as he did to set up the Lublin government: Mao and his lieutenants were already there. Jiang did not want a "Polish solution" for the northern half of China, and he could not act as stubbornly and unyieldingly as the Polish government-in-exile. The Sino-Soviet pact was concluded on 14 August, and on the same day, Jiang cabled Mao to invite him to negotiate in Chongqing. Jiang seemed confident that Stalin would have instructed Mao to come to terms with him this time.[14]

Mao and his colleagues, however, had a very different perspective on the Sino-Soviet pact. On 3 August, Wang Roufei, the CCP's chief delegate in

Chongqing, voiced the Party's view at a meeting in Yan'an on the forthcoming result of the Chongqing-Moscow bargaining. He stated that the deal would have to reflect the interests of both the U.S. and the USSR in China, and thus, it would not be a deal which would support the CCP against the GMD. There-fore, the CCP should no longer hope that the Soviet Union would deliver "direct support" to the CCP to fight the GMD. Wang was speaking of a wide-spread belief among the CCP members that when the Red Army appeared in the Far East, it would support their struggle against the GMD for national power in a direct and forceful manner. What was the exact form of Soviet "direct support" the CCP had hoped for? The Red Army's direct participation in the Chinese civil war just like the British did in Greece? Or, turning over the Red Army–liberated area and the Japanese weapons to the CCP just like the Russians did in Poland? Wang did not, and probably could not, specify what the CCP should no longer hope for, and what was still hopeful. He, nonethe-less, pointed out two basic principles which could be taken for granted: First, he said, the USSR would not allow a U.S.-supported GMD-dominated "fascist China" to emerge in postwar Asia; second, as a Marxist, Stalin would not sign a treaty which would constrain Chinese revolution. Mao agreed with Wang, and he believed that the Soviet presence in China would at least constrain the U.S. from outright intervention on the GMD's behalf against the CCP.[15] Mao and his colleagues understood perfectly that the exact form of Soviet support would be played out in the CCP-USSR vs. GMD-U.S. game.

Since the CCP was convinced that Stalin would not allow the pro-Ameri-can GMD to prevail in China, he would come to the CCP's aid, in one form or another, when it was necessary. Mao also understood that Stalin, as a Marx-ist revolutionary leader, might not act outright on the CCP's behalf, but he would certainly support the Party's revolution, and the newly signed Sino-Soviet pact would not change the basic direction of Stalin's policy. Mao knew from his previous experience that if the official state-to-state relations between Moscow and Jiang's government did not prevent Stalin from supporting an antigovernment regime secretly in China's northwest in the 1930s, the new pact would not "constrain" the CCP revolution; it was merely one more diplo-matic maneuver of Stalin. In fact, after the pact was signed on 14 August, Mao not only rejected Jiang's invitation for negotiations, his military strategy became more aggressive, especially regarding his plan to seize Shanghai, the traditional home base of the GMD.

Mao planned to seize Shanghai the day after the Red Army started its cam-paign against the Japanese in Manchuria. On 10 August, Mao cabled the Cen-tral China Bureau, instructing the NFA to "concentrate main forces to occupy major cities and key strategic points."[16] Consequently, preparations for seiz-ing Shanghai and Nanjing were under way. To accomplish such an ambitious plan, the Communists extended their united front to embrace the defeated Japanese and the collaborationist regime. A liaison mission was sent to Nanjing and Shanghai to persuade the Japanese and collaborators to cooperate with the CCP. Attached to the NFA, this liaison mission was directed by Yan'an. At first, the Communists attempted to meet with the Japanese Commander-in-Chief in Nanjing, but for unknown reasons, Yan'an instructed its agent to drop the plan.[17] Chongqing detected the CCP's move and reacted promptly. The GMD secret service assassinated two top officials of the puppet regime, who were believed to be cooperating with the CCP. On 16 August, Jiang appointed Zhou Fuhai, the puppet mayor of Shanghai, as the Acting Commander-in-Chief responsible for the defense of Shanghai, Nanjing, Hangzhou, and the surrounding areas. Zhou Fuhai and Chen Gongbo, another key figure in the collaboration regime, replied immediately to show their loyalty to Jiang.[18]

The Communists' attempt to win over their old enemies failed, but they went ahead on their own. On 15 August, 3,000 undercover CCP troops went into Shanghai to prepare for a general uprising. The same day, however, Zhang Zhiyi, the CCP-appointed mayor, reported to the Party Center that unless a major military campaign was launched to attack Shanghai, the internal uprising alone had a slim chance of winning. At the time, the former Chinese collaborator military forces in the city had switched their loyalty to Jiang, and General Douglas MacArthur issued General Order No. 1 on 15 August, instructing the Japanese troops to surrender to the GMD authority only. Thus, the CCP forces in Shanghai were utterly outnumbered and outgunned. However, Mao disregarded the situation and overruled Zhang's opinion. On 20 August, he approved the insurrection plan submitted by the Central Bureau, and issued an order to carry out an armed revolt and occupy Shanghai immediately without waiting for the main forces of the NFA. At the same time, Mao also ordered his lieutenants in North China to prepare for seizing Beiping and Tianjin immediately.[19] Had Mao's orders been carried out, the CCP would have suffered a disaster more severe than that of the Li Lisan "left-deviationist adventurism" in the 1930s.

Such ruthless military conduct does not seem to fit Mao's usual behavior pattern. Why was he so eager to take Shanghai without sufficient preparation and adequate forces? Considering the fact that Shanghai was the GMD's home base and the traditional Anglo-American sphere of influence in China, is it possible that Mao might have tried to start a direct confrontation with *Mei-Jiang* so that the Soviets would act more forcefully on behalf of the CCP? In any case, Stalin rejected Mao's military plan and sent him a telegram on 20 August. Stalin said that if China were to have a civil war, the nation would have been ruined. Apparently, Mao had reported his military plan to Stalin who figured out that Mao wanted a civil war right away. This could not fit Stalin's China policy, and he wanted Mao to stop his plan. Mao was reportedly angry, and in a later day he would complain that Stalin did not allow him to "carry out revolution." Given how much Mao had hoped for "direct support" from the USSR, it is not difficult to imagine how disappointed he was upon receiving Stalin's telegram. Nonetheless, as usual, he followed Stalin's advice closely. Within twenty-four hours after he ordered the insurrection in Shanghai, he fired two cables in a row on 21 August to stop the action. At the same time, Mao's attitude toward Jiang's invitation for negotiation became more flexible. On 22 August, he responded to Jiang that he would send Zhou Enlai to Chongqing. Then, Stalin sent Mao a second cable in which he said that because the international community and the Chinese people desired peace, Mao should go to Chongqing to negotiate with Jiang, and the U.S. and the USSR would guarantee Mao's personal safety. If Mao refused to negotiate, the CCP would take the blame when the civil war erupted, and that would be disadvantageous to the CCP. On 24 August, Mao telegraphed Jiang that he would go to Chongqing to talk peace in person.[20]

Having received Stalin's advice, not only did Mao change his military plan instantly, he also started to formulate a theoretical understanding of the postwar world order and China's role in it. On 23 August, Mao made a lengthy speech at the politburo meeting. He said that the Soviet Union, the United States, and Britain all desired peace, and disapproved of a civil war in China. "It is certain that a third world war should be avoided. . . . If the Soviet Union were to support us [the CCP], the United States would certainly support Jiang, and a third world war would erupt." Therefore, Mao continued, the Soviet struggle against the U.S. in China had to be kept within certain limits. "For maintaining world peace and being constrained by the Sino-Soviet pact, the Soviet Union cannot help us"; thus, the CCP could not seize the major cities. "We have to live with this fact," Mao grumbled. He proposed that the Party adopt a new political slogan: "For peace, democracy, and unity."[21]

Reading Mao's speech, two points become apparent: First, Mao's military plan to seize major cities and to fight the GMD in a civil war was at least partially based on the assumption that Stalin would come to his aid in one way or another. Thus, when Stalin's first telegram was received, Mao knew he had placed too much hope for a "Polish solution" with massive Red Army "direct support." No matter how emotionally disappointed Mao was, he heeded Stalin's advice thoroughly. Second, not only did Mao change his policy in accordance with Stalin's position, he also tried to rationalize Stalin's policy within the framework of the U.S.-GMD vs. USSR-CCP postwar alignment. Mao understood that the Soviet Union needed peace to gain breathing space before it was ready for the next armed conflict; and therefore, Stalin had to maintain the status quo with western powers and consolidate Soviet power in its sphere of influence. Unfortunately for Mao, China did not belong to the Soviet sphere of influence. Mao said at the same meeting that the USSR acted forcefully in supporting the communists in Bulgaria, but passively in Greece; that was simply because Greece was Britain's sphere of influence. He went on to identify China as Asia's Greece, an American sphere of influence in which

Stalin could not support the CCP openly. The best Stalin could do was to strive for influence in Manchuria and Outer Mongolia so that the U.S. influence could not penetrate into the north.[22]

Mao did not stop here; he went further to implement his understanding of Stalin's strategic thinking in his policy. On 26 August, he said at another polit-buro meeting that in appearance it was up to the Chinese to sort out China's domestic problems; but in reality, it was a three-power intervention. "The Red Army does not cross the Great Wall, America does not land on China's shore," was a tacit understanding of maintaining the status quo in China between the U.S. and the USSR, Mao believed. Accordingly, Mao delineated a three-step military strategy: Depending on the situation, the CCP would give up, first, the area from Henan to Guangdong; second, the base area south of the Yangzi; and third, the NFA's base area north of the Yangzi. But, the Party would fight for control over the area between the Long-hai Railway and Outer Mongolia.[23] Mao thought that although China was America's sphere of influence, Manchuria and Mongolia were exceptional. Consequently, Stalin would cer-tainly support the CCP in those areas to create an authority friendly to the USSR. He sensed that due to the Sino-Soviet pact, whether or not Stalin would allow the CCP military to enter Manchuria was yet to be clarified. But it was certain that Stalin would welcome the CCP forces to go to the northeast. On the same day, he ordered that a regiment of 1,200 cadres be sent to Manchuria immediately.[24] Mao was soon to find out that Stalin wanted him to do much more in Manchuria to make sure that it remained in the hands of friendly Chi-nese forces.

CCP-SOVIET COOPERATION IN MANCHURIA

Stalin understood that "this war is not as in the past. Whoever occupies a ter-ritory also imposes on it his own social system" as far "as his army can reach."[25] When the northeast of China was occupied by the Red Army, Stalin did not make it an exception. Although he struck a deal with Jiang, whom he considered an Anglo-American lackey, Stalin instructed his generals in the Far East to support the CCP secretly. The first CCP group operating in Manchuria was in fact brought back from the USSR by the Red Army. When the CCP resistance forces were crushed in the region by the Japanese in the 1930s, they retreated to Siberia where they were organized into the 88th Brigade of the Red Army led by Zhou Baozhong, together with some well-trained Chinese-speaking Soviet officers. On 16 August 1945, the Red Army authority instructed Zhou that after the brigade was sent back to Manchuria, it should prepare itself for three possible scenarios: First, the CCP's main forces would enter into the region, so the task of the brigade was to prepare the ground for their arrival; second, the CCP main forces might be cut off from Manchuria and the GMD might take over the region, in which case the brigade should prepare for protracted guerrilla warfare; third, should the situation turn worse, the brigade should retreat back into the USSR. For their protection, the members of the unit were given dual identities: officers of the Chinese resistance force, and of the Red Army as well. To avoid possible diplomatic complications in case one of them should fall into the hands of the Chinese government, they all used fake names on their officer's identifications. For instance, Zhou Baozhong became Huang Shaoyuan. Altogether, they were brought to fifty-seven locations all over Manchuria and were appointed as commanders of city garrisons and administrative heads, etc. On 20 August, the Red Army airborne force brought Liu Yalou, later Commander-in-Chief of the PRC's Air Force, to Harbin to take over the radio station of the former Manchuguo, and turn it into the first CCP radio broadcasting station in the region. Once the CCP main forces arrived in Manchuria, the 88th Brigade members and their organizations were fully integrated into one system under the authority of the CCP's Northeast Bureau.[26]

If Mao was uncertain on 26 August whether or not Stalin would allow the CCP military to enter Manchuria, the uncertainty was clarified in two days. On 29 August, the CCP Central Committee issued a directive which ordered that the CCP cadres and troops waiting to enter Manchuria should depart swiftly. The troops should disguise themselves by using the name of Northeastern Army or Resistance Army, and they should occupy rural areas where the Red Army was not present. As long as the CCP operations in Manchuria did not create problems for the USSR to fulfill its diplomatic obligations defined by the Sino-Soviet pact, the directive stated, "the Soviet Union will take a laissez-faire attitude [*fangren taidu*] and give us [the CCP] great sympathy."[27] As Liu Shaoqi, the Acting Chairman of the Party while Mao was in Chongqing, stated at a meeting: "They [the Soviets] are Red Army, we are Red Army, too; they are Communists, so are we."[28] This CCP ideologically defined perception was soon to be proven true by their experience in Manchuria.[29]

On 30 August, a CCP regiment under Zeng Kelin's command moved into Shanhaiguan, the gateway to Manchuria. When the Japanese refused to surrender to Zeng's troops, the Red Army units nearby assisted Zeng in launching an offensive to take over the city. Then, the Soviets let Zeng's troops take a train heading north. When they arrived in Jinzhou, a major city in southern Manchuria, the Soviets allowed them to leave one unit to take over the city, of which Zeng's deputy was now the garrison commander. The rest of Zeng's troops sailed into Shengyang (Mukden) on 5 September, and the Soviets there let them set up their headquarters in the former city hall. Two days later, the Soviet occupation authority invited Zeng and his comrades for dinner. The Soviets told them that because of state relations between the USSR and the GMD government, the CCP troops should not use their well-known name as the "Eighth Route Army." Zeng decided to rename his unit "The People's

Autonomous Army of the Northeast." Thereafter, the Red Army issued an order to allow Zeng's troops to take over various locations in the region with Soviet direct assistance. Zeng became the Shengyang garrison commander, and a "People's Municipal Government" was also established. In the next two months, Zeng's original 4,000 troops were to grow to 60,000 men, equipped with 30 Japanese airplanes turned over to them by the Soviets.[30]

At the same time, the CCP military forces from Shandong across the Bohai Strait also received welcome and cooperation from the Soviet authority in the Dalian area. The good news was reported back to Yan'an quickly, and the Party Center decided on 11 September that 30,000 troops be sent to Manchuria from Shandong, and more from North China and the Yan'an area would follow. To delay the GMD's move toward the Northeast, the CCP also started to prepare campaigns along the railroads leading toward Manchuria. On 14 September, Marshal Malinovsky sent a colonel to Yan'an accompanied by Zeng Kelin. At a public meeting, the colonel relayed an official statement of Malinovsky that before the Soviet withdrawal the CCP troops should not enter into Manchuria, and those who were already there should withdraw. Once retreated to a private setting, however, the colonel made it clear that the Red Army would support the CCP military operations insofar as they were in the name of local armed forces. He also encouraged the CCP to send a group of high-ranking officials to Manchuria so that the CCP-Soviet coordination could be more efficient. In response, the CCP Center formed the Northeast Bureau, which included one-third of the politburo members, thereby acquiring the nickname "Small Politburo" within the Party's rank and file. The available members of the Bureau boarded the Soviet airplane before dawn and took off for Manchuria together with the Soviet colonel.[31]

The very next day, more good news arrived in Yan'an. Through the CCP's Jin-Cha-Ji Bureau's radio transmitting station, the Red Army authorities urged the CCP to move into Inner Mongolia and Manchuria as quickly as possible, and the Red Army would provide them with assistance there. If it became necessary later on, the Soviets indicated, the CCP forces could also retreat to Outer Mongolia. The overall strategy of the CCP, the Soviets suggested, was to concentrate on the north first, and give up the southern base areas if necessary. At the same time, the Soviet ambassador in Chongqing advised that the CCP make sure to defend the Zhangjiakou-Gubeikou-Shanhaiguan line to block the GMD's way toward Manchuria.[32] Stalin now made it clear to Mao that he would fully support the CCP's action to seize Manchuria before the Red Army's scheduled withdrawal in November, although this should be done in a disguised manner.

Mao and his comrades realized that it was "the golden opportunity that hardly occurs once in a thousand years [*qianzai nanfeng zhiji*]," and they acted quickly and boldly to take the opportunity. On 17 September, they decided to send 100,000–150,000 troops to Manchuria from Shandong, while the main forces of the NFA moved into North China to block the path toward Manchuria. A new military strategy was formulated: strive for the Northeast, take control over Rehe and Chahar—offensive in the north, defensive in the south. Mao said that once the Party controlled the Northeast, Rehe, and Chahar, "there will be nothing to fear."[33] This Soviet-inspired strategy was carried out rather successfully and the CCP spared no effort to pour into Manchuria as swiftly as they could. By the end of November, the CCP military in Manchuria reached 130,000, plus 20,000 civilian cadres.[34]

However, the speed with which the CCP troops were pouring into Manchuria was unsatisfying to Yan'an, especially when the Americans began to transport GMD troops from the southwest to North China with planes and warships. On 24 September, Liu Shaoqi telegraphed the Northeast Bureau: U.S. forces would land in Tianjin and Dalian and would help Jiang transport his troops to Tianjin, Beiping, and the Northeast. Therefore, the most urgent need of the Bureau was to transfer the Party's troops and cadres in Shandong to Manchuria; otherwise, the Party would lose its favorable position in the Northeast.[35] On 28 and 29 September, Liu cabled CCP leaders in both Shandong and Manchuria again, urging them to move 20,000 to 30,000 Shandong troops within 20 days via the Bohai Strait. He warned of the possibility of U.S. Navy intervention, but stressed that the operation should not be deterred by the presence of American naval patrols.[36] On 30 September, U.S. Marines landed in Tanggu, which was an ominous sign for the CCP. Liu Shaoqi cabled various leaders again on the same day. Using harshly critical language, he ordered that 30,000 to 40,000 Shandong troops be swiftly moved into Manchuria.[37] Yan'an realized that it was a race between the Communists and the GMD, and timing could be decisive.

The GMD and the United States realized this, too. Early in September, Jiang asked the Americans to furnish vessels for transporting divisions from Guangdong to Dalian. Jiang brought this matter directly to President Truman's attention through Dean Acheson. Ambassador Song told the Secretary that "according to present advice, transportation for Chinese troops to Manchuria would not be available until December which would, manifestly, be too late . . . if National Government troops were not in Manchuria . . . Chinese Communist troops would be likely to move into the area."[38] President Truman acted rapidly. On 18 September, he informed Acheson that the Joint Chiefs of Staff guaranteed that "adequate transportation for the Chinese troops will be available on the dates when they are ready to embark for Manchuria."[39]

A race was taking place between the American warships, airplanes, and the Communists' feet. The latter were apparently at a disadvantage. For example, the third division of the NFA under the command of Huang Kecheng received orders to go to Manchuria on 23 September, when the division was in Jiangsu Province. And then, the 35,000 troops spent two months walking through five provinces. When they finally got there, not only were they exhausted, but the situation had changed as well. The GMD forces in southern Manchuria were then much stronger than those of the CCP.[40]

Stalin, however, understood Mao's problem in competing with *Mei-Jiang*, and was ready to extend helping hands to the Communists. While the Americans were conspicuously backing the GMD, the Soviets were covertly supporting the CCP, and their aid became increasingly generous. Before the end of September, the CCP policy was rather cautious. Yan'an ordered its forces to take over only those remote areas neighboring Mongolia, the Soviet Union, and North Korea, and to wait for the right moment to seize southern and central Manchuria where major cities and railway lines were located. The CCP directive of 28 September stated that the Party's main forces should be widely spread out to take over the rural counties, and they should not be concentrated in southern Manchuria to block the entry of the GMD troops.[41] This cautious position started to change early in October.

While Moscow informed Chongqing that the Red Army would begin to pull out of Manchuria, the Soviet authority in the Far East was encouraging the CCP to take over the whole region. The Soviets were apparently aggravated by the news that U.S. Marines would land in North China on 30 September. With an American military presence just south of the Manchurian gate, Moscow felt uneasy about pulling the Red Army out, and letting the GMD take over. To counterbalance *Mei-Jiang*, the Soviets advised the CCP to deploy 250,000–300,000 troops in southern Manchuria "to hold the gate." They also told the Northeast Bureau explicitly that the Communists should abandon their previous cautious policy and go ahead and take over all of Manchuria. The Soviets even promised that before 15 November the Red Army would combat the GMD directly, should it launch an offensive in Manchuria against the CCP.[42] To the Soviets, a CCP-controlled Manchuria would certainly offer them a strong strategic foothold in the Far East, while the GMD's control over the region would turn it into a potential outpost of hostile forces threatening their security in Asia. Thus, the Soviets advised the CCP to send all its armed forces, at least 500,000 troops, to Manchuria, even at the risk of losing Central and North China. They reasoned that because of its advanced industrial base and its friendly surrounding neighbors, Manchuria provided the CCP an ideal base. If the CCP could hold Manchuria, it could expand later to take over the whole of China. Due to the Soviet encouragement, Mao ordered on 19 October that the previous cautious policy be abandoned. The main forces should be concentrated in southern and central Manchuria, namely, in the Jingzhou, Yingkou, and Shenyang areas, and any GMD troops that entered into Manchuria should be annihilated thoroughly and decisively. Mao's new aim was to "take control over the whole Northeast [*duzhan dongbei*]."[43]

But, to Yan'an's best estimation, an additional 100,000 troops could reach Manchuria by the end of October, while 50,000–80,000 troops would be ready to start their journey toward the Northeast. That was not enough to match the speed with which U.S. airplanes and warships were moving GMD troops into this area. Thus, Yan'an requested that the Red Army delay its withdrawal for one and a half months, and that the Soviets deny the GMD entry into Manchuria until the end of December. Mao dispatched a cable to the Northeast Bureau: "Ask our friends to hold up the arrival of the Guomindang troops in Manchuria for as long as possible."[44] The Soviets responded favorably to Mao's appeal.

Early in October, large numbers of GMD troops arrived in Dalian on American warships, but the Soviet military authority in Manchuria denied them landing. On 6 October, the Soviet Ambassador in Chongqing informed the GMD Government that the USSR objected to the landing of Chinese troops at Dalian. Negotiations between the GMD and the Soviet authority in Manchuria started but no agreement was reached. In late October, Marshal Malinovsky informed the GMD that the USSR would have no objection to Chinese troops disembarking at certain Manchurian ports such as Huludao and Yingkou where the Red Army would guarantee their security. When the Americans and the Nationalists arrived there, however, these two ports had already been taken over by the Communists, who categorically denied them access. Now we know that before the American warships arrived at Huludao and Yingkou, the CCP proposed to the Soviets that the CCP take over these ports, and the Soviets agreed.[45] Eventually the GMD had to give up landing at any Manchurian port. Instead, they landed at Qinhuangdao, a small port outside Manchuria, where the U.S. Marines had been in control since late September.[46] In the same time period, the Soviets publicly acknowledged that the GMD could use U.S. airplanes to transport troops to Changchun and Shenyang. But secretly, they encouraged the CCP to take over the area surrounding the airports. This made it impossible for U.S. airplanes to land there.[47]

The Soviets also turned over an enormous number of Japanese weapons to the CCP, thereby Communist military strength was dramatically increased. In early October, the Soviet authorities in Manchuria officially informed the Northeast Bureau that all weapons of the 700,000 Japanese Guangdong Army would be turned over to the CCP.[48] Although there is no reliable figure of how many weapons the CCP actually received, it is apparent that from that time on, the lack of weapons was no longer a major concern of the CCP. In fact, the Communists were so optimistic that they told their troops in China proper to leave their arms with local forces before they left for Manchuria. They were assured that they would get better weapons when they arrived there.[49] By the end of 1945, the CCP armed forces in Manchuria were 274,000 strong and were divided into ten military zones, some of which had artillery brigades or regiments attached. Moreover, at the end of 1945, the CCP in Manchuria possessed more stockpiles of war materials for further military expansion. When the Communists were forced to retreat from major cities, they made special efforts to transfer those stockpiles to safe places. A party directive of 7 December instructed that an additional 150,000-man field army and a 200,000-man local army be established during that winter. This suggests that the CCP's arsenal in Manchuria at the time was capable of arming at least 350,000 additional troops. By the end of February 1946, the number of Communist troops in Manchuria reached 319,000.[50] Without the large quantity of weapons that the Soviets turned over to the CCP, such a rapid growth of CCP military strength in Manchuria would have been impossible.

Moreover, the CCP-Soviets harassed the existing GMD agencies in Manchuria in every possible way in an attempt to drive them out of the region. For instance, on 24 October, Soviet troops searched the GMD Jilin Provincial Office in Changchun. All its documents were seized and its personnel interrogated. The Soviet authorities insisted that all GMD publications undergo Soviet censorship, and that the GMD party organizations terminate their activities. The Soviets even forbade the GMD Northeast Headquarters' staff to go to Rehe to purchase winter clothing. In addition, the GMD Headquarters' telephone lines were cut by the Communists.[51] Mao was honest when he wrote Peng Zhen in November 1945: "As a result of support from our elder brother and the development of our Party in Manchuria, Jiang Jieshi's troops could not successfully advance in Manchuria and also failed to assume power there."[52]

With Moscow's support, Mao became increasingly ambitious and bold. He not only intended to occupy the northeast exclusively (*duzhan dongbei*), but also take control over North China and much of central China as well. He even planned to make CCP-controlled Manchuria and North China "autonomous regions." In his telegram to the Northeast Bureau on 28 October, Mao revealed his plan:

> Jiang has already mobilized 800,000 troops to attack us in North and Central China, and they are preparing for attacking the Northeast as well. Our Party is determined to mobilize all our resources to take control of the Northeast, to defend North and Central China. Within six months, we must smash all Jiang's military offensives. And then, we can start negotiating with him and force him to recognize the autonomous status of North China and the Northeast.[53]

The next day, and again on 3 November, Mao cabled Zhou twice to reiterate his scheme of the CCP autonomy in Manchuria and North China. He claimed that, according to Sun Yat-sen's principle of local autonomy, the central government had no right to appoint officials in Manchuria and North China; those who had been appointed should be recalled. "The Northeastern People's Autonomous Army will protect the security of Manchuria," Mao continued to assert, "thus, the army of the central government should not come into the region. Otherwise, the central government will be responsible for inciting a civil war." Obviously, with Soviet support, Mao intended to create a CCP autonomous government in Manchuria and North China against the GMD central government.[54]

MAO READJUSTS TO STALIN'S CHANGING POLICY

To control Manchuria and North China under an autonomous government, however, Mao needed superior military strength against the GMD. Yet, the CCP's forces were much weaker than their enemies. When the CCP was defeated militarily, Stalin could not possibly take part in the conflict against the U.S.-backed Chinese government. He had to make a diplomatic retreat while the CCP military was retreating. The Soviets in Manchuria thus became more cooperative with the GMD, asking the CCP to turn over the major cities and railroads to the government forces. Mao had to readjust to the new situation, which he did quite well.

Immediately after the GMD forces landed at Qinhuangdao, Mao was very alarmed. On 1 November, he drafted a directive which stated that in November the CCP's main military operations should concentrate in the Northeast, and Lin Biao's forces should block the GMD forces along the Huludao-Jinzhou-Yingkou line, while waiting for the arrival of more troops. Then, a major campaign would be organized in southern Manchuria to destroy the GMD forces there.[55] The next day, Mao cabled the Northeast Bureau: "We must concentrate all possible strength [in the area] to win this strategically decisive battle in order to consolidate our base [in the Northeast]."[56] With Soviet backing, Mao was quite confident about his plan, and he said on 4 November: "If [we] can eliminate two GMD divisions in November, and then, after consolidation, eliminate all GMD offensive forces, [we] can control the whole Northeast."[57] On 15 November, Mao cabled Lin Biao and Peng Zhen with detailed instructions on the strategic deployment of troops for the anticipated battle. Mao claimed that the CCP could gather 70,000 troops in southern Manchuria, and they should be able to engage the GMD forces in several major battles, in each of which the CCP should wipe out two to three GMD divisions.[58]

The reality, however, shattered Mao's utterly unrealistic expectations. The day that Mao sent out this directive, five GMD divisions launched an offensive in Shanhaiguan. Mao had anticipated that the CCP troops there would hold their position and wear down the enemy forces before retreating toward Jinzhou, where the main CCP forces would deliver a fatal blow to the GMD. Nonetheless, the CCP forces in Shanhaiguan could not maintain their position for more than one day. On 16 November, they were forced to retreat, and Shanhaiguan was now under GMD control. In the following week, the Nationalists pushed their way toward Jinzhou, and the CCP was unable to slow down the

GMD march.[59] This military setback sobered up the Communist leaders. Mao suddenly fell ill and was bedridden until the middle of December.[60] On 22 November, Lin Biao proposed that to avoid being defeated one by one, the CCP should not engage in major battle for the time being. The planned Jinzhou campaign should be called off, and CCP forces should prepare to give up Jinzhou and the railway north of Jinzhou as well. Yan'an approved Lin's proposal on 28 November.[61]

To the CCP's further dismay, under diplomatic pressure from both Washington and Chongqing, Stalin changed his policy in Manchuria. On 15 November, the GMD government ordered the withdrawal of its Northeast Headquarters from the region in order to "counter Soviet efforts to obstruct our [the GMD's] takeover and secretly assist" the CCP.[62] Chongqing informed Washington of this move immediately, and complained that the Soviets failed to honor the Sino-Soviet pact of 1945.[63] At the time, Stalin did not want to have an all-out confrontation with *Mei-Jiang* in Manchuria. When the Soviets encouraged the CCP to seize Manchuria, they also cautioned that in Manchuria the CCP could "act," but not "speak out," especially not to advocate publicly the autonomy of Manchuria and not to publicly challenge the GMD government's rights to take over the region. If the CCP did so, "it would provide *Mei-Jiang* a pretext to put the Soviet Union in a difficult spot . . . and Jiang would have a pretext to invite the U.S. to attack the CCP."[64] Apparently, while aware of the danger of GMD-U.S. control over Manchuria, Moscow did not want to confront the U.S. directly in China, nor did it intend to overthrow the Yalta protocol outright. There were limits how far Stalin would go in supporting the CCP in Manchuria.

After the CCP's defeat, Stalin realized that the CCP was not ready to take over and keep Manchuria by itself. In order to save Soviet interest in the region defined by the Yalta protocol, and under U.S.-GMD diplomatic pressure, Stalin became more cooperative with the GMD government, at least in appearance. On 17 November, Moscow sent Jiang's government a note, proposing that the Red Army postpone its withdrawal to help the GMD takeover. The Soviets also promised to "eradicate all mob action" against the GMD authorities in Manchuria.[65] On 19 November, Chongqing agreed that if the Soviets would assist the GMD's airlift operation in both Shenyang and Changchun, facilitate the GMD's transportation effort by sea and land, and disarm the CCP military units in Manchuria, the Red Army could delay its withdrawal for one or two months. On 20 November, Moscow informed Chongqing that the Red Army would guarantee the safe landing of GMD troops in Shenyang and Changchun.[66] Mao had requested that the Soviet withdrawal from Manchuria be delayed; now, Moscow got the deal to stay in Manchuria for a few more months, which proved to be advantageous to the CCP.

But, Stalin had to do something in appearance as a trade-off to the GMD. On 19 November, the Soviets officially notified the Northeast Bureau that the

Communists should withdraw from major cities and the Changchun railway area by 50 kilometers. These areas had to be handed over to the Central Government of China, and the CCP could not fight the GMD forces in these places.[67] However, the Soviets soon modified the limits they put on the CCP: Only the armed forces of the CCP needed to withdraw from the above-mentioned areas by 20 kilometers, while the Bureau and other CCP agencies could stay. The Soviet authority in Manchuria even supported the "Northeastern People's Representative Convention" held in Changchun on 22 November. To counterbalance the increased GMD forces in Manchuria, the Soviets continued to furnish the CCP with military materials from their bases in Dalian and North Korea.[68]

The CCP might have felt it emotionally difficult to swallow the new Soviet policy, but it understood the reason behind the Soviet move. On 20 November, Yan'an dispatched a directive to the Northeast Bureau to propose a new strategy:

> [We] must place our main force in southern, northern, eastern, and western Manchuria, i.e., in the broad area surrounding the Changchun Railway from Shenyang to Harbin. By taking middle and small cities, and minor railways as the focal points, and backed against the Soviet Union, Korea, Outer Mongolia, and Rehe, [we can] create powerful base areas. [We] will face the Changchun Railway, and surround Shenyang, Changchun, Harbin, and other major cities, so that [we can] capture them when the Soviet troops are withdrawing.[69]

On 28 November, Yan'an went further to rationalize Stalin's new move and the consequent CCP strategic change in the "Directive on the Strategy of Struggle against *Mei-Jiang*" (*Guanyu dui mei-Jiang douzheng de zhishi*). It reads: "The central problem in the [postwar] world is the struggle between the United States and the Soviet Union. The reflection of this struggle in China is the struggle between Jiang and the CCP." In an effort to explain why the Soviets demanded to keep the CCP-USSR cooperation secret, the directive stated that although the U.S.-USSR struggle and the GMD-CCP struggle were inherently interrelated in substance (*benzhi*), sometimes it was necessary to separate them in appearance (*xingshi*). The U.S. China policy was to "support Jiang, suppress the CCP, and confront the USSR." Nonetheless, to minimize U.S. involvement in China, the Soviet Union decided "to separate itself in appearance from the CCP." Accordingly, the CCP should "on the one hand, certainly pretend that the CCP has no connection with the Soviet Union; on the other hand, when the CCP opposes Jiang, it should sometimes try to neutralize the United States as well."[70]

The CCP's perception of the new development in Manchuria was also expressed in a Northeast Bureau document on 29 November:

> Because of the development of our Party and armed forces in the Northeast, and Jiang's inability to enter into Manchuria to restore his power there smoothly, the

U.S. government has already launched a diplomatic offensive against the Soviet Union, and Sino-Soviet diplomacy is in a crisis. This is a global struggle; there-fore, [we] must strive for the initiative to stabilize our [the CCP-USSR] position in the diplomatic battle. . . . [We] must withdraw from the cities quickly and deci-sively, and retreat to areas where the Red Army is not present, so that the Soviet Union can honor the Sino-Soviet Treaty without any difficulty. This is a necessary condition to defeat the U.S.-Jiang diplomatic offensive, and frustrate the Ameri-can plot of intervening in China's internal affairs.[71]

In response to some complaints within the rank and file, the same document explained that the CCP's withdrawal from the major cities "is not because of the unreasonable restriction or the 'rightist deviation' of the Red Army. Instead, [we] should look at the whole situation [in the world], and engage *Mei-Jiang* in a global diplomatic struggle successfully."[72] The CCP's under-standing of and cooperation with Moscow's maneuvers were richly rewarded by covert Soviet assistance. For instance, on 20 November, Yan'an directed the Northeast Bureau to seek the Red Army's consent to the CCP's military actions in the railway area south of Jinzhou.[73] This CCP request was met by the Soviet authorities in Manchuria. On 5 December, when Malinovsky agreed to allow GMD troops to use the Manchurian railway, he excluded the area south of Jinzhou.[74] Therefore, this bottleneck area in the Manchurian rail sys-tem continued to be at least partially blocked by the CCP. Identifying the CCP's interest with that of the USSR, Mao and his comrades were willing to adjust their policy to suit Moscow's diplomatic move; the Soviets also recog-nized the CCP as their comrade-in-arms and continued their secret support whenever possible, short of publicly siding with the CCP. On the contrary, CCP-U.S. relations were another matter altogether.

THE CCP DEALS WITH THE AMERICANS, AUGUST–NOVEMBER 1945

In Mao's eyes, the formidable force which could derail his plan for an autonomous Manchuria was not the GMD, but the U.S. In his telegram to Peng Zhen on 2 November, Mao said that whether or not the CCP would be able to prevent the GMD from taking Shenyang was determined by whether or not the Americans assist the GMD directly. He predicted that if the Americans were not to assist Jiang, the CCP could surely defeat the GMD. When the U.S. decided to assist the GMD in Manchuria, Mao said, the CCP would have to retreat to the border areas of the region.[75] Mao's policy toward the Americans was a mixture of caution and hostility.

Considering how actively the U.S. was supporting the GMD, the CCP cer-tainly had sufficient reasons to hate the Americans. But the Communists also had their own reasons to be diplomatic. In order to avert U.S. involvement on behalf of the GMD as much as possible, the CCP intended to handle the Americans with some diplomatic courtesy. On the other hand, the Communists were skeptical that the Americans would behave themselves, and they determined to fight back if U.S. troops engaged in hostilities. Thus, there were two sides to the CCP's policy in dealing with the Americans in North China. Since the Americans were actively supporting the GMD in the last months of 1945, the side of military resistance to American intervention became more pronounced than the side of diplomatic courtesy.

This two-sided CCP policy was depicted by an inner-party directive of 29 October in which Yan'an gave instructions to its commanders in North China on how to deal with the landed U.S. troops. It stated: "If they respect our interest, [we] welcome their cooperation with us. But, when their action damages our interest, [we] must reject it in the name of opposing intervention in China's internal affairs." If the American troops tried to force their way into CCP areas, "we should formally inform them of our objection . . . as [we] should be prepared militarily for resistance. When [we] are forced to take a self-defense stand militarily, we should resolutely do so, but never fire the first shot." In dealing with small groups of American soldiers who happened to enter into CCP areas by mistake, "[we] should clarify the situation, and then, send them back courteously."[76]

The Communists did not want to involve the Americans in the civil war, but they were prepared for resistance to U.S. military intervention. On 30 September, the same day the U.S. Marines landed, Yan'an voiced that

> the purpose of the GMD regime asking the U.S. Army to land in the Beiping and Tianjin area is obviously not for the disarmament of the Japanese but to make use of the U.S. Army to oppose the Eighth Route Army. . . . Thus, no matter what the intention of the Americans is, their landing will in fact interfere in China's internal affairs, and inevitably assist the GMD to oppose the CCP and 100 million people in the liberated areas.[77]

A few days later, Yan'an further warned that the U.S. Marine presence in China should be "temporary and regional," and that it should not expand to "places which have already been liberated and where there are no Japanese troops."[78] The hostility between CCP forces and U.S. landing troops became evident immediately. A one-hour engagement between the Americans and CCP forces took place right after the Americans' landing at Qinhuangdao on 1 October.[79] With the presence of the U.S. forces in China proper, the whole month of October witnessed mounting CCP-U.S. tension and armed conflict. In early October, U.S. naval forces approached Yantai which was an important departing point for the CCP to send troops into Manchuria from Shandong. The Americans requested that the CCP troops withdraw from the city and turn it over to them. Yan'an was alarmed. Ye Jianying informed American headquarters that Yantai had no Japanese forces; therefore, U.S. Marines had no right to land there. The Americans would be responsible for the consequences should they insist on landing by force.[80] At the same time, Yan'an instructed its Shandong leaders to reinforce their fortifications there, and to resist any American landing action resolutely. Yan'an should be immediately informed of any development there, so that the CCP's propaganda machine could create a "public opinion storm" in the international community, if the Americans did not behave themselves.[81] Eventually, due to the CCP's firm rejection and military preparedness in Yantai, the Americans had to give up.

Elsewhere, however, the CCP-U.S. confrontation was getting uglier. According to a CCP official statement of the time, on 18 October thirty American soldiers surrounded and searched an ERA office in Tianjin, and arrested five CCP officers there.[82] On 21 October ten U.S. warplanes harassed Bei'an, Hebei, where a CCP mass rally was taking place. The American planes allegedly opened fire on the crowd. At the same time, about ten U.S. planes harassed Gu'an, Hebei, for one hour, and dropped leaflets which ordered the CCP's troops there to leave, otherwise the U.S. Army would attack Gu'an.[83]

What was really a dangerous sign to Yan'an was U.S. Marine movements in the narrow corridor between Qinhuangdao and Shanhaiguan, then under CCP control. From the middle of October, the U.S. Marines began to repair the railway there in order to transport the GMD from Qinhuangdao to attack Shanhaiguan. Yan'an instructed its troops to stop the American attempt by building a defense line on the railway. The CCP was to notify the marines of the existence of the line and warn them not to cross it. Should the Americans launch an offensive, resistance must be resolute and retreat would be allowed only when ultimate resistance failed. If the situation was favorable, a counteroffensive would be advisable.[84] According to CCP sources, by the end of October, the marines began to move on the Communists. On the 30th, the Nationalists accompanied by U.S. Marines attacked Haiyangzheng, and 18 CCP soldiers there were disarmed. The next day, some U.S. Marines together with GMD troops attacked the Beitaihe railway station and forced the CCP troops to retreat.[85] Backed by U.S. Marines and air force, GMD troops disembarked from U.S. ships at Qinhuangdao, and pushed north toward Shanhaiguan, which was finally occupied by the Nationalists on 16 November.

Yan'an was now convinced that General Wedemeyer was playing the role of General Scobie in China. Yan'an voiced on 14 November that, while continuing to tell the lie of "nonintervention," Wedemeyer made the U.S. Army in China "the vanguard of the anti-Communist war."[86] Yan'an held a mass rally on 7 November and used slogans such as "Oppose Wedemeyer's armed intervention in China's internal affairs," and "Demand the withdrawal of the U.S. Army in China."[87] At this point, the Communists' ideological conviction must have been reconfirmed by what they experienced in the months following Japan's defeat. They believed that following the law of capitalist development the U.S. economy would inevitably run into a serious crisis with overproduction and unemployment. Consequently, "class relations in the United States will inevitably become much tenser."[88] According to Leninism, the Communists believed that U.S. domestic tension would lead its ruling classes toward reactionary moves by oppressing the people at home while shifting the responsibility of the problems on to other countries, thus oppressing other peoples as well. Even some famous progressive figures in the eyes of the CCP, such as Henry Wallace, were becoming more conservative.[89] Although it recognized the differences between the Republicans and the Democrats, the CCP now tended to view the two parties as similar in their bourgeois nature.[90] Therefore, they pinned their hopes on the "good" people in America as opposed to the "bad" government.[91]

In short, if Mao's two-camp vision of the postwar world order was initially ideologically inspired, the unfolding reality in the immediate postwar period seemed to reinforce his belief. What happened in Manchuria in the months following Japan's defeat reconfirmed Mao's perception of the CCP-Moscow vs. GMD-Washington alignment as naturally determined by the "class nature" of parties involved. Thus, no matter how emotionally discomforting it was for him to accept Stalin's changing policy in Manchuria, Mao adjusted and readjusted his own policy to meet Moscow's position. At the same time, the CCP's hostility toward the U.S. was mounting, although Mao intended to be more "diplomatic" in order to avert more direct U.S. intervention on behalf of the GMD. Instead of making the CCP's policy simplistic, Mao's two-camp vision manifested itself through an intricate game play among the four parties; yet, the simplicity of Mao's conviction was never obscured by the intricacy of the situation. This will repeat itself in Mao's policy conduct in 1946, when George Marshall played an essential role in China.

CHAPTER VI

Mao Deals with George Marshall, November 1945–December 1946

The [world] bourgeoisie was divided into two
major camps [during the war], the Anglo-American-French
camp and the German-Italian-Japanese camp. The
bourgeois division will continue in the postwar era. It will
split into two major parts: one is anti-Soviet and anti-CCP;
the other wants peace with the USSR and the CCP.
We should promote such a division.
—Mao Zedong, March 1946

THE simplicity of Mao's two-camp vision on the postwar world order did not make the CCP's policy toward the U.S. simplistic during the Marshall Mission. On the contrary, the CCP's handling of Marshall proved to be tactful and flexible; yet, its identification of the U.S. as the No. 1 enemy was never obscured, and its policy continued to change in accordance with Moscow's changing positions. Marshall's mission in China can be divided into two phases along the line of March–April 1946. In the first phase, due to its military setback in southern Manchuria and the change in Moscow's policy, the CCP adjusted its strategy of shutting the GMD out of the region, and came back to the negotiating table with the GMD under Marshall's mediation. The CCP's new strategy was what Zhou Enlai called combining "talk" with "fight" (*tan-tan da-da*). Talks offered the Communists time to consolidate their military position as well as a political forum on which they could "expose" how "fascist" and corruptive the GMD regime was, and how hypocritical Washington was in sustaining such a regime.

Against the background of an intensifying cold war earmarked by Stalin's "inevitability-of-war" speech and Churchill's "iron-curtain" speech in February and March 1946, respectively, the CCP followed Moscow's lead and resumed an aggressive policy especially in Manchuria. While the Red Army was pulling out, Stalin encouraged Mao to take over the region, at least the northern half of it. Mao vowed to turn Changchun into China's Madrid in order to secure CCP-Moscow control over northern Manchuria against the *Mei-Jiang* forces' penetration. Marshall's optimism about a possible peace was thus shattered, and a full-scale civil war soon ravaged the entire nation. Yet, the CCP continued "talking" with the GMD under Marshall's mediation until the

end of 1946 while the "fighting" took precedence in the Party's policy priority. If Marshall's intentions in China were either to incorporate a disarmed
CCP into a GMD-dominated government or to assist the GMD to destroy an
"intransigent" CCP, neither was accomplished. Mao frustrated the Marshall
Mission, yet he did not leave enough reason, or "pretext," as he would put it,
for Washington to intervene directly in China to save the GMD. In other
words, Mao's handling of Marshall was tactful enough not to provoke American direct participation in the civil war on the GMD's behalf.

THE CCP'S PERCEPTION OF MARSHALL'S MISSION

Regarding short-term tactics, the CCP believed there were contradictions
between the GMD and Washington, which should be taken advantage of in
order to reduce the degree of U.S. involvement in the civil war. The CCP also
understood that its domestic struggle with the GMD was tied to the USSR-
U.S. global struggle; therefore, the superpowers' diplomatic maneuvers
became essential conditions in which the Party had to alter its policy.

In early December 1945, the CCP sensed that in accordance with the
upcoming Moscow Conference of the three foreign ministers of the U.S., the
USSR, and Britain, the GMD-CCP negotiations would likely resume. Zhou
Enlai wrote a report to the Center on 5 December in which he said that there
had been no indication of an immediate threat of a third world war between
the Soviet Union and the West; both sides, though in conflict, were to negotiate. Thus, the GMD-CCP relations in the coming era would feature a mixture
of "fight and talk." If the CCP maintained its policy of "democracy and peace,"
taking a position of "political offensive, and military defensive," the Americans would probably accept the idea about China's political reform; but, Jiang
would never go along with it. Thus, there was contradiction between the U.S.
and the GMD. On the other hand, if Jiang invited the CCP leaders to participate in the National Government, and demanded that the CCP give up control
over its armed forces, the Americans would also be in agreement with Jiang;
but, the CCP would never accept it.[1] The Communists correctly foresaw that
the Americans intended to trade the GMD's political reform for the CCP's
control over its armed forces, thereby eliminating a potential threat to U.S.
hegemony in China. To the Americans, the disarmament of the CCP was
essential for maintaining the unification of China under the pro-American
GMD regime. With this in mind, the CCP formulated its basic two-sided strategy in dealing with the Marshall Mission: to get the Americans to push for
political reform in order to undermine the GMD's credibility; and to avoid the
possibility of being disarmed.

After the announcement of Truman's China policy on 15 December, the
Party Center dispatched the "Directive on the Shift of U.S. China Policy and

Our Party's Response." It stated that the adjustment of U.S. China policy did not indicate any fundamental change from the policy of supporting Jiang, and the Communists should discard any illusions that the U.S. might change this stand in the future. Nonetheless, the U.S. decided not to participate in China's civil war directly, and Truman also acknowledged the "one-party-dictatorship" nature of the GMD regime and the need for political reform. These changes were in favor of the CCP cause and the Party should use Truman's policy statement to "launch a political offensive against the GMD in the Political Consultation Conference [PCC]."[2]

The CCP's suspicion of U.S. intentions and impartiality was not groundless. Before Marshall's departure for China, he and Truman came to an understanding that if the Communists would not cooperate in the pursuit of political unification, the U.S. would support the GMD in an all-out offensive to defeat the CCP. But if Jiang Jieshi "failed to make reasonable concessions, and this resulted in the breakdown of the efforts to secure a political unification," the U.S. would continue to support the GMD. Otherwise, "there would follow the tragic consequences of a divided China and of a probable Russian reassumption of power in Manchuria, the combined effort of this resulting in the defeat or loss of the major purpose of our war in the Pacific."[3] Washington was committed to the GMD regime, because it fundamentally shared with Mao the same vision of the CCP-Moscow vs. GMD-Washington alignment.

Yan'an had no illusions about the American peace move; it, nonetheless, also recognized that there were differences and conflict between Washington and the GMD, which should be taken advantage of. The CCP found some points in the Truman policy statement useful to its purposes. Truman stated that Marshall was

> to facilitate arrangement for cessation of hostilities. . . . National Government troops will not be transported by the U.S. into areas, such as north China, when their introduction would prejudice the objectives of the military truce and the political negotiations. . . . The U.S. is cognizant that the present National Government of China is a "one-party government" and believes that peace, unity and democratic reform in China would be furthered if the basis of this Government is broadened to include other political elements in the country. Hence, the U.S. strongly advocates that the national conference of representatives of major political elements in the country agree upon arrangements which would give these elements a fair and effective representation in the Chinese National Government.[4]

The CCP could see two favorable points here. First, after the military setback in Manchuria and the withholding of overt Soviet support, the Communists needed more time to prepare for a military showdown. If U.S. mediation could restrain Jiang's offensive by applying political pressure and withholding transportation assistance, the CCP would win much needed breathing space. In fact, Yan'an instructed the Northeast Bureau on 7 December that the CCP troops in Manchuria should use the winter to consolidate and expand, not to fight. The goal was to recruit 150,000 field troops and 200,000 local troops in order to prepare for the "great showdown next spring."[5] That was after the withdrawal of the Red Army. The U.S. proposal was thus useful to the CCP.

Second, Truman officially acknowledged that the GMD government was not a democratic one, and needed structural reform. The "one-party dictator-ship" had been the major target for CCP attacks on the GMD for years, and the Communists knew that Jiang would not share power with anyone else. This was a vital weakness of the GMD which not only pushed the "third force" in China to the CCP side, but also alienated public opinion abroad. The main political strategy of the CCP was to cash in on the GMD's weak point, and sep-arate the U.S. and the "third force" from Jiang. The U.S. had to take a politi-cal risk if it insisted on supporting a dictatorial regime.

Furthermore, Mao combined this political strategy with a military program. He was fully aware of how disunited the GMD troops were, and how badly the Chinese people wanted peace and democracy. Should the CCP win over pub-lic opinion at home, some GMD troops could be encouraged to switch sides. On 30 October, Gao Shuxun, a GMD general, defected to the CCP with one army and one column of troops. Mao used the event to initiate psychological warfare designed to demoralize the GMD troops. Appealing to the GMD gen-erals and soldiers to engage in anti-Jiang rebellions, Mao told the Party that "we must prepare and organize uprisings within the GMD army and spread the Gao Shuxun movement, so that, at crucial moments in the fighting, large num-bers of GMD troops will follow Gao Shuxun's example and come over to the people, oppose the civil war and take a stand for peace."[6] To a large extent, what happened in the civil war proved Mao's psychological warfare success-ful. To gain time for military consolidation, to win over the "third force" in China, and to dismantle the GMD from within—-these were the three goals Mao tried to attain by making use of Marshall's mediation.

Thus, Yan'an appeared to be more enthusiastic than Chongqing in welcom-ing Marshall. On 17 December, Wang Bingnan went to the U.S. embassy to inform the Americans that Zhou Enlai had arrived in Chongqing, and was preparing for negotiations with the GMD under Marshall's mediation. When Marshall arrived on 22 December, Zhou went to the airport to greet him. He told Marshall that there were many things worth learning from the U.S., such as (1) George Washington's spirit of national independence; (2) Abraham Lin-coln's principles of "from the people, by the people, and for the people"; and (3) American agricultural reform and national industrialization. Zhou further stated that the CCP firmly opposed a civil war, and advocated a political con-ference for drawing up a constitution and conducting governmental reform.[7]

Zhou's welcoming address was well thought-out. His three points corre-sponded with the Communist interpretation of Sun Yat-sen's three "people's principles." By stressing Washington's spirit of national independence, Zhou was telling Marshall that the CCP would firmly oppose anyone's attempt to turn China into a colony, which was what the Communists suspected the Americans would try to do. By emphasizing democracy and peace, Zhou was criticizing the GMD's dictatorship and a military solution toward the CCP. By talking about China's future modernization and industrialization, Zhou tried to hint that a CCP-dominated China would sate the U.S. hunger for business. This had been, and would continue to be, a point that the CCP tried to sell to the Americans in order to soften their hostility to the CCP and to neutralize them politically. Yan'an was well prepared to deal with Marshall in its own way.

THE CCP'S COOPERATION WITH MARSHALL

There were two contradictory factors in Communist thinking during the first stage of the Marshall Mission: the hope for peace, and the desire to fight. Because the CCP perceived the GMD-CCP struggle as a part of the U.S.-USSR global conflict, when the Moscow Conference reached a series of agreements on 27 December, the CCP sensed that a GMD-CCP compromise was necessary and possible. In early January 1946, the CCP consulted Moscow as to what China's future should be. On 17 January, Zhou Enlai informed Yan'an of Moscow's response. The message from Moscow stated that due to the lack of knowledge of the Chinese situation, the Communist Party of the Soviet Union (CPSU) could not provide a detailed agenda for the CCP. Nevertheless, the CCP should not attempt to sovietize China, but should determinedly stop the civil war and democratize China in cooperation with Jiang. If the CCP could not stop a civil war from breaking out, the U.S. army and air force would jump on the CCP, and Yan'an should not underestimate the strength of the United States.[8] Considering what Truman told Marshall about an all-out U.S. support of the GMD military campaign against the CCP in case of CCP failure to go along with the peace process, Stalin's warning of a possible U.S. direct intervention against the CCP was not off the mark. Stalin would continue to sound the alarm to Mao throughout the entire Chinese civil war period, and Stalin's caution served as a balancing mechanism to Mao's often impulsive and radical policy, as we have seen, and will see later on.

The impact of Moscow's message on the CCP was felt immediately. On 1 February, the Party Center dispatched the "Directive on the Current Situation and Task," which stated that China had "entered a new stage of development of peaceful and democratic reconstruction. . . . Currently, the main form of Chinese revolution has changed from armed struggle to nonarmed parliamentary struggle of the masses. The domestic issues should be settled through political means; and therefore, the whole work of the Party should be adjusted according to the new situation." Since Moscow was in agreement with Marshall's mediation effort, Yan'an further considered that "Marshall not only represents the United States, in fact, he is the representative [of the international community] to carry out the agreement of the Moscow Conference of the three Powers."[9]

This, however, should not be taken as an indication that Mao abandoned his belief in armed struggle. Mao had repeatedly concluded that the parliamentary path did not fit China's reality, and he would in a later day blame this "parliamentary attempt" on Liu Shaoqi's "rightist deviationism." It appeared that Mao's flirtation with the parliamentary path was one more repetition of an old pattern: when Stalin speaks, Mao listens and complies, willingly or not. Later, Mao explained to Yudin why he heeded Stalin's advice so closely and sometimes unwillingly: he had no other choice because it was something Stalin wanted him to do.[10] If the parliamentary path was Mao's lip service to Stalin, Stalin's peace approach followed by Mao benefited the CCP a great deal at the time. Soon, Mao was also to learn that Stalin did not really ask the CCP to lay down its arms.

The Communists' fundamental distrust of both the GMD and the United States urged them not to lay down their arms. Although the CCP publicly welcomed Truman's China policy statement of 15 December, it maintained that the nature of the U.S. China policy was still "supporting Jiang, containing the USSR, and suppressing the CCP." Thus, although the CCP declared that the armed struggle was to be replaced by peaceful parliamentary struggle, the Communists refused to disarm themselves. In the same directive of 1 February, which was revised and approved by Mao in person, it was stated that "the GMD is still likely to launch a military assault on us, and we should tighten our vigilance. Generally speaking, armed struggle is over now; but, to safeguard peace, the CCP everywhere shall make use of the current situation to launch a three-month campaign to train our troops."[11]

In reality, what Mao meant by "parliamentary struggle" was only another way of expressing his coalition agenda. The paradoxical coexistence of a peaceful political struggle and the expansion of military strength was a typical feature of Maoist dualism. The CCP intended to hold on to its military forces, and at the same time, to take part in the "parliamentary struggle" to undermine the GMD's political institutions and to enhance the CCP's political power. One of Mao's reasons to cooperate with Marshall was to pursue the political destruction of the GMD by using American democratic principles.

On the other hand, Jiang had always been opposed to any CCP power-sharing scheme. He said that a coalition government was the vital step in Moscow's scheme of "peaceful competition," which would put China under Russia's control.[12] Jiang did not want to share power with the CCP, but intended to use Marshall to induce the Communists to give up their armed forces. To a large extent, Marshall shared Jiang's concern. In January 1946, he told the Generalissimo that two factors made it imperative to find an agreement with the Communists for a unified government and army at an early date. First, "China is very vulnerable to low-level Russian infiltration methods to the strengthening of the Communist regime." Second, the U.S. military and naval presence in China "can not be continued for long."[13] Marshall made it clear that Jiang should "absorb" the CCP politically and militarily before it became stronger with covert Russian assistance, and before the U.S. military leaves China.

The difference between Marshall and Jiang was that the former intended to trade a minority position in a representative government system for CCP surrender of its army, and the latter did not want a coalition at all. It seemed beyond Marshall's comprehension that in the estimation of both the GMD and the CCP, the CCP would soon gain the upper hand in the political struggle, should a democratic system be in place. Jiang did not want to take any chance of facilitating what he called "Moscow's scheme," while Marshall tried hard to push him to democratize the government, to include the CCP in a coalition. Mao was well aware of this U.S.-GMD contradiction, and intended to make use of it. To dismantle GMD political institutions, the CCP waged its "parliamentary struggle" in the newly established PCC, which was composed of representatives of the GMD, the CCP, the Democratic League, the Youth Party, and nonpartisan delegates. From 10 to 31 January 1946, the PCC was in session and Marshall was actively involved to ensure that the American spirit of democracy and representative government would hold the ground. As a result of intensive bargaining and political maneuvers, the PCC reached final resolutions on various issues regarding the democratization of the government. The CCP saw the resolutions as a political victory because the seats which the CCP and the Democratic League would occupy in the State Council constituted the minimum one-third necessary to make proposals and to veto any government nomination of nonpartisan personnel to the Council whom they considered undesirable.[14]

The results of the PCC seemed encouraging for a "parliamentary struggle" of the CCP. The Communists believed, at least for the moment, that "the GMD one-party dictatorship is being destroyed, and nationwide democratization has started. . . . From now on, China will enter into a new era of peaceful and democratic reconstruction. . . . The Party will cease to lead the army directly (to be carried out after several months)."[15] On 6 February, the Politburo discussed the question of participation in the government, and it decided to nominate Zhou Enlai for vice president of the Executive Yuan of the coalition government, and the Party's headquarters would move to a major city in the future.[16]

Mao appeared very enthusiastic about the recent result of the PCC. On 2 February, he cabled Chen Yi, saying that the CCP's military control over eastern China must be reinforced, because it was possible that the Party Center would move to Huaiying (a city in northern Jiangsu Province). Mao made this idea more explicit one month later. On 4 March, Marshall, Zhang Zhizhong, and Zhou Enlai, namely, the Committee of Three, arrived in Yan'an. In the conversation, Zhang said to Mao that now that the government had been reformed, the CCP Center should move to Nanjing, and Mao should take up residence in the capital as well. Mao replied, "Of course, we'll go to Nanjing in the near future. But, I heard that it is very hot in Nanjing, and I hate heat. So, I think I would take residence in Huaiying, and go to Nanjing whenever it's necessary to attend a meeting."[17] On 9 February, he also told a United Press reporter that "the all-around achievement of the PCC is very encouraging; but [we] shall continue to strive to overcome difficulties in the days to come. I deeply believe that we can cast aside various obstacles. . . . Generally speaking, China has stepped into a stage of democracy. Marshall's effort to bring an end to the civil war, to facilitate peace, unity, and democracy, is undeniably outstanding."[18]

Mao was encouraged enough by Stalin's advice and the PCC result to think about how to participate in a representative government in Nanjing. But, his ideology, which was reinforced by his experience in the past, made his distrust of *Mei-Jiang* so intense that he would not live in Nanjing. Instead, he would take up residence in Huaiying where the CCP's military reinforcement would safeguard him. Although he declared the coming of a new era of peaceful parliamentary struggle, he was not prepared to give up the Party's military. Mao's hope for peace was soon overshadowed by his concept of armed class struggle. After the PCC resolutions on government reform had been reached, Marshall made a proposal on military integration according to the western tradition of nonintervention of the military in political matters. On 5 February, Zhou cabled Yan'an for instructions, and Mao replied the next day: "Marshall's proposal is thorough in the destruction of the GMD's original military system. But in reality, it is not feasible today. [We] can agree with his proposal in principle. The military issue is of the first and foremost importance, and must be dealt with cautiously."[19] Three days after he publicly praised Marshall and his effort, Mao had something entirely different to say in a private occasion. On 12 February, he chaired a Politburo meeting to discuss the agenda of military reorganization. Mao said:

> The United States and Jiang Jieshi intend to eliminate us by way of nationwide military unification. We want unification, but we do not want to be eliminated. The principle of separating political parties and military troops is not most dangerous to us; it is most dangerous to let Jiang integrate our troops and to deploy them in different places. . . . This danger can be avoided only if we are going to manage the situation carefully and properly. In principle, we have to advocate national military unification; but, how we shall go about it should be decided according to the concrete circumstances of the time. This is the difference between our way and the way of the French Communists.[20]

Mao was very reluctant to agree to an early integration of the CCP's armed forces into the national army. He did not want to start the integration program for another thirteen months.[21] The Communists refused to lay down their weapons until they saw that Jiang was deprived of the power to hurt them. If the French Communist Party had handed over the weapons its members aquired during the resistance movement in France, and then participated and lost in the parliamentary process, Mao was probably wiser than Maurice Thorez, the FCP leader, in deciding to hold his guns long enough to see if the revolutionary interests could be preserved and promoted without an armed struggle. He soon came to realize its impossibility on what he saw as solid evidence.

On 16–19 January, Guo Moruo, Zhang Dongsun, and other non-GMD representatives of the PCC were physically attacked, presumably by the GMD secret service, when they delivered speeches at a rally in Chongqing.[22] On 26 January, policemen in Chongqing searched the home of Huang Yanpei, a leader of the Democratic League and a close ally of the CCP. On 10 February, when non-GMD elements held a meeting to celebrate the PCC's resolutions, the GMD sent people to attack and disrupt the meeting, and many preeminent and politically active intellectuals were mercilessly beaten. Finally, at the GMD plenum from 1 to 17 March, the "extreme reactionaries" within the GMD (Marshall's term) violently opposed the PCC resolutions, and forced the plenum to call for the revision of the resolutions. All these events, plus the military confrontation in Manchuria, convinced Mao that the "parliamentary path" was only an illusion in China. By the middle of March, the relations between Moscow and *Mei-Jiang* also deteriorated, and the Soviets once again encouraged the CCP to take over Manchuria when the Red Army was pulling out. Mao now thoroughly cast away any hope for peace with the GMD, and an agenda of armed struggle came to the fore. On 15 March, Mao asserted at a Politburo meeting that in the Allied nations the pro-fascist forces had launched an anti-Soviet and anti-Communist movement, and they intended to stir up a third world war; thus, they were the main enemies of the CCP.[23]

Within this broad picture of world struggle in the postwar era, Mao continued to claim, Jiang was determined to destroy all revolutionary partisans whenever he was capable of doing so. "People tend to forget this, especially when the situation quiets down a little. We forgot this in 1–9 February; but, we remembered this again after the Jiaochangkou Incident [of 10 February]," Mao said. Clearly, he was renouncing the "parliamentary path." With his armed class struggle vision coming to the fore, Mao became more resentful than grateful to Marshall. He said that Marshall was very good at putting out a "long cord" with a hook at the end, trying to catch the "big fish," the CCP's armed forces. On 16 March, Mao cabled Zhou in Nanjing: "All that has happened lately proves that Jiang's anti-Soviet, anti-CCP, and anti-democratic nature will not change." Thus, only through severe struggle could it be possible to gain a bit of democracy.[24] On 18 March, the day after the conclusion of the GMD plenum, Mao instructed Zhou Enlai that the CCP would not take part in the national assembly and government reform.[25] China's revolution had to be won on the battlefield.

Fundamentally, Mao distrusted Marshall from beginning to end. On 30 December 1945, the GMD proposed that a committee be established to include one representative from each of the two parties plus Marshall. This committee of three would be responsible for maintaining the truce and supervising the program of halting troop movements on both sides. The CCP was worried about being at a disadvantage on the committee since Marshall was essentially pro-Jiang. Thus, Zhou Enlai proposed that the USSR should be included. To make it more presentable, the CCP also suggested the participation of the British government. In his telegrams to Zhou on 2 and 3 January 1946, Mao stated that

China's independence has always relied upon the checks and balances of several powers, and the so-called policy of "using barbarian to check barbarian." China would have been extinguished a long time ago, had it been dominated by one power. . . . [Therefore,] it will be better to have both Britain and the Soviet Union participating [in the mediation]. Only after this is proved impossible, do [we] have to let Marshall take part in the mediation alone.[26]

Using the traditional Chinese expression of realpolitik diplomacy, Mao obviously had a strategic preference as to which "barbarian" he feared the most and which he expected help from. In Mao's mind, to prevent China from being turned into an American "colony" under the GMD, Soviet intervention in China's politics became indispensable. However, Moscow didn't find Yan'an's proposal diplomatically sound and was unwilling to participate in it. This must have confirmed Mao's assumption that in the postwar division of spheres of influence, China belonged to the U.S., just like Greece to Britain and East Europe to the USSR.

But, Yan'an understood that according to the Yalta deal Manchuria fell under the Soviet sphere of influence, and it would thus be a safe haven to the CCP. This hope was strengthened in the beginning of 1946 when the Soviets suggested that the CCP propose to Marshall that in the GMD-CCP negotiations Manchuria be excluded. The Soviets demanded to exclude Manchuria from the realm of Marshall's mediation because they did not want to see any American presence in this region. When General Wedemeyer was conducting an inspection tour of China in November 1945, the Soviets told the CCP that America's unspoken goal in China was to monopolize control over all of China, including Manchuria.[27] The Soviets seemed very nervous about the possibility of U.S. influence penetrating into Manchuria.

The CCP foresaw the disadvantage of excluding Manchuria from the truce settlement, because it knew that its military forces there were not yet ready to compete with the GMD. On the other hand, Yan'an also recognized that if the U.S.-led mediation included Manchuria, "the Soviet Union will be disadvantaged, thus, it will be disadvantageous to us [the CCP] as well."[28] Since the Soviets insisted, Zhou officially proposed to Marshall that Manchuria should not be included in the negotiations in Chongqing.[29] Yan'an hoped that since Manchuria was excluded from the Marshall mediation, the Soviet Union would play the role as "Manchuria's Marshall," to head a separate committee of three to settle the business there. With the Soviets in a leading position, Yan'an could be at ease. However, although Yan'an suggested this to Moscow several times, the Soviets declined the proposal.[30] The truce agreement of 10 January officially recognized the exclusion of Manchuria from the settlement. The CCP immediately realized that a CCP-GMD military confrontation in Manchuria was inevitable. Yan'an instructed the Northeast Bureau to propose to the Soviet authorities that the number of GMD troops moving into Manchuria should be limited, but the Soviets were not in a position to make such a demand. Then, since the GMD troops were supposed to take over places under Soviet occupation, not places under CCP control, Yan'an requested that the Red Army transfer some territory to the CCP before GMD arrival, and the Soviets agreed.[31] Yan'an also ordered on 27 January that a major decisive battle be organized in order to "take the wind out of the GMD's sail."[32]

The Soviets, however, warned the CCP that it could not launch attacks on the GMD in Manchuria; otherwise, "the danger of U.S. troops' entry into Manchuria is imminent."[33] Yan'an thus concluded that the Soviet Union would not assist the CCP to launch a civil war in Manchuria, but would support the CCP's peace move diplomatically. But without the Soviets playing the role of "Manchuria's Marshall," the CCP proposed in February, certainly with Soviet consent, that the mediation under Marshall be extended into Manchuria, where the CCP was losing ground to the GMD. Yan'an told the Northeast Bureau that although Soviet mediation in Manchuria might be advantageous to the CCP in the long run, to demonstrate its impartiality, the USSR might have to ask the CCP to yield more ground to the GMD than Marshall might. "Thus, it has its up side that the Soviets don't come to the fore for the moment."[34] The Communists were convinced that unless it was defeated militarily, the GMD would not come to terms with them. Therefore, while the CCP was pursuing a peace move under the Marshall mission, it was simultaneously preparing for war on the grounds of self-defense. The CCP-GMD military conflict in Manchuria continued in a limited scope throughout the first three months of 1946, when the CCP was most cooperative with Marshall.

Due to the recent military and diplomatic successes in Manchuria, Jiang was confident that he could gain control over Manchuria by force. Therefore, the GMD did not want a truce with the CCP in Manchuria. From 7 to 14 January, the GMD and the CCP fought in Yingkou, the same time as the cessation of hostilities was negotiated and agreed upon by both sides. This worried Marshall, who agreed with the CCP on the inclusion of Manchuria in the negotiations, and proposed on 24 January that the Executive Headquarters in Beiping send a field team to Yingkou immediately. But, the GMD rejected it on the grounds that Manchuria was excluded from the Cessation of Hostilities Order, and Marshall was aware of Jiang's intention.[35]

On the contrary, the CCP was eager to reach a settlement in Manchuria. Worried that the possibility of fighting in Manchuria might wreck all his previous achievements, Marshall was then pushing Jiang to include Manchuria in the Cessation of Hostilities Order. Yan'an's cooperation with Marshall on this issue was impressive to the Americans.[36] But Yan'an had its own reason to be more diplomatic than militant. Despite the CCP's desire to win a decisive victory in Manchuria in order to force the GMD to accept its equal position in the region, the CCP forces there were not strong enough to deter the GMD. In fact, in February, the CCP suffered further setbacks with the anti-CCP "bandits" disturbance and the defection of newly established CCP troops. On 25 February, Chen Yun acknowledged the reality and reiterated the strategy of consolidating base areas in the countryside.[37] For the CCP, facing such a situation in Manchuria, continued cooperation with Marshall to seek a settlement with the GMD was desirable. On 11 March, just before Marshall's departure for Washington, Zhou told him that

> I hope, before you leave this evening, specific measures can be worked out so that General Gillem following your footsteps will assist us to achieve a settlement for the Northeast. We believe that only you have the capacity to promote the fulfillment of this matter.[38]

Although the CCP was eager to use Marshall's mediation to stabilize the situation in Manchuria, the GMD refused to budge. While Marshall was absent from China, the Soviet policy in Manchuria changed in March, as did the world situation after Stalin's inevitability-of-war speech of 9 February 1946, followed by George Kennan's long telegram of 22 February, and Churchill's Fulton speech of 5 March. In an intensifying cold-war atmosphere, the CCP was soon to become more militant than diplomatic in dealing with both the GMD and Marshall. When Marshall came back from the U.S. on 18 April, much had changed.

MAO'S NEW MANCHURIA POLICY: MARCH–MAY 1946

If the CCP's cooperation with Marshall was intended to win more time to consolidate its military position in Manchuria, Mao and his colleagues soon found out that neither Marshall nor Jiang was very enthusiastic about a truce in the Northeast. Zhou cabled Mao on 27 February, reporting that *Mei-Jiang* intended to delay a settlement on the Manchurian problem until the Soviet withdrawal was completed. And then, the GMD would mount its attack against the CCP.[39] Mao's response to this "delaying strategy" of *Mei-Jiang* was to expand its territorial control in the Northeast as vigorously as it could before the Red Army's evacuation was completed. This was greatly encouraged and assisted by the Soviets.

Against the background of the intensifying cold war, Moscow-GMD relations also deteriorated rapidly in February. On 11 February, the secret Yalta protocol specifying the restoration of Russian privileges in Manchuria was made public. The Russian delay in withdrawing from Manchuria and their dismantling and exporting of Manchurian industrial equipment also fueled Chinese resentment. Moreover, Zhang Xingfu, a well-known geographer and then a member of GMD Northeast Headquarters, was killed in the Soviet occupation zone. On 22 February, about 10,000 Chongqing students took to the streets in a mass anti-Soviet demonstration characterized by slogans such as "The U.S.S.R. = Germany + Japan," "Stalin = Hitler + Hirohito," and so on. During the demonstration, the offices of the *Xinhua ribao* (New China Daily), the CCP official organ in Chongqing, and the *Minzhubao* (Democracy Daily), the organ of the Democratic League, were attacked.

Yan'an did not see this event as an isolated or incidental "anti-foreign" student demonstration, but as an integral part of the global anti-Soviet and anti-Communist reactionary trend. In a press conference on 22 February, Zhou Enlai attributed the demonstration to what he called the organized and planned schemes of the GMD secret service.[40] The Communists believed that immediately after the Moscow Conference of foreign ministers in December 1945, the West began to embark on an anti-Soviet crusade. Yan'an interpreted the "Gouzenko Case" in Canada as a signal of the world "anti-Soviet countercurrent" which reached its peak with Churchill's "Iron Curtain" speech on 5 March.[41] On 10 March, Zhou cabled Mao: "We think Jiang is trying to use the [Manchurian issue] to stimulate the USSR-U.S. conflict, and therefore refuses to have a settlement in the Northeast."[42] The CCP was convinced that Jiang wanted to take advantage of USSR-U.S. tension in order to secure more direct U.S. involvement in China on his behalf.

Moscow shared the CCP's interpretation and reacted strongly to the Chongqing anti-Soviet demonstration. The Soviet newspapers published many articles attacking the GMD; they were translated and reprinted in *Jiefang ribao*.[43] Moreover, the USSR-GMD negotiations on economic issues in Manchuria broke off when the GMD negotiators left Changchun to protest the continued Soviet occupation after the 1 February deadline. After the withdrawal of the Red Army from some locations in Manchuria, Soviet citizens and officials there were attacked, and some of them were murdered by members of the GMD. According to Marshall's information, more than thirty Soviet citizens in Changchun were tortured, mutilated, and murdered by GMD troops. The Soviets thus began using language such as "Fascist Chiang Kai-shek thugs."[44]

Mao welcomed the deterioration of GMD-Moscow relations. In his directive to the Northeast Bureau on 5 March, he said that the Soviet Union wanted an arrangement of Sino-Soviet economic cooperation in Manchuria, but so far,

Mei-Jiang had refused it, and they even stirred up a nationwide anti-Soviet movement. In response, the Red Army postponed its withdrawal. While the struggle between the USSR and *Mei-Jiang* continued in Manchuria, Mao claimed, a CCP-GMD compromise there was impossible. Mao then said that due to the GMD anti-Soviet move, the Red Army in Manchuria was likely to be more willing to give the CCP a free hand to operate. The Bureau should, therefore, take advantage of the situation, and approach the *Cheng xiong* (a benevolent brother) immediately; Mao demanded a report on the result of the Bureau's meeting with the Soviet authorities as soon as possible.[45]

In the same directive, Mao specified two requests to be discussed with the Soviets. First, he suggested that the Soviets help the CCP wipe out all the "bandits," that is, armed local anti-CCP forces, before the Red Army's withdrawal. He said the elimination of the "bandits" would destroy the anti-Soviet anti-CCP forces in the region; if this could be accomplished, the five GMD armies in the Northeast could do little harm to the CCP. Second, he suggested that the Soviet authorities not promise to hand over medium-sized cities to the GMD. Mao worried that if a Sino-Soviet agreement on economic cooperation was reached, the Soviets would promise to hand over more locations in Manchuria to Jiang. He specifically mentioned the areas and cities along the southern portion of the Southern Manchurian Railway and the western portion of the Eastern China Railway as essential to the CCP.[46]

It turned out that the *Cheng xiong* was more cooperative than Mao had hoped for. By then, the Soviets had no doubt that a GMD-dominated Manchuria would become an anti-Soviet outpost, and the U.S. would penetrate into this region. Thus, they changed their previous cautious policy and started to encourage the CCP to act boldly in Manchuria again. On 8 March, a Red Army representative officially notified the Northeast Bureau that the Soviet troops would start to pull out of the Fushun, Jiling, and Shenyang areas, the Red Army would not hand over these areas to the GMD, and the CCP troops could have a free hand to take action. As a result, while the Red Army was pulling out, the Communists poured in and seized a series of cities in southern Manchuria with large industrial capacities, such as Andong, Benxi, Liaoyang, Haicheng, Fushun, and Tonghua.[47]

In the same period, American warships had just carried an additional five GMD armies into Manchuria, and an offensive was soon launched to regain those places newly occupied by the CCP. The Soviets in Manchuria were displeased with the CCP's performance, and they criticized their Chinese comrades of being "too courteous to the Americans" and unable to stop the entry of GMD armies into Manchuria. They told the Northeast Bureau that in all places of Manchuria, including Shenyang and Sipingjie, the CCP should launch an all-out offensive, and should gain firm control over the areas north of Changchun. Apparently, Moscow now wanted the CCP to take control over at least the northern half of Manchuria after the Soviet withdrawal. This could provide a buffer zone between the USSR and the hostile *Mei-Jiang*, and the Soviet interest in the Eastern China Railway would be better served as well. As soon as Mao was informed of the Soviet advice, he instructed the Northeast Bureau on 16 March to follow Moscow's direction by taking the whole of the Eastern China Railway and the Southern Manchurian Railway north of Shenyang, even at the risk of a "full-scale civil war."[48] This same instruction was repeated the next day by Mao.[49] On 18 March, Mao stressed in a Party Center's directive that "we shall be psychologically prepared for a split [with the GMD] and not be afraid of a civil war [with it]."[50]

Finally, a new CCP strategy emerged around 20 March, which aimed at the creation of a north-south division in the Northeast with Changchun as the dividing point: the GMD controlling the south and the CCP the north. To carry out this new strategy, the Communists, with the Red Army's help, started to sabotage railways in the area south of Shenyang in order to delay the northward advancement of the GMD troops transported by the Americans.[51] The military aspects of this plan were further detailed in Mao's telegram of 24 March. This directive reads: "Our Party's policy is to use all our strength to control Changchun, Harbin, and the whole Changchun Railway. No matter how much sacrifice that may take, [we must] prevent Jiang's troops from occupying these two cities and the railway. Southern and western Manchuria should function as auxiliaries." The cable designated Sipingjie as the main point to defend.[52] To firmly control the northern half of the Northeast, Mao needed the Soviets' help. In the same directive of 24 March, Mao instructed the Northeast Bureau to contact the *Cheng xiong* and to gain their cooperation in both Changchun and Harbin. Three days later, Mao cabled Lin Biao: although the CCP had decided to seize Changchun and Harbin, and the railway in between, it would largely depend on the decision of the *youren* (the "friends").[53] Given the intensification of the cold war and the deterioration of the GMD-Soviet relations, Stalin certainly did not want to see Manchuria under the pro-American GMD control after the Red Army's withdrawal. Moscow apparently gave Mao the go-ahead. If, from 15 November 1945 to 8 March 1946, there was a discrepancy between what Mao wanted to do in Manchuria and what the Soviets allowed him to do, it disappeared now. The new gap was between how much Mao wanted to do and how much he could do.

When the Soviets were pulling out of southern Manchurian cities, they wanted the CCP to take over the whole of the Northeast. However, what had been handed over to the CCP by the Red Army in southern Manchuria was quickly lost to the GMD forces carried by the American war machines. When the Red Army left Shenyang on 11 March, the CCP attempted to seize it, but the GMD military strength proved superior again. On 13 March, the GMD drove the CCP forces away from Shenyang, and continued to push them northward. The next major city the CCP wanted to defend was Changchun, the capital of former Manchuguo. To secure the CCP's occupation of

Changchun when the Red Army pulled out, Mao ordered his lieutenants to capture Sipingjie, a strategic point south of Changchun.[54] This was accomplished on 18 March. In the following two months, Sipingjie became the battleground for the CCP-GMD conflict. Mao was determined to defend Changchun at any cost, because the loss of Changchun meant the failure of the new strategy of north-south division. On 20 April, Mao cabled Lin Biao to order that more troops be sent to Sipingjie. Eventually, there were 100,000 CCP troops gathered in the Sipingjie front. Mao vowed that if necessary, "[we] are prepared to turn Changchun into China's Madrid."[55] Although Mao's comparison between Changchun in the Chinese civil war and Madrid in the Spanish civil war was irrelevant, it revealed that his thinking was along the lines of a Moscow-led world revolution and he spoke in the parlance of international communism. His new Manchuria policy suited Moscow's new position more than it did "Chinese national interest."

The CCP forces at Sipingjie, nevertheless, were driven out by the GMD on 18 May, and Changchun fell four days later. It appears that Mao frequently overestimated what he could do, and would be quite upset, to say the least, if someone told him he could not do something he wanted to do. For instance, regarding the CCP's policy in Manchuria in March 1946, the Soviets in Chongqing were more cautious and diplomatic than their counterparts in Manchuria and their advice was "too soft" for Mao's taste. On 15 March, Mao told Zhou that the CCP should not take the advice of the Soviet *youren* in Chongqing for granted because it tended to be less aggressive and more conciliatory than that of the Soviets in Manchuria.[56] Mao was not very happy either when Stalin advised him to stop fighting and go to Chongqing to negotiate in August 1945, although he complied and benefited from following Stalin's advice, as has been shown. If we are going to interpret this kind of tactical discrepancy as a type of confrontation between Chinese national interest and Soviet imperialism, we have to twist our common-sense logic first.

MAO'S STRATEGY OF COMBINING "TALK" WITH "FIGHT"

Having decided to fight, Mao, nevertheless, had no intention to terminate the talks under Marshall's mediation. In fact, the CCP worked hard to use the CCP-GMD negotiations to fulfill its new Manchuria plan. On 25 March, one day after the CCP's directive on seizing northern Manchuria, Mao sent another cable to Lin Biao and Peng Zhen. This time, he said that Zhou Enlai had arrived in Chongqing and a GMD-CCP agreement on cessation of hostilities in Manchuria would be signed soon. But, before this,

the GMD will launch attacks fiercely in order to control more strategic points and resources. Therefore, you should do all you can to defend these strategic points no matter how much it will cost. Northern Manchuria is of special importance. . . . You must gain control over Changchun, Harbin, and Qiqihar within one or two days after the withdrawal of the Soviet Army. Otherwise, when the field team arrives in these cities, it will guarantee the GMD's occupation. But if [these cities] are occupied by us, the field team will also guarantee our occupation.[57]

In other words, Mao believed that the field team under the Committee of Three would recognize the status quo in Manchuria, and the more the CCP could gain before the arrival of the field team, the better. This perception was repeated by Mao in the following few weeks. For instance, on 13 April, Mao learned that Marshall was leaving the U.S. for China and he cabled Lin Biao: Since Marshall's arrival would result in a truce in Manchuria, the GMD would for certain launch an all-out attack on Sipingjie and Benxi. The CCP there must defend these two places so that its position in the negotiations could be enhanced. On 16 April, Mao told the Northeast Bureau that the Committee of Three would arrive in Manchuria on 20–25 April, and a truce would possibly be reached then; thus, Changchun, Harbin, and Qiqihar must be seized immediately.[58] Apparently, Mao tried to incorporate fight with talk, and he regarded fight as a primary means to gain more, while using talk to secure the gain.

To continue talks with the GMD under Marshall's mediation, the CCP also tried to make use of the "*Mei-Jiang* contradictions" so that Americans would, hopefully, withhold loans and limit the U.S. operation in transporting the GMD troops to Manchuria. In his telegram of 19 March, Zhou Enlai stated that

> Jiang tries to postpone a settlement; but, the United States wants China to be stable, then, large loans would be given. Therefore, Jiang does not dare to break [the negotiations] at the present time. Accordingly, our current policy should make use of this *Mei-Jiang* contradiction and Jiang's weak point of his two-sided policy, and launch an all-out attack on his reactionary side. This policy analysis has been explained to the Democratic League. They agreed one hundred percent and promised to take action together.[59]

By "Jiang's weak point of his two-sided policy," Zhou meant that the GMD intended to eliminate the CCP by force, but in order to get the American loans and assistance, Jiang had to go along with the Marshall Mission which insisted on a political settlement between the two parties. Therefore, Jiang's desire for conditional American aid became his vulnerable point, which could be exploited to the CCP's advantage.

The validity of Zhou's analysis was confirmed by Jiang's conversation with Marshall on 10 March, when Jiang told Marshall that the precondition for U.S. aid to China mentioned in Truman's China policy statement had unwittingly helped the Communist Party. He hoped that any loan which might be granted to China should have no conditions attached to it. At least there should be no public announcement of such conditions.[60] But the Americans still believed that a coalition with a disarmed CCP was the best solution for China; in order to keep the Russians away, a peaceful settlement between the GMD and the

CCP was necessary. The gap between Jiang's desire to defeat the CCP by force with unconditional American assistance and the U.S. insistence on a peaceful solution became what the CCP called the *Mei-Jiang* contradiction.

Zhou Enlai was determined to utilize this contradiction, and his immediate goal was to reduce U.S. aid to the GMD in terms of loans and transportation facilities. On 26 March, he told General Gillem, Marshall's representative when he was in the U.S., that the GMD Government was continuing to pour troops into the Northeast to enlarge the civil war. Therefore, it would be better for Marshall to seek loans for China after the completion of government reform and the completion of the constitutional process. Otherwise, any loan would make the reactionaries more arrogant and government reform more difficult. It would also affect the realization of the military reorganization program.[61] When the Americans continued to ship the GMD troops into Manchuria, Zhou hardened his attitude to exercise political pressure on the Marshall mission. On 31 March, Zhou delivered a statement to Gillem:

> In case the U.S. Forces Headquarters shall continue to move Government troops into Manchuria, we would deem such action as a change of the U.S. policy toward China, and lack of faith on the part of the Government to implement a real truce in Manchuria. Consequently we shall feel obliged to contemplate seriously what countermeasures we shall have to take.[62]

In April, it became evident to the CCP that the United States was helping the GMD to take over Manchuria even at the risk of a peaceful settlement. The Communists were thus progressively leaning toward a more militant position. In his cables to Yan'an on 5 and 8 April, Zhou stated that the situation regarding the Manchurian problem had changed, and a policy reassessment was necessary. "The GMD would attempt to take over Changchun, Harbin, and Qiqihar, while the United States intended to help Jiang take over the Changchun Railway. Therefore, [we] shall prepare for a great battle in the Northeast, and never have any illusions that the GMD would make concessions." Mao replied immediately to confirm Zhou's opinion. Mao once again linked the changing situation in China with the global struggle between the two camps. He said that "considering the international and domestic reactionary tides, our Party must have an overall plan to smash the reactionaries' offensive."[63] In his telegram of 10 April, Mao further concluded that the U.S. and the GMD were plotting together in order to take over not only Manchuria but also Rehe and Chahar, and turn them into anti-Soviet and anti-CCP outposts. The CCP, therefore, should spare no effort to consolidate these two provinces as well as Manchuria.[64]

By "international reactionary tide," Mao was referring to the mounting cold-war tension in early 1946 symbolized by Churchill's Fulton Speech. Yan'an had been very sensitive to, and carefully monitoring, developments in Soviet relations with the West. In the Communists' opinion, because of the conflicting policies between Moscow and the West over the issues of Iran, Greece, Indo-China, East Europe, and the Middle East, the British and the Americans were forming an alliance, which led a "worldwide anti-Soviet countercurrent." Yan'an recorded Churchill's every speech after he arrived in the U.S. on 15 January 1946, and summarized what Churchill advocated in three points: (1) the Anglo-American alliance for maintaining the world *status quo*, (2) the monopoly of nuclear technology by the West, and (3) the permanent stationing of U.S. forces in Western Europe in order to counterbalance the Soviet Red Army.[65] The Communists regarded Churchill's Fulton Speech as an appeal for the formation of an Anglo-American military anti-Soviet alliance, and President Truman apparently stood with Churchill.[66]

Linking these international developments with China's domestic situation, Mao was of the opinion that the GMD was delighted with, and aided and abetted the Anglo-American anti-Soviet move. Yan'an's press pointed out that the GMD-controlled press deliberately omitted the criticism of Churchill in the U.S. and Britain, while spreading the rumor that "all British people, except Communists, agreed with Churchill's speech." To counterattack the GMD's pro-Churchill propaganda, *Jiefang ribao* reported various criticisms of the Fulton Speech by non-Communists in the U.S. and Britain.[67] The Communists went so far as to say that the GMD "pins its hopes on the outbreak of the Third World War" between the West and the Soviet Union because the U.S.-USSR conflict would make the U.S. fully committed to the GMD's cause of eliminating the CCP.[68] This line of thinking not only demonstrated how deeply the Communists embraced the concept of the USSR-CCP vs. U.S.-GMD alignment, it also made them greatly concerned with the possibility of a third war throughout the postwar era. Intertwined with the bipolar vision of postwar politics at home and abroad, the CCP's Leninist perception of the inevitability of war played a major role in the Party's foreign policy for years to come.

To both Moscow and Yan'an, the natural alignment between the GMD and the U.S. was obvious and a good USSR-GMD relationship seemed hopeless in the face of deteriorating U.S.-USSR relations. Thus, while Moscow's verbal attack on Jiang's government accelerated, Yan'an openly charged that Washington's policy was to squeeze U.S. interests into Manchuria.[69] The Americans continued to transport more GMD troops into the Northeast regardless of the civil war there and the CCP's repeated protests. The Communists thus concluded that U.S. behavior in China was a part of its imperialist policy in postwar East Asia. The issue that concerned the CCP was no longer U.S. partiality in the GMD-CCP conflict, but U.S. intention to use the GMD to achieve its imperialist goal. To fight the U.S.-GMD alliance, the USSR-CCP cooperation in Manchuria was naturally strengthened.

Early in April, Red Army representatives in Manchuria informed the CCP that Soviet troops would pull out from Changchun, Harbin, and Qiqihar on 15 and 25 April, respectively. The Soviets then suggested that CCP troops

advance to the suburban areas of these cities in order to take them over immediately after the withdrawal of the Red Army. The Soviets stated that the U.S.
was supporting the GMD to take over Manchuria as an anti-Soviet outpost,
while Jiang allied with the U.S. against the USSR and the CCP. Since the
Soviet Union didn't want to take part directly in Manchurian affairs, the CCP
needed to do its utmost to hold Manchuria to frustrate *Mei-Jiang*.[70]

Against this background, Mao put the CCP-GMD confrontation in the
Sipingjie-Changchun area into an international context. On 5 April, he said
that "currently, the counterrevolutionary tide is on the rise at home and abroad.
[The CCP] should keep its vigilance," and be prepared for the enemies' sudden attack. He believed that *Mei-Jiang* had decided to mobilize fifteen armies
to attack the CCP in Manchuria, and then, sit down to negotiate after their victory. In response, Mao said, the CCP should use Marshall to reach a truce; but,
at the same time, the Party should prepare to fight the fifteen GMD armies. The
key, Mao stated on 6 April, was to win two upcoming battles in Sipingjie and
Benxi.[71] Encouraged by the recent Soviet advice, Zhou Enlai was also eager to
fight, although he was personally engaged in the negotiations for a truce. After
he met with GMD and U.S. representatives on the Committee of Three on 8
April, Zhou cabled Mao: *Mei-Jiang* could not be stopped in Manchuria without suffering a major military defeat. Mao was fully in agreement with Zhou,
and told him on 10 April that "the reason for which the GMD and the U.S. are
eager to send the Committee of Three to Shenyang is to force us to recognize
the GMD's right to take over Changchun, Harbin, and Qiqihar, and the railway
between them." He instructed Zhou to refuse the *Mei-Jiang* demand categorically. The next day, when Zhou learned that the GMD had suddenly changed
its previous attitude and expressed willingness to reach a truce in Manchuria,
he reasoned that it was only because the GMD realized it could not breach the
CCP's defense line at Sipingjie and reach Changchun on 15 April, the date for
the Soviet withdrawal. Therefore, the GMD proposed a truce in order to win
more time to reinforce its military strength. Zhou thus suggested that the CCP
take over Changchun in the next two days. Mao turned over Zhou's telegram
to the Northeast Bureau, and ordered that Zhou's idea be followed.[72]

As a result of close USSR-CCP cooperation, within an hour after the Soviet
withdrawal from Changchun on 14 April, CCP troops attacked the 15,000
GMD troops previously flown to Changchun by the Americans. Tanks oper-
ated by Japanese crews were employed by the CCP. The airport was taken first,
then the whole city. Marshall was deeply puzzled by the CCP's action, since
he had been under the impression that Zhou was reasonable and conciliatory
in pursuing a settlement.[73] Apparently, Marshall could hardly understand the
CCP's dualistic pattern which combined "fight" with "talk"; he hardly knew
Moscow's secret role in the making of CCP policy. Changchun was taken by
the CCP on 18 April; this literally deadlocked the negotiations under Marshall's mediation.

Mao was confident of the outcome of a full-scale military confrontation with the GMD in Manchuria. On 17 April, having learned of the success of the Communists in resisting the GMD's offensive in both Sipingjie and Benxi, Mao believed that "the situation in the Northeast has fundamentally turned in our favor.... Unless [the GMD] transfers several additional armies to the Northeast, they cannot maintain an offensive posture [any more]."[74] Based on this judgment, Mao ordered the Northeast Bureau on 19 April to move its headquarters into Changchun and to prepare for the Convention of the Northeast People's Autonomy Assembly, and the proclamation of the Northeast Autonomous Government. In another directive of the same day, Mao further stressed that the centerpiece of CCP Manchuria policy was to defend Changchun, Harbin, and Qiqihar; whether this could be done successfully or not would depend on the battle in the Sipingjie area.[75]

Mao's analysis and military plan was shared by Zhou and other CCP leaders. On 22 April, Zhou cabled Mao that "Jiang does not want to have a truce in the Northeast, and he is waiting for reinforcements now. Marshall probably intends to let Jiang fight, and appears not eager to see me. We should destroy the transportation line in southern Manchuria, preparing for a great victorious battle within ten days."[76] Luo Ronghuan, then hospitalized in Soviet occupied Dalian, cabled the Northeast Bureau on 23 April: "The current situation in the Northeast has turned to be favorable for us. The Red Army withdrew from the north of Shenyang, while the GMD troops are blocked and under attack in the south of Sipingjie. That makes it possible for us to take control over Changchun, Harbin, Qiqihar, and other major cities [in the north]."[77] According to Mao's ambitious plan, immediately after the Soviet withdrawal, the Communist forces launched an offensive and occupied Qiqihar and Harbin on 24 and 28 April, respectively, and 27,000 GMD troops were reportedly annihilated in these battles.[78]

When Marshall returned to China on 18 April, the impasse was complete. Neither the Nationalists nor the Communists were willing to make further compromises. After the Communist occupation of Changchun and other major cities in the northern half of Manchuria, a north-south division became a reality. To legalize and consolidate the CCP's control over the northern half of Manchuria, and in the face of its relatively weak military strength, Zhou tried to use Marshall's mediation to reach a truce in Chongqing, while the CCP military men were consolidating their position in the Northeast. Marshall was afraid that if the military conflict in Manchuria could not be checked, it would spread everywhere else, and his previous achievements would be jeopardized. Therefore, on 23 and 28 April, he presented two draft agreements on the immediate cessation of hostilities in Manchuria to the Committee of Three. He suggested that all troop movements in Manchuria be frozen, and the movements of the National Army, previously free from any limits, should be authorized by the Committee of Three.[79]

Marshall's proposal was just what the CCP wanted at the moment. However, Jiang did not want a truce before his armies could retake Changchun from the Communists. He presented a draft in which the essential condition for the cessation of hostilities was the CCP's evacuation from Changchun. Jiang also demanded the reestablishment of government control over the railways and the surrounding areas.[80] When Marshall presented Jiang's proposal to Zhou on 29 April, Zhou immediately rejected it. He argued that since Soviet troops had already left, the question of restoring Chinese sovereignty became irrelevant. He insisted on separating the two sides in the battlefield and prohibiting troop movements. That was to cement the north-south division in Manchuria, which the GMD could not accept. A negotiated truce seemed hopeless. Marshall announced that he had exhausted his resources and that he had to withdraw from mediation on the Manchurian problem.[81]

Zhou did not want to make any more concessions to sustain Marshall's mediation efforts, especially considering the Soviet Union's hardened attitude toward the GMD and the deteriorating U.S.-USSR relations. Early in May, the war in Manchuria spilled out into China proper. In Hubei province, the 5th Division of the CCP under Li Xiannian's command was surrounded by GMD troops who started an attack, but Yan'an had no military strength to reinforce the division. Thus, Zhou tried to use Marshall to persuade the GMD to let the division go. On 4 May, Zhou told Marshall that the GMD attack on the 5th division would mean a renewed civil war in China proper. To avoid a total wreckage of his previous achievement, Marshall agreed to send an American member of the field team in to mediate, and he persuaded the GMD to send a representative to go with the American officer. On 10 May, a temporary truce agreement was reached in central China.[82]

Nonetheless, this did not make Zhou any more conciliatory on the Manchurian issue. On 12 May, Marshall and Xu Yongchang, the GMD's new representative on the Committee of Three, proposed that when the team was having difficulty in reaching a unanimous decision, the American representative should have the final say. Distrustful of the Americans' impartiality, the Communists regarded this proposal as a scheme of *Mei-Jiang* intended to trap the CCP. Zhou rejected it outright.[83] On 13 May, Marshall brought up the issue again, and this made Zhou even more suspicious of Marshall's intentions. He told Marshall that he needed to consult Yan'an.[84] But, in his cable to Yan'an on the same day, Zhou did not advise Yan'an to consider Marshall's proposal; instead, he told Mao that on the Manchurian issue, Marshall's position was not very far from that of Jiang Jieshi; on the issues concerning China proper, the U.S. position was increasingly in conflict with that of the CCP. Any real improvement of this situation became absolutely impossible, and the ultimate settlement would be decided by the relative military strengths of both sides. Therefore, Zhou concluded, "[we] must mobilize the masses in order to prepare for a final showdown."[85]

The situation on the battlefield, however, was not going as well as Mao had expected. After their seizure of Changchun on 18 April, the Communists concentrated their major forces in the Northeast on the Sipingjie front to resist the GMD's northward offensive. Nonetheless, they were forced to retreat on 18 May. During their retreat, the GMD's pursuit inflicted more casualties on the Communists. The defeat in the Sipingjie battle was so distressful to the CCP troops that morale became a major concern of the Northeast Bureau, which decided to retreat further north to defend the Sungari River.[86]

Before its final defeat at Sipingjie, Yan'an tried again to make use of Marshall to reach a truce to stabilize its position. On 15 May, a telegram from Yan'an stated that on the one hand, "the Sipingjie defense should be sustained, the longer, the better." On the other hand, "our negotiating people should press and strive for a truce."[87] Zhou made one more effort to talk to Marshall, but Marshall told him that it was useless to attempt to persuade Jiang to abandon his demand for the CCP's evacuation from Changchun. Marshall would not reenter into the negotiations unless the CCP could assure him a favorable outcome.[88] On the next day, the GMD occupied Sipingjie. On 23 May, Changchun fell into the hands of the Nationalists.

Since the Sipingjie battle had proved that CCP troops were not strong enough to win positional warfare, Mao ordered on 19 May the resumption of mobile warfare, the Communists' traditional strong point. To distract the GMD's northward move, the Communists in southern Manchuria launched an attack on the Anshan-Haicheng area on 25 May, and occupied Anshan, Yingkou, and other strategic points. But when GMD reinforcements reached this area on 30 May, the Communists had already disappeared.[89] Shortly thereafter, the GMD army was stretched beyond its ability to effectively defend its position or to attack its enemy, while the CCP's mobile warfare spread not only all over the Northeast, but also in China proper. On 6 June, a temporary truce was separately announced by both sides, but it was a "short-lived propaganda truce," as Marshall put it. On 7 June, the CCP launched an attack in Shandong along the Qingdao-Jinan railway, and the GMD sent in two armies to fight back. On 8 June, the CCP and the GMD clashed in Lafa, a city east of Changchun. Charge and countercharge followed.[90] Hopes for peace were diminishing rapidly.

This, nonetheless, did not exclude the Party from continuing profitable negotiations. In fact, the Communists tried their best to coordinate their actions on the battlefield and at the negotiating table. On 21 May, three days after the CCP's defeat at Sipingjie, Mao wrote: "Regarding the eruption of a nationwide civil war, [we] must try to delay it as much as possible, so that we can be in an advantageous position. If we cannot delay it for six months, three months, two months, or one month will be alright, too. We can then be better prepared."[91] For this purpose, Marshall's service was still useful to the CCP.

The Communists, however, were progressively distrustful of Marshall. On

18 June, Zhou told Mao that the differences between Marshall and Jiang were diminishing, and that they were increasingly coordinating their actions against the CCP. Mao concluded the next day that only if the CCP was to gain the upper hand in battle, or both sides were to reach a stalemate, would negotiations for peace be possible.[92] The Communists closely tied the negotiations with the outcome on the battlefield, and it was obvious to them that only military victory could secure political gains at the bargaining table. When they were at a disadvantage, they needed Marshall's help to gain breathing room. For instance, when Mao learned that Jiang had agreed with Marshall's proposal on a fifteen-day truce on 5 June, he immediately cabled his lieutenants in Manchuria: "In the fifteen days, while our delegates are negotiating with the GMD in Nanjing, our units in the Northeast should use this period to have a rest, to have logistics taken care of, to enhance the morale, so that we can continue to fight again.[93]

On the other hand, how much the CCP would yield at the negotiations depended upon how much the Party's military strength could hold on by force. In late June, it seemed likely that the GMD forces would push further north along the railways to regain Harbin and Qiqihar. If this was unavoidable, Zhou wanted to take the initiative to yield these places to the GMD in negotiation before the GMD troops took them. In this way, the CCP might gain some bargaining chips to advance its interest somewhere else. Therefore, on 23 June, Zhou telegraphed the Northeast Bureau, asking whether or not the CCP should take the initiative to give up Harbin and Qiqihar to the GMD. The next day, the Bureau replied that the CCP should not make concessions to the GMD without a fight. The degree of limited concessions should be decided according to how many troops the GMD could muster. The concessions should not exceed the limit of the CCP's estimation as to how far the GMD could push. Yan'an endorsed the Bureau's idea.[94] On June 24, the Committee of Three met, but Zhou made no concessions in Manchuria. After the meeting, Zhou cabled Yan'an: "Negotiations are drawing close to the end," and he asked Mao's permission to act freely according to the circumstances so that the final breakdown of the negotiations could be made in a way which was advantageous to the CCP. Mao replied the next day and gave Zhou the authority to go ahead.[95] By the end of June, a full-scale civil war had started in both Manchuria and China proper, and the situation grew worse. On 10 August, Marshall and the new U.S. Ambassador, Leighton Stuart, issued a joint statement, recognizing the failure of U.S. mediation. Zhou, however, stayed in Nanjing, the restored capital of China, until 19 November, and he continued to exploit the U.S.-GMD "contradictions" to reduce Washington's commitment to the GMD.

Zhou's effort was not wasted. On 22 July, afraid of a possible total breakdown of the GMD-CCP negotiations, and Soviet overt intervention on behalf of the CCP, Marshall cabled Washington to suggest a delay in the passage of

China aid legislation.[96] To press the GMD to move toward political reform, which would have involved the CCP in a coalition, Dean Acheson wrote to the War Assets Administration on 6 August to ask them to add a proviso to the U.S. munition sales agreement with China. The request stated: "It is the desire of the United States Government that these munitions be destined for an integrated and representative National Army under a coalition government." On 23 August, the Munitions Division informed the GMD that "in the light of the foregoing, and in view of existing circumstances, the Department of State regrets that it is not in a position to grant, at this time, an export license for the subject rifle ammunition."[97]

U.S. China policy, however, was inconsistent. In the same period, the U.S. government was making arrangements to furnish the GMD with Pacific surpluses from the war against Japan. On 28 August, Marshall endorsed this deal, and further suggested that the Export-Import Bank extend a line of credit to China for the purchase of spare parts in the U.S. As far as the Communists were concerned, the deal in the surplus materials made a joke of the arms embargo itself.[98] In the summer of 1946, in the face of continued U.S. assistance to the GMD when the CCP-GMD confrontation was escalating, Yan'an was becoming openly critical of U.S. policy. On 10 June, Zhou frankly told Marshall that the CCP believed that America's China policy was a "self-contradiction," and that America had a "two-track policy toward China."[99] On 24 June, the Party Center dispatched a directive, "Mobilizing the Masses to Press the U.S. to Change Its Supporting-Jiang Policy," which stated that the American policy of military intervention was becoming increasingly probable, while the Jiang government's policy of turning China into a U.S. colony was increasingly obvious. Therefore, the Party must mobilize the masses to struggle against *Mei-Jiang*.[100] The statement of the CCP spokesman on 1 July and the declaration of the CCP Central Committee on 7 July marked a turning point in the CCP's U.S. policy. From this point on an open confrontational attitude became the predominant feature in the CCP's dealings with the United States.[101] On 31 August, Zhou Enlai concluded:

> *Mei-Jiang* have reached an identical view on three issues, that is, to deny the reality of the nationwide civil war; to deny the failure of [U.S.] mediation; to refuse to withdraw U.S. forces [from China]. . . . Now, the struggle has come to the last stage, during which the focus is on the United States. If only [we] can leave Leighton Stuart and Marshall nothing to blame [us] in regards to both military and political issues, then all the responsibility [for the final split] will be self-evident. The American deception can no longer continue.[102]

Given the fact that before his departure for China, Marshall had reached an understanding with President Truman that if the Communists proved intransigent and obstructive, the U.S. would give the GMD all-out support in eliminating them, Zhou's continuation of working with Marshall did not provoke the Americans to take a more aggressive policy in assisting the GMD. Mao's political purpose of continuing the "talks" was clearly spelled out in his telegram to Zhou on 13 October:

> In the situation of a nationwide civil war, all negotiations are for the purpose of exposing the reactionary feature of *Mei-Jiang*, and educating the masses. As long as *Mei-Jiang* do not give up political negotiations so that they can continue to deceive the masses, we shall not take the initiative to announce the breakdown of the negotiations with *Mei-Jiang*. If we did it, that would put us in an unfavorable light.[103]

Although Marshall did not leave China until early in 1947, it was obvious that his mission there had failed completely by the fall of 1946. When he left China, a full-scale civil war had already erupted. Yet, the U.S. government could not cut off its ties with the GMD government, as Marshall understood before his mission started. To do so would mean Soviet dominance over at least part of East Asia, especially Manchuria. On the other hand, Marshall's Mission also failed to find an opportunity to lay the blame on the CCP for starting the war, which could have justified the U.S. giving all-out support to the GMD. In that regard, the Maoist pattern of combining "fight" with "talk" was successful in out-maneuvering Marshall and achieving its own political and military ends.

Direct official Communist contact with the U.S. government started in 1944, when the Dixie Mission arrived in Yan'an, and ended in early 1947, when the Marshall Mission finished disastrously. This direct CCP-U.S. contact did not resume until the early 1970s. The break with the United States was not because of the CCP's lack of flexibility in choosing a course of action according to the changing situation, but because of its perception, and therefore, distrust of, the U.S. government as the representative of the American grand bourgeoisie, and natural ally of the GMD. This ideological perception was confirmed and reinforced by the U.S. China policy as seen by the CCP. At the same time, the Communists' self-identification with Moscow led them to consider their struggle with the GMD as closely linked with the U.S.-USSR postwar global struggle. Their experience in the struggle over Manchuria also confirmed their "two-camp" perception. This perception would further manifest itself in the following three years, when the cold war dramatically intensified.

CHAPTER VII

The CCP and the Cold War in Asia

MAO'S "INTERMEDIATE-ZONE" THEORY AND

THE ANTI-AMERICAN UNITED FRONT, 1946–1947

> The postwar world has evolved into a standoff
> between U.S. reactionaries and the people of the world.
> The situation in China reflects this standoff; thus,
> our struggle in China is intimately related to that of the
> world. . . . The world is progressing, the USSR
> is uplifting itself, and the U.S. is facing crisis.
> —*Mao Zedong, November 1946*

EARLY in 1946, Stalin's militant speech inspired George Kennan's long dispatch, and Churchill's Fulton Speech announced the drop of the "iron curtain" between Eastern and Western Europe. Before the end of 1947, the eastern-bloc countries gathered to form the Cominform, which proclaimed the inevitable confrontation between the camp of the "people's democracies" of the East and the "imperialist camp" of the West. Coinciding with this irreversible trend toward the cold war, the CCP-GMD conflict escalated, and a full-scale civil war had raged all over Manchuria and China proper before George Marshall left that country. The Party thereafter was under a total war situation, and its united front–style diplomacy with the U.S. ended.

The civil war at home and the cold war abroad further convinced the CCP that its struggle with the GMD was a reflection of the U.S.-USSR global conflict; its commitment to the Soviet-led world revolutionary cause was thus reconfirmed. Within this framework, Mao's theory of "intermediate zone" emerged. In August 1946, Mao offered American journalist Anna Louise Strong a lengthy interview and he intended to let Strong spread his new theory.[1] This theory was further elaborated on by Lu Dingyi, the head of the Party's Propaganda Department, in an article published in early 1947.[2]

What was the essence of Mao's new theory? How did it fit into the CCP's rationale of the relationship between the Chinese civil war and the U.S.-USSR cold war? Against the background of the Sino-Soviet split and the Sino-American detente in the late 1960s and early 1970s, some scholars came to interpret Mao's intermediate-zone theory of the 1940s as the origin of his "three-world" theory of the 1970s. They believe that the CCP was independent of Moscow, and Mao was a rival, rather than a comrade, of Stalin; the new theory was Mao's first effort to pull together a "third bloc" in between the two superpowers to advance China's national interests.[3]

Based on new CCP historical materials, however, a close reexamination of Mao's theory challenges this "third-bloc" interpretation. Mao's intermediate-zone theory was not a departure from the CCP's long-standing "two camp" concept, but a continuation of it with new intention. Mao separated the intermediate zone from both the U.S. and the Soviet Union for two interrelated reasons. First, he wanted to encourage the anti-American struggle in China and other colonial and semicolonial countries, as the CCP put it, even if the Soviet Union continued her diplomatic maneuvers and reached some temporary compromise with the United States at a certain point in time. He held that the more boldly the world revolutionary forces fought U.S. imperialism, the more likely that the U.S. would be forced to reach a temporary compromise with the Soviet Union, the vital pillar of what Mao called the world democratic forces. Second, Mao intended to apply the united front principle to separate other capitalist countries from U.S. reactionaries, and to form a people's united front at home and abroad to oppose U.S. imperialism. In other words, Mao's intermediate-zone theory reflected Mao's intention to use his dualistic pattern in the international arena. Just like at home, the existence of the "third force" and various different anti-Jiang factions in the GMD provided the basis for the CCP to utilize united front tactics, Mao's creation of an intermediate zone, including the oppressed nations and the non-American western capitalist nations, served as a theoretical foundation for the Communists to develop their united front diplomacy against the U.S.

MAO'S RADICAL ANTI-AMERICAN-IMPERIALISM STAND

In fact, the evolutionary process of the intermediate-zone theory can be traced back as early as April 1946. It started as a means to justify Mao's decision to fight at home in the face of a seemingly conciliatory international atmosphere. As has been shown, Mao had kept its course of action in close coordination with Moscow's diplomatic maneuvers. For instance, only a week after Moscow signed the Sino-Soviet pact of 1945, the CCP reversed its military strategy and Mao went to Chongqing to talk peace; and in accordance with the forthcoming Moscow Conference of the foreign ministers of the Big Three in December 1945, Mao shifted his policy again to welcome Marshall's mission in China. Whenever the Soviets sat down with *Mei-Jiang*, the CCP felt that a certain type of CCP-GMD compromise would, and should, follow.

If the Red Army's presence in Manchuria justified this type of micromanaging coordination with Moscow, it became a liability and an impedance to the CCP after March 1946, when the Red Army had pulled out of Manchuria. In the spring of 1946, under the Soviets' encouragement, Mao took an aggressive position which led the CCP to occupy Changchun. But, the world situation then did not seem congenial to Mao's hardening position at home. At the time, the Soviets sat down again with the western allies in Paris. As Huan Xiang, a leading CCP commentator on international affairs, observed, "The atmosphere of the Paris Conference of the Big Four Foreign Ministers has been good so far." He predicted that some minor compromise between the Soviet Union and the West would be reached at Paris.[4] If it was so, should the CCP follow suit to sit down with the GMD to reach some sort of settlement?

Mao was apparently concerned with the incompatibility between the CCP's hard-line policy at home and the conciliatory tone of the U.S.-USSR talks in Paris. To justify his militant position and to encourage the Party to continue fighting, Mao tried to set loose the previous micromanaging cooperation between the CCP's domestic struggle and the Soviet diplomatic maneuver. Chiefly for this purpose, Mao wrote "Some Points in Appraisal of the Present International Situation" in April 1946, in which he predicted that sooner or later the USSR and the West would reach some compromise, but it did not mean that the U.S.-USSR confrontation would disappear. "That is impossible so long as the United States, Britain, and France continue to be ruled by reactionaries," Mao said. Certain compromise between the USSR and the West "does not require the people in the countries of the capitalist world to follow suit and make compromises at home. The people in those countries will continue to wage different struggles in accordance with their different conditions."[5]

The logic behind Mao's justification for Yan'an's hard-line position was twofold. First, Mao believed that an all-out war between the U.S. and the USSR was unlikely in the near future. Even if the CCP fought *Mei-Jiang* forces in China resolutely, it would not trigger a new world war. At the time, there was a major concern among Mao's colleagues that the U.S.-USSR conflict might escalate into a third world war, which America would win because of its atomic bomb. Should this happen, the GMD with U.S. support would defeat the CCP. Based on this estimation, they were inclined to a more reconciling position in dealing with the GMD at home in order to avoid triggering a U.S.-USSR confrontation.[6] To redress this "erroneous rightist deviation," and to encourage the Party's morale, Mao went on to state:

> The forces of world reaction are definitely preparing a third world war, and the danger of war exists. But the democratic forces of the people of the world have surpassed the reactionary forces and are forging ahead; they must and certainly can overcome the danger of war.[7]

The second half of Mao's logic was that any compromise or peace between world revolutionary forces and reactionary forces could be achieved only when the former had shown their strength and determination, and the latter were temporarily deterred. A third world war could be best prevented by increasing revolutionary strength. Mao asserted:

[The] compromise between the United States, Britain, France, and the Soviet Union can be the outcome only of resolute, effective struggle by all the democratic forces of the world against the reactionary forces of the United States, Britain, and France.[8]

Clearly, Mao's intention to change the CCP's previous practice of step-by-step micromanaging coordination with Moscow was not to separate the CCP to form a "third bloc"; rather, it was to encourage the Chinese Communists to fight U.S. imperialism in a more aggressive and uncompromising way, even in the face of a temporary detente in U.S.-USSR relations. This technical change in CCP-Moscow relations, however, seemed too weighty to be taken lightly; Mao took extra caution. His directive was circulated in a very small group of top CCP leaders; it was not widely circulated within the Party until the end of 1947.[9] Maybe Mao's caution indicated that he knew how suspicious Stalin could be; thus, in order not to cause the "old brother" to question the CCP's loyalty, Mao wanted to keep his proposed change on the existing pattern of CCP-Moscow cooperation discrete. Maybe Mao did not want to leave any impression in the minds of his rank and file with a weakened CCP-Moscow solidarity.

Given the nature of their personality, it is not surprising that Mao and Stalin were often suspicious of each other, just as they were of their closest comrades. This, however, did not change the fact that they trusted one another's basic value system and commitment. They in fact tried hard to avoid conflict and to cultivate good feelings toward each other. Early in 1946, as we may recall, Stalin sent two physicians to take care of Mao.[10] After Mao had favored Jiang Qing, he sent He Zizheng, his soon-to-be ex-wife, to the USSR for "psychiatric care," and Stalin was readily helpful to provide such care.

In June 1947, thanks to the Soviets' assistance, the CCP had secured its control over northern Manchuria. Mao then told Stalin that he wanted He to take residence in Harbin. Stalin was most cooperative and accommodated Mao's request.[11] On Mao's side, whenever a CCP official was to go to the USSR, Mao would ask the person to pay Stalin a visit on his behalf. For instance, Mao on 30 June 1946 cabled Luo Ronghuan who was about to go to Moscow for medical treatment. Mao told Luo that after his arrival in Moscow, he should go to see "Filipov," Stalin's codified name, to report on the situation in Manchuria.[12]

If Mao was concerned with the incompatibility of his hard-line policy at home and the Soviet conciliatory position at the Paris conference in April 1946, his concern would be alleviated one month later. The Paris foreign ministers' conference ended in the middle of May with no settlement reached. Secretary Byrnes made a militant speech on 20 May, calling for an "offensive to secure peace." Two days later, Senator Vandenberg endorsed Byrnes's report, adding that "eastern Communism and western democracy were unable . . . to see eye to eye on most matters." He disclosed a bipartisan foreign policy of which "getting tough with the Soviets" was its overtone.[13] The CCP immediately sensed the intensification of the cold war atmosphere. Huan Xiang wrote another commentary at the end of May, and he not only summarized the speeches of Byrnes and Vandenberg, but also quoted Molotov's charge that "the U.S. and Britain have already formed an anti-Soviet front." Huan voiced Yan'an's opinion:

> The American policy is twofold. First, it tries to use "dollar diplomacy" to draw Britain and France [into its camp]. The conclusion of huge U.S. loans to Britain and France . . . indicated the U.S. intention to form a U.S.-Britain alliance as a center; and then, surrounding this center, to sustain a western European bloc. . . . Second, the U.S. is using the psychology of fear of the atomic bomb to launch a continuous nerve-warfare against the Soviet Union, hoping that the USSR would come to American terms.[14]

When the cold war tension between the U.S. and the USSR escalated in the latter half of 1946, Yan'an noticed signs of Moscow's willingness to openly stand behind the CCP against *Mei-Jiang*. For instance, on 3 July, Moscow radio broadcast that "if there were no U.S. assistance, the Chinese reactionaries would not dare to act blatantly. However, the scheme of the Chinese reactionaries has been met with determined opposition from the Chinese ordinary people . . . the CCP and other democratic parties have developed into a powerful force. . . ." This message was immediately translated and printed in a CCP publication.[15]

In early July, Yan'an observed that the atmosphere of the second Paris Conference of the foreign ministers appeared conciliatory again. But, Yan'an also noticed that Moscow's conciliatory attitude toward European issues paralleled its hardening position against the GMD government in China. On 5 July, the Americans and the British proposed to invite the Chinese Government to the European Peace Conference, but the Soviet Union refused to endorse it. On the same day, both *Pravda* and *Izvestia* published articles condemning the GMD for inciting civil war and jeopardizing the PCC resolutions. The Soviets also condemned the U.S. policy of colonizing China.[16] Yan'an had no doubt that Moscow approved its position to fight in China regardless of the temporary decrease of tension between the U.S. and the USSR.

MAO'S ATTEMPT TO FORM AN ANTI-AMERICAN UNITED FRONT

The CCP's concept of the united front was operating in three different dimensions in late 1946. If the CCP continued to search for rifts between the U.S. and the GMD in the early half of 1946, the united front tactics aiming at winning over the United States gradually turned into a united front against the United States after June 1946. In the face of a total civil war and continued U.S. aid to the GMD, the Communists' effort in using the Americans to check Jiang was diminishing. Since the CCP had come to identify the U.S. as their primary enemy at home and abroad, the priority of the CCP's united front tactics shifted to the other two dimensions: an attempt to organize a "domestic patriotic united front," and an "international united front for peace."

The last week of June was a turning point in the CCP's united front policy from "with" to "against" the United States. Due to the continuous U.S. military assistance to the GMD in the face of a full-scale war between the CCP and the GMD, Yan'an came to the conclusion that the U.S. government was manipulating the GMD, which was only a "running dog" of American imperialism. On 25 June, Yan'an issued a statement which read:

> Under the slogan of the "open door" policy, the United States is imposing all demands [defined by] the unequal treaties on China, in order to turn China into America's Philippines and Latin America, to let U.S. imperialists control China's domestic and foreign policy, to make China a puppet serving the imperialists' armed anti-Soviet, anti-Communist purpose. . . . As for the price, the U.S. imperialists mobilize all military, financial, and diplomatic resources to support the dictatorial and civil-war-loving GMD government.[17]

The CCP's anti-American position was further hardened due to the U.S. Marines' clash with the CCP in Anping on 29 July, and the GMD's air raid on Yan'an on 2 August. Yan'an took these events as a serious challenge directly from the United States.[18] In order to defeat the "*Mei-Jiang* reactionary clique," Mao labored hard to form an anti-American united front with other political forces in China. However, there were not many Chinese who were willing to fight the Americans for the sake of the Russians, and people tended to view the CCP as a client of Moscow. During the Sino-Soviet conflict in 1929 over the Manchurian railway, the CCP was on the side of the USSR, publicly upholding the slogan of "defending the Soviet Union, the socialist fatherland," and that made the Communists very embarrassed in front of their countrymen. To avoid such a political setback, they became more careful in projecting their relations with Moscow in public.

The CCP also noticed that the U.S. press had been arguing that U.S. policy was to contain Soviet expansion, and many Chinese people believed that the U.S. had to support Jiang as the only choice to prevent China from falling under Russia's dominance and becoming a Soviet satellite.[19] Therefore, to label U.S. foreign policy as anti-Soviet was to identify any anti-American program as pro-Soviet. To breach this logic in people's minds, Mao tried hard to portray U.S. anti-Soviet rhetoric as a "smoke screen," intended to cover Washington's policy of global expansion, of which the victims were not the Soviet Union but nations in the intermediate zone, such as China. If the CCP had argued that the United States intended to turn China into an anti-Soviet base before June 1946, this argument was noticeably minimized in the CCP press by the end of 1946. The CCP now wanted people to believe that the U.S. intention in China was to turn it into an American colony, and the anti-Soviet rhetoric was only a mask to cover Washington's true designs. Qiaomu (Qiao guanhua's pen name), another leading CCP commentator on international affairs, wrote an article entitled "Unmask the U.S. Imperialists." He claimed that "the U.S. goal of colonizing China under the name of establishing an anti-Soviet base has been deeply shaken by the Chinese people's heroic struggle."[20] A CCP editorial made the point more explicit. It was entitled "Enlarge the Patriotic United Front," which stated:

> For sixteen months, the U.S. imperialists have been selling the idea of an anti-Soviet war in China, but their intention is to make anti-Soviet noise to mask their anti-Chinese interventionist policy. . . . [We] regard the Sino-American Commercial and Navigation Agreement signed on November 14 as a new national humiliation [*guochi*]. . . . We shall resolutely resist [the U.S. invasion] to protect China's national independence, to purge the new national humiliation. . . .[21]

Parallel with this anti-American patriotic united front, the CCP also intended to form an international anti-American united front. Mao and his colleagues were keenly aware that there was conflict within the United States and between the U.S. and European capitalist countries. The attempt to establish an international anti-American united front was precisely Mao's purpose when he explained his "international-zone" theory to Anna Louis Strong. Mao put two tea cups on the table to represent the U.S. and the USSR; then, he put a few small liquor cups to surround the "U.S. tea cup" to indicate the people in the U.S. He told Strong that the current propaganda about an anti-Soviet war "is a smoke screen put up by the U.S. reactionaries to cover many actual contradictions between the U.S. reactionaries and the American people, and the contradictions between U.S. imperialism with European capitalist countries and with the colonial and semicolonial countries."[22] The contradictions between the U.S. government and the people were the basis for the united front from below, and the contradictions between the U.S. and European capitalist countries were the basis for the united front from above. Mao tried to promote both.

Since Strong was an American journalist, Mao wanted her to pass on his message. He said that

> at present, the actual significance of the U.S. slogan of waging an anti-Soviet war is the oppression of the American people. . . . To start a war, the U.S. reactionaries must first attack the American people. They are already attacking the American people—oppressing the workers and democratic circles in the United States politically and economically and preparing to impose fascism there. The people of the United States should stand up and resist the attacks of the U.S. reactionaries. I believe they will.[23]

Throughout 1946–47, CCP newspapers and magazines continuously reported news about U.S. workers' strikes, and the "get-the-boys-home" movement, and Wallace's opposition to Truman's policy gained attention in the CCP's press as well. The Communists believed that after the end of the external war, the internal class conflict in the U.S. would naturally worsen. Activating popular opposition to the U.S. government, the CCP hoped, would check U.S. imperialist world expansion.

If the U.S. reactionaries overcome their domestic opposition, Mao continued to tell Strong, they would run counter to European capitalist countries. To illustrate his point, he put cups of various sizes, a matchbox, and an ashtray in between cups representing the U.S. and the USSR, and explained:

> The United States and the Soviet Union are separated by a vast zone which includes many capitalist, colonial, and semicolonial countries in Europe, Asia, and Africa. Before the U.S. reactionaries have subjugated these countries, an attack on the Soviet Union is out of the question. . . . Using various pretexts, the United States is making large-scale military arrangements and setting up military bases in many countries. . . . True, these military bases are directly against the Soviet Union. At present, however, it is not the Soviet Union but the countries in which these military bases are located that are the first to suffer U.S. aggression.[24]

Apparently, the CCP saw the world democratic forces as consisting of three parts: the people in the United States, in other capitalist countries, and in colonial and semicolonial countries. The Soviet Union was the pillar of these world democratic forces. In opposition were the reactionary elements in these countries, such as Churchill in Britain and de Gaulle in France, who were pursuing a policy of relying upon the U.S. and opposing their own people, and people wanted independence and cooperation with the Soviet Union. The famous article by Lu Dingyi called for a "worldwide united front against U.S. imperialism and its running dogs, for world peace and democracy, for the independence of every nation."[25]

Mao's effort to forge an anti-American international united front was in close coordination with Stalin's policy in late 1946. The CCP observed that on 24 September and 28 October, Stalin had interviews with western journalists, in which he claimed that there was no immediate danger of war, and he was optimistic about the UN's role in maintaining world peace. On 29 October, Molotov proposed a plan for arms reduction at a UN conference and expressed Soviet willingness to compromise with England and France. The CCP seized the opportunity to emphasize that the Soviet concession was made in places where the Americans pretended to be the protector of British interests. With Soviet concessions in these areas, the Anglo-American conflict would rise to the surface.[26] The CCP also insisted that the Soviet socialist system guaranteed its commitment to world peace, which was further strengthened by two factors in the West. First, the people in other countries supported the peace policy, and they were, to a certain extent, capable of forcing their governments to accept the Soviet peace initiative. Second, the ruling circles in these countries were in conflict with each other. They could not unite to form an anti-Soviet "holy alliance."[27]

Since the CCP identified the Soviet Union with the "world democratic forces" in opposition to the U.S.-led reactionary forces, and considered its own struggle against the *Mei-Jiang* a part of the global struggle, it was absolutely impossible for Mao to even think about creating a third bloc independent of both the U.S. and the USSR. As Mao stated to Strong,

> The Soviet Union is a defender of world peace and a powerful factor preventing the domination of the world by the U.S. reactionaries. Because of the existence of the Soviet Union, it is absolutely impossible for the reactionaries in the United States and the world to realize their ambitions. That is why the U.S. reactionaries rabidly hate the Soviet Union and actually dream of destroying this socialist state.[28]

In fact, Mao's intermediate-zone theory, which downplayed the link between the "peoples' struggle against U.S. imperialism" in China and elsewhere and the Soviet interest, was only for public consumption. Privately, Mao continued to speak of "cooperation with the Soviet Union." For instance, he said to Zhou Enlai and others on 1 September 1946 that "the consciousness of the people in various countries is rising daily, and progressive public opinion is also developing rapidly. In cooperation with the Soviet Union, people's determined actions against reactionaries in various countries have made the world situation in favor of the democratic camp, not the reactionary camp."[29] His internationalistic outlook was made most explicit in his private conversation with Liu Shaoqi and Zhou Enlai on 21 November, as quoted in the outset of this chapter. He also asserted that the contradiction between the U.S. and other capitalist nations had become the main contradiction of the world; therefore, the CCP's united front had a broad basis.[30]

Evidently, Mao's intermediate-zone theory was not a departure from the Party's traditional view of a polarized postwar world, but a repetition of it with some new elaborations. The CCP's two-camp concept of the postwar world order was vividly depicted by Mao's "two-cup" layout: one represented the U.S. and the other the USSR. The small cups, the matchbox, and the ashtray which stood in between did not and should not form a separate bloc. In Mao's opinion, they should be mobilized or utilized to fight the "U.S. cup." Because this "two-cup" outlook underlined the intermediate-zone theory, the CCP was well positioned to endorse the "two-camp" concept when the Cominform officially adopted it at the end of 1947.

THE CCP AND THE COLD WAR: 1947

The essential message conveyed in Mao's intermediate-zone theory was the determination to fight U.S. imperialism and its "running dog" in China, and the formation of an anti-American united front at home and abroad. Formulated in the latter half of 1946, these concepts in Mao's theory also provided the Party the principles for its action in 1947. As a matter of fact, Mao's interview with Strong was made public by the CCP media only in the middle of 1947, while Mao's "Some Points in Appraisal of the Present International Situation" was made known to the Party at large only at the end of that year. If the intermediate-zone theory was a manifestation of Mao's ideology of communist internationalism, it also dictated the CCP's policy in 1947.

The year 1947 began with the end of the Marshall Mission, which was followed by the announcement of the "Truman Doctrine" and the GMD's successful attack on Yan'an in March. The intensification of both the cold war and the civil war made the Communists' anti-American sentiment much stronger, and their perception of the evil nature of U.S. imperialism much sharper. On 7 January, Marshall was appointed Secretary of State, and three days later, the Truman administration announced its 1948 budget, of which military related expenditures counted 70 percent of the total, according to CCP propaganda. The Communists also observed that Wallace went on the air to say that the United States was marching toward war against the Soviet Union, but his voice was weak and unheeded by Washington. Truman, with his "get-tough" attitude, won the upper hand. The Communists came to embrace the idea that the U.S. was on the path toward "military imperialism."[31]

Mao and his colleagues came to view the postwar domestic development in the U.S. along the ideological line of Marxism-Leninism and they believed that due to the wartime economic boom the United States had developed an unprecedented level of monopoly capitalism. Wartime profit went into the pockets of about one hundred big firms which received 67 percent of the government military contracts. Wartime profit made these monopoly businesses economically powerful and politically influential. On the other hand, the war had produced a group of "warlords," such as Leahy, MacArthur, Wedemeyer, and Marshall, who, in the opinion of the CCP, controlled U.S. domestic and foreign policy making. The Communists concluded that "the master of the White House now is not really a representative of a particular party, but that of a fascist clique of financial magnates and reactionary warlords." To consolidate their power and to create the situation for more wartime profit, this "fascist clique" in the White House was pursuing a policy of war. The Communists predicted that with the inevitable and forthcoming economic crisis, this U.S. reactionary trend would worsen.[32]

Regarding the U.S. role in China, Mao and his comrades concluded that American imperialists intended to colonize China along the same lines as the United States did the Philippines. They saw that the independence of the Philippines in 1946 was a political joke: the Philippine President was a former Japanese puppet, and the U.S. forced the Philippine Parliament to accept the Bell Act which imposed on the Filipinos a system of preferential tariffs and forced the Philippines to give special constitutional rights to U.S. capital. The U.S. also supported the reactionaries and collaborators there, in exchange for the maintenance of U.S. military bases. The CCP declared that such "democracy" and "independence" given by the United States was virtually worthless. "What the Chinese people need is the kind of democracy that is won by the people," not that "granted" by the U.S.[33] On 1 February 1947, Mao addressed the Party:

> The circumstances . . . [in China] are that U.S. imperialism and its running dog Jiang Jieshi have replaced Japanese imperialism and its running dog Wang Ching-wei and have adopted the policies of turning China into a U.S. colony, launching a civil war, and strengthening the fascist dictatorship.[34]

The other side of the coin of CCP hostility toward the United States was the intimate relationship between the CCP and Moscow, which both sides involved tried to conceal as much as possible. In the face of the GMD-CCP civil war raging throughout the nation, the United States continued to assist the GMD overtly, while the Soviet Union was covertly backing the CCP with military supplies and diplomatic coordination. This CCP-Moscow vs. GMD-Washington conflict continued throughout 1946–47, which was an important part of the hidden history of the cold war in Asia.[35]

According to recent CCP sources of information, Soviet material support to the CCP after the withdrawal of the Red Army was essentially delivered from the city of Dalian and North Korea, both of which were under Soviet direct control. For instance, Xiao Jingguang, the deputy commander of CCP forces in Manchuria, went to Dalian in July 1946 to arrange the Party's military production in the city. At the time, the GMD had occupied the south of the Songhua (Sungari) River, which made it impossible to keep the CCP troops in southern Manchuria supplied from the northern base. The only point in southern Manchuria which could keep producing military supplies for the CCP forces was Dalian, because it was occupied by the Soviets. Xiao went there, and was pleased to find that, from the head of the police force to the head of the financial department, all administrative posts of the municipal government were in the hands of Communist cadres. Relying upon these cadres, CCP military production in that city was well maintained throughout the period of the civil war. There are no available statistics on the volume of Dalian's military production for the CCP's war effort during these years. According to Xiao, however, it "made a great contribution to the victory in the Liberation War."[36]

The other place which served as the source of the CCP's military supplies was North Korea. After his trip to Dalian, Xiao spent two months in North Korea to establish the "Delegation of the Northeast Bureau to Korea" (*Dongbeiju zhu chaoxian banshichu*), known publicly as the Pyongyang Limin Company. It had four branches in Korea, whose main task was to organize the supply, storage, and transportation of military materials for the CCP forces. Zhu Lizhi, later the deputy of the Logistics Department of the CCP forces in Manchuria, was in charge of this "Limin Company." The number of people working in one of the branches exceeded five hundred at one time. According to incomplete statistics, in the first seven months of 1947, there were 210,000 tons of war materials transferred to the CCP through North Korea. The figure in 1948 increased to 300,900 tons. Before the "Company" was closed in February 1949, it obtained enough military cargo from the Soviet–North Korea source to fill more than 2,000 rail cars to ship to Manchuria. It also helped the CCP Shandong logistics department to buy and ship military supplies from North Korea.[37]

At the same time, CCP-Moscow mutual consultation and coordination on diplomatic matters was also becoming closer in 1947. On 17 February 1947, just before the second Moscow conference of the Big Four foreign ministers in March, Moscow consulted Mao as to whether or not the Chinese domestic situation should be included in the discussion at the conference, and what Mao had to suggest in terms of a common position taken at the forthcoming conference in relation to the China issue. Zhou Enlai replied immediately on behalf of Mao, and suggested that the noninterference of foreign powers in China's domestic affairs and the withdrawal of U.S. forces from China be raised at the conference. He also proposed that in principle the U.S. should terminate its military and financial aid to Jiang in the civil war, and the CCP should be given equal recognition in any international discussions on China's situation. If the conference would not accept these terms, Zhou said, Molotov should raise them anyway just for the sake of propaganda.[38]

On 12 March, when the Moscow conference was held to review the agreements on China's postwar settlement reached at the first Moscow Foreign Ministers' Conference in December 1945, Molotov criticized the United States for stationing U.S. troops in China and taking sides in China's domestic conflict. To coordinate with the Soviet diplomatic move, Zhou made a public statement, which condemned U.S. imperialism in China along a similar line.[39] Moreover, the Soviets refused the GMD's request to take part in the discussion on China's situation at the conference. In response, the GMD stirred up mass protests in China against the USSR, arguing that as one of the five permanent members of the UN Security Council, the Chinese government had the right to take part in any postwar settlement, let alone those related to China. The CCP promptly came to the defense of the Soviet position by condemning the GMD for its treasonous collaboration with U.S. imperialism, which was inflicting much damage on China in the civil war and would reduce China to the status of a U.S. colony. The CCP also demanded the right to represent China in international discussions should the GMD be invited.[40] Apparently, a close coordination between Moscow and the CCP in what they called the "diplomatic front" started then, and it was to be greatly enhanced as the CCP approached a nationwide victory in 1949.

Although the CCP was fully occupied with military affairs in 1947, especially after Yan'an was taken by the GMD army in March, the Party's involvement in eastern-bloc activities was as active as it could have been under the circumstances. Shortly before the CCP was forced out of Yan'an, Zhou Enlai organized the Foreign Affairs Group (*waishizhu*) under which there were offices of foreign affairs in the structure of the Northeast and Hong Kong Bureaus.[41] Situated in those locations, the CCP was actively participating in the bloc activities sponsored by Moscow. For instance, Zhou cabled the Northeast Bureau on 24 May 1946, which disclosed that Liu Ningyi, the CCP's leading figure in trade union activities, had already become a regular representative in the World Federation of Trade Unions. Zhou demanded that efforts be made to send regular representatives to work in the World Federation of Democratic Youth and the Women's International Democratic Federation as well.[42] When Zhou learned that the International Organization of Journalists was established in Prague, he cabled the Northeast Bureau again on 19 June 1947, instructing that a CCP compatible organization be established immediately, and its representatives sent to Prague.[43] Although the CCP and its Liberated Areas were not officially recognized by Moscow and other Eastern European countries, the partnership, bloc solidarity, and diplomatic ties between them were obvious.

The CCP's perception of a polarized world well prepared it to adopt the "two-camp" formula expounded by Zhdanov in his inaugural speech at the Cominform at the end of 1947. To Moscow, the "warmongers" of the anti-Soviet camp included not only the western governments, but also "their socialist lackeys."[44] Apparently, Stalin was concerned that the Marshall Plan would undermine the loyalty of the Eastern European countries toward Moscow. Thus, the emphasis on the "national particularity" of various countries' anti-American struggle would damage the unity of the socialist camp and Moscow's leadership in it. If the Zhdanov two-camp formula reflected Stalin's turn toward an antinationalist position in order to secure Soviet control over Eastern Europe, Mao followed Stalin's lead very quickly. He addressed a meeting of the Party Center in December 1947:

> After the victorious conclusion of the antifascist Second World War, U.S. imperialism and its lackeys in various countries stepped into the shoes of German and Japanese imperialism and their lackeys had formed a reactionary camp against the Soviet Union, against the People's Democracies in Europe, against the workers' movement in the capitalist countries, against the national movements in the colonies and semicolonies and against the liberation of the Chinese people.... The anti-imperialist camp headed by the Soviet Union has already been formed.[45]

Evidently, in line with Stalin's change of policy, Mao's intermediate-zone theory was quietly replaced by a more rigid formula of two-camp struggle, which Mao held true until the end of the 1950s. Since there was not much room for the CCP to carry out its united-front diplomacy in the international community, the Party's united front activities in 1947 actually concentrated on the domestic scene, namely, the effort to constitute a "second front" of national struggle against *Mei-Jiang* under the name of patriotism.

THE "SECOND FRONT" OF THE CCP: 1947

In late 1946, the popularity of the United States and the GMD government suffered a great setback in the Chinese political arena. Two preeminent professors and members of the Democratic League, Li Gongpu and Wen Yiduo, were assassinated by GMD extremists because of their sharp criticism of the GMD regime. That triggered a massive wave of anti-GMD protests in Chinese urban areas. Students, often supported by their professors, were the front-runners of the movement, while the Democratic League and other small parties of the "third force" hardened their policy in opposition to the GMD. When the GMD convened the National Assembly in November without CCP participation, these alienated "third forces" boycotted the GMD assembly as well.[46] The rape by a U.S. Marine of a female student in Beijing University on Christmas Eve made the CCP effort in stirring up anti-American sentiment among the Chinese more successful. In Beiping, Shanghai, and other major Chinese cities, students walked out of their classrooms, and took to the streets. Mass demonstrations and rallies against the Americans made U.S. prestige drop rapidly among the Chinese population.

To muster popular support for their struggle against *Mei-Jiang*, the Communists had made every effort to identify the United States with Japan, and Jiang's regime with that of Wang Jingwei. They had been calling for a patriotic united front for independence, democracy, and peace, in opposition to the GMD policy of "selling out China, dictatorship, and civil war." Now, in the beginning of 1947, their efforts seemed to be working well. They were encouraged to enlarge their influence in China's urban areas to form a "second front" in cooperation with their military front in combating the U.S.-backed GMD in the countryside. On 6 January, the Party Center telegraphed its leaders in the GMD-controlled areas that

> regarding the [organization of] students' anti-American demonstrations in Beiping, Tianjin, Nanjing, and Shanghai, the result is very good, the influence great. . . . [Now,] the base of the patriotic and democratic movement is enlarging daily. It starts to be able to cooperate with the self-defense war in the Liberated Areas. . . . In order to make the patriotic and democratic movement under the banner of nationalism persistent for a long time to come, our Party should help the newly emerged activists to get organized.[47]

On 1 February, Zhou Enlai formally suggested at a CCP Politburo meeting that the people's movement in the urban areas should be taken as the "second front" against *Mei-Jiang*. His proposal was incorporated into the directive of the meeting, which called for brave actions to welcome the forthcoming high tide of the Chinese revolution.[48] The CCP tactics in attracting the people's political sympathy and support were twofold: first, to place the responsibility for the civil war solely on the GMD; and second, to identify the GMD as treasonous, selling out Chinese sovereignty and interests to the United States. It is worth noting that in a few rare cases the word "nationalism" (*minzu zhuyi*) was used in the CCP document. The CCP's use of nationalism here was obviously a propaganda technique, catering to an audience of urban dwellers who were, by Marxist definition, "petty bourgeoisie"; therefore, receptive to the appeal of nationalism. This utilitarian, if not cynical, use of the concept revealed that nationalism was not the "faith" of the Communists, who nevertheless would use it for their specific purposes.

The CCP's use of "nationalism" to incite hatred of the U.S. among urban populations was rather effective. In the postwar era the GMD regime faced a profound economic-financial crisis, and the people in the GMD-controlled urban areas suffered the most. The Communists spared no effort to exploit the difficulties of their foe. On 8 March, a Party Center directive to Liu Xiao, the CCP leader in Shanghai, stated that the general policy of the CCP was to overthrow the dictatorship of the GMD through coordination between the "patriotic self-defense war" in the countryside and the people's "patriotic and democratic movement" in urban areas. The Party should consider programs which related to the hardship of people's livelihood and their struggle for survival, so as to mobilize the masses for further and lasting struggle against *Mei-Jiang*.[49]

To this end, the Communists made efforts to link China's economic crisis and the civil war with the U.S. policy of "colonizing China." They emphasized that the roots of China's hyperinflation were the U.S.-sponsored civil war, the flood of U.S. goods and surpluses into China's market, and the monopoly of "bureaucratic capitalism" headed by the four families of Jiang and his henchmen.[50] The CCP's efforts in agitating and organizing the people, especially the students, in the GMD-held urban areas were highly successful. In the week following 20 May, China's major cities witnessed a massive wave of student protests against the civil war and the poverty allegedly caused by *Mei-Jiang*. Mao was so excited by these protests that he wrote an article for the New China News Agency to be broadcast on 30 May. This article became the guideline for the CCP propaganda. It reads:

> Now a second front has emerged, that is, the sharp struggle between the great and righteous student movement and the reactionary Jiang Jieshi government. The slogan of the student movement is "Food, Peace, Freedom" or "Against Hunger, Against Civil War, Against Persecution". . . . Since U.S. imperialism and its running dog Jiang Jieshi have taken the place of Japanese imperialism and its running dog Wang Jingwei and adopted the policy of turning China into a U.S. colony . . . they have declared themselves to be enemies of the entire Chinese people and driven all strata of the people to the brink of starvation and death. . . .[51]

Although the eight-year war with Japan was over, painful memories and anti-Japanese sentiment remained strong among the Chinese population. In 1947, the U.S. started to pursue a policy of restoring Japan as its ally in the Far East as a part of its "containment strategy." The Chinese were furious about this new development, and the CCP tried immediately to cash in on it. When the GMD government also protested against U.S. policy on the issue of Japanese reparations, the New China News Agency in North Shaanxi described the GMD as the "concubine of America," jealously courting favor in competition with Japan, as well as deceiving the Chinese people.[52] The CCP's tactics worked well in shifting the Chinese anti-Japanese patriotism toward a new anti-*Mei-Jiang* direction.

When President Truman sent General Wedemeyer to China on a "fact-finding" tour in the summer of 1947, the CCP's anti-American activities intensified. On 21 August, the Party instructed its underground organizations in the GMD area to "propagate the facts" of Jiang's treasonable activities and the U.S. evil deeds in China, "in order to inspire the people's nationalist sentiment."[53] On the same day, the CCP broadcast in North Shaanxi told its audience a story: Admiral Cooke, the Commander in Chief of U.S. Marines in Qingtao, was said to be upset because his dog disappeared on 29 June. "The GMD authorities were greatly disturbed by the irritation and moodiness of the master." The mayor of Qingdao dispatched policemen to find the missing pet. At the same time, five innocent Chinese people were killed by U.S. sentries in Qingtao within one week. "But these successive events went by without causing any concern to the GMD authorities who were even too lazy to find out victims' names."[54] The aforementioned Party directive instructed CCP local organizations that the New China News Agency would broadcast a commentary of importance and they should listen attentively. Apparently, such CCP anti-American propaganda was directed by the highest leadership of the Party. Those propaganda materials would be repeated by other CCP propaganda organs throughout China.

The CCP tried to seize every opportunity to "expose U.S. imperialism" to "educate" the people so that the anti-American "patriotic united front" could be enlarged. It is no surprise that when the Communists were triumphantly marching into major cities in 1948–49, their fundamental anti-American-imperialism continued to direct the Party's policy toward the United States, while the united front technique would be utilized at the same time.

CHAPTER VIII

Mao's Revolutionary Diplomacy and the Cold War in Asia, 1948–1949

American imperialists' China policy has shifted
from a one-sided policy of supporting the GMD's military
effort against the CCP to a two-sided policy. . . .
They will send their running dogs to penetrate into the
revolutionary camp to organize so-called opposition in
order to sabotage the revolution from within. When
the PLA is close to nationwide victory, [the U.S.] will
use the recognition of the People's Republic as a means
to achieve legal status so that they can carry out
such a policy of sabotage from within.
—*Mao Zedong, January 1949*

In 1948–49, the cold war in Europe was escalating drastically, leading toward the explosive situation during the Berlin crisis. In China, Mao's communist forces turned from a defensive position to an offensive one first, and then began wiping out the GMD troops in a series of stunning military victories. Nanjing fell in the spring of 1949; the CCP Beijing regime was established in the fall. Mao then went to Moscow to sign a treaty of military alliance with Stalin early in 1950; and by the end of that year, Mao's "volunteers" were fighting the Americans in Korea. The cold war confrontation thus evolved into an armed conflict in Asia, while it reached a status quo in Europe.

Some scholars view Mao as a beholder of "Chinese national interest" which was being threatened by Stalin's Russian imperialism. In order to counterbalance the pressure from China's northern border, Mao passed on a series of friendly overtures to the United States, seeking recognition and help from Washington on the eve of the proclamation of the PRC. It was, they argue, the unevenhanded U.S. China policy and U.S. rejection of Mao's pursuit of friendship and diplomatic accommodation with the U.S. that forced the CCP into Moscow's embrace.[1] In short, Mao's "lean-to-one-side" policy was only a response to the "mistaken" policy made by the United States.[2] However, the new historical evidence suggests that Mao was driven by his revolutionary commitment which had been confirmed and reinforced by the "reality" as he saw it. The Mao-Stalin secret radio communications became more active than ever before, due to the need to coordinate their policies. Yet, Mao continued to play "diplomacy" with the U.S. including sending out disinformation to confuse the Americans so that a possible U.S. direct intervention against the CCP's takeover could be avoided or delayed. The CCP's ideological-psychological, political-institutional, and military-strategic ties with Moscow determined the Beijing regime a natural ally of Moscow, and a hostile opponent to Washington in the cold war international environment; the Sino-Soviet alliance of 1950 was only a logical end-product of the long history of the CCP-Moscow partnership. There was never a "chance" for Washington to win over the CCP as an ally in the anti-Soviet front.

The basic principles of Mao's diplomacy in 1948–49 were best summarized by Zhou Enlai in 1952, when he made a speech to the staff of the PRC Foreign Ministry. Using Mao's typical peasant language, Zhou described these principles as follows: First, *lingqi luzao* (to build a new stove), which meant to cook one's food in a new way. Zhou explained that the new regime established after the victory of the 1911 revolution inherited the old Sino-West relations characterized by the unequal treaties because the new government hoped to obtain foreign recognition quickly. "We should not do the same. . . ." Zhou claimed, "*lingqi luzao* is not to recognize the old diplomatic relations between the GMD government and various countries, but to establish totally new diplomatic relations on a new basis. . . . We shall wait and see whether or not they [western powers] will accept our principles for establishing diplomatic relations."[3] The CCP was determined not to follow the diplomatic convention of the international community, but to revolutionize China's relations with the West through isolating the nation from the West for a period of time, until the western powers were ready to accept the CCP's terms.

Second, "*dasao ganjing wuzi zai qingke*," meaning to clean up the house first, then invite guests. The CCP was well aware that the West and the United States would be hostile to their domestic programs, namely, the establishment of the "proletarian dictatorship" and a state-controlled economy. To prevent unwanted interference from hostile outsiders, the simplest if not the best way was to shut them out when the Party was putting the house in order. Clearly, the CCP took its domestic programs as the highest priority, and considered them as being in conflict with inviting diplomatic recognition by the West; therefore, the invitation of western "guests" had to be postponed in order to safeguard the Party's efforts to consolidate its power at home. In other words, the CCP's priority in establishing a Soviet-style "house order" necessitated a self-imposed isolation from the West.

Third, "*Yibiandao*," meaning "lean to one side," the Soviet side. Since the CCP had decided to revolutionize China's relations with western powers and to impose self-isolation from the West, it naturally desired a close alliance with the Soviet Union and the eastern bloc. The Communists were convinced that Moscow would surely support its revolutionary diplomacy and radical domestic programs. With the Soviet Union and the "socialist camp" behind it, the

CCP would find it easier to ride out this period of self-isolation from the West. Mao-Stalin relations became more intimate than ever before.

CCP-MOSCOW SOLIDARITY

Although the formula of *yibiandao* first appeared in Mao's article published in the summer of 1949, the CCP's ideological, political, and historical ties with Moscow determined the Party's natural inclination toward a pro-Soviet policy. Zhou Enlai reportedly said to Marshall early on that "of course we will lean to one side. But how far depends upon you."[4] With the intensification of both the cold war abroad and the civil war at home, Mao felt a greater need to consult and coordinate with Stalin in 1948–49, especially when he sensed that the U.S. was the only force that could block his way to national power.

In January 1948, Mao had several conversations with Chen Yi, the CCP commander in eastern China. Mao said that due to CCP victory in 1947, a "nationwide revolutionary offensive" to topple Jiang's regime had started. The question the CCP faced at the time was how to march into Sichuan, Guangdong, and Guangxi provinces. The United States, Mao claimed, advised Jiang to give up Manchuria, to defend North China, to reinforce the defense line along the Yangzi River, and to consolidate South China. Mao was apparently concerned with the possibility of U.S. direct intervention on Jiang's behalf as the CCP marched toward the South. He said:

> [We] are not going to eliminate Jiang as a person; we are going to extinguish his clique and the class he represents. Imperialist countries will, [therefore] for sure, intervene in our revolutionary country, and their ways of intervention can vary. If [the U.S.] sends its armies to participate in the war, [we] can defeat them as well. . . . The United States has a few years to play tough. If we are going to be scared by this, we will be playing right into their hand; but if we are not going to be scared by the U.S., we can win.[5]

In Mao's mind, it was clear that the U.S. was the main enemy of his revolution. In his telegram to the Hong Kong and Shanghai Bureaus on 7 May 1948, Mao said that the Party was to establish a "democratic coalition," and the first step was to convene a political consultation conference. The non-CCP organizations and personnel should be selected, and the essential criteria for the selection was one's "anti-American and anti-Jiang stand," Mao claimed. There was no indication whatsoever throughout 1948 that Mao thought about a possible compromise, let alone a friendship, with the U.S.

In the summer of 1948, a rumor reached Mao that the U.S. was considering replacing Jiang with the Guangxi Clique led by Li Zhongren. The possible U.S. abandonment of Jiang could no longer please Mao and reduce his animosity toward the U.S. He and Zhou wrote a directive on 1 August:

The current policy of the U.S. State Department is still to sustain Jiang's anti-CCP activities. At the same time, the U.S. is discontent with Jiang's inability and military defeat. [The U.S. recent move] was to force Jiang to yield more power so that when the Jiang camp collapses the U.S. can unite various other reactionary cliques (including possibly a portion of the bourgeoisie) for the common cause of anti-communism. Thus, the State Department is plotting all sorts of activities in the dark, including exploring the possibility of negotiating with our Party. . . . We should expose this sort of U.S. plot; but, we should make use of the rift and the anti-Jiang move within the reactionary ruling circle in order to promote more rifts among them.[6]

Mao thought his suspicion of the "U.S. new plot" proven true when he received a report on the observation by an unnamed U.S. news reporter in Hong Kong in December 1948. According to the reporter, the centerpiece of current China policy of the U.S. State Department was how to create an effective opposition to resist the CCP in China's new coalition government. The U.S. would recognize the new coalition under the conditions that the composition of the new government would be acceptable to the U.S., and that American rights to acquire naval and military bases in Shanghai, Qingdao, etc. would be guaranteed by the new government. The U.S. would then resume trade with, and invest in, China. By so doing, the reporter said, the U.S. hoped to sustain the non-CCP forces in the coalition so that they could undermine the CCP's united front with other political forces. Mao took this report so seriously that he immediately sent it to every member of the politburo to read, and he also commented that "this kind of U.S. plot must be watched out by us from now on. We cannot let the American imperialist plot, which aims at the new Political Consultation Conference and coalition, to gain ground." At the Politburo meeting of January 1949, Mao made his point more explicit in the quotation at the outset of this chapter. He also said that "when the PLA is close to nationwide victory, [the U.S.] will even use the recognition of the People's Republic as a means to achieve legal status, in order to carry out such a policy of sabotage from within. We must arouse our vigilance, watching out for this imperialist plot and defeat it resolutely."[7]

Mao's fear of possible U.S. intervention against the CCP in different forms almost reached the state of phobia. In February 1949, Liu Xiao, later China's ambassador to Moscow, went to see Kovalev, Stalin's liaison in China, to pass on a "top secret plan" of the U.S. obtained by a CCP secret agent. According to Liu's information, the U.S. would fight a third world war with the USSR in Asia by allying with Japan and GMD forces. After atomic bomb strikes on targets in Manchuria and Siberia, three million U.S. troops together with millions of GMD and Japanese troops would launch a general offensive to defeat the PLA and Soviet forces in the Far East, and further attacks in the general direction of the Urals would follow. Kovalev immediately reported the CCP intelligence to Stalin, who replied:

War is not profitable for the imperialists. Their crisis has begun and they are not ready to go to war. They try to scare us with the atomic bomb, but we are not afraid of it. . . . The way things are now, America is less prepared for mounting an attack than the USSR is for repulsing one. . . . But history has shown us that there are persons who are not normal. . . . We are prepared to repulse an attack.[8]

It was against this background that Mao intended to go to Moscow to see Stalin in person. If Stalin would stand behind him firmly, Mao had nothing to fear in his struggle against the Americans. As early as the summer of 1947, Mao started planning a personal visit to Moscow in order to discuss with Stalin important issues then facing the CCP. On 15 June 1947, Stalin cabled Mao to suggest that he come to Moscow secretly via Manchuria, and an airplane would be prepared for him. Stalin, however, changed his mind, and sent another cable to Mao on 1 July: "In view of the forthcoming [military] operations, and in view of the fact that Mao Zedong's absence may adversely affect these operations, we consider it preferable to postpone the visit."[9]

Mao, however, persisted that it was necessary to meet Stalin in person. In spring 1948, Stalin agreed that Mao come to Moscow in mid-July. Mao was so excited about the invitation that he cabled Stalin on 26 April 1948 that he would set off for the USSR earlier, because, he said, "I shall take advice and request directions from comrades in the RCP (Russian Communist Party) Central Committee on political, military, economic, and other important issues. . . . In addition, if it is possible, I would like to visit the countries of Eastern and Southeastern Europe to study the work of the popular front and other kinds of work." Mao also mapped out his travel route to Stalin, who gave his consent to Mao's plan on 29 April. On 10 May, apparently based on Mao's further reports on the military situation in China, Stalin suggested that Mao delay his departure, because of the military developments in the areas Mao planned to travel through. In particular, Stalin mentioned the advance of the GMD forces under Fu Zuoyi in Yuxian. "We are worried lest your absence should adversely affect the course of events, and also about the safety of your journey," Stalin said to Mao. "Would it not be better, therefore, for you to postpone your visit to us for a while? Should you decide not to postpone your visit, please let us know where and when we should send an airplane. We await your reply." Mao replied the same day with many thanks to Stalin, and agreed to postpone his trip.[10]

Mao seemed so eager to go to Moscow that he could hardly wait. On 4 July, he cabled Stalin again to propose that he would like to set off on the trip by the end of that month. Stalin replied on 14 July, and asked Mao to postpone the trip until November. This time, Stalin's reason was that it was harvest season, and top party officials would leave for the provinces. Mao seemed skeptical about this, and he told Stalin on 28 August that there were many things he wished to discuss with Stalin, including the CCP's relations with the "third forces" in China, the unity among communist parties in the East, China's economic reconstruction under the CCP, a $30 million (U.S. dollar) loan from the USSR, and the policy regarding the new China's diplomatic relations with the West. Mao emphasized that "we need to agree to ensure that our policy fully coincides with that of the USSR." On 28 September 1948, he telegraphed Stalin to duly report the details of the recently concluded CCP politburo meeting and repeated that there were many important issues "to report personally to the RCP Central Committee and the boss to receive instructions." On 16 October, Mao cabled Stalin again, and this time he added one more issue to discuss, namely, "regarding the convention of the Political Consultation Conference and the establishment of the provisional central government." On 30 December, Mao sent one more telegram to Stalin to report that a CCP leadership meeting was in session and they were discussing military and political strategies for the coming year and the convention of the Second Plenum of the Party. Mao proposed that he visit Moscow immediately after the meeting, and the Second Plenum would be held only after he came back from the Kremlin.[11]

The politburo meeting Mao mentioned was in session on 6–8 January 1949. Immediately after the meeting, Mao cabled Stalin again. This time, Stalin said in his telegram of 14 January that "It is very necessary for you to stay in China right now. If you like, I can send a leading member of our politburo to your place immediately." Mao replied on 17 January: "I decided not to come to Moscow right now. We wholeheartedly welcome you sending a comrade of the politburo to China . . . and he can discuss many issues with the five members of our Central Secretariat. Currently, the main issues [to be discussed] are of the Political Consultation Conference, the coalition government, and diplomatic policy."[12] That was how Mikoyan came to Xibopo in January 1949 to confer with Mao.[13]

Evidently, Mao's persistent request for a personal visit to Moscow was not to have a "showdown" with Stalin to set the record straight, nor did he intend to discuss the bilateral relations between the soon-to-be CCP regime and Moscow, as some popular writers and scholars in the West believe.[14] Rather, Mao wanted to make sure Stalin understood and approved the CCP's policies at home and abroad, thereby improving coordination between the CCP and Moscow in their struggle against *Mei-Jiang*. Mikoyan later explained why Stalin hesitated to let Mao come to Moscow: Besides technical problems such as the current military situation, the safety of the journey and the secrecy of Mao's trip were Stalin's main concerns. Should the secret trip become public knowledge, Mao could have been "named a Moscow agent. This would have been detrimental to the prestige of the CCP and would have been exploited by the imperialists and the Chiang Kaishek clique against the Chinese Communists."[15]

Mikoyan's secret visit started on 30 January 1949. He flew from the Soviet military base in Dalian to Xibopo, and stayed until 8 February. According to Shi Zhe, Mao dominated their talks during the first three days, and his topics ranged from the CCP's military planning and the structure of the proposed CCP government, to economic reconstruction and foreign policy. Regarding foreign policy, Mao stressed two principles: First, the CCP had decided to clean house before inviting guests; second, the new regime would thoroughly abolish all special privileges of western powers in China. "Imperialists have always despised Chinese people, [we should] teach them a lesson now," Mao said. Zhou Enlai met with Mikoyan separately to talk in detail about how to organize the new government, how to conduct its foreign policy, how to control foreign trade, and so on.[16]

There was no sign that the issue of Soviet recognition of the CCP government was ever brought up for serious discussion, simply because it was taken for granted.[17] On the contrary, it was Mikoyan, following Stalin's instruction, who insisted that the CCP take over major cities such as Shanghai and Nanjing, and not to postpone the formation of a revolutionary government in China. Mao, on the other hand, argued that it would be more advantageous to be without a government, because if "we [the CCP] had a government, that would be a coalition government, and that means that we would also have to answer to other parties for our actions, which would only complicate things." Acting as a "revolutionary committee," instead of a coalition government, Mao said, it would help the CCP "purge the country of counterrevolutionary elements."[18] Here, an old pattern in Mao-Stalin relations manifested itself again: Mao was more of a radical revolutionary inclined to simple solutions, while Stalin was more of a tactful statesman who tutored Mao to form a united front with the GMD during the anti-Japanese war, and he continued to correct Mao's radicalism. Had Stalin lived ten years longer, would Mao's Anti-Rightist movement and the Great Leap Forward have happened? One might well argue that from a CCP retrospective, Stalin died too early and Mao lived too long. As will soon be demonstrated, Mao's simplistic radical policy toward western capitalist countries was to shut them out while the CCP was "cleaning its house," and it was again Stalin who advised Mao to seek diplomatic accommodation with the U.S. and other western nations. Mao remained to be more of a radical revolutionary than a mature statesman until his death.

In 1948–49, however, Mao was still maintaining his absolute loyalty to Stalin and the Moscow-led international revolution. When Tito was denounced by Moscow, the CCP promptly published the article "On Internationalism and Nationalism," denouncing "nationalism" in general and Tito's "betrayal" in particular. The article was reprinted in the Cominform's organ immediately.[19] If this article was only a public statement designed to show the CCP's loyalty, a series of inner-party directives at the time addressing the same issue clearly indicated that Mao and the CCP were fully and wholeheartedly in line with Stalin, not Tito. In one of these documents, it was stated that "if the Chinese people hope to win a thorough victory in their revolution, they must reinforce their brother-like alliance with the Soviet Union."[20]

Stalin, too, understood very well the importance of the victory of Chinese revolution to the USSR and to the cause of world communism. He told his aide that

> we will of course give the new China all possible assistance. If socialism is victorious in China and our countries follow a single path, then the victory of socialism in the world will virtually be guaranteed. Nothing will threaten us. Therefore, we cannot withhold any effort or means in our support of the Chinese Communists.[21]

Stalin valued the CCP's cause so highly that he took all the matters related to Mao's Party into his own hands. After Kovalev was sent to China, he addressed a few questions to Molotov and Vyshinsky. But, they replied, "Henceforth address all questions concerning our mission to China to Filipov only." According to Kovalev, "even the most insignificant, parochial requests of Mao Zedong were sent only to him [Stalin]."[22]

The frequency and substance of the Mao-Stalin secret policy consultation in the pre-1950 period are vividly illustrated by seven telegrams of the two men on 10–17 January 1949. Immediately after receiving the GMD government's request for international mediation in the Chinese civil war, Stalin sent Mao a telegram on 10 January 1949. He told Mao that the GMD peace move "was inspired by the Americans," and then he gave Mao the full content of the Soviet government response to the GMD request, asking Mao to offer "a more expedient answer" in case he disagreed with Moscow's draft. The essence of Stalin's response to the GMD was that the CCP must be informed of, and agreeable upon, the conditions of peace negotiations before the Soviet government would offer its "good office." Then, Stalin advised Mao what to say when he was approached by the GMD. Stalin told Mao that the CCP's precondition for negotiations was the exclusion of the GMD "war criminals who provoked the civil war," and that the CCP was "in favor of direct negotiations with the GMD without any foreign mediators," especially "those foreign powers which have played a role in the civil war against the Chinese People's Liberation Army with their armed forces and navy." Stalin was obviously pointing his finger at the United States and Great Britain. To make his position unequivocal, Stalin followed up with another telegram the next day, in which he told Mao that his policy proposal was "designed to undermine the peace negotiations," because the GMD "would not agree to hold peace negotiations without the mediation of foreign countries, especially the United States." "Consequently," Stalin concluded, "the peace overtures from the GMD and the U.S. would be in vain, and you would be able to continue your victorious war of liberation."[23] These telegrams clearly indicate that Stalin did not intend to force Mao to negotiate in 1949, thereby creating a divided China along the Yangzi River, as some scholars have argued.

Mao, however, appeared to be unwilling to negotiate with the GMD at all.

In his reply to Stalin on 12 January, Mao was not the least hesitant to give Stalin his version of what the Soviet response to the GMD ought to be. In essence, he wanted Stalin to reject the GMD request for mediation outright. Mao even told Stalin that if the Soviet Union agreed to mediate in principle, despite the impossible preconditions attached, "it would convince the United States, Britain, and France that it is appropriate for them to participate in the mediation while at the same time providing the GMD with a pretext to accuse us of being warmongers." In conclusion, Mao told Comrade Stalin that "the balance of class power in China has already experienced a fundamental change. We do not need to take politically evasive action again."

In response, Stalin sent Mao a telegram on 14 January, arguing that an out-right rejection meant that "you put your trump card on the table and give away an important weapon—the banner of peace—to the GMD," and that also would give the U.S. an excuse for armed intervention against the CCP. Despite a slight sense of being annoyed, the basic tone of Stalin's message was more persuasive than instructive or argumentative. He altered his response to the GMD to include Mao's idea that foreign mediation was not needed, and he offered Mao detailed advice on what the CCP should do if the GMD either rejected or accepted Mao's terms. He even went out of his way to reassure Mao that his policy proposal was "a piece of advice only, which should not bind you to anything," and his response to the GMD "will be in accordance with your [Mao's] opinion."

Mao responded to Stalin's telegram on the same day, stating that he com-pletely agreed with Stalin. He also informed Stalin that he had just announced eight conditions for negotiations with the GMD, the first of which was Stalin's invention: the punishment and exclusion of the "war criminals." The next day, Stalin sent Mao a brief message, stating that the CCP "has already started its 'peace' campaign. The issue should now be considered resolved." The type of equal partnership reflected in these Mao-Stalin communications would cer-tainly strengthen the CCP-Moscow links, and there is no room for the specu-lation that Stalin wanted to prevent the CCP from achieving nationwide vic-tory, and thus kept China divided and weak, as some scholars argued.[24] Stalin had backed Mao's revolution all along, and had treated Mao as an equal part-ner. A China under Mao's CCP, according to Stalin, was in the best interests of the USSR as well as of the socialist world revolution.

If Stalin's words are not enough, his deeds, which soon followed, should make it clear that he did not want to keep Mao's China weak and divided. In fact, he was so committed to the victory of the CCP revolution against the West that he was prepared to confront the western "imperialists" militarily on the CCP's behalf. Shortly after the cross-Yangzi campaign started, CCP artillery fired on the British gunboat *Amethyst*.[25] Consequently, some Parlia-ment members in London called for retaliation to "punish the Communists" and tension in the Far East rose. Both the CCP leadership and Moscow were thus alarmed. To prepare for the possibility that the Anglo-American forces would enter into China's civil war against the CCP, Stalin gave orders to put the Soviet troops on the Liaodong Peninsula and the naval forces at Port Arthur on full combat alert.[26] This Soviet action might have encouraged the Communists to request direct Soviet involvement in its military campaign against Taiwan and Hong Kong two months later. Mao certainly had no reason to doubt Stalin's willingness to support him; nor would he think that Stalin was against his decision to cross the Yangzi because he intended to keep China divided and weak.

If this is still not enough to demonstrate that Stalin saw a united and strong China under the rule of the CCP as in the best interests of the USSR, let's examine Stalin's policy regarding Xinjiang which had been divided with strong Soviet influence in the northern part. When Xinjiang was transferred from Sheng Shichai's hands to the GMD's control in the mid-1940s, the Soviets supported the anti-GMD regime and its separatist stance in the Yili area. This made the GMD leaders worried about the future of China's northwest; the United States was also anxiously monitoring developments in the region.[27] On the eve of the CCP's nationwide victory in 1949, however, Moscow took the initiative to help the CCP incorporate this remote province into the Beijing regime.

The CCP originally planned to take over control of this province in 1950. However, when the CCP delegation headed by Liu Shaoqi was in Moscow in the summer of 1949, Stalin personally advised the CCP to accelerate its takeover of Xinjiang. He warned that the U.S. was encouraging Muslim leaders in northwest China to concentrate their forces in Xinjiang in order to form an anti-Communist Muslim state. If this plot succeeded, China's internal conflict would be internationalized. Stalin also promised that the Soviets would "give direct assistance in the liberation of Xinjiang."[28] Acting on Stalin's advice, Mao decided to take over Xinjiang immediately. Deng Liqun, one of the members of the CCP delegation to the USSR, was sent to Xinjiang directly from Moscow with a radio communication team, and they were accompanied and assisted by the Soviet consuls in that Chinese frontier. At the time, the province was divided, with the pro-Soviet revolutionary regime controlling the north and the GMD authorities the south. Since the Yili regime in the north was actually controlled by the Soviets, and most of its leaders held Soviet citizenship, it immediately joined the Beijing regime when Deng Liqun arrived at Yili accompanied by the Soviets. The pro-Soviet leaders in Xinjiang left for Beijing on 24 August on a Soviet airplane to participate in the CCP-controlled Political Consultation Conference.[29]

Not only did the Soviets help incorporate the Yili regime into Beijing's orbit at a time when Moscow still had an official diplomatic relationship with the GMD government, they also persuaded the GMD authorities in Xinjiang to switch sides before the arrival of Deng in Dihua (Urumchi), the capital of Xinjiang. A Soviet consul at Dihua went to Yili to advise Deng that he should go to the GMD-controlled capital to talk to the GMD authorities who were willing to defect. When he arrived on 15 September, Deng stayed at the home of Bao Erhan, the GMD governor of the province. Obviously, everything had been arranged by the Soviets, and the GMD authorities in Xinjiang had already decided to defect before the arrival of Deng, who only functioned as a messenger between the GMD authorities in Xinjiang and CCP headquarters. After the CCP took over control of Xinjiang, according to Deng, then the head of the foreign affairs office of the province, the Communist policy toward the American and British consulate there was firm: to "squeeze them out." All foreigners, except the Soviets, had to leave.[30] The Mao-Stalin solidarity on the eve of the CCP nationwide victory was self-evident.

CCP-MOSCOW COOPERATION AND MAO'S RADICAL DIPLOMACY

The Soviet advice was also instrumental in the making of CCP revolutionary diplomacy which started to emerge when the CCP military took over major cities in Manchuria. On 1 November 1948, one day before the Communists' entry into Shenyang, the Party Center dispatched a directive to the Northeast Bureau as a guideline in dealing with foreigners in the city. This directive instructed that because of the special circumstances in the Northeast, foreign banks and businesses should not be suspended for the moment; that the foreign consulates should be protected, and neither body searches nor office searches should be imposed on these diplomats and their consulates; that since the Communists were not familiar with diplomatic practices and international customs, they should consult the Soviet comrades in Manchuria for advice. The directive also emphasized that matters related to foreign policy should be reported to the Center for instruction before taking any action.[31] This directive in fact repeated the principles outlined in an earlier document of 7 February 1948, which stated that the CCP local authorities should protect foreign residents and foreign governments' establishments. If the staff of a foreign consulate contact the local CCP, "no matter whether this country has recognized our [the CCP's] democratic government or not," they should be received as the country's "diplomatic representatives."[32]

It seems apparent that up to early November, the CCP remained cautious not to provoke international incidents against foreign establishments in China. The CCP did not want to repeat the "Nanjing Incident" of 1927, when the revolutionary soldiers attacked foreign establishments in the city, and foreign gunboats retaliated. This cautious approach in turn resulted in the friendly and reasonable attitude of the CCP new mayor of Shenyang, Zhu Qiwen, toward the Americans in the city. Zhu visited the U.S. consulate in Shenyang on 8 November and his friendliness impressed Angus Ward so much that he reported to Ambassador Stuart that the CCP left a "definite impression of desiring to be friendly and helpful.[33] The situation was soon to change and Ward and his staff were detained for an entire year. This change of CCP policy toward the U.S. consulate in Shenyang signified the beginning of Mao's radical diplomacy which was later expressed as *lingqi luzao* (building a new store). This sudden change was from Mao himself, with Stalin's advice, of course.[34]

Earlier in the year, Stalin sent I. V. Kovalev to China as a liaison between Stalin himself and Mao. After the CCP entered into Shenyang, Kovalev suggested that the U.S. consulate had a powerful radio station serving as a U.S.-GMD intelligence-gathering center. He advised the CCP to blockade the U.S. consulate and not allow its staff to leave freely. He also suggested that the CCP take control of the radio station in the U.S. consulate. When Mao learned Kovalev's advice, he telegraphed Stalin immediately to ask for further clarification. But Stalin didn't reply, indicating that he had no further advice to offer, nor did he have objections to the ideas of his man in China.[35] Consequently, a dramatic change in the CCP's foreign policy took place. On 10 November, Zhou Enlai drafted a directive to the Northeast Bureau in which he said that since the governments of Britain, the United States, and France had not recognized the CCP, the Communists should not recognize the legal status of those countries' consulates. Western diplomats should be treated only as ordinary foreign citizens.[36] The CCP's previous policy stated in the directives of 7 February and 1 November was abandoned.

In accordance with Kovalev's advice, Zhou's directive went on to suggest that certain measures be taken to confine western diplomats' freedom of movement. He reasoned that because of wartime circumstances the westerners had no sufficient reason to object to certain restrictions such as surrounding western consulates with CCP guards and "escorting" the diplomats wherever they went. Zhou then spelled out the real purpose of the CCP policy: "We should use such measures in order to confine and isolate them [western diplomats]. [If we] do not give them freedom of movement for some time, they will have to withdraw."[37] To force the western diplomatic presence in Manchuria to withdraw "voluntarily" through measured harassment was the goal of the "nonrecognition" policy, which was soon phrased by the CCP as the "squeeze out" policy (*jizou fangzhen*). This may have been, at the outset, a policy applicable only to Manchuria in order to please the Soviets, but it soon became an important part of the Party's overall foreign policy toward the West in general, and the U.S. in particular. Radical revolutionary diplomacy was thus set in motion by the CCP's treatment of the "Ward case."

One day after Zhou's directive, six soldiers were on guard at the American Consulate and two at Ward's residence. It was immediately apparent to the Americans that the action was really for the purpose of monitoring and confining Ward and his staff.[38] On 14 November, the CCP authorities in Shenyang ordered that all foreign radio transmitting and receiving equipment was to be taken into custody within thirty-six hours. A few days later, the Communists went into the U.S. consulate and seized the radio equipment. Ward and his staff were then detained for more than a year.[39] This chain of events was set in motion by Mao. After a talk with the Soviets in Manchuria, probably Kovalev, Gao Gang sent Mao a telegram on 16 November, suggesting that the CCP take further action to "squeeze out" the western diplomatic establishments.[40] Mao replied the next day:

1) [We] agree with your policy of squeezing out the U.S., British, and French consulates from Shenyang; (2) [regarding] the naive actions of Zhu Qiwen . . . let Chen Yun redress it; (3) please tell Malining [transliteration of the name of a Soviet official in Manchuria] that regarding [the CCP's] foreign policy in the Northeast and everywhere in China, we will certainly consult with the Soviet Union in advance so that we can achieve common ground.[41]

Following Kovalev's advice, now confirmed by Mao, the Northeast Bureau had issued an ultimatum to have the Americans surrender their radio equipment within thirty-six hours, but when the deadline passed there was no action taken by the CCP. Mao was furious when he learned this, and he cabled Gao again on 18 November. He first criticized the Bureau for failing to ask permission before issuing the ultimatum, and then failing to show the westerners that the CCP meant what it said. He went on to order that the U.S. radio equipment be taken into custody resolutely and immediately. Mao explicitly told Gao that communications between the western consulate in Shenyang and the outside world be severed in order to make the life of western diplomats more difficult, so that "our [the CCP's] purpose of squeezing them out" could be achieved. Mao also suggested that the western diplomats' freedom of movement be further restricted. If they wanted to go out of their consulate, Mao said, armed personnel should follow them for "their own protection."[42] The next day, Mao's order was thoroughly implemented.

The CCP's strategy for detaining Ward and his staff was carefully calculated so that the measured harassment would force the Americans to leave, but not provoke direct U.S. hostility against the CCP. Since communications between Shenyang and the outside were cut off, Washington was in the dark about what was really happening there. At the same time, rumors about a moderate CCP Center versus a radical pro-Soviet faction in Manchuria were circulated, as were rumors about a pro-Soviet faction versus a pro-American one within the Party Center. The Americans were confused and found themselves unable to take any definite action such as limited retaliatory bombing or armed rescue, although these options were discussed among U.S. diplomats. Dean Acheson telegraphed O. E. Clubb, the U.S. consul at Beiping, on 15 April 1949, protesting that the CCP's blocking of communications with Mukden created an intolerable situation "while [the] reported confinement [of the] consular staff, if true, [is] so clearly contrary [to] universally accepted principles [within the] international community." Acheson warned that unless the Communists promptly corrected the unsatisfactory situation in Mukden, the U.S. government "will have no alternative but to withdraw them [consular personnel]."[43] The Secretary of State apparently couldn't understand that the withdrawal of the U.S. diplomatic establishments in China was precisely what Mao desired.

The CCP's "squeeze out" policy was implemented throughout 1949. In January 1950, the Americans couldn't take any more, and they packed up and left. The last CCP action against the Americans was also authorized by Mao, who was then in Moscow. Early in 1950, the Communists decided to requisition the military barracks in foreign diplomatic compounds, which eventually made Washington irritated enough to withdraw all its diplomatic representatives from mainland China. In his telegram to Liu Shaoqi on 13 January 1950, Mao issued a "go-ahead" order to take over the barracks. He explicitly stated that the CCP should be "prepared that the U.S. will withdraw all consulates in China." On 18 January, having heard Washington's decision of withdrawal, Mao cabled Liu again, stating that "the U.S. withdrawal of all officials in China is extremely advantageous to us. Only those bourgeois democrats who were afraid of the U.S. would oppose the CCP's action."[44] From the "Ward case" in November 1948, to the requisition of foreign military barracks in January 1950, Mao and his colleagues eventually succeeded in "squeezing" the Americans out of China without provoking direct confrontation. In the whole process, the CCP-Moscow policy consultation played a significant role, which indicated that a strong Moscow-CCP alliance against the United States had already been in place before the Sino-Soviet pact was signed in 1950.

"LINGQI LUZAO": THE CCP'S DETERMINATION FOR A REVOLUTION

Why did Mao and his colleagues intend to "squeeze out" the westerners, especially the Americans, and thus refuse to recognize the legal position of western diplomatic establishments? The answer seems to lie in the CCP's determination to revolutionize China's relationship with the West. The State Department and some U.S. diplomats in China tended to perceive the Ward Case as an isolated event plotted by the Soviets and pro-Soviet elements within the CCP. This perception was wrong on two counts: it perceived Moscow's policy in conflict with that of Mao, and it also wishfully projected a conflict between a pro-Soviet and a pro-American faction. The new historical evidence suggests that Mao actively sought Stalin's advice and heeded Moscow's policy closely. More often than not, however, Mao appeared to be more radical than Stalin, and he often went too far in pursuing his revolutionary goal. If Moscow took the initiative on the CCP's policy toward the U.S. consulate in Shenyang, because the Soviets considered Manchuria their exclusive sphere of influence, Mao soon took over the Soviet initiative to apply this "squeeze out" policy nationwide as the core of the Party policy toward the West. He had his own rationale for doing so.

In the last few months of 1948, the CCP's military victory forced the West to prepare for a Communist regime in China, and both Washington and London undertook the search for a feasible China policy. The common ground shared by the Americans and the British was to "stay where we are, to have de facto relations with the Chinese Communists." By "keeping a foot in the door," that is, maintaining consulates and embassies in the cities taken by the CCP, Washington and London intended to "prevent China from becoming an adjunct of the Soviet Union," and to protect and salvage as much as possible American and British interests in China. To achieve these goals, they felt it desirable to maintain flexibility and avoid "irrevocable commitment to any one course of action or to any one faction."[45] The fundamental assumption behind this "stay-put" policy was that the CCP was not Moscow's "adjunct," and a Titoist prospect was likely. U.S. policy makers apparently failed to imagine a "third type" of CCP-Moscow relations, a genuine partnership defined by a shared ideology and a long history of common struggle, other than the "Tito type" or the "adjunct type."

At the same time, as if he had known the American intention to stay, Mao was determined to drive U.S. influence out of China altogether. From 8 to 13 September 1948, a CCP Politburo meeting was held to decide the general policy line in the final phase of its war of liberation. Regarding the Party's foreign policy toward the West, the CCP decided on a general goal, to "drive imperialist influence out" after the CCP victory.[46] Early in 1949, a Politburo meeting took place from 6–8 January, and the Second Plenum followed early in March. It was at these two meetings that Mao further elaborated on the CCP's foreign policy principles, and "*Lingqi luzao*" became the backbone of the Party's revolutionary diplomacy. It meant the CCP would unilaterally abolish all existing treaties between China and the West outright, instead of negotiating to revise the old "unequal treaties." It also meant that the western countries had to accept the CCP's terms, otherwise, the new regime would rather have no relations with them at all. Mao put it rather bluntly when he said that the Party intended "*to force*" western countries to "recognize [CCP] China *unconditionally*, to abolish [all the] old treaties, and to conclude entirely new treaties."[47]

By the end of 1949, Dean Acheson correctly sensed the nature of the CCP position vis-à-vis the U.S. position. On 8 December, he told the British Ambassador to Washington that

> it seemed to us that the inclination of the Chinese Communists was to follow the Russian example of considering themselves not an evolutionary regime which . . . entailed that they assumed both the rights and the obligations of the former regime, but a revolutionary one which would seek to assume all the rights and only those obligations they choose to undertake.[48]

Mao, too, was well aware of the difference between the CCP's revolutionary determination and the "evolutionary" demand of the West, and he was convinced that the western "imperialist countries" would not accept the CCP's terms. Therefore, Mao decided not to seek recognition by the West for a fairly long period of time after the proclamation of the People's Republic. He believed that a period of isolation from the West would bring western countries to their knees. For commercial reasons, the capitalist countries would eventually come back to seek restoration of diplomatic relations. The CCP could then dictate the terms and the western powers would have no claim for any special rights as defined by the old treaty system. He told the Party Plenum on 5 March 1949:

> Thoroughly anti-imperialist in character, the Chinese people's democratic revolution has incurred the bitter hatred of the imperialists. . . . At the same time the whole imperialist system is very much weakened after World War II, while the strength of the world anti-imperialist front headed by the Soviet Union is greater than ever before. In these circumstances, we can and should adopt a policy of systematically and completely destroying imperialist domination in China. . . . Refuse to recognize the legal status of any foreign diplomatic establishments and personnel of the Kuomintang period, refuse to recognize all the treasonable treaties of the Kuomintang period, abolish all imperialist propaganda agencies in China, take immediate control of foreign trade and reform the customs system— these are the first steps we must take upon entering the big cities.[49]

That was precisely the CCP's rationale which inspired Mao to revolutionize China's relations with the West. The CCP's "nonrecognition" policy was clearly a message that the CCP wanted western legal representations out of the country, and the "Ward case" was a device to facilitate the fulfillment of this "squeeze out" goal.

The nonrecognition policy of the CCP was reconfirmed repeatedly throughout 1949. On 25 April the Center cabled the headquarters on the Yangzi front, stating that after entering into Nanjing, since the CCP did not have diplomatic relations with western countries, the Communists should not have any official contact with western embassies. The following day, the Center sent another telegram to the front, reiterating that anything related to foreign affairs should be reported to the Center before any action was taken.[50] After the clash between the PLA and the British gunboat *Amethyst*, the Center telegraphed its Nanjing Committee, instructing that "we should hold negotiations with the commander of this ship directly. If the British Embassy in Nanjing sends personnel to take part in negotiations, we should only recognize them as individuals. . . ."[51] The Party Center was extremely careful not to grant any de facto recognition of legal status to the western diplomatic establishments, not even the British, who were eager to develop official relations with the new regime.

Washington seemed incapable of understanding the CCP position. When

Acheson realized the revolutionary nature of the CCP diplomacy at the end of 1949, he continued to believe that the "Chinese Communists do want recognition by other powers than the USSR and its satellites," and therefore, the Americans should seize the opportunity to bring "pressure to bear [on the CCP] for recognition of existing obligations."[52] Obviously, thinking in "evolutionary" terms within the framework of normal international practice, Acheson failed to understand a revolutionary regime's foreign policy and the rationale behind it.

"CLEAN THE HOUSE FIRST BEFORE INVITING GUESTS"

The CCP's desire for a revolution in China's relations with the West derived also from its determination to establish a "people's dictatorship," a domestic political structure molded after the Soviet system. Using earthy language, Mao spelled out the second principle of CCP revolutionary diplomacy: to clean the house first before inviting guests. That meant to give precedence to the fulfillment of the CCP's domestic political program over seeking diplomatic recognition by the West.

Since the CCP was determined to build a "people's dictatorship," western democratic influence was utterly incompatible with the CCP's domestic agenda. The CCP thus utilized nationalistic sentiment among the general population, and presented itself as the national leader against the continued danger of western imperialist encroachment, now led by the U.S. The Soviet Union was thus put in a favorable light as an ally of China vis-à-vis her old foe in the West. In so doing, the CCP's domestic goal was served by its aggressive foreign policy, which sought no compromise and no conventional negotiations with, nor recognition by, the western powers, especially the United States. In this regard, the U.S. policy of containment in Asia, which necessitated the restoration of Japan, worked to the CCP's advantage. The tension between Communist China and the U.S. in the post-1949 era, which was greatly escalated by the Korean War, actually facilitated the CCP's domestic establishment of a "people's dictatorship."

The CCP foresaw the hostile response of the U.S. to its domestic policy. The fundamental American hostility was depicted by Leighton Stuart who sent a long letter on 10 March 1949 to Washington, asking for permission to meet the CCP leaders. In describing what he would say to the Communists, Stuart stated that the CCP action led him to

> envisage the attempt to establish a totalitarian state in China, on the Russian model, in which all free intercourse of thought and action, of information and belief, will be banned and the usual coercive methods will [be] employed to enforce uniformity in harmony with communist ideology. . . . So far from bring-

ing "liberation" and "new democracy" it seems to us to be a more subtle and sinister form of despotism, the last phase of outmoded domination of the whole by a highly organized minority.[53]

Stuart did not intend to conceal the possible U.S. reaction toward a communized China either. He continued:

My Government might therefore feel called upon to assist any nucleus of organized opposition first in arousing the Chinese people to the danger of their national sovereignty and personal liberties and then in using all possible means for their self-protection. If this were undertaken at all I had reason to believe that we would use every available resource we possessed to restore real liberation to the Chinese people.[54]

The Communists would not doubt for a minute the truth expressed by Stuart as to how the U.S. would treat them if they intended to pursue their deeply cherished belief. Although Washington did not permit Stuart to see the CCP leaders, the Communists did not need to be told what the American Ambassador intended. In fact, their ideology of worldwide class struggle sharpened their vision, which led them to conclude in late 1948 that from then on the main danger to the Chinese revolution was direct American intervention or U.S.-sponsored sabotage from within. In order to subvert the new order, Mao believed, the United States would probably offer recognition to the People's Republic, thereby achieving legal status enabling them to stay in China. In so doing, the U.S. influence could undermine the CCP rule through its plot of "sabotage from within," as Mao said in January 1949. It was plain to Mao that in order to put the house in order the Communists needed to shut out Westerners, especially the unfriendly Americans, for "a fairly long period of time."

THE CCP'S DILEMMA: HOSTILITY OR FRIENDLINESS?

The CCP's ideological and political hostility toward the U.S. resulted in an exaggerated fear of possible U.S. military intervention on behalf of the GMD. Mao wrote a resolution for the Politburo in January 1949 and predicted that a nationwide victory would be soon achieved. There would be no force which could stop the PLA other than possible U.S. direct intervention. Therefore, the resolution stated, the Party's military planning should take into account that U.S. troops could possibly intervene by landing on the coast, occupy cities there, and confront the CCP troops directly. To stiffen his comrades' boldness to confront the Americans, Mao also called for continued efforts to redress the "erroneous point of view" which overestimated U.S. strength, and dared not to fight.[55]

Stalin contributed to fuel the CCP's fear of U.S. military intervention and exacerbated its combative mood against the Americans. In April 1949, while the CCP military was preparing for the "cross-Yangzi" campaign, Stalin cabled Mao warning that when the CCP marched toward southern China, the West might intervene with any number of measures, ranging from a blockade to a direct military confrontation. He also predicted that it was increasingly likely that the Anglo-American forces would land in the CCP rear in northern coastal areas. He then recommended:

a) Do not hurry but prepare the PLA well for a march southward to the borders of neighboring countries;

b) Detach two good [field] armies from the main forces of the PLA [which are] moving southward, and send them to the coastal regions to reinforce the area and maintain a state of readiness in case of [foreign] enemy attack.[56]

As usual, Mao followed Stalin's advice closely, and changed the CCP's military planning and troop deployment accordingly. In a military plan drafted by Deng Xiaoping on 31 March 1949, there were no steps taken to deal with the perceived danger of foreign intervention in China's eastern coastal area.[57] On 23 May, after receiving Stalin's telegram, Mao dispatched the "Directive on the Deployment of Each Field Army," which ordered the Second Field Army under Liu Bocheng and Deng Xiaoping to assist the Third Field Army in dealing with a possible American assault. Mao reasoned that in the following two months the Liu-Deng Army should not march toward the southwest hinterland because before the coastal cities of Shanghai, Ningbo, Fuzhou, and especially Qingdao, were taken, the possibility of U.S. direct intervention would remain high.[58]

Five days later, Mao's sense of crisis became more acute. According to his information, the American naval force in Qingdao and British troops in Hong Kong all increased their activities, and western embassies in Nanjing were preparing to withdraw. Mao thus concluded that the danger of imperialist intervention increased, and he telegraphed the generals at the front on 28 May to adjust military planning. In accordance with Stalin's advice, Mao ordered that the CCP deploy enough forces in the coastal areas from Tianjin to Shanghai, that the Second Field Army delay its southward move for two months, that the Third Field Army surround Qingdao and defend the Shanghai area, and that troops moving southward to attack Fujian be limited to two armies. He also urged that the CCP should achieve economic self-reliance in order to face a blockade imposed by the U.S. and other western powers.[59]

Given the CCP's long-standing suspicion of and hostility toward the U.S., it is no surprise that the Communists' fear of American intervention was so intense that they were ready to engage U.S. troops in the battlefield. What is interesting and puzzling is the fact that while the CCP was intensely in fear of and preparing for a military conflict with the U.S., it also sent out a series of friendly overtures for accommodation and trade relations with the U.S. For instance, in mid-April, before the PLA's "cross-Yangzi" campaign was launched, a CCP-GMD agreement was reached which amounts to the GMD's surrender. In his telegrams of 16 and 17 April, Mao stated that "whether or not Nanjing will sign [this agreement] will be determined by the attitude of the U.S. Government and Jiang Jieshi." Therefore, Mao concluded that there was not much hope for Nanjing's signature, and the plan for the campaign on 22 April should be carried out decisively.[60] Mao's deeply harbored enmity toward the U.S. was obvious. Paradoxically, at the same time, the CCP's public statements expressed interest in establishing trade and diplomatic relations with the West, including the U.S.[61] In fact, this appears to be one more example of how closely Mao heeded Stalin's advice. In the above-mentioned cable, Stalin also stated:

> We believe that the democratic government of China should not reject establishing official relations with some capitalist states, including the United States, if these governments officially renounce military, economic, and political support for Chiang Kaishek's Kuomintang government.[62]

Stalin's advice came as an alternative to Mao's radical "squeeze out" policy, and Mao adopted it quickly as the line of CCP public diplomatic policy toward the West. This, however, did not mean that Mao had abandoned his revolutionary radicalism, nor that Stalin wanted Mao to do so. It only made Mao more careful in building a moderate public image, while pursuing a radical revolution in China's international relations. Mao even found this technique useful in confusing the foe so that the possible U.S. military intervention could be delayed or avoided.

In the month of May, Mao was intensely alarmed by the possibility of U.S. intervention. He, however, sent Huang Hua, a former student of Stuart, to Nanjing to see the U.S. Ambassador. On 13 May, in a friendly and informal way, Huang talked with Stuart about U.S. recognition of the CCP regime.[63] Before the first Huang-Stuart meeting took place, Philip Fugh, Stuart's secretary, visited Huang, and expressed that the U.S. was willing to establish new relations with the CCP regime, and the Sino-American Commercial and Navigation Treaty, which the CCP denounced, could be revised. Huang said that empty words were useless, the U.S. should do something beneficial for the Chinese people. Huang reported this meeting to Mao immediately, and Mao in response sent a lengthy directive to Huang on 10 May, instructing him on how to conduct the talk with Stuart. Mao said Huang should listen more and talk less, since his first task was to sound out the Americans' intention. Mao was harshly critical of Huang's wording about the U.S. doing something beneficial for the Chinese people. He said that it sounded as if the U.S. had done something good to China in the past, that it would give the Americans the false impression that the CCP was hoping for U.S. assistance. Mao also instructed Huang that it should be made clear to the Americans that his meeting with Stuart was unofficial.[64] Mao was clearly resentful of the U.S. and had no interest in negotiating normalization of relations. Why, then, did he send Huang to Nanjing in the first place?

While Huang stayed in Nanjing, the so-called "Zhou Demarche" occurred at the end of May. Through Michael Keon, an Australian journalist, a message which allegedly came from Zhou Enlai reached the Americans. This message was intended to reveal the division between Zhou and Liu Shaoqi regarding the CCP's policy toward the U.S. and the USSR. The former was reportedly supportive of a friendly policy toward the U.S. for possible U.S. economic assistance in the reconstruction of China. The latter was portrayed as a pro-Soviet hard-liner who was strongly opposed to friendly relations with the U.S. Mao was depicted as undecided and the CCP was thus at a crossroad, and could lean to either side.[65]

During the same period, a series of overtures for trade relations with the U.S. was sent to the Americans. In March 1949, the U.S. Consul General in Tianjin reported that the Communist foreign affairs group invited the Chairman of the Tianjin American Chamber of Commerce to discuss foreign trade problems. The Chairman commented that the Communists were cordial during the interview and displayed increasing interest in trading with the U.S.[66] In late April, Yao Yilin, who was in charge of economic matters in CCP-controlled North China, sent a representative to see Clubb in Beiping. He expressed interest in trading with U.S.-occupied Japan, and restoring Sino-American trade to its prewar level. Clubb mentioned the case of a U.S. oil firm which could not get entry permission from the Communist North China authorities, and the bad effect of anti-American propaganda on trade relations. In response, Clubb's guest indicated that Mao's political thinking about the "new democracy" was "along moderate lines," but some "lower Communist levels" were "along more strictly Communist lines." He promised that "there was reason to believe there would shortly be [a] political veering to [the] right."[67] This message of "radical following vs. moderate leadership" from the CCP appears in the same line as the Zhou Demarche; combining the following similar pattern of behavior, it suggests an orchestrated disinformation campaign by the highest authorities of the CCP.

On 6 June, Chen Yi, now the mayor of Shanghai, stated that as the USSR might not be able to offer assistance to China for the time being, aid from the U.S. and Britain would be acceptable. The aid could include loans, technical assistance, or aid in the nature of the Marshall Plan in Europe. Ordinary trade was "naturally" desired by the CCP as well. Although this speech was allegedly for "internal consumption," it found its way to the U.S. Consul General in Shanghai on the same day.[68] Similar messages were delivered to the U.S. Consul General in Hong Kong on 7 June.[69] The next day, Huang Hua told Philip Fugh that the CCP was anxious to bring about an economic recovery, which was contingent upon American aid.[70]

We are obviously confronted with a puzzle. On one hand, the recently available CCP documents suggest that the Party consistently pursued a policy of "squeezing" the Americans out, that the Communists were intensely looking out and preparing for U.S. direct intervention. On the other hand, the U.S. documents recorded a series of CCP friendly overtures for a better relationship. There are two alternative explanations for the coexistence of hostility and friendliness in the CCP's behavior. First, Mao and his colleagues were realistic enough to see the advantages of having a better relationship with the U.S.; thus when such a possibility arose, they could not help but respond spontaneously. In other words, there were moments when the CCP leaders were attracted by the advantages of having a friendly relationship with the West. For instance, Mao telegraphed his lieutenants at the Yangzi front on 28 April that the U.S. was sending signals to explore the possibility of establishing diplomatic relations with the CCP. Mao felt that if the U.S. and Britain could sever their relations with the GMD, the CCP would consider the establishment of normal foreign relations with them.[71]

This explanation of "momentary spontaneity" becomes inadequate if one notices that the series of the CCP's friendly overtures were apparently orchestrated in terms of their timing and coherence. It should be remembered that the CCP Center constantly reiterated that no one on the local level had the right to take diplomatic action without authorization from the Center in advance. Therefore, the second explanation seems more logical: the friendly overtures were disinformation designed to confuse the Americans in order to reduce or delay the possibility of U.S. military intervention on behalf of the GMD. In Mao's 10 May directive to Huang, despite its overtone of animosity, Mao told Huang not to express objection if Stuart proposed to stay on and negotiate with the new government. In the final stage of the Party's war of liberation, concerned with possible U.S. intervention, the CCP did not want to provoke the Americans. If the Americans could be led to think that a CCP regime, with a Titoist nationalistic tendency, might not be a bad thing, the CCP's purpose of averting or delaying U.S. intervention would be better served. Huang Hua reportedly said in 1991 that his mission to see Stuart in 1949 had two purposes. The first was to "explore the intentions of the U.S. Government," and the second was to use the meeting as a "diplomacy of impediment" (*waijiao qianzhi*) in coordination with the CCP's "military action."[72] In other words, when CCP military forces were sweeping the GMD out of the mainland, Huang's diplomacy was designed to keep the Americans at bay by confusing them, making them indecisive.

No matter what intention the CCP had in mind, which may never be revealed, Washington was misled by Huang's visit as well as the orchestrated disinformation campaign. For instance, Dean Acheson signed the aforementioned report from Tianjin in March in order to have it circulated among the

U.S. foreign service worldwide. Acheson appeared to believe that the Tianjin report was a significant indication of a possible Titoist tendency in the CCP leadership. Fugh interpreted Huang's message of 8 June as a sign that the CCP, or at least the so-called liberal wing led by Zhou Enlai, placed industrialization ahead of communization.[73] Until the end of 1949, Acheson was still of the opinion that the CCP did want recognition by the West. The CCP's friendly gestures encouraged Washington's hopes for a Titoist prospect in China, and the "hands off" policy followed. Since a large part of the CCP's friendly overtures related to establishing a trade partnership with the U.S., we need to examine whether or not the CCP was sincere in this regard.

THE CCP'S ATTITUDE TOWARD TRADE RELATIONS WITH THE U.S.

From the vantage point of both contemporary U.S. statesmen and later scholars, the immense economic problems the CCP would have to face could not be solved without America's trade and aid, which the Russians were unable to provide. Therefore, "the temptation [for the CCP] to seek trade and financing in Britain and the United States arose." As a result, Mao's "adherence to ideological desiderata" gave way to China's national economic needs. As "a conscientious ruler," Mao had to look for help from the United States. Based on this judgment, the "lost chance" scholars further concluded that it was "American behavior" which "presented a serious obstacle to diplomatic intercourse and trade in the late 1940s [with Communist China]."[74] Did the Communists really want American trade and loans in 1948–50?

It should be recalled that as early as 1922, the Communists were convinced that American imperialists intended to use their economic superiority to breach Anglo-Japanese hegemony in China, and Washington's open door policy was an imperialist weapon to use economic power to dominate China.[75] After the establishment of the GMD's Nanjing Government in 1927, the CCP believed that because of the lack of a particular sphere of influence in China, Washington strongly supported the Central Government in Nanjing under Jiang Jieshi. A unified China under a pro-American regime would be advantageous to U.S. economic expansion under the open door policy. Therefore, Jiang, the CCP's chief enemy, became the U.S. "running dog," and the United States the principal imperialist power that the CCP was determined to fight.[76]

The CCP's hostility toward the U.S. and its perception of the imperialist nature of the open door policy were deep-seated. When Lauchlin Currie visited China in early 1941, the CCP tried hard to woo the Americans in public, but in private inner-party communications, the Communists did not conceal their suspicion of American "evil intentions." Zhou Enlai told Mao that one of

Currie's purposes was to use wartime loans to secure America's postwar occupation of Hainan Island as a U.S. concession.[77] In the Communists' mind, any American economic aid or financial loan was intended to encroach on China's sovereignty.

On the eve of nationwide victory, the Communists did not lose their Leninist view of western trade and capital investment as instrumental to American neo-imperialist expansion. Although Mao did state that "we will also trade with capitalist countries," he was distrustful of western business institutions in China. He said that "they can be allowed to exist for the time being, subject to our supervision and control, to be dealt with by us after countrywide victory."[78] Furthermore, Mao considered China's economic underdevelopment "the result of imperialist and feudal oppression." Therefore, when he addressed the question of China's economic reconstruction, he attributed no importance to foreign trade with the capitalist countries. Instead, he argued for rigid control over it:

> The restoration and development of the national economy of the people's republic would be impossible without a policy of controlling foreign trade . . . after the victory of the people's democratic revolution, the state power of the people's republic under the leadership of the working class must not be weakened but must be strengthened. The two basic policies of the state in the economic struggle will be regulation of capital at home and control of foreign trade [abroad]. Whoever overlooks or belittles this point will commit extremely serious mistakes.[79]

The CCP wanted to establish a "proletarian dictatorship," and to match this superstructure, they desired a state-controlled economy. A "free-trade" capitalist economy was incompatible with their blueprint of a socialist-communist society. Therefore, they confiscated "bureaucratic capital" and "regulated" private capital at home as soon as they took over national power. For the same reason, they could not allow foreign capital to operate freely in China either. The Communists did not believe that U.S. capital would come to the new China without political consequences. In fact, Mao placed his hope for speedy economic development on the CCP leadership, state power, and Soviet support. He said:

> With the victory of the Chinese people's revolution and the founding of the people's republic, and with the leadership of the Communist Party of China, plus the support of the working class of the countries of the world and chiefly the support of the Soviet Union, the speed of China's economic construction will not be very slow, but may be fairly fast.[80]

On the other hand, Mao believed in the myth of the "China market," and intended to use foreign trade as political leverage. In the imperial period, the Chinese "barbarian managers" were convinced that China needed no overseas trade, while the "barbarians" could not survive without trade with China. To allow the westerners to trade with China was to show the mercy and superiority of the "Middle Kingdom" over the "barbarians." The Communists inherited this attitude, and reinforced it with their Leninist theory on imperialism. Mao told the Party in March 1949 that several capitalist countries had already been competing to do business with the Liberated Areas. He assumed that all capitalist countries, especially the United States, were eager to trade with China, to exploit the "China market." Therefore, he tried to use trade as a political instrument just as the Americans did. He said that "So far as possible, we must first of all trade with the socialist and people's democratic countries" in East Europe. In 1944–45, on the assumption that the U.S. badly wanted overseas trade with China, Mao talked about the bright future of Sino-American business cooperation when he was trying to court the Americans. In 1949, a series of signals was sent out to the Americans to show a bright picture of future Sino-U.S. trade. In so doing, the CCP hoped that it would reduce the possibility of U.S. intervention.

If the Americans were encouraged by the CCP's friendly words, they were soon dismayed by its deeds. As Edwin Martin discovered, although the U.S. and British private businessmen were originally flexible in trying to stay in China after the CCP takeover, they soon found it impossible. On 26 June 1949, twenty days after Chen Yi's friendly message was sent to the Americans, Washington received a report from Shanghai which said that "incidents of [the] last few weeks involving foreigners have dampened any initial optimism with which the foreign colony may have regarded the future under Communist rule. . . . Increasing mood among American businessmen is that of packing up and leaving Shanghai rather than submit to humiliations and insecurities of the present situation [sic]."[81]

The harassment imposed upon the U.S. consulate at Shanghai made it difficult for the diplomats to stay as well. Cabot recorded in his diary in late June that "we discuss using hoses and tear gas if [the] mob invades [the consulate] building, but I find other senior officers are opposed—and probably rightly. . . . I feel utterly discouraged, frustrated, sick, nervously exhausted, anxious only to get away [sic]."[82] The Communists' deeds strongly indicated that they did not intend to do business with the West, nor did they want the western diplomatic establishments to stay on. They succeeded in squeezing them out of China by irritating them, but they did not provoke foreign intervention by creating a scandalous event such as the "Nanjing Incident" in 1927. Instead, they sent friendly messages to the foreigners, while encouraging the "lower levels" of Communists and employees to harass their western bosses.[83] One has to admit that this tactic was highly successful as far as the CCP's real goal—to squeeze westerners out of China without provoking direct hostility—was concerned.

In short, the CCP's historical experiences, its ideological convictions, its perception of the contemporary world order, and the pursuit of its domestic political program, all came together to determine the direction of the CCP's revolutionary diplomacy toward the West in general and the U.S. in particular. There was no "chance" for Washington to lose, especially when one examines CCP-Moscow relations in the same period. Mao's Beijing regime was born anti-American and pro-Soviet, and the Sino-Soviet military alliance established by the the combined efforts of Mao and Stalin was only a logical extension of the history of CCP-Moscow relations in the decades prior to the proclamation of the PRC in 1949.

Conclusion

EARLY in 1935, when Mao succeeded in taking over the Party leadership in Zunyi, he could not even have entertained the prospect that fifteen years later he would rule all of China. In the following fifteen years, the world was changing rapidly, and China was ever tightly entangled with the global struggle. The Japanese invasion and China's need for survival propelled its political leaders to search for a solution which would not only win them the war against Japan, but also realize their ideas for a "new China." As history so repeats itself, different competing ideas weigh heavier in shaping the future when the world is in a transitional period from the old to new. Chinese history in 1935–50 proves no exception: it was an age of ideology.

When the old-fashioned capitalist-imperialist world order was apparently in crises of economic depression and war, other political ideas, such as nationalism and communism, naturally became more assertive. People embracing different persuasions in the United States had different or conflicting views on what was American national interest in the postwar world and how to bring it about. FDR's postwar foreign policy was nothing but a far cry from the "national consensus." Such being the case, how could anyone expect a holistic view of Chinese "national interest" shared by a quarter of the entire population on earth?

In fact, as I have documented, the CCP's idea for the future of China was so radically in opposition to that of the GMD that Mao and his comrades cherished an idea which came close to China's defeat by Japan, if one recognizes the GMD regime as the "state" of China. Mao in the early forties did not want to see an American-boosted GMD defeat Japan; and by the end of the war, he wished the Japanese would "mop up" more Chinese military forces under the GMD. To the Communists, a U.S.-GMD dominated China was worse than a war-torn China, simply because the Party's revolution had a better chance to survive and win in the latter scenario. Thus, to conclude our story, I shall revisit the question of what motivated the CCP's foreign policy.

NATIONALISM OR INTERNATIONALISM?

I appreciate many scholars' efforts to explain the uniqueness of "nationalism" in modern Chinese history and their invention of terminologies such as "anti-foreign nationalism," "cultural nationalism," "revolutionary nationalism," "nationless state nationalism," and so on.[1] In reviewing historical evidence of CCP behavior in 1935–50, however, I find that none of these different types of "nationalism" is really adequate to serve as an interpretive framework of the CCP's diplomatic history. No matter how diversified different movements of nationalism around the world were, nationalism needs a fundamental qualification—to locate the source of individual identity within a "nation" as a "people," that is, the "nation" commands individuals' loyalty. Where did the Communists channel their loyalty? Did the concept of "nation-state," or the "Chinese nation" as a unique and unified "people" ever exist in the minds of Mao and his colleagues?

Since the Communists drew a line not along the national boundaries of territory, language, ethnicity, or common history, but along the social class boundaries of bourgeoisie, petty bourgeoisie, or proletariat, certain factions of Chinese society were seen as enemies whose destruction, even by the Japanese, was what the CCP desired. In contrast, the Outer Mongols and the Soviets were taken as "brothers," whose friendship and assistance were expected and sought by the Party. It is thus clear that Mao and his generation of radical revolutionaries shared no such concept of the Chinese nation as a holistic "people," let alone their devotion to the "nation" which did not exist in their conceptual world.

Ironically, the CCP's lack of the concept of "Chinese nation" was exactly a reflection of the uniqueness of the "Chinese people," a "nationless people." As many scholars have pointed out, there is no such word in Chinese which conveys the concept of "nation." The word "*minzhu*" refers to the ethnic or racial identity of a group of people, such as "*Hanzhu*" and "*Zhangzhu*," which does not constitute a political entity by its own virtue, nor does it command the loyalty of its own people. What Sun Yat-sen meant by "nationalism" (*minzu zhuyi*) amounts to the "anti-Manchu-ism." In order to get rid of the Manchu imperial rule Sun tried very hard to enlist help from the Japanese and the British. In this regard, Sun's 1911 revolution was more of an ethnic struggle than a "national revolution," simply because he failed to define what the "Chinese nation" was. In Sun's perspective before 1911, the ethnic difference between the Han and the Manchu "nations" seemed more conspicuous and antagonistic than that between China and Japan or other western nations, and the Manchu people were more "foreign" than the Japanese or westerners.

With the concept of "nation" missing, "*guojia*," or "state" figures large in the Chinese political culture, as many scholars have noted. *Guojia*, however, has two meanings: "country" in a geopolitical sense, and "state" as "government." If the U.S. "Government" claims its policy represents the U.S. as a "Nation" or a "Country," the indistinctness of notions among "state," "nation," and "country" is a political deliberation within the framework of "nation-state," which claims the "state" as representing the "nation" as a "people" and the "country" as a geopolitical entity. The linguistic impreciseness of *guojia*, however, reflects a fundamental conception that the "state" in and of itself is in fact the "country" with its geopolitical boundaries, which includes "all under heaven," from the viewpoint of the "son of heaven." In Chinese, *tianxia* (all under heaven) is also synonymous with *guojia*. In this sense, Chinese traditional political culture is multinational, or "international" by nature. Mao and his comrades had no difficulty embracing internationalism, but found "nationalism" very alien indeed.

Since the concept of "nation" was missing, a Chinese ruler couldn't possibly perceive the state authority as representing the "nation," nor would he think of his power as being delegated by the "people." Instead, he claimed that his power was sanctioned by the "mandate of heaven," the ultimate moral authority.[2] This imperial cult of Confucian moral absolutism was so deep-rooted in Chinese political culture that even non-Chinese invaders, such as the Manchus, could claim for the "mandate" to rule. Thus, the ethnic identity of a "people" (*minzu*) was further detached from "state." The Chinese imperial state had always been a "multinational" empire in which the Han people amounted to more than 90 percent of the total population, and they had always managed to assimilate the "invaders" culturally and politically. Thus, from the Chinese perspective, it did not matter whether the imperial house was the Han "nation," or the Manchu "nation," it had the right to rule as long as it could claim for the sanction of the "mandate," which meant the continuation of Chinese cultural and political tradition. The way for a ruler to claim the imperial power has been the same throughout China's history: military conquest in the name of "heaven's will," an odd combination of brutality and moral absolutism.

When the imperial history came to an end in 1911, the specificity of the Confucian cult died. However, the age-old authoritarian framework of moral absolutism proved to die hard. According to the CCP's Marxist perspective, communism represents the ultimate moral ideal of the entire human race, and the proletariat, the most advanced class in human history, plays a leading role in the struggle for the ultimate destiny of the human race. The Communist Party, the logic goes on, is the vanguard of the proletarian class; it thus represents the highest moral authority. Therefore, the Party is above the "state," providing it with the moral core. In other words, the Party itself is the "mandate" to rule. Since the "people" are categorized into different classes, it is impossible for them to represent themselves through the "state" without the Party. Henceforth, the CCP, the most radical political institution in modern Chinese history, has come full circle, and confined itself in the oldest political tradition of imperial authoritarianism. In the Communists' minds, there was only the concept of "party-state," not "nation-state."

It is, therefore, understandable why in the CCP political culture the Party was placed in the highest position to absorb all its followers' loyalty. Only those loyal to the Party were considered the "people," and, according to the current CCP constitution, anyone who is opposed to the Party is a "class enemy," not one of the "people." Clearly, the CCP locates individual identity and loyalty not within the "Chinese nation" as a "homogeneous people," nor even the "unitary state"; it was with the Party. Along the Leninist line, the CCP considered the state a tool of class oppression, and the "proletarian dictatorship" was necessary in the transitional period toward communism. Thus, the class nature of the state would be determined not only by the class nature of the people who controlled it, but also by a "higher moral authority" which would determine whether or not the people in control were "corrupted." When Mao determined that his own government became "bureaucratic," controlled by the "capitalist-roaders," he launched the "Great Cultural Revolution" to dismantle the "party-state" in the name of the "proletarian ideology" (*wuchang jieji yishi xingtai*), the "higher moral authority." This highly abstract moral absolutism was a new expression of the old concept of "mandate of heaven," which continued to sanction one man's rule. At the Lushan Conference of 1959, Mao threatened that if the Party and the state would not listen to him, he would bring the PLA to the mountain to fight a civil war all over again; if the PLA would not follow him, he would invite the Soviet Red Army to intervene.[3] Mao was deadly serious, not so much about the military action he threatened to take, but about the "higher moral authority" which would legitimize any action against an "immoral" state or the Party itself. If Mao's words and deeds could be interpreted as one man's "irrationality" or "insanity," it is more denotative to point out the fact that no one in the Party, or in the entire country, questioned his principle of moral absolutism, which sanctioned his action to destroy the state and the Party during the Cultural Revolution. Mao was only acting within the norm of the CCP political culture.

The later expression of CCP political culture helps to explain the CCP's earlier behavior which this study is about. If for the sake of the "proletarian ideology," Mao was allowed to destroy the CCP party-state apparatus, there was absolutely nothing the CCP could not do to topple the GMD state. Mao and his colleagues felt that they were morally sanctioned to desire that the more GMD forces annihilated by the Japanese, the better. By the same token, China's territorial and administrative integrity under the "bad" GMD state was worth nothing to the CCP. As we have documented, in fifteen years the CCP attempted three times to establish its own "autonomous state" in opposition to the GMD government. The CCP's separatist plans took place in the Northwest in 1935–36, in all the "liberated areas" in 1945, and in the Northeast in 1946; and all these plans were contingent upon Soviet support. To be fair to the CCP, we must also note that when the GMD was facing a total defeat early in 1949, the Nanjing regime intended to use international influence to separate China along the Yangzi River, with the CCP controlling the north, and the GMD the south. This time, it was Mao who was determined to put the whole country under a single CCP state, because he was sure that the CCP military was strong enough to do the job. Given the fact that both the CCP and the GMD morally upheld their parties' interests above the territorial and administrative integrity of the nation due to the lack of "nationalism" in Chinese tradition, China could very well have been divided early in 1949, had the CCP been a bit weaker, or the GMD a bit stronger; and the world would have faced a much bigger "Korea" or "Vietnam" in the postwar Asian mainland.

Due to their outlook of moral absolutism, the Communists effectively pushed any national boundaries into the obscure background of their conceptual world. In their mind, since the Soviet government was a "proletarian state," it was not only better than the Chinese GMD state, it was also their source of inspiration and material assistance. That was the fundamental reason for Mao to assert repeatedly the inseparability of Chinese and Soviet interests. More often than not, as we have seen, Stalin had to persuade Mao to conceal the "illegal relations" between the CCP and Moscow, and to pay more lip service to the concept of national boundaries. For instance, when Mao intended to declare Manchurian autonomy early in 1946, the Soviets disuaded him. In 1949, when Mao requested Soviet direct involvement in the planned assault on Taiwan, it was Stalin who said "no" softly but firmly. Without distorting the facts or our own minds, the last label that may fit the reality of the CCP behavior in 1935–50 is "nationalism." Unlike Tito, Mao and his comrades were inherently "internationalists," or "universalists," as Chen Jian put it.[4]

Conditioned by its "proletarian mandate," the CCP's anti-Americanism was a fundamental characteristic rooted in its self-identification. It was not because the U.S. was perceived to be dangerous to China's "national interest" that triggered the CCP's hostility toward the U.S. Instead, it was because the Party consistently viewed the United States as the "foreign master" of the GMD, inherently hostile to the CCP revolution, that the CCP was born anti-American, as it was born pro-Soviet. Only when Mao felt that the American factors could be played out in favor of the CCP cause against the GMD, did he decide to extend the united front doctrine and technique to court the Americans. To do so, as we have seen, he had specific short-term goals in mind, and when these goals failed to materialize, Mao quickly reversed his friendly gesture toward "American imperialists." If Mao had understood the concept of western nationalism, he would have taken the "third path" as the pro-CCP "third force" had suggested. In contrast, for the sake of consolidating the Party's power at home and advancing the "international proletarian cause" abroad, Mao not only repudiated the "middle-of-the-road" approach and took the "lean-to-one-side" policy, but he also sent the CPV to Korea to engage the Americans in a shooting war, which he saw as inevitable.[5]

One decade later, when Sino-American tension was still running high, Mao decided to split with the Soviet Union. From a conventional international perspective in the "nation-state" framework, it was a highly "irrational" diplomatic move, which literally isolated China from the outside world. It, however, was perfectly rational for Mao and his colleagues who were convinced that the new elite in the Kremlin were "revisionists" who betrayed the "proletarian cause." In their mind, by declaring the Soviet state as an "all-people" state, Khrushchev betrayed the class-struggle doctrine, thereby putting the "proletarian revolution" to an end at home. And by going to Camp David to shake hands with Eisenhower, Khrushchev sold out the international proletarian cause of anti-imperialism. Having lost the "proletarian mandate," the Soviet party-state was no longer a friend of the CCP. Where was the "Chinese national interest" located in Mao's conceptual world when he decided to split with the USSR? In the fierce "war of words" Mao personally directed against the Soviet "revisionists" early in the 1960s, there is no such term as "Chinese national interest" found anywhere in Beijing's extensive texts of polemic. If in the 1960s, more than a decade after the CCP had become the ruler of China, the concept of "nation" was still obscure in the minds of Mao and his colleagues, how could it be possible that "nationalism" was the driving force of CCP foreign policy before 1950, when the Party was but a rebel force against the established Chinese state?

THE ROLE OF IDEOLOGY IN CCP FOREIGN POLICY MAKING

Unlike those who argue for the "structural" existence and supremacy of the "Chinese national security interest" in shaping China's foreign policy, I contend that different political groups of individuals did not share a consensus on what China's national interest was and how to bring it about. Thus, the ideology of a person, such as Mao, or a group, such as the CCP, became essential in shaping their perception of the situation they found themselves in, and their policy toward the perceived reality. I also suggest that an ideology, such as Maoism, should be seen as the bedrock of a particular culture, with which the group of people involved identified themselves, for which they found their purposes of life. I not only identify the CCP-controlled military forces and the rural base areas as the historical agents of Maoist class-struggle ideology, I also demonstrate how the CCP's policy was influenced by the dualistic Maoism which, in addition to its "hard core," possessed a "soft layer" of united front doctrine. Thus, the CCP ideology was no longer a set of rhetorical principles or doctrines which could be hung high and dry; it was the spiritual matrix from which Mao and his comrades formed their visions of reality and policy guidelines.

Scholars have discovered the complex of socioeconomic and political-intellectual circumstances in which Marxist-Leninist ideology took roots in China. Inspired by psychoanalytical theory of identification, I come to conceptualize the role of ideology in the CCP policy-making structure within the framework of a CCP political culture, which had its own dynamics. After Mao and his generation had completed their conversion to the class-struggle ideology, it became the foundation of the "psychological self" of them as individuals, and the Party as a group. For their survival and well-being, they acquired a self-generated momentum to defend and enhance their collective identity. In so doing, they needed to modify their program to achieve gratification of their identity. The process of the modification of their program was in and of itself the Party's policy-making process, which was driven by the inner dynamics of the CCP culture. In this instance, outside factors, such as how the U.S. behaved, were only some of the components of the subjective environment with which the Party came to interact. In general, we have good reason to consider a nation's foreign policy as the extension of its domestic policy. If it is absurd to argue that U.S. policy during the Gulf War was essentially determined by the behavior of Saddam Hussein, it is equally, if not more, absurd to assume that the CCP's foreign policy was determined by what the Americans did or didn't do. In fact, as I have documented, the CCP's policy toward the U.S. often changed rapidly and radically not because of a change in U.S. behavior, but because of a change in Moscow's policy. The CCP identified itself with Moscow, and it viewed its relations with the USSR as matters of "internal affairs" within the world socialist movement.

Since the CCP's policy-making process was first of all driven by the inner dynamics of its political culture, the limits of the Party's tactical flexibility were by and large confined by the boundaries of the culture. If the Communists were to change the fundamentals of their identity/ideology for the sake of short-term gains, they would have used their means to defeat their ends. The CCP's policy flexibility was sanctioned and guided by the united front doctrine, and Mao unequivocally stated that the united front policy was a class policy. This meant that after the Maoist ideology helped select the CCP's friends and enemies, the united front policy was to use tomorrow's enemies to defeat today's enemies. In so doing, the CCP should nonetheless never identify itself with its bedfellows. Had the Communists come to identify themselves with the Nationalists as "Chinese" for the sake of defeating the Japanese, they should have turned their armed forces and base areas into an integral part of the GMD establishment; and then they would have found themselves totally at the mercy of Jiang when Japan was defeated. By the same token, to use the Americans' ideal of "democracy" against the GMD "dictatorship" was not to identify the Communists themselves with the Americans. This explains why there was a two-sided pattern in the CCP's dealing with the Americans in 1942–45, and again in 1948–49: on the "*yang* side," the Communists were friendly and flexible; on the "*ying* side," they kept watchful eyes on their "bedfellows" with deep-seated distrust. In contrast to the argument that ideology only influenced the CCP's theoretical and abstract selection of enemy and friend and its concrete policy-making was determined by the "Chinese national interest," I conclude that the concrete manner in which the Communists dealt with the Soviets and Americans was also conditioned by their identity/ideology as well.

When the Communists embraced and fought for their ideology for years, ideology was not only their self-identity, but also their "trademark" and "selling point" with which they recruited new converts and appealed to the general public. Thus, had they decided to change the fundamentals of their ideology, they would have risked great political danger of internal disarray and external defeat. It would be absurd to suggest that it would be advisable for Newt Gingrich to turn himself from a conservative into a liberal, should the political environment in the future so recommend, in order to gain more votes. By the same token, I contend that only by utter ignorance could one expect Mao and his comrades to accept Marshall's mediation in 1946 by turning themselves from Communists into liberal parliamentarians. Had they taken the "French path" in 1946 by giving up their military forces and participating in a genuine democratic process, what would have happened to them? Not only would they have suffered from personality breakdown, but also, in a democratic environment, what they had done in the past would have become political liability, and Mao could have been charged with treason for his secret conduct during the anti-Japanese war, or for his ruthless persecution of innocent people such as Wang Shiwei whose only "sin" was writing an article. Mao was keenly aware of how dangerous it could be if the Party gave up its military and territorial control, and he refused to change the Party's identity, although he tried to mislead the Americans to believe that the CCP's cause was only "liberal" in the American sense of the word. The point is that, once the CCP culture was established, it not only possessed the defining power in terms of who they were and what they would do, it also had the self-restraining power which even the creators of it could not breach. Thus, by the very nature of its culture, the CCP could not but continue to follow the "Russian path," and Mao remained a Stalinist in essence until his last day. Mao was a prisoner of the CCP culture which he helped a great deal to build. Thus, the CCP foreign policy has to be understood within the framework of the CCP political culture.

To safeguard the Party from self-destruction by losing its identity, the CCP created a set of ritualized activities such as group study, endless rectification through criticism and self-criticism, and inner-party struggle against the "rightist" or "leftist deviations," and so on. These activities, which became an important part of the CCP culture, generated a strong tendency toward enhancing the group identity by weeding out the "less-purified" (*buchun*) elements among party members. Thus, from Mao down to the rank and file, the Party demonstrated an inclination toward radicalism. Within the Party, to be criticized as a "left-deviationist," one was only an "immature revolutionary"; while to be condemned as a "right-deviationist," one's revolutionary identity was questioned. Consequently, the Party's capacity for being more tactical and flexible was limited and the process toward adopting a compromising policy often painstaking. Stalin, therefore, often came onto the scene as a balancing mechanism in the CCP policy process. In this sense, I argue that after the death of Stalin the CCP's road toward self-destructing ultra-leftism during the Great Leap Forward and the Cultural Revolution should also be seen as the working of the CCP political culture. The CCP's radical tendency explains why its policy adjustment toward a united front with the GMD in 1935–37, and with the U.S. in 1937–42, was so dragging and torturous, while its policy reverse by the end of World War II against both the GMD and the U.S. was so summary and painless. To the Communists, it was easier to be "leftish" than to be "rightish" in policy matter. Thus, to invoke the united front to make CCP policy more flexible, the Party often needed Moscow to take the lead.

By the same logic, whenever Mao felt strong enough to achieve gratification without taking a detour, he would naturally become more reluctant to compromise, and military conquest would always take precedence over the united front. Only after suffering a defeat would Mao's "monkey spirit" rise and his "tiger spirit" temporarily recede. With the cold war intensifying after 1947, Mao and his comrades were greatly encouraged by their military success at home; consequently, they became more uncompromising with both the GMD and the U.S., even when Stalin advised for more tactical caution. It is worth noting that the Communists have grasped the psychological dimension of the cold war as early as 1946, when they called it *shenjingzhan* ("the war of nerve," or "psychological warfare"). As I have demonstrated, during both the civil war and the Korean War, Mao's "credibility concern" had two dimensions: to raise morale within the revolutionary camp, and to frustrate the morale of the enemies to force them to retreat (*zhinan ertui*). Therefore, by announcing the "hands-off" policy, the Truman Administration conveyed a sense of hopelessness, and Mao's "tiger spirit" was thus encouraged, which made him more inclined to adopt a hard-line policy in Korea when the crisis erupted there. On the other hand, by reverse logic, Mao could have temporarily accepted the reality of a divided China along the Yangzi River in 1949, had the U.S.-GMD managed to stop the CCP's southward march militarily.

By so arguing, I do not endorse the "lost China" school of interpretation which insists that since the CCP was a part of the Moscow-led worldwide communist expansion, the U.S. should have used more forceful means to check the CCP. From my perspective, this "lost China" school shares the same problem with the "lost chance" school, assuming that the outcome of Chinese development was determined by what the U.S. did or did not do, and the power of the U.S. was unlimited. Given the characteristic of Mao's behavior pattern and Stalin's inclination to avoid direct confrontation with the U.S. in Asia, I assume that Mao could have been forced to accept a divided China, had the U.S. managed to defeat the CCP by massive intervention. This does not mean that the Truman administration should have intervened on a large scale, because I believe that U.S. foreign policy was not determined by what the Chinese did or did not do, and there were limits of U.S. power. Had the U.S. managed to hold the southern half of China in 1949, would the American people have prepared to face a "bigger Vietnam" in the 1950s?

My study confirms the "traditionalist" arguments that there was a "systemwide Soviet bloc threat" to the U.S. and the West, and that this bloc was "held together" by a shared ideology of Marxism-Leninism, "largely as defined in Moscow."[6] I nonetheless do not consider myself a "traditionalist," one of whose essential points is that the U.S. response toward the CCP revolution should have been more forceful and direct, and the failure of so doing "lost China" to communism. If one does not take the free-market doctrine of capitalism for granted as a "God-given" system, one has to admit that Washington's foreign policy wasn't, and isn't, ideology-free. When FDR whistled to Jiang, cautioning him to watch out for the Soviets, an ally of the U.S. at the time, he made it obvious that he shared an ideologically driven anti-Soviet "threat perception." One can also make an argument that the CCP-Moscow's "threat-perception" was not entirely ideologically driven, if one considers the western armed intervention against the Soviet Union in 1917–21, the British intervention in postwar Greece against the communists there, and U.S. hostility toward the CCP during the Chinese civil war. The hostility between the two ideologically defined systems, namely, communism and capitalism, was inherently and mutually interactive. Thus, if one takes ideology into account in explaining foreign policy, one has to do so consistently. "Active" and "reactive" are relevant terms; the CCP-Moscow's "active" expansion did not necessarily make Washington's policy, even in its modest form of "hands-off" China policy, any more "reactive," if one sees its ideological components and internal dynamics.

In conclusion, I appeal to my colleagues for a fresh start in studying international history by placing more emphasis on the inner dynamics of each party involved, and perceiving its foreign policy as, first of all, the extension or expression of its own internal logic. Thus, instead of repeating the fruitless "chicken-egg" argument, we approach the interaction between two parties in the international arena as the encounter between two autonomous economic, political, and cultural entities driven by their own inner dynamics. Consequently, misunderstanding, hostility, and war become a "norm" in international history. On the other hand, the striving for a better understanding of all parties involved may provide hope for the otherwise hopeless world order.

Notes

Introduction

1. J. Reardon-Anderson, *Yenan and the Great Powers*, New York: Columbia University Press, 1980, Introduction.

2. Sergei Goncharov, John Lewis, Xue Litai, *Uncertain Partners, Stalin, Mao and the Korean War*, Stanford: Stanford University Press, 1993, pp. 203–25; Donald Zagoria, "Containment and China," *Caging the Bear*, ed. by C. Gati, Indianapolis: Bobbs-Merrill, 1974, pp. 109–27; Barbara Tuchman, "If Mao Had Come to Washington," *Foreign Affairs*, v. 51, October 1972, pp. 44–64. This is a revisionist interpretation against an earlier "lost China" school of thought, for which see Anthony Kubek, *How the Far East Was Lost, American Policy and the Creation of Communist China*, Chicago, 1963; Tang Tsou, *America's Failure in China*, Chicago, 1963.

3. See E. P. Thompson, *The Poverty of Theory and Other Essays*, New York: Monthly Review Press, 1978. Much of the paragraph is based on Richard Ashley, "The Poverty of Neorealism," *International Organization*, v. 38, no. 2, Spring 1984, pp. 225–86; Alexander Wendt, "The Agent-Structure Problem in International Relations Theory," *International Organization*, v. 41, no. 3, Summer 1987, pp. 337–70.

4. John Fairbank, *Cambridge History of China* (CHOC), Cambridge University Press, 1983, v. 12, pp. 14–15.

5. See Lucian Pye, "How China's Nationalism was Shanghaied," *Australian Journal of Chinese Affairs*, no. 29, January 1993, pp. 105–33; Arthur Waldron, "Representing China: The Great Wall and Cultural Nationalism in the Twentieth Century," *Cultural Nationalism in East Asia*, ed. by Harumi Befu, Institute of East Asian Studies, University of California, Berkeley, 1993.

6. Michael Hunt points out that Garver's book, *Chinese-Soviet Relations, 1937–45: The Diplomacy of Chinese Nationalism*, "stresses the CCP's policy of maneuver and places Mao alongside Jiang Jieshi as a nationalist whose outlook drove him into rebellion against Moscow." *Bulletin*, Cold War International History Project, Woodrow Wilson International Center, Issue 6–7. Winter 1995/96, p. 138. Garver is not alone to characterize Mao as a Chinese nationalist "alongside Jiang." It seems that the "nationalism theory" takes the view of a "holistic China," disregarding social, political, and ideological divisions in China.

7. Liah Greenfeld, *Nationalism, Five Roads to Modernity*, Cambridge, Mass.: Harvard University Press, 1992, pp. 2–7.

8. Hereafter "the Communists" refers to "Chinese Communists," unless otherwise specified.

9. Fairbank, CHOC, v. 12, p. 2.

10. Jerome Chen, "The Communist Movement to 1927," CHOC, v. 12, pp. 507–9.

11. *Mao's Road to Power, Revolutionary Writings, 1912–1920*, ed. by S. Schram, New York: M. E. Sharpe, 1992, pp. 250, 399, 505. For a comprehensive overview of Mao's conversion to communism, see Schram's introduction to the collection.

12. Scholars of the "nationalism theory" tend to use the scarcity of Soviet aid to the

CCP as an explanation for Mao's alleged anti-Stalin attitude, as if Mao was as opportunistic toward the Soviet Union as Jiang.

13. S. Schram, *Mao's Road*, p. xvii.

14. Quoted from Benjamin Schwartz, *Chinese Communism and the Rise of Mao*, Harvard University Press, 1968, p. 28.

15. This CCP concept of *guojia* (state) in relation to *minzu* (nation) and *dang* (the Party) is symbolized by the PRC's national five-star emblem: the four small stars represent the four major *minzu* in China (namely, the *Han*, *Meng*, *Zhang*, and *Hui*), or four social classes (namely, proletariat, the poor-middle peasants, petty bourgeoisie, and the national bourgeoisie); and they surround and hold up one bigger star which emblematizes the CCP. Why the Party not the "state"? According to Leninist theory, the state apparatus, including the bureaucracy, the armed forces, police, jails, courts, etc., is only a tool which can be utilized by any class. The Party, which embraces the highest value and morality—communism—provides the "state" the ultimate source of legitimacy to rule the "peoples." As the latest Chinese constitution specifies, the Party is above the state, and the Party's policy above the law. This is deeply embedded in the Chinese traditional culture of moral absolutism, and should not be dismissed lightly as merely a propaganda scheme in the Western context.

16. Professor Akira Iriye convincingly argues that there are three categories exercising their influence to determine international relations: power, economy, and culture, and they "overlap and affect one another," although they are not synonymous or interchangeable. See *China and Japan in the Global Setting*, Cambridge, Mass.: Harvard University Press, 1992, pp. 3–8.

17. The CCP's world vision in relation to its domestic program was shaped at its Second National Congress in 1922. See Zhongyang dang'an guan (The Central Archives of the CCP), ed. *Zhonggong zhongyang wenjian xuanji* (Selected Documents of the CCP Party Center, hereafter, *Xuanji*), Beijing: Zhonggong zhongyang dangxiao chubanshe, 1988–92, v. 1, pp. 59–125.

18. For a theoretical discussion on the relevance of the united front doctrine and CCP diplomacy, see J. D. Armstrong, *Revolutionary Diplomacy, Chinese Foreign Policy and the United Front Doctrine*, Berkeley: University of California Press, 1977.

19. See *Zhou Enlai nianpu* (Chronology of Zhou Enlai), ed. by Zhongyang wenxian yanjiushe (Document Research Office of the CCP Center), Beijing: Renmin chubanshe, 1989 (thereafter, *Zhou nianpu*). This volume is filled with examples of how Zhou was involved in various united front operations and how Mao's role figured in them. For Stalin's involvement, see Michael Sheng, "Mao, Stalin, and the Formation of the Anti-Japanese United Front, 1935–37," *China quarterly*, no. 129, March 1992, pp. 149–70.

20. Mao Zedong, *Selected Works of Mao Tse-tung*, Beijing: Foreign Languages Press, 1966–68 (hereafter, SW), v. 2, pp. 443–44.

21. *Xuanji*, v. 14, pp. 314–18.

22. For the text of the telegram, see *Wenxian he yanjiu*, 1986, no. 5; for Zhou's comments, see *Yanjiu Zhou Enlai* (Studies on Zhou Enlai), ed. by Waijiaobu, Waijiaoshi bianjishe (Diplomatic History Research Office, the Foreign Ministry of the PRC), Beijing: Shijie zhishi chubanshe, 1989, p. 20.

23. *Zhou nianpu*, p. 725, 828. Ronald Keith describes Wang as the deputy director of the group in 1947. (*The Diplomacy of Zhou Enlai*, 1989, p. 34.) Actually, Wang was secretary of the party branch of the group; thus, he was in charge.

24. Erik Erikson, *Identity, Youth, and Crisis*, London: W. W. Norton, 1968; William Bloom, *Personal Identity, National Identity and International Relations*, Cambridge: Cambridge University Press, 1990, pp. 35–40.

25. Ibid.

26. Since Mao and his comrades, who often differed from Mao in tactical details, were all the makers and prisoners of the CCP culture, and shared the fundamentals of the CCP ideology/identity, I will treat the CCP leadership under Mao as a whole. Terms such as "the Party" and the "Party Center," are used in an interchangeable way with "Mao and his comrades," or the "Mao generation." New evidence suggests that even between Mao and Wang Ming, the most frequently mentioned by the "two-line-struggle" school, there was not much substantial difference in terms of the basics of the CCP's policy toward the GMD. See M. Sheng, *China Quarterly*, pp. 149–70.

27. For more discussion, see M. Sheng, "America's Lost Chance in China? A Reappraisal of Chinese Communist Policy toward the United States before 1945," *Australian Journal of Chinese Affairs*, no. 29, 1993, pp. 135–57. For Mao's statement of March 1945, see Yang Kuisong, *Zhongjian de dai de geming* (Revolution in the Middle Zone), Beijing: Zhongyang dangxiao chubanshe, 1992, p. 393. This will be further discussed in chapter 6.

28. See Paul Cohen, *Discovering History in China*, New York: Columbia University Press, 1984.

Chapter I
The Roots of Mao's Pro-Soviet Policy before 1937

1. The most systematic expression of Mao's allegation of Stalin's "mistakes" can be found in his conversation with P. F. Yudin on 31 March 1956. The transcript of the conversation is in the Modern Documents Depository Center in Moscow, and its English translation is in *Far Eastern Affairs*, no. 4–5, 1994, pp. 132–43 (hereafter, Mao-Yudin, 1956).

2. Some scholars take Mao's allegation at face value, and talk about the "bitter memories and past betrayal" between Mao and Stalin as characteristic of their relationship. As Harrison Salisbury put it, " 'Cool' is too weak a word to describe the nature of Soviet-Chinese and Stalin-Mao relations over those years. . . . He [Mao] had not forgotten the times since 1926 that he had been forced by the Soviets to eat humble pie, the reprimands, the expulsions from Party and office because he had failed to follow Moscow's orders, or the mistaken policies Soviet advisers had insisted the Chinese carry out at the cost of death and disaster." (*The New Emperors: China in the Era of Mao and Deng*, Boston: Little, Brown, 1992, p. 84.) I recognize that Salisbury was a journalist, not a historian. He is, however, quoted here because his statement represents a popular assumption of the Mao-Stalin antagonism taken for granted by many, such as the authors of *Uncertain Partners*. The latest example of this popular assumption can be found in Brian Murray, "Stalin, the Cold War, and the Division of China," Working Paper No. 12, Cold War International History Project, Woodrow Wilson International Center for Scholars, June 1995.

3. Mao-Yudin, 1956, p. 135.

4. For more on this period, see Martin Wilbur, "The Nationalist Revolution: From Canton to Nanking, 1923–28," CHOC, v. 12, pp. 527–721.

5. See *Mao Zedong Nianpu* (Chronology of Mao Zedong), ed. by Zhonggong

zhongyang wenxian yanjiushe (The Document Research Office of the CCP Center), Beijing: Renmin chubanshe, 1993 (hereafter, *Mao nianpu*), v. 1, pp. 153–59.

6. See Yang Kuisong, *Zhongjian dedai de geming* (Revolution in the Intermediate Zone), Beijing: Zhongyang dangxiao chubanshe, 1992 (hereafter, *Zhongjian dedai*), pp. 108–10.

7. Influenced by Maoist history, a popular assumption in the West is that while the CCP-Comintern leadership followed conventional Marxist-Leninist doctrine and placed emphasis on the mobilization of the working class in the urban centers, Mao alone recognized the importance of peasants in rural China. See, for instance, the narrative of "China in Revolution," an award-winning television documentary.

8. See Yang Kuisong, *Zhongjian didai*, p. 81.

9. R. North and X. Eudin, *M. N. Roy's Mission to China*, Berkeley: University of California Press, 1963, pp. 137–39.

10. See footnote 2 in *Mao nianpu*, v. 1, p. 185.

11. R. North, *Moscow and Chinese Communists*, Stanford: Stanford University Press, 1965, pp. 105–6.

12. *Mao nianpu*, v. 1, p. 209.

13. Ibid., v. 1, pp. 210–11, 216–19, 255.

14. Ibid., pp. 311–27.

15. Ibid., pp. 339–40.

16. Ibid., pp. 415–16.

17. Ibid., pp. 377–91. The exact date of the Ningdu meeting isn't clear; therefore, it is also unclear whether the Shanghai Center's telegram of 6 October was received before or after the meeting. Given the fact that there is no mention of the Center's telegram, it is safe to assume that the telegram from Shanghai was received after the meeting. Otherwise, the meeting would have been unnecessary, or at least there would have been a mention of the telegram at the meeting.

18. Ibid., p. 420.

19. Ibid., p. 398.

20. Ibid., p. 435.

21. See Yang Kuisong, "kangzhan shiqi gongchan guoji, Sulian, yu Zhongguo gongchandang guanxi zhongde jige wenti" (Several Issues in the Relations between the Comintern, the USSR, and the CCP in the Period of the War of Resistance), *Dangshi yanjiu*, no. 6, 1987, pp. 132–49.

22. Ibid.

23. *Mao nianpu*, v. 1, pp. 438–40.

24. The Zunyi conference of 15–17 January 1935 abandoned the decision made on 12 December 1934, and decided to head toward western Sichuan area. Ibid., p. 443.

25. According to Garver, "Mao won leadership of the CCP if not in the face of Comintern opposition, at least without Comintern support," and "The severance of radio contact between the CCP Politburo and the Comintern was critical to Mao's victory at the expanded Politburo conference at Zunyi." *Chinese-Soviet Relations*, pp. 10–13, 58–62. For an opposite argument, see M. Sheng, *China Quarterly*, pp. 149–70.

26. For more details on Mao's effort in this regard, see M. Sheng, *China Quarterly*, pp. 149–70.

27. Zhang Kuitang, "Zhonggong zhongyang heping jieju Xi'an shibian fangzhen de ziding" (The Formation of the CCP Center's Policy of Peaceful Solution to the Xi'an Incident), *Jindaishi yanjiu*, no. 2, 1991, pp. 243–55.

28. Five of those telegrams from the ECCI to the CCP have been published in *Zhonggong dangshi yanjiu* (1988, no. 3), and it is reasonable to infer that there are still more in the CCP and Moscow archives.

29. See *Zhou nianpu*, pp. 448–54; Shi Zhe, *Zai lishi juren shenbian: Shi Zhe huiyilu* (With the Historical Heroes: Shi Zhe Memoirs), Beijing: Zhongyang wenxian chubanshe, 1991, pp. 136–46.

30. Shi Zhe, ibid., pp. 200–204.

31. Ibid.

32. See Yang Kuisong, "*Sulian daguimo yuanzhu zhongguo hongjun de yici changshi*" (The Soviet Attempt to Deliver Massive Aid to the Chinese Red Army), *Jindaishi yanjiu*, 1995, no. 1, pp. 254–75 (hereafter, "Soviet Attempt). Yang's article is based on his recent research in Moscow's archives. This author is grateful to Mr. Yang for sharing some of his research materials with me.

33. See Wang Ming's letter to CCP politburo, 16 September 1934, ibid., p. 257.

34. A document in Modern Documents Depository Center, Moscow, dated 16 September 1934, ibid.

35. Ibid.

36. Some scholars argue that Stalin did not decide to support Mao's CCP until 1946, or even later, due to a deterioration in the U.S.-Soviet and GMD-Soviet relations. See Odd Arne Westad, *Cold War and Revolution: Soviet-American Rivalry and the Origins of the Chinese Civil War*, New York: Columbia University Press, 1993; Brian Murray, "Stalin, the Cold War."

37. See *Mao nianpu*, v. 1, pp. 442–54.

38. Ibid., pp. 458–59.

39. Ibid., pp. 460–65; Yang Kuisong, *Makesi zhuyi zhongguohua de lishi jingcheng* (The Historical Process of Sinicizing Marxism), Henan: Renmin chubanshe, 1994 (hereafter, *Historical Process*), p. 387; "Soviet Attempt," p. 260.

40. Huang Qijun, *Dangshi yanjiu*, 1987, no. 2; Yang Kuisong, *The Historical Process*, pp. 388–89; Yang Zhongmei, *Zunyi Huiyi yu Yan'an zhengfeng* (The Zunyi Conference and the Yan'an Rectification), Hong Kong: Bengma chubanshe, 1989, p. 64.

41. Yang Kuisong, *Historical Process*, p. 388.

42. Mao Zedong, *Mao Zedong wenji* (The Collection of Mao Zedong's Writings), Beijing: Renmin chubanshe, 1993, v. 1, pp. 363–71.

43. See Mao's telegram to Zhang, 30 November 1935; Mao's letter to Zhang, 1 December 1935, *Mao Zedong junshi wenji* (Collection of Mao Zedong's Military Writings), Beijing: Zhongyang wenxian chubanshe, 1993 (hereafter, *Military Writings*), v. 1, pp. 396–409.

44. See Yang Yunruo, Yang Kuisong, *Gongchang guoji he zhongguo geming* (The Comintern and Chinese Revolution), Shanghai: remin chubanshe, 1988, p. 375.

45. Mao's telegram to Zhou Enlai and Zhang Wentian, 20 April 1936, cited in Yang Kuisong, *Historical Process*, p. 389.

46. *Mao nianpu*, v. 1, p. 530.

47. Mao, *Military Writings*, v. 1, pp. 529–32.

48. Yang and Yang, pp. 378–79.

49. Mao's Telegram of 25 May 1936, *Military Writings*, v. 1, pp. 523–35.

50. See Mao's telegram of 20 May 1935, *Xuanbian*, v. 2, pp. 147–49.

51. Yang Kuisong, "Soviet Attempt," pp. 263–64.

52. The full texts of the two cables are in *Military Writings*, v. 1, pp. 551–55.
53. Ibid., p. 551.
54. *Mao nianpu*, v. 1, p. 532.
55. Mao, *Military Writings*, v. 1, pp. 551–55.
56. Yang Kuisong, "Soviet Attempt," pp. 265–66.
57. Ibid.
58. *Military Writings*, v. 1, pp. 578–93.
59. Yang Kuisong, "Soviet Attempt," pp. 267–68.
60. *Military Writings*, v. 1, pp. 627–55.
61. Yang Kuisong, "Soviet Attempt," p. 267.
62. Ibid.

Chapter II
CCP-Moscow Relations during the Anti-Japanese War, 1937–1945

1. *Mao nianpu*, v. 1, pp. 645–46. For more background information on what Mao was referring to, see M. Sheng, *China Quarterly*, pp. 149–70.
2. Mao-Yudin, 1956.
3. For example, Garver says that Mao resisted the Comintern's new line of a united front with Jiang, and when he finally accepted the united front in principle, he continued to defy Moscow on many concrete issues. Thus, Stalin "had plenty of reason to view Mao as a dissident Communist who refused to accept the 'iron discipline' of the International Workers Movement." *Chinese-Soviet Relations*, p. 13.
4. This point is subtly made in the resolution of the CCP's Third Plenum of the Eighth Congress shortly after the death of Mao. It criticizes Mao's "undemocratic" behavior in the post-1949 era, and officially put an end to Mao's Cultural Revolution, thereby signifying the rise of Deng Xiaoping.
5. Quoted from Yang Kuisong, *Zhongjian didai*, pp. 193–94.
6. Mao, *Military Writings*, v. 1, pp. 402–3.
7. Quoted from Yang and Yang, pp. 351–53.
8. Ibid.
9. Ibid.
10. See *Jiuguo shibao*, 12 July 1936; M. Sheng, *China Quarterly*, pp. 155–56.
11. For Dimitrov's speech on 23 July and the ECCI's directive of 15 August 1936, see *Zhonggong dangshi yanjiu*, no. 2, 1988, pp. 84–86.
12. Some scholars are of the opinion that on the eve of the German-Japanese "Anti-Comintern Pact" of November 1936, Stalin desperately wanted to strike a deal with Jiang and ordered the CCP to compromise with Jiang to serve Moscow's security needs. But Mao was unwilling to sacrifice the Party's military and political independence for Moscow's sake; therefore, he continued to defy the ECCI's policy of "uniting with Jiang." See Garver, "The Origins of the Second United Front," p. 56; "The Soviet Union and the Xi'an Incident," *The Australian Journal of Chinese Affairs*, no. 26, 1991, pp. 145–75.
13. *Xuanbian*, v. 2, pp. 235–55. Also see M. Sheng, *China Quarterly*, pp. 156–58.
14. Yang Kuisong, *Zhongjian didai*, p. 289.
15. See the Party's directive on "Compelling Jiang to resist Japan," 1 September 1936, Zhongyang dang'anguan, zhongyang tongzhanbu (Central Archives and the

Department of the United Front of the CCP), ed., *Zhonggong zhongyang kangri zhanzheng shiqi tongyi zhanxian wenjian xu*anbian*mm133* (Selected Documents of the Party Center on the United Front during the War of Resistance), Beijing: Dang'an chubanshe, 1984–84 (hereafter, *Xuanbian*), v. 2, pp. 251–52.

16. See *Wenxian he yanjiu*, no. 6, 1986, pp. 25–29. In this issue, 34 pieces of CCP telegrams regarding the Xi'an Incident are released.

17. Ibid.; Yang Kuisong, "Guanyu gongchan guoki yu zhongguo gongchandang lian-Jiang kang-ri fangzheng de guanxi wenti" (About the Relations between the CCP and the Comintern Regarding the Policy of Uniting with Jiang to Resist Japan), *Zhonggong dangshi yanjiu*, no. 4., 1989, pp. 51–59.

18. Kong Xiangxi, "Xi'an shibian huiyilu" (Recollection on the Xi'an Incident), *zhuanji wenxue* (Taibei), v. 9, no. 6, 1966; Deng Wenyi, "Xi'an shibian yu zhongguo mingyun" (Xi'an Incident and China's Fate), *Zhuanji wenxue*, v. 32, no. 2, 1978. Garver provides an accurate and detailed account of the Nanjing-Moscow interaction in his article, "The Soviet Union and the Xi'an Incident," pp. 164–68.

19. For this telegram of Mao, see *Zhonggong dangshi yanjiu*, no. 6, 1988, pp. 27–28.

20. Ibid.

21. Ibid.; also see *Zhou nianpu*, p. 337.

22. See *Zhou nianpu*, p. 335.

23. For Zhou's telegram, see *Zhonggong dangshi yanjiu*, no. 6, 1986.

24. Garver speculates that Mao would have adopted a peaceful resolution of the Xi'an Incident without Comintern intervention. Based on Zhou's telegram of 17 December, I agree with Garver on this point. But I don't agree with his statement: "A central element of Mao's leadership of the CCP was his determination to emancipate the Chinese revolution from Soviet direction." ("The Soviet Union and the Xi'an Incident," pp. 172–73.)

25. See *Zhou nianpu*, p. 337. According to the researchers in Beijing, the ECCI's telegram was sent out with a "wrong code," and Mao could not decipher it. Thus, Mao sent Moscow another cable on 18 December, asking Moscow to redispatch the directive of 16 December, and Moscow did so on 20 December. (Yang and Yang, pp. 392–94.) Garver speculates that it might have been Mao's tactic to gain time to hash out the issue in order to present Moscow with a *fait accompli.* ("The Soviet Union and the Xi'an Incident," pp. 171–72.) I agree that the alleged "wrong code" seems to be Mao's way of gaining time to hash out the issue; but I think Mao in the given situation would have had little intention to show that he outsmarted Moscow. Rather, he needed time to carry out the transition of policy initiated by Moscow.

26. See *Mao nianpu*, v. 1, pp. 624–27.

27. See Mao's telegram of 8 January 1937, ibid., p. 640.

28. For the ECCI's telegram, see *Zhonggong dangshi yanjiu*, 1988, no. 3, pp. 78–80.

29. Ibid.

30. *Xuanbian*, pp. 370–71, 373, 385–86.

31. *Zhonggong dangshi yanjiu*, 1988, no. 3, p. 79.

32. See *xuanbian*, pp. 514–16, 522–23.

33. See Yang Kuisong, "Kangri zhanzheng baofahou zhongguo gongchandang duiri junshi zhanlue fangzhen de yanbian" (The Evolution of the CCP's Military Strategy After the Eruption of the Anti-Japanese War), *Jindaishi yanjiu*, 1988, no. 2, pp. 105–27.

34. *Zhou Nianpu*, pp. 370–75.

35. Influenced by the myth of Mao's own making, some scholars depict a fierce debate over military strategy within the CCP in which Mao stood firm for dispersed and independent guerrilla warfare while his opponents advocated a concentrated mobile warfare in cooperation with the GMD. "Mao's strategy," they believe, "was admirably designed to carry out an eventual social revolution in China," but was detrimental to Moscow's security and foreign policy planning, whereas the strategy of Mao's opponents in the CCP was in accordance with Stalin's will. See Garver, pp. 58–67.

36. For Dimitrov's speech, see *zhonggong dangshi yanjiu*, 1988, no. 3, pp. 80–82.

37. See Mao's telegrams of 16 and 28 July 1937, *Military Writings*, v. 2, pp. 5–6, 18–19; also Yang Kuisong, *Jindaishi yanjiu*, 1988, no. 2, pp. 105–27.

38. Yang Kuisong, ibid.

39. *Military Writings*, v. 2, pp. 20, 22–24; also see *Zhou nianpu*, pp. 373–74.

40. *Zhou nianpu*, pp. 374–75; also *Military Writings*, p. 26, note 2; Yang Kuisong, "The Evolution."

41. See Mao, *Military Writings*, pp. 25–27; Yang Kuisong, "The Evolution."

42. Ibid.

43. Yang Kuisong, "The Evolution." Mao's telegram to Zhang Chong on August 17 is in *Military Writings*, p. 30.

44. *Military Writings*, pp. 32–33; Yang Kuisong, ibid.

45. Yang Kuisong, ibid.

46. For Zhou's attitude at the Conference, see *Zhou nianpu*, pp. 378–79.

47. *Military Writings*, pp. 40–41; Yang Kuisong, "The Evolution."

48. For the texts of Mao's cables of 17 and 21 September, see *Mao Zedong Junshi Wenxuan, neibuben* (Selected Military Works of Mao, Inner-circulating version), ed. by Zhongguo renmin jiefangjun junshi kexueyuan (Military Academy of the PLA), Beijing: Jiefangjun zhanshi chubanshe, 1981 (hereafter, *Junshi wenxuan*), pp. 82–85.

49. *Zhou nianpu*, p. 383.

50. For the text of this cable, see *Junshi wenxuan*, pp. 85–86.

51. Ibid., pp. 86–87.

52. See *Military Writings*, pp. 76–79; Yang Kuisong, "The Evolution."

53. Garver takes the document of 8 October as key evidence of the strong opposition of CCP generals in the front to Mao's guerrilla strategy. (*Chinese-Soviet Relations*, pp. 63–64.)

54. *Zhou nianpu*, pp. 386–87.

55. Garver believes that the campaign "was a dramatic departure from Mao's strategy of protracted guerrilla war." Like many other scholars, he also stresses that Peng launched the campaign before Mao gave his approval (pp. 140–42). However, he does not ask and try to answer the question which will immediately challenge the conventional interpretation on this issue: Why didn't Mao stop Peng? Why did he allow Peng to pursue the campaign for months? Was there any sign which would suggest that in 1940 Mao's power to make final decisions was weakened, and that he was incapable of stopping Peng?

56. Yang and Yang, pp. 433–35.

57. Ibid., pp. 435–37.

58. These messages were revealed by Wang Jiaxiang at a Party Secretariat meeting on 8 October 1941. See Xu Zehao, "Wang Jiaxiang yu Yan'an zhengfeng yundong"

(Wang Jiaxiang and the Rectification Movement), *Zhonggong dangshi yanjiu*, 1989, no. 5, pp. 81–85.

59. Ibid.; Yang Kuisong, *Zhongjian didai*, pp. 315–16.

60. Yang Kuisong, *Dangshi yanjiu*, 1987, no. 6, pp. 132–49. Conventional wisdom suggests that the Conference did not have a resolution because Mao resisted it. See Garver, p. 66.

61. Garver argues that Wang Ming "forced Mao into accepting a drastic reorientation of the Party line," because Wang had "special Comintern powers"(p. 66). If this were the case, what made Mao reconcile with Zhou Enlai and others on the issue of military strategy before Wang's arrival?

62. For Mao's interview with the report and his speech, see *Mao Zedong ji* (Collected Writings of Mao Zedong), ed. by Takeuchi Minoru, Tokyo: Hokubosha, 1971–72, v. 5, pp. 323–33.

63. For the two documents, see Wang Jianmin, *Zhongguo gongchandang shigao* (Draft History of the CCP), Hong Kong, 1974, v. 3, pp. 148–50.

64. *Zhou nianpu*, p. 420.

65. Kui-Kwong Shum states that "Mao meant exactly what he said at the time," because Mao understood that the expansion of the rural base relied upon the continuation of a united front with the GMD. *The Chinese Communist Road to Power: The Anti-Japanese National United Front, 1935–1945*, Hong Kong: Oxford University Press, 1988, p. 141.

66. SW, v. 2, pp. 219–25.

67. See Yang and Yang, pp. 457–69; Wang Jiaxiang, "Huiyi Mao Zedong yu Wang Ming jihui zhuyi de douzhen" (Recollection on Mao's Struggle against Wang Ming's Opportunist Line), *Renmin ribao*, 27 December 1979; "Guoji zhishi baogao" (Report on the Comintern Directives), *Wenxian he yanjiu*, no. 4, 1986.

68. Ibid.

69. Yang Kuisong, *Dangshi yanjiu*, 1987, no. 6; *Zhou nianpu*, pp. 473–74.

70. Ibid. The whole text of Mao's cable to Peng is available in *Junshi wenxuan*, pp. 231–32.

71. See Yang Kuisong, *Dangshi yanjiu*, 1987, no. 6. Shum takes this document as key evidence indicating that Mao personally directed "all these developments" in maintaining GMD-CCP cooperation (p. 182). Had Shum known that this document was really Mao's self-criticism in the face of Moscow's rejection of his radical plan to split the united front, he might have reconsidered his entire interpretation.

72. See Mao's telegram of 14 January 1941, *Junshi wenxuan*, p. 234; *Zhou nianpu*, p. 486.

73. See *Zhonggong dangshi yanjiu*, 1988, v. 3, pp. 87–88.

74. See Yang Kuisong, *Dangshi yanjiu*, 1987, no. 6.

75. Yang and Yang, pp. 521–22; *Zhou Nianpu*, pp. 491–92.

76. Yang Kuisong, *Dangshi yanjiu*, 1987, no. 6.

77. Ibid.

78. *Mao nianpu*, v. 2, p. 402.

79. Some scholars believe that the German-Soviet War offered Mao an "opportunity to push [to] a successful conclusion his struggle against the Internationalists of the CCP." The Rectification Movement is seen as a means to "break once and for all the influence of Wang [Ming] and Moscow within the CCP." One event often referred to by

some to demonstrate Mao's "Chinese nationalism" versus Stalin's "Russian imperialism" was Mao's alleged rejection of Moscow's order of an offensive against Japan shortly after the eruption of the German-Soviet war. See Garver, pp. 237–41.

80. *Mao nianpu,* v. 2, p. 312.

81. Ibid., p. 311.

82. For instance, Chen Yi and Liu Shaoqi cabled Mao on 12 July and proposed that when Japan attacks the USSR, the CCP should launch an all-out offensive against the Japanese, even if the GMD would not budge, and even if some strongholds of the CCP behind enemy lines had to be abandoned. Ibid., p. 312.

83. Ibid.; also see Yang Kuisong, *Dangshi yanjiu,* 1987, no. 6.

84. Ibid., pp. 312–13.

85. Ibid., p. 325; Yang and Yang, p. 537; Yang Kuisong, *Zhongjian didai,* p. 361. The meeting on 8 September is based on this author's interviews with informed researchers in Beijing who have privileged access to the Party Central Archives. In 1992–93, the author made three trips to China to do research, including interviewing contemporaries and their associates, researchers and historians in various Party-associated organizations such as *Zhongyang wenxian yanjiushi* (The CCP Center's Archival Research Office). The materials based on these interviews will be referred to hereafter as "Interviews."

86. According to Yang and Yang, Dimitrov's telegram of 7 October disturbed the CCP leadership severely, and the CCP, "for the sake of the unity of the international proletariat, and due to respect for the Comintern," made changes on its policy along the Moscow line (p. 537).

87. *Mao nianpu,* v. 2, p. 314.

88. For instance, see Mao's article of 18 February 1942 on the occasion of the Soviet Red Army's 24th anniversary, *Mao nianpu,* p. 364.

89. *Zhou nianpu,* p. 508.

90. Ibid., p. 509.

91. *Mao nianpu,* v. 2, pp. 347–48.

92. See Mao's statement of 20 February; statement at the politburo meeting of 13 April; telegram to Zhou on 21 April; and statement at the politburo meeting of 18 August 1942, ibid., pp. 365, 374–75, 377, 399.

93. See Mao's speech at a politburo meeting of 18 August; a Mao-revised CCP statement of 25 August 1942, ibid., pp. 399–400.

94. Mao told Yudin in 1956 that the CCP was happy when the Comintern dissolved itself. This is not true at all. Influenced by the Maoist myth, Garver believes that the Comintern dissolution was a "windfall" for Mao. (Garver, p. 248.)

95. *Zhou nianpu,* pp. 555–56.

96. Yang Kuisong, *Zhongjian didai,* p. 371.

97. Shi Zhe, *Memoirs,* pp. 200–209.

98. *Mao nianpu,* v. 2, pp. 386, 394.

99. Cao Zhongbing, *Wang Ming Zhuan* (Biography of Wang Ming), Changchun: wenshi chubanshe, 1991, pp. 348–49.

100. This document is in Russian and is kept in Moscow's archives. A Chinese translation is available in *Zhonggong dangshi yanjiu,* 1988, no. 3, pp. 61, 88.

101. Ibid.

102. *Vladimirov Diaries, Yenan, China, 1942–1945,* New York, Doubleday, 1975,

pp. 190–94. As a whole, *Diaries* was Moscow's fabrication in the 1970s designed to discredit Mao as a "narrow bourgeois nationalist." In the process of compiling the book, however, some historical materials, such as Vladimirov's letters and notes, were used. It is tricky to determine which parts of the book are fabricated, and which are not. I think the parts quoted here are not fabricated, because they prove Mao was an "internationalist" and loyal to Moscow, a theme that directly contradicts the fabricators' basic purpose.

103. *Mao nianpu*, v. 2, pp. 492–94.

104. Cao Zhongbing, pp. 355–58.

Chapter III
From Enemies to Friends
CCP Policy toward the United States before Pearl Harbor

1. Some scholars contend that ideology was important for Mao and Stalin only "on the most general level . . . especially in the selection and treatment of enemies." When the question boiled down to a particular policy issue, "the ultimate concern on both sides was not class struggle, but state interest." (*Uncertain Partners*, p. 220.) I find it logically incoherent to separate "the selection and treatment of enemies" from the concrete policy process, as if one's policy perception has nothing to do with one's policy. Again, "state interest" is always a subjective matter, necessarily tainted by the color of one's ideological lens.

2. For the text of this Manifesto, see *Xuanji*, v. 1, pp. 99–118.

3. See Chen Duxiu's letter on 6 April 1922. Ibid., pp. 31–32.

4. Ibid.

5. Ibid., pp. 174–78. The Diplomatic Clique referred to some American-trained politicians and diplomats such as Wellington Koo.

6. See Stuart Schram, *The Political Thought of Mao Tse-tung*, p. 266.

7. "Zhongyangju baogao" (The Central Bureau's Report), 5 December 1926, *Xuanji*, v. 2, pp. 476–502.

8. *Xuanji*, v. 4, pp. 590–603. Warren Cohen's source identifies the same document as "Circular No. 65," dated September 19. See "The Development of Chinese Communist Policy toward the United States, 1922–33," *Orbis*, v. 11, no. 1, p. 229.

9. "Why Is It That Red Political Power Can Exist In China?" SW, v. 1, pp. 63–72.

10. *Xuanji*, v. 4, pp. 596–97.

11. *Hongse wenxian* (Red Documents), Jiefang chubanshe, 1938. The English translation is Cohen's; *Orbis*, p. 230.

12. See Cohen, *Orbis*, pp. 232–33.

13. E. Snow, *Red Star Over China*, New York: Random House, 1938, pp. 80–81.

14. Ibid.

15. *Jiefang*, no. 12, August 1937.

16. *Jiefang*, no. 13, 16 September 1937.

17. A Chinese translation of Stalin's speech is in *Jiefang*, no. 74, June 25, 1939.

18. See Mao's speech at the meeting of CCP Central Secretariat in February 1939; *Mao nianpu*, v. 2, pp. 112–13.

19. Ibid., p. 125.

20. Ibid., p. 126.

21. See Mao's statement at the CCP Central Secretariat meeting on 7 June 1939; Mao's conclusion at the Party high-Ranking cadres' meeting on 13 June 1939; the Party's directive of 29 July 1939 on the "Far Eastern Munich Plot"; ibid., pp. 126–28, 131.

22. This and previous paragraphs are based on *Jiefang*, nos. 83, 85, 20 & 30, September 1939.

23. "Zhonggong zhongyang guanyu shiju quxiang de zhishi" (The Party Center's directive on the changing situation), 10 September 1940, *Wannan shibian: ziliao xuanji* (The New Fourth Army Incident: Material Collection), ed. by Zhongyang dang'anguan (CCP Central Archives), Beijing: Zhongyang dangxiao chubanshe, 1982 (hereafter, *Wannan shibian*), pp. 14–19.

24. See *Xuanji*, v. 12, pp. 521–22.

25. *Wannan shibian*, pp. 34–36.

26. See *Nanfangju dangshi ziliao* (Materials of the History of the CCP Southern Bureau), Chongqing: Chongqing chubanshe, 1990, p. 25.

27. "Mao Zedong guanyu muqian shiju de zhishi" (Mao's directive on the current situation), 1 November 1940. In his telegram to Zhou Enlai on November 3, Mao further elaborated on this judgment. Ibid., pp. 38–39, 71–73.

28. Ibid.

29. Ibid., p. 39.

30. Ibid., pp. 75–77.

31. Mao to Dimitrov, 4 November 1940, "Interview"; also see Yang and Yang, p. 517.

32. Mao to Li Kenong, 6 November 1940, "Interview"; also see *Wannan shibian*, pp. 80–81.

33. Mao to Zhou Enlai, 6 November 1940, "Interview."

34. *Zhou nianpu*, p. 492.

35. Ibid., p. 496.

36. See Mao's telegram to Zhou on 4 March 1941; Mao's statement at the CCP politburo meeting on 5 March 1941; *Mao nianpu*, v. 2, pp. 279–80.

37. *Zhou nianpu*, p. 503.

38. SW, v. 2, p. 21.

39. See JFRB, 25, 29, 30, 31 May & 4, 19 June 1941.

40. *Mao nianpu*, v. 2, p. 283.

41. See Mao's telegram to Peng Dehuai and other military leaders on 13 April 1941, "interview"; also, *Mao nianpu*, v. 2, p. 287.

42. See Mao's telegrams to Zhou on 14 & 17 April 1941; Mao's speech at the politburo meeting on 16 April 1941, "Interview"; also, *Mao nianpu*, v. 2, pp. 287–88. Being sure of the CCP's nationalistic nature and lack of sufficient historical evidence, conventional wisdom holds that Mao and other CCP leaders were reproachful of the Moscow-Tokyo pact of neutrality. See, for example, Gittings, *The World and China*, pp. 81–85.

43. See Mao's telegram to Zhou on 20 April 1941, *Mao nianpu*, v. 2, p. 290.

44. See Mao's telegrams of 25, 26 May 1941, and Mao's speech at the politburo meeting on 26 May 1941; *Mao nianpu*, v. 2, pp. 300–301.

45. See the editorial of *Jiefang ribao*, 20 June 1941.

46. For the CCP's view on the resumed international united front, also see JFRB editorials on 8, 11, 15, 16 July, 4, 15, 21, 26 August, Zhou Enlai's article on 31 July,

and the CCP's official statement on 20 August. Noticeably, the CCP was now attacking U.S. isolationists such as Charles Lindbergh and Herbert Hoover, instead of those previous "warmongers" such as Knox and Stimson.

47. Mao to Zhou Enlai, 6 July 1941, interview; also Niu Jun, *Cong Yan'an zouxiang shijie* (From Yan'an toward the World), Fujian renmin chubanshe, 1992, p. 103.

Chapter IV
Courting the Americans
The CCP's United Front Policy toward the U.S., 1942–1945

1. John Gittings put these quotations in the beginning of a chapter entitled "From Moscow to Washington . . . , 1943–5." Like many other scholars in the West, Gittings believes that Mao struggled to bring the CCP out of Stalin's shadow during the Second World War; at the same time, Mao's welcome of the U.S. presence and intervention in China is not mere "calculated flattery." In other words, Mao was leaving Moscow to lean toward Washington. See Gittings, *The World and China*, pp. 91–99.

2. *Zhou nianpu*, pp. 578–81; for the text of the directive, see *Xuanji*, v. 14, pp. 314–18. This text was not available in China until the late 1980s, but it was published in Moscow in the early 1970s.

3. "Zhonggong zhongyang guanyu duiyu guoneiwai shili lianhe huo fandui de biaozhun de zhishi" (The Party Centre's Directive on the Criteria of Uniting or Opposing Various Domestic and Foreign Forces), 12 July 1941; Mao to Zhou Enlai, 15 July 1941, interview.

4. For Mao's analysis, see *Mao nianpu*, v. 2, pp. 221–22.

5. Ibid., pp. 343–44.

6. See Mao's speech on 28 May 1942, ibid., p. 384.

7. See *Jiefan ribao*, 7 July 1942; *Mao nianpu*, v. 2, pp. 392, 396, 399–400.

8. *Zhou nianpu*, p. 537.

9. Mao Zedong to Liu Shaoqi, 31 July 1942, interview.

10. *Zhou nianpu*, pp. 554–59.

11. For Mao's telegram of 13 July 1943, see *Nanfanju dangshi zilao*, p. 93.

12. See FRUS, 1942, China, pp. 99–102, 207–11, 277–28. 1943, pp. 193–99.

13. FRUS, 1943, China, p. 260.

14. Service, *Lost Chance in China*, pp. 308–16.

15. FRUS, 1943, China, p. 97; Jiang Jieshi, *Jiangzongtong milu* (Secret Records of President Jiang), pp. 91–92.

16. Yang kuisong, *Zhongjian didai*, pp. 379–80.

17. Niu Jun, *Cong Yan'an zouxiang shijie*, p. 135.

18. Memo by Davis, 6 August 1942; 16 March 1943, FRUS, 1942, China, p. 227; 1943, China, pp. 214–16.

19. Memo by Service and Davis in January, June, and December 1943, FRUS, 1943, China, pp. 193–99, 258–66, 397–99.

20. Memo by Davis, 31 December, FRUS, 1943, China, p. 399.

21. Memo by Davis, 24 June 1943, ibid., p. 258.

22. FRUS, 1944, China, p. 329.

23. Ibid., pp. 373–74, 394.

24. *The China White Paper*, pp. 551–57.

25. *Zhou Nianpu*, p. 576.

26. *Mao nianpu*, v. 2, p. 519.

27. Ibid., pp. 519–20.

28. Ibid., pp. 521–22.

29. *Zhou nianpu*, p. 577.

30. D. Barrett, *Dixie Mission*, Berkeley, 1970, pp. 29–48.

31. FRUS, 1944, China, p. 518.

32. "Nanfangju tongzhi dui waijiao de yijian ji dui zhongyang de jianyi" (The Analysis on Diplomacy and Suggestions to the Party Center by the Comrades in the Southern China Bureau), 16 August 1944, *Nanfanju dangshi zilao*, pp. 110–17.

33. Ibid.

34. Ibid.

35. "Guanyu waijiao gongzuo de zhishi" (The Directive on Diplomatic Work), 18 August 1944, Xuanji, v. 14, pp. 314–18.

36. Ibid.

37. Memo by Service, 23 August, FRUS, 1944, China, pp. 608–14.

38. JFRB, 15 September 1944.

39. *Zhou nianpu*, p. 583.

40. Mao Zedong to Li Xiannian, 19 July 1944, interview; also see Niu Jun, *Cong Yan'an zouxiang shijie*, p. 147.

41. Memo by Service, 23 August, FRUS, 1944, China, pp. 610–11.

42. Reardon-Anderson, p. 39, note 8.

43. Romanus and Sunderland, *Stilwell's Command Problems*, Washington, D.C.: Office of the Chief of Military History, 1956, pp. 431–32.

44. For details, see Zhang Yimin, "Kangri zhanzheng shengli qianhou wodang zhanlue fanzheng de zhuanbian" (The Shift of Our Party's Strategy Before and After the End of the War of Resistance), *Dangshi yanjiu*, 1984, no. 1; Xu Yan, "Kangri zhanzheng shengli qianxi zi shenglihou wodang zhanlue fangzheng de zhuanbian" (The Shift of Our Party's Strategy Before and After the Victory of the War of Resistance), *Dangshi yanjiu ziliao*, v. 7, ed. by Zhonggou geming bowuguan (Museum of Chinese Revolution), Sichuan: Renmin Chubanshe, 1987, pp. 231–49; Zhao Shude, "Zhonggong zhongyan guanyu kaipi Wulin kangri minzhu gengjudi de zhanlue juche de yanbian" (The Evolution of the Party Center's Strategy on Opening Up Wulin Base Area of Resistance," *Dangshi yanjiu*, 1986, no. 4, pp. 49–56.

45. Report by Service, 31 August, FRUS, 1944, China, pp. 530–31.

46. See *Junshi wenxuan*, pp. 265–67.

47. *Zhou Nianpu*, p. 594.

48. Ibid., pp. 605–6.

49. See Mao's telegram to Li Xiannian on 19 July 1944, *Mao nianpu*, v. 2, p. 530.

50. Gauss to Hull, 4 July 1944; Hull to Gauss, 9 September 1944, FRUS, 1944, China, pp. 116–17, 568.

51. *Mao nianpu*, v. 2, p. 534.

52. Ibid., v. 2, p. 539. This is a CCP version of the Mao-Service interview, which reflects more accurately the true meaning of Mao's words than Service's report in FRUS, which reflects Service's understanding of Mao's words.

53. For Mao's speech, see Yang Kuisong, *Chinese Historian*, v. 5, p. 21.

54. *Mao nianpu*, v. 2, pp. 541–42.

55. Telegrams of Dong Biwu and Li Boqu to Mao, 17, 18, 24 October 1944, interview; also see Niu Jun, *Cong Yan'an zouxiang shijie*, p. 152; *Mao nianpu*, v. 2, pp. 551–52.

56. See telegrams from Lin and Dong to Mao on 18 and 24 October 1944, *Mao nianpu*, v. 2, p. 552.

57. Niu Jun, *Cang Yan'an zouxiangshijie*, p. 152; *Mao nianpu*, v. 2, p. 555.

58. *Zhou nianpu*, pp. 586–87; Niu Jun, ibid., p. 153; *Mao nianpu*, v. 2, pp. 555–58.

59. *Mao nianpu*, v. 2, pp. 557–58.

60. *Zhou nianpu*, p. 588.

61. Ibid., pp. 588–89; *Mao nianpu*, v. 2, p. 560.

62. *Zhou nianpu*, p. 590; *Mao nianpu*, v. 2, pp. 560–61.

63. *Zhou nianpu*, pp. 590–91; *Mao nianpu*, v. 2, p. 563.

64. Barrett to Wedemeyer, 10 December, FRUS, 1944, China, p. 730.

65. *Zhou Nianpu*, p. 598.

66. *Mao nianpu*, v. 2, p. 564.

67. *Zhou nianpu*, pp. 591–92; *Mao nianpu*, v. 2, p. 564.

68. Ibid.

69. Ibid.

70. See the CCP's directive on the current situation and the Party's task, 25 December 1994, which was revised by Mao. *Mao nianpu*, v. 2, pp. 568–69.

71. *Zhou nianpu*, p. 593.

72. Entry for Thursday, 14 December 1944, Stimson Diary, quoted from Odd Arne Westard, *Cold War and Revolution*, New York: Columbia University Press, 1993, p. 27.

73. See Reardon-Anderson, p. 61.

74. *Zhou nianpu*, pp. 592–93; *Mao nianpu*, v. 2, pp. 566–70.

75. Barrett, pp. 77–78; ibid.

76. Barbara Tuchman, "If Mao Had Come to Washington," *Foreign Affairs*, v. 51, October 1972, pp. 51–52. The next day, the CCP sent Wedemeyer another message which alleged that the Party had evidence to prove that the GMD was negotiating with the Japanese "for a sell-out of American interest in China." See Reardon-Anderson, p. 64. The CCP still appears sensitive about its dealings with the U.S. and there is no Chinese material released recently on this matter, nor on the matter of the "Ward Case" in 1949.

77. Ibid.

78. *Zhou nianpu*, pp. 596–97.

79. See telegrams of Zhou to Mao, 11 February, Mao to Zhou, 12 February; Mao's statement, 17 February 1945, *Mao nianpu*, v. 2, pp. 578–81.

80. Mao's telegram to Zhou, 3 February 1945, *Xuanbian*, v. 3, p. 790. In the document, Mao said that "Stalin is meeting Churchill and Roosevelt," and the result of the meeting would be made available in a few days. Judging from the fact that there was no one who could inform Mao about Yalta beforehand, and the Mao-Stalin radio communication had been active, it is reasonable to assume that Mao was informed by Stalin directly on this matter.

81. Hurley to the Secretary of State, 19 February, FRUS, 1945, China, pp. 234–35.

82. *Zhou nianpu*, pp. 600–603.

83. He Di, "Kangri zhanzheng houqi meiguo duihua zhengce di yanbian" (The Evolution of U.S. China Policy in the Late Period of the War of Resistance), *Jindaishi yanjiu*, 1981, no. 4.

84. FRUS, 1945, China, pp. 242–46.

85. Roosevelt to Mao, FRUS, 1945 China, p. 267.

86. FRUS, 1945, China, pp. 273–78.

87. FRUS, 1945, China, p. 318.

88. JFRB, 9, 10 April 1945.

89. *Nanfanju dangshi ziliao*, pp. 112–14.

90. For details, see Anthony Kubek, ed., *The Amerasia Papers: A Clue to the Catastrophe of China*, The Government Printing Office, Washington, D.C., 1970. See also John Service, *The Amerasia Papers, Some Problems in the History of U.S.-China Relations*, Univ. of California, 1971. For more about the Amerasia Case, see Harvey Klehr and Ronald Radosh, *The Amerasia Spy Case: Prelude to McCarthyism*, University of North Carolina Press, 1996.

91. JFRB, 25 June 1945.

92. *Zhou Nianpu*, pp. 608–10.

93. *Mao nianpu*, v. 2, p. 597.

94. CCP Center's directive on how to handle the anti-CCP civil war launched by *Mei-Jiang*, 17 June 1954, interview; also Yang Kuisong, *Zhongjian didai*, p. 394.

95. Niu Jun, *Cong Yan'an zouxiang shijie*, p. 165.

96. Cited in Wang Chieh-min, v. 3, p. 476.

97. See JFRB, 10, 12, and 19 July. These articles used the name of "the correspondent of the Hsinhua News Agency." The first two have been collected in Mao's *Selected Works* (v. 3, pp. 331–34, 335–36). The last one begins with the sentence: "On Hurley's policy, the correspondent of the Hsinhua News Agency continues to have some comments" (JFRB, 20 July). It is clear that the last one was also written by Mao.

Chapter V
Postwar Alignment
CCP-Moscow versus GMD-Washington in Manchuria, August–December 1945

1. For Mao's prediction, see his telegram on 15 June 1945, *Military Writings*, v. 2, pp. 797–98.

2. For the quotation of Mao in the outset of the chapter, see *Xuanji*, v. 15, pp. 455–56.

3. Some scholars consider the CCP as a party independent from both Moscow and Washington, and they argue that while the Soviets were "betting on all the horses," Mao tried to play in between the superpowers in order to win support from whomever possible. Others even argue that the "tense and sometimes suspicious nature" of the relationship between Mao and Stalin in the summer of 1945 "was driven both by the zero-sum character of their immediate strategic interests and by their bitter recollections of earlier betrayals." See Steven Levine, "Soviet-American Rivalry in Manchuria and the Cold War," *Dimensions of China's Foreign Relations*, ed. by Chun-tu Hsueh, New York: Praeger Publishers, 1977, pp. 10–43; *Uncertain Partners*, p. 8.

4. See JFRB, 18 January, 3 February, 4 March, 31 August, 9 September, 3 October, 7 November, and 15, 16 December 1944.

5. See Suzanne Pepper, *Civil War in China*, Univ. of California, 1978, p. 11.

6. FRUS, 1944, China, pp. 703, 738.

7. *Mao nianpu*, v. 2, pp. 616–17.

8. *Military Writings*, v. 3, pp. 18–19.

9. *Mao nianpu*, v. 2, pp. 616–18.

10. Ibid., v. 3, p. 1.

11. Ibid., v. 2, p. 617; v. 3, pp. 3, 8.

12. See the CCP resolution drafted by Mao on 11 August 1945; Mao's telegrams of 16, 19 August, *Military Writings*, v. 3, pp. 1–3, 34–35, 42–43; *Zhonggong Shanghai dangshi dashiji* (The Chronology of the CCP in Shanghai), Shanghai: Zhishi chubanshe, 1988, pp. 597–98; Zhang Yimin, *Dangshi yanjiu*, 1984, no. 1; Xu Yan, *Dangshi yanjiu ziliao*, pp. 231–49.

13. Qin Xiaoyi, ed., *Zhonghua minguo zhongyao shiliao chubian* (The Preliminary Collection of Important Historical Materials of the Republic of China), Taiwan: The Party History Committee of the GMD, part 3, v. 2, pp. 591–94.

14. Some scholars believe that the Sino-Soviet pact infuriated Mao because it "undermined Mao's widely publicized pronouncement of 1936 that Outer Mongolia should become a part of the Chinese federation after the victory of the revolution." (*Uncertain Partners*, p. 6.) They seem to argue that Mao in 1945, still a rebel against Jiang's nation-state, was more nationalistic than Jiang. They fail to note that when Mao made that statement in 1936 publicly to E. Snow, he was secretly working with Stalin to create a Soviet-supported northwest military base in conjunction with Outer Mongolia, from where Mao expected Soviet war materials to be delivered.

15. Nui Jun, *Chong Yanan zouxiang shijie*, pp. 172–73.

16. Junshi kexueyuan junshi lishi yanjiubu (The Military History Research Department, Military Science Academy), *Zhongguo renmin jiefangjun zhanshi* (The Military History of the PLA), Beijing: Junshi kexue chubanshe (Military Science Press), 1987, v. 2, p. 509.

17. For details, see Tai Dong, "Feng Shaobai sijin Shanghai" (Feng Shaobai's Four Missions to Shanghai), *Renwu* (People), 1987, no. 6, pp. 41–48.

18. *Zhonggong Shanghai dangshi dashiji*, pp. 597–98.

19. *Shanghai dashiji*, pp. 597–600; Xu Yan, *Dangshi yanjiu zilao*, pp. 231–49; *Mao nianpu*, v. 3, pp. 8–9.

20. Shi Zhe Memoir, pp. 307–8; *Shanghai dashiji*, p. 600; *Mao nianpu*, v. 3, pp. 8–10.

21. *Mao nianpu*, v. 3, pp. 10–13; Yang Kuisong, "*Zhongguo gongchangdang duoqu dongbei de zhanlue yanbian yu sulian*" (The USSR and the Evolution of the CCP Manchuria Policy), *Zhonggong dangshi yanjiu*, 1990, special edition, pp. 60–71.

22. Ibid.

23. *Mao nianpu*, v. 3, pp. 13–15.

24. Ibid.

25. Milovan Djilas, *Conversations with Stalin*, New York, 1961, p. 114.

26. Ding Shaochun, *Dongbei jiefang zhanzheng dashiji* (Chronology of the Liberation War in the Northeast), Beijing: Zhonggong dangshi ziliao chubanshe (The Publishing House of CCP Historical Materials), 1987 (hereafter, DJZD), pp. 3–8, 15–16; Wang Minggui, "Dongbei kanglian renyuan qu sulian zhengxun de jinli" (The Experience of the Members of the Manchurian Resistance Force in the USSR), *Junshi ziliao* (Military History Materials), 1985, no. 7, pp. 34–39; Peng Shilu, "Zai dongbei kangri lianjun de yiduan huiyi, sulian beiyeying de wunian" (Recollections about the Northeast Union Army of Resistance to Japan, Five Years in the Northern Camp in the

USSR), *Junshi ziliao*, 1984, no. 2, pp. 60–91. Some scholars argue that Stalin plotted an independent Manchuria by using the 88th Brigade, and Mao was thus resentful of Stalin's attempt to violate China's territorial integrity. See James Reardon-Anderson, pp. 119–22; *Uncertain Partners*, pp. 9–10. They are obviously uninformed of the materials presented here.

27. *xuanji*, v. 15, pp. 257–59.

28. Zhu Yuanshi, "Liu Shaoqi and the Struggle over the Northeast after the End of the War of Resistance," *Jindaishi yanjiu*, 1988, no. 5, pp. 124–45.

29. Other than Stalin's two above-mentioned telegrams, the author is not aware of direct Mao-Stalin radio communications in August 1945. Rather than directly contacting Mao, Stalin seemed to be cautious, passing on information to Mao via the Red Army authorities in the Far East or Soviet embassy in China. Maybe Stalin was uncertain about his China policy for a while, given the sudden ending of the Pacific War due to the A-bombs.

30. Zeng Kelin, "Recover the Land: Recollections of Marching into the Northeast," *Renwu*, 1984, no. 5, pp. 73–82.

31. Yang Kuisong, *zhonggong dangshi yanjiu*, 1990, pp. 60–71; Zeng Kelin, ibid. According to an interview conducted by this author with an informed CCP military historian, the public statement of the Soviet representative was made for the consumption of the Americans in the Dixie Mission. To avoid being noticed, the members of the newly formed Northeast Bureau boarded the Soviet plane before dawn. The overloaded plane crashed on the runway while landing at Dalian, injuring many passengers. Some scholars emphasize that the Red Army representative demanded the withdrawal of the CCP forces, and even declared that if they refused to do so, the Soviets would use tanks to drive them out. However, these scholars do not note, or choose to ignore, the fact that the Bureau was formed overnight and went to Manchuria on board the same Soviet airplane; and thousands of CCP troops poured into Manchuria in the following two months. See, for example, Brian Murray, Working Paper No. 12, Woodrow Wilson Center, 1995.

32. Yang Kuisong, *zhonggong dangshi yanjiu*, 1990, pp. 60–71.

33. *Mao nianpu*, v. 3, pp. 26–27.

34. Yuan Wai, *Zhongguo renmin jiefangjun wuda yezhan budui fazhan shilue* (The Development of the Five Field Armies of the PLA), Beijing: Jiefangjun chubanshe, 1987, pp. 175–76.

35. "Liu Shaoqi zhi dongbeiju dian" (Liu's Cable to the Northeast Bureau), 24 September 1945, interview; also Zhu Yuanshi, *Jindaishi yanjiu*, 1988, no. 5, pp. 124–45.

36. "Zhonggong zhongyang junwei zhi Teng Taiyuan, Bo Yibo, Liu Bocheng, Deng Xiaoping dian, 28 September 1945" (The Cable of the Central Military Committee of the CCP to Teng . . .); "Junwei zhi Luo Ronghuan, Li Yu, Peng Zhen, Chen Yun . . . dian, 29 September 1945" (The Cable of the Central Military Committee of the CCP to Luo . . .), interview; also Zhu Yuanshi, ibid.

37. DJZD, p. 13; Zhu Yuanshi, ibid.

38. Acheson to Truman, 12 Sept. 1945, FRUS, 1945, v. 7, p. 1027.

39. Truman to Acheson, ibid., p. 1028.

40. Huang Kecheng, "Chong subei dao dongbei" (From Northern Jiangsu to the Northeast), *Zhonggong dangshi ziliao*, v. 16, 1985, pp. 56–81. Also see "Luo Ronghuan tongzhi tan dongbei jiefang zhanzheng" (Comrade Luo Ronghuan Talks about the Liberation War in the Northeast), *Junshi shilin*, 1988, no. 4, pp. 22–26.

41. See CCP Military Committee Directive to the Northeast Bureau, 28 September 1945, interview; *Mao nianpu*, v. 3, p. 30.

42. Yang Kuisong, *zhonggong dangshi yanjiu*, 1990, pp. 60–71.

43. *Military Writings*, v. 3, p. 64.

44. See Borisov, *The Soviet Union and the Manchurian Revolutionary Base, 1945–1949*, Moscow: Progress Publishers, 1982, p. 107. Borisov wrote as a polemicist in the 1960s and 1970s; precaution is thus advised in using his writings. In this instance, Borisov's account is confirmed by recent CCP publications. For instance, Xu Yan states that "because of our Party's request, the USSR refused the landing of GMD troops in Dalian, in the excuse that Dalian was a commercial port." (*Lishi jiaoxue*, 1988, no. 12, p. 23.)

45. Yang Kuisong, *zhonggong dangshi yanjiu*, 1990, pp. 60–71.

46. Robertson to the Secretary of State, November 16, FRUS, 1945, v. 7, pp. 1040–42; Feis, pp. 383–86.

47. See Qin Xiaoyi, ed., *zhonghua minguo zhongyao shiliao chubian*, v. 7, "Zhanhou zhongguo" (Postwar China), part 1, pp. 140–48.

48. Xu Yan, *Lishi jiaoxue*, 1988, no. 12, pp. 21–24. Yang Kuisong, *zhonggong dangshi yanjiu*, 1990, pp. 60–71.

49. See Luo's and Huang's memoirs.

50. See *Xiao Jingguang huiyilu* (Xiao Jingguang's memoirs), Beijing: Jiefangjun chubanshe, 1987, pp. 330–31. Also see Yuan Wei, pp. 180–84. That was before the major CCP-GMD military clash, and the Communists had not yet received weapons from defeated GMD troops. As a matter of fact, the CCP's armed forces in Manchuria had expanded so rapidly that their quality deteriorated. According to the CCP's own statistics, by the end of 1945, 33,200 of the newly expanded CCP troops deserted and became "bandits." To solve this problem, the CCP launched a major campaign to tighten army discipline in July 1946. See Yuan Wei, pp. 187–89; Chen Yun, pp. 229–35.

51. Yao Songlin, ed., *Zhang Gongquan xiansheng nianpu* (Chronology of Zhang Gongquan). Cited from *Zhuanji wenxue* (Biographical Literature, Taiwan), v. 63, no. 3, p. 73. The English translation of Zhang's diary is now available, and is entitled *Last Chance in Manchuria*, trans. by Dolores Zen, ed. by D. Gillin and R. Myers, Stanford: Hoover Institution Press, 1989.

52. O. Borisov, p. 106. The CCP today seems to be quite sensitive about these types of documents, and the author has no Chinese language materials to confirm this particular letter.

53. *Mao nianpu*, v. 3, pp. 42–43.

54. Ibid., pp. 43–45. Mao's argument for autonomy in Manchuria and North China challenged a hitherto widely accepted notion that Stalin plotted to separate Manchuria from China in the name of autonomy and Mao, as a Chinese nationalistic leader, was opposed to Stalin's scheme. See, for example, Reardon-Anderson. In light of the above-mentioned documents, however, it becomes clear that if there was a scheme for Manchuria's autonomy, it was Mao's, not Stalin's.

55. *Mao nianpu*, v. 3, pp. 43–44.

56. "Zhongyang junwei guanyu 11 yue zuozhan bushu ji zhishidian" (The Directive of the Military Committee on the Strategic Deployment in November), 2 November 1945, interview.

57. "Zhongyang junwei zhishidian, 4 November 1945" (Directive of the Military Committee), interview.

58. Mao Zedong, "Guanyu neixian zuozhan fangzheng" (On the Inner-line Combat Strategy), DJZD, p. 20. Also see Yang Guoqing, *Luo Ronghuan zai dongbei jiefang zhanzheng zhong* (Luo Ronghuan in the Liberation War in the Northeast), Beijing: Jiefangjun chubanshe, 1986, pp. 42–45.

59. Ibid.

60. When Stalin heard that Mao was ill, he sent two Soviet medical doctors to treat him, and they arrived at Yan'an on 7 January 1946. Mao's eldest son, who had been studying in the USSR, was on board the same plane. See Shi Zhe Memoir, pp. 313–18; also *Mao nianpu*, v. 3, p. 53.

61. *Xuanji*, v. 15, pp. 447–48.

62. Chang Kia-ngau, *Last Chance in Manchuria*, pp. 118–19.

63. FRUS, 1945, v. 7, p. 1044.

64. This is from a telegram of the Northeast Bureau to Yan'an to report a conversation with Soviet representatives. See Yang kuisong, *zhonggong dangshi yanjiu*, 1990, pp. 60–71.

65. Chang Kia-ngau, pp. 126–27.

66. Ibid., pp. 132–36.

67. DJZD, p. 22.

68. Yang Kuisong, *zhonggong dangshi yanjiu*, 1990, pp. 60–71.

69. *Xuanji*, v. 15, pp. 447–52.

70. *Zhonggong zhongyang jiefang zhanzheng shiqi tongyi zhanxian wenjian xuanbian* (Selected Documents of the Party Center on the United Front during the War of Liberation), ed. by Zhongyang tongzhanbu (The United Front Department of the Center), Zhongyang dan'anguan (The Archives of the Center), Beijing: Dang'an chubanshe, 1988, p. 32; also, *Xuanji*, v. 15, pp. 455–56.

71. *Xuanji*, v. 15, pp. 449–52.

72. Ibid.

73. "Zhonggong zhongyang gei dongbeiju zhishidian" (The Directive Telegram of the Party Center of the CCP to the Northeast Bureau, 20 November 1945), ibid., pp. 431–32.

74. Chang Kia-ngau, pp. 146–47.

75. *Mao nianpu*, v. 3, p. 44.

76. "Zhongyang guanyu yingfu huabei meijun huodong gei fenju he qudangwei de zhishi" (The Center's Directive to North China Bureau and Regional Party Committees Regarding Dealing with U.S. Troops' Action in North China), 29 October 1945, interview; also Niu Jun, *Jindaishi yanjiu*, 1987, no. 1, p. 226.

77. JFRB, 30 September 1945.

78. *Xinhua ribao* (New China Daily), 4 September 1945. See Reardon-Anderson, p. 111.

79. JFRB, 4 November 1945.

80. JFRB, 8 October 1945.

81. "Zhonggong zhongyang gei jiaodong quwei zhishidian" (The Party Center's Cable to the Committee of Jiaodong District), 6 October 1945, interview.

82. See Zhu De's protest of 4 November, JFRB, 6 November 1945. Interestingly enough, one week after the event, the Red Army in Manchuria took almost the same action against a GMD office in Changchun as retaliation.

83. Ibid.

84. "Zhonggong zhongyang zhishidian" (the CCP Center's Telegram of Instruction), 25 October 1945, interview.

85. JFRB, 4 November 1945.

86. Ibid., 14 November 1945.

87. Ibid., 8 November 1945.

88. Ibid., 19 August 1945.

89. Ibid., 3 November 1945. The CCP criticized Wallace for repeating an anti-Soviet cliche in order to win the approval of some conservatives.

90. Ibid., 2–3 November 1945.

91. For instance, *Liberation Daily* of 14 November delightedly reported that the U.S. working class and their unions were protesting against their government's China policy, demanding the recall of both U.S. armed forces and supplies from China.

Chapter VI
Mao Deals with George Marshall, November 1945–December 1946

1. *Zhou nianpu*, p. 629; *Zhou Enlai yanjiu xueshu taolunhui lunwenji* (Collection of Articles Presented on the Academic Conference on Zhou Enlai), Beijing: Zhongyang wenxian chubanshe, 1988, p. 260; Zhang Baijia, "Yingxiang zhonggong duimei zhengce de sange yinsu" (Three Elements Influencing the Changes in CCP Policy Toward the U.S., 1945–46), a presentation at the Conference of "Modern China and the World," Beijing, 1990. The manuscript is in my possession.

2. *Xuanji*, v. 15, pp. 494–95.

3. FRUS, 1945, v. 7, p. 768.

4. Ibid., pp. 770–73.

5. DJZD, p. 28.

6. SW, v. 4, p. 75.

7. *Zhou nianpu*, pp. 629–31.

8. Ibid., p. 638.

9. Liu Shaoqi, "Shiju wenti de baogao (Report on the current situation)"; see Niu Jun, *Cong Yanan zouxiang shijie*, p. 219. Also Yang Kuisong, "1946 nian guogong liangdang douzheng yu Marshall tiaozhu" (The GMD-CCP Struggle and the Marshall Mediation in 1946), *Lishi yanjiu*, 1990, no. 5, pp. 52–67; He Di, "1945–1949 nian zhongguo gongchandang duimei zhengce de yanbian" (The Changing of CCP Policy Toward the U.S., 1945–49), *Lishi yanjiu*, 1987, no. 3, pp. 15–23.

10. Mao-Yudin, p. 137.

11. *Mao nianpu*, v. 3, pp. 55.

12. Chiang Kai-shek, *Soviet Russia in China*, New York: Farrar, Straus & Giroux, 1965, pp. 104–5. Jiang had a vision of USSR-CCP vs. U.S.-GMD alignment, just as strong as the CCP's.

13. FRUS, 1946, v. 9, p. 143.

14. *Marshall's Mission to China*, v. 1, pp. 23–32.

15. "Guanyu muqian xingshi yu renwu de zhishi" (Directive on the Current Situation and Tasks, 1 February 1946), *Zhou nianpu*, pp. 640–42.

16. Ibid.

17. *Mao nianpu*, v. 3, p. 58.

18. Ibid., p. 56.

19. Ibid.

20. Ibid., v. 3, p. 57.

21. *Marshall's Mission to China*, v. 1, pp. 440–46.

22. Guo was a prominent pro-CCP intellectual, and Zhang was the leader of a non-GMD minor party. Both of them were considered representatives in the "third force."

23. *Mao nianpu*, v. 3, pp. 60–61. Mao's quotation at the outset of this chapter is a part of this speech.

24. Ibid., pp. 60–62.

25. *Zhou nianpu*, p. 652.

26. Mao to Zhou Enlai, 2 & 3 January 1946, interview; also Niu Jun, *Cong Yanan zouxiang shijie*, p. 215.

27. Telegrams between Zhou in Chongqing and Yan'an Center, 7 and 12 November 1945. See Niu Jun, *Cong Yanan zouxiang shijie*, p. 202.

28. "Zhongyang guanyu manzhou wendi zi tanpan yingqu ruhe fangzheng zi Zhou Enlai dian" (The Party Center's telegram to Zhou on how to deal with the Manchuria issue in negotiations), 9 January 1946, interview; Yang Kuisong, *zhonggong dangshi yanjiu*, 1990, pp. 60–71.

29. Yang Kuisong, ibid.

30. Ibid.

31. "Zhonggong zhongyang gei dongbeiju de dianbao" (The Party Center's telegram to the Northeast Bureau), 11 January 1946, interview; also Niu Jun, *Cong Yanan zouxiang shijie*, pp. 230–31.

32. "Zhonggong zhongyang guanyu dayi dazhang juiding dongbei daju gei dongbeiju de zhishi" (The Party Center's directive to the Northeast Bureau on planning a major battle to settle the score in Manchuria), 27 January 1946, interview; also Yang Kuisong, *zhonggong dangshi yanjiu*, 1990, pp. 60–71.

33. Peng Zhen's telegram to the Party Center, 26 January 1946, interview; also Niu Jun, *Cong Yanan zouxiang shijie*, p. 228.

34. The Party Center's telegram to the Northeast Bureau, 12 February 1946, interview; also Niu Jun, *Cong Yanan zouxiang shijie*, p. 232.

35. *Marshall's Mission to China*, v. 1, pp. 50–52.

36. Ibid., v. 1, pp. 49–63.

37. DJZD, pp. 34–44.

38. FRUS, 1946, v. 9, pp. 535–38.

39. *Zhou nianpu*, p. 647.

40. Ibid., p. 646.

41. JFRB, 14 March 1946. For the Gouzenko Case—the investigation of a Soviet nuclear spy ring in Canada in February 1946—see *The Gouzenko Transcripts*, ed. by R. Bothwell and J. Granatstein, Ottawa: Deneau Publishers, 1982.

42. *Zhou nianpu*, p. 651.

43. For instance, see JFRB, 3 March, 10, 25, 27 May, and 3 June 1946.

44. See Borisov and Koloskov, pp. 50–51; *Marshall's Mission to China*, p. 99.

45. "Zhongyang guanyu dongbei wendi de zhishi" (The CCP Center Directive on the Manchurian Issues), 5 March 1946, interview.

46. Ibid.

47. Yang Kuisong, *Lishi yanjiu*, 1990, no. 5, p. 58.

48. "Zhongyang guanyu buneng chengren guomindang tiaojian gei Chongqing

daibiaotuan de zhishi" (The Party Center's directive to the Chongqing delegation instructing it not to accept the GMD proposal), 16 March 1946; interview.

49. *Mao nianpu*, v. 3, p. 62.

50. *Xuanji*, v. 16, pp. 96–98.

51. Ibid.

52. DJZD, pp. 46–47; also *Xuanji*, v. 16, pp. 100–101.

53. Ibid., pp. 100–104.

54. Yang Kuisong, *Lishi yanjiu*, 1990, no. 5.

55. *Mao nianpu*, v. 3, pp. 70–71.

56. *Zhou nianpu*, p. 651; *Mao nianpu*, v. 3, p. 60.

57. *Xuanji*, v. 16, pp. 102–3; DJZD, p. 47.

58. *Mao nianpu*, v. 3, pp. 68–69.

59. *Zhou nianpu*, pp. 652–53.

60. FRUS, 1946, v. 9, p. 529.

61. *Zhou nianpu*, p. 655.

62. FRUS, 1946, v. 9, pp. 719–20.

63. *Zhou nianpu*, pp. 655–56. This suggests that Zhou Enlai initiated a hard-line policy and Mao endorsed it. But, in front of Marshall, Zhou presented himself as a conciliatory person, caught in the middle between the unyielding GMD and his increasingly dissatisfied and militant colleagues in Manchuria. By spreading such disinformation, Zhou's bargaining position was strengthened, and Marshall, as well as some later historians, was confused. They tended to believe that Zhou was more conciliatory and easier to work with, and that the CCP was divided. They also believed that Yan'an had little control over its generals in Manchuria. We will later see more examples of the CCP's technique of disinformation designed to mislead the Americans.

64. *Xuanji*, v. 16, p. 114.

65. JFRB, 14 March 1946.

66. JFRB, 10, 14 March 1946. Stalin's comment on Churchill's speech was reported on 15 March, JFRB.

67. JFRB, 10 March 1946.

68. Ibid.

69. Moscow's radio broadcast on 3 March, for instance, condemned Jiang as the instigator and organizer of the anti-Soviet demonstrations then taking place in many Chinese cities. *Jiefang ribao* reprinted the Soviet commentary on the same day. Also see JFRB, 10 & 21 March.

70. Yang Kuisong, *Lishi yanjiu*, 1990, v. 5.

71. *Mao nianpu*, v. 3, pp. 64–65.

72. *Zhou nianpu*, pp. 656–57.

73. *Marshall's Mission to China*, pp. 99–100.

74. "Zhonggong zhongyang guanyu dongbei jushi yi genben haozhuang zhi Chongqing daibiaotuan dian" (The Party Center's Cable to the Delegation in Chongqing on the Manchurian Situation's Fundamental Turning in [the CCP's] Favor), 17 April 1946, interview; also Yang Kuisong, *Lishi yanjiu*, 1990, v. 5, p. 61.

75. "Zhonggong zhongyang guanyu dongbeiju qian Changchun deng wenti de zhishi" (The Party Center's Directive on the Northeast Bureau Moving to Changchun and Other Issues), 19 April 1946, interview; also Yang Kuisong, ibid.; *Xuanji*, v. 16, pp. 132–33; *Military Writings*, v. 3, pp. 171–74.

76. *Zhou nianpu*, p. 660.
77. Yang Guoqing, pp. 70–71.
78. Ibid.
79. FRUS, 1946, v. 9, pp. 792–93, 801–2.
80. Ibid., pp. 795–96.
81. Ibid., pp. 802–5; also *Marshall's Mission to China*, pp. 105–8.
82. *Zhou nianpu*, pp. 663–64.
83. Ibid., p. 665.
84. *Marshall's Mission to China*, pp. 112–20. Also *Zhou nianpu*, p. 665.
85. *Zhou nianpu*, p. 665.
86. Yang Guoqing, pp. 72–73.
87. Ibid.
88. *Marshall's Mission to China*, pp. 115–16.
89. DJZD, pp. 58–60.
90. *Marshall's Mission to China*, pp. 136–37.
91. *Mao nianpu*, v. 3, pp. 84–85.
92. *Zhou nianpu*, p. 674.
93. *Mao nianpu*, v. 3, p. 89.
94. Yang Guoqing, pp. 83–84.
95. *Zhou nianpu*, p. 676.
96. FRUS, 1946, v. 10, p. 753.
97. Ibid., pp. 755–57.
98. Ibid., pp. 1047–54.
99. FRUS, 1946, v. 9, pp. 1009–11.
100. *Xuanji*, v. 16, pp. 216–17.
101. JFRB, 2 & 7 July 1946.
102. *Zhou nianpu*, p. 688.
103. Ibid., pp. 697-98.

Chapter VII
The CCP and the Cold War in Asia
Mao's "Intermediate-Zone" Theory and the Anti-American United Front, 1946–1947

1. SW, v. 4, pp. 87–88; *Mao Zedong ji*, v. 10, pp. 47–56.
2. For the text, see *Zhonggong dangshi cankao ziliao* (Reference Materials on CCP History), Beijing: renmin chubanshe, 1979, v. 6, pp. 208–19. Although the article was under Lu's name, it was revised by Mao in person. See *Mao nianpu*, v. 3, p. 158.
3. See Gittings, *The World and China*, p. 142; Okabe Tatsumi, "The Cold War and China," *The Origins of the Cold War in Asia*, ed. by Yonosuke Nagai and Akira Iriye, New York: Columbia Univ. Press, 1977, p. 232. Gittings poses the question, "Relations with Moscow, 1946–50: Ally or Rival?" while Tatsumi argues that the CCP tried to be neutral in the U.S.-USSR fight, but was "drawn into the Cold War structure of the postwar period." The authors of *Uncertain Partners* also believe that Mao's theory was a sign of his Titoist tendency, seeking independence from Moscow. (P. 27.)
4. *Xin Zhonghua* (New China, a CCP biweekly published in Hong Kong), v. 10, 1 May 1946.

5. SW, v. 4, p. 87.

6. According to the editors of *Selected Works of Mao Tse-tung*, "Some comrades overestimated the strength of imperialism, underestimated the strength of the people, feared U.S. imperialism, and feared the outbreak of a new world war. They showed weakness in the face of the armed attacks of the U.S.–Jiang Jieshi reactionary gang and dared not resolutely oppose counterrevolutionary war with revolutionary war." SW, v. 4, pp. 87–88.

7. Ibid. Furthermore, the Communists believed, Jiang Jieshi was hoping for a new world war between the U.S. and the USSR, starting from full-scale American military intervention in China on the GMD's behalf. See *zhengbao* (Righteousness, a weekly CCP publication in Shanghai, later relocated to Hong Kong), editorial, 11 October 1946. To rebuff the GMD, Mao felt it necessary to deny the immediate possibility of a third world war.

8. SW, v. 4, pp. 87–88.

9. Ibid.

10. See Shi Zhe; also *Mao nianpu*, v. 3, p. 53.

11. Ibid., p. 194.

12. Ibid., p. 102.

13. For the texts of both addresses, see *New York Times*, 21 & 22 May 1946.

14. *Xin Zhonghua*, v. 12, 30 May 1946.

15. See *Qunzhong*, 7 July 1946.

16. Zhuo Yun, "Guoji guanxi xinfazhan" (The New Development in International Relations), *Qunzhong*, 14 July 1946.

17. JFRB, 25 June 1946. This was a public version of the Party Center's directive of 24 June; see *Xuanji*, v. 16, pp. 216–17.

18. *Jiefang ribao* published an editorial on the Anping incident, and *Qunzhong*'s editorial called the air raid on Yan'an a signal of full-scale civil war. See *Qunzhong*, 10 August 1946.

19. See *Qunzhong*, 30 December 1946.

20. *Zhengbao*, 30 December 1946.

21. *Qunzhong*, 30 December 1946.

22. A Chinese version of Strong's interview with Mao is available in *Qunzhong*, 5 June 1947. The English quotation is from SW, v. 4, pp. 97–101.

23. SW, v. 4, pp. 97–101.

24. Ibid.

25. Lu Dingyi, "Duiyu zhanhou guoji xingshi zong jige jiben wenti de jieshi" (Explanation for Several Basic Issues Regarding the Postwar International Situation), JFRB, 4 & 5 January 1947.

26. Qiao Mu, *Zhengbao*, 30 December 1946.

27. Ding Si, "Sulian heping waijiao zhengce de genju yu tiaojian" (The Basis and Conditions of Soviet Peace Policy), *Qunzhong*, 16 December 1946.

28. SW, v. 4, pp. 97–101.

29. *Mao nianpu*, v. 3, p. 129.

30. Ibid., pp. 150–51.

31. Su Han, "Truman zhengfu de dongxiang" (The Tendency of the Truman Administration), *Zhengbao*, 18 January 1947.

32. Su Han, "Junguo zhuyi yu jingji xiaotiao" (Military Imperialism and Economic

Recession), *Zhengbao*, 8 February 1947; *Jiefang ribao*, editorial, 12 September 1946; Chen Jiakang, "Kuoda guoji heping tongyi zhanxian" (Enlarge the International United Front for Peace), Ting Si, "Dui mei diguozhuyi de kanfa" (A View on U.S. Imperialism), *Qunzhong*, 30 December 1946.

33. *Qunzhong*, 14 July 1946.

34. SW, v. 4, pp. 120–21.

35. This hidden history of cold war in Asia has not attracted much scholarly attention until recently. Many western scholars argued that Stalin gave Mao little assistance, and the CCP achieved victory independently. For more historiographical debate on this issue, See D. Macdonald, "Communist Bloc Expansion in the Early Cold War," *International Security*, v. 20, no. 3, pp. 172–79.

36. Xiao Jingguang, *Memoirs*, pp. 338–40.

37. *Zhonggong dangshi ziliao*, Beijing: Zhonggong dangshi ziliao chubanshe, 1986, v. 17, pp. 197–210.

38. *Zhou nianpu*, p. 720.

39. *Zhengbao*, 22 March 1937.

40. Ibid.

41. After the GMD-CCP negotiations ended and all CCP delegations in the GMD area withdrew in early 1947, the Shanghai and Hong Kong bureaus were established to be in charge of the CCP affairs in eastern and southern China, respectively.

42. *Zhou nianpu*, p. 736. Another main activity of these foreign affairs organizations in 1947 was to translate some of Mao's writings and Liu Shaoqi's report on the revision of the Party constitution into English. See ibid., pp. 741, 743, 754.

43. Ibid., pp. 737–38.

44. For the Zhdanov and Malenkov speeches, see *For a Lasting Peace, For People's Democracy*, the newspaper of the Cominform, 1 December 1947. Historians are still debating Stalin's role in the origins of the cold war and his motive in organizing the Cominform. But it is clear that the "two-camp" formula was initially expounded by Zhdanov at the Szklarska Poreba meeting in late September 1947. For a stimulating discussion on this issue, see William McCagg, Jr., *Stalin Embattled, 1943–1948*, Detroit: Wayne State University Press, 1978.

45. SW, v. 4, pp. 157–73.

46. For new information about the CCP's effort to win over the "third force" to boycott the GMD assembly, see *Zhou nianpu*, pp. 700–706. For a general discussion on the "third force" issue and the student anti-GMD movements in this period, see Suzanne Pepper, *Civil War in China: The Political Struggle, 1945–49*, University of California Press, 1978; "The Student Movement and the Chinese Civil War, 1945–49," *China Quarterly*, v. 48, 1971, pp. 726–35. Carsun Chang's *The Third Force in China* (N.Y.: Bookman Associates, 1952) offers a participant's accounts. However, these works do not use the inner-party documents which reveal how the CCP tried to engineer the anti-GMD activities in the GMD-controlled urban areas. A new study by Joseph Yick, *Making Urban Revolution* (M. E. Sharpe, 1995), has shed new light on the CCP's activities in Beijing and Tianjin during the civil war period.

47. *Zhou nianpu*, p. 715.

48. Ibid., pp. 718–19.

49. Ibid., p. 725.

50. *Zhengbao*, 1 March 1947.

51. SW, v. 4, pp. 135–39. For Zhou's directive to the Shanghai Bureau on 23 May, see *Zhou nianpu*, p. 734.

52. "NCNA, Yenan Broadcasts, 1946–1948." These are records of CCP broadcasts made by the U.S., and they are available at the Fairbank Center, Harvard University.

53. *Zhou nianpu*, p. 745.

54. "Yenan Broadcasts," 21 August 1947.

Chapter VIII
Mao's Revolutionary Diplomacy and the Cold War in Asia, 1948–1949

1. For examples of this school of interpretation, see D. Zagoria, *Caging the Bear*, pp. 109–27; J. Gittings, *The World and China*, chapter 8. I believe that by exaggerating technical differences in the Mao-Stalin strategic coordination and personality friction between the two dictators into a matter of national conflict, the authors of *Uncertain Partners* leave the readers the impression that Washington could have somehow made use of the fundamental Sino-Soviet conflict to win Beijing over. For a different interpretation, see M. Sheng, "Chinese Communist Policy toward the United States and the Myth of the 'Lost Chance,' 1948–50," *Modern Asian Studies*, v. xx, 1994; Chen Jian, "The Ward Case and the Emergence of Sino-American Confrontation," *Australian Journal of Chinese Affairs*, no. 30, July 1993.

2. Based on American and British materials, Edwin Martin convincingly shows that Washington was interested in exploring a possible working relationship with the CCP, and took some reasonable steps to meet the CCP's friendly overtures halfway, but nothing positive came out of it. See *Divided Council*, Kentucky: the University of Kentucky Press, 1986.

3. The Office of Diplomatic History, the Foreign Ministry of the PRC, ed., *Yanjiu Zhou Enlai* (Study Zhou Enlai), Beijing: Shijie zhishi chubanshe, 1989, p. 240. R. Keith interprets this metaphor to mean building a new foreign ministry, thereby reducing the importance of this principle to a technicality. See *The Diplomacy of Zhou Enlai*, pp. 33–36. Zhou's explanation was fully in accordance with the Party's directive of 19 January 1949 on its foreign policy. See *Xuanji*, v. 18, pp. 44–46.

4. Whiting Testimony, 24 September 1970, *China and U.S. Foreign Policy*, Congressional Quarterly, Washington, D.C., 1973, p. 68.

5. *Mao nianpu*, v. 3, pp. 274–75.

6. Ibid., pp. 329–30.

7. *Junshi wenxuan*, pp. 326–32.

8. S. N. Goncharov, "Stalin's Dialogue with Mao Zedong," *Journal of Northeast Asian Studies*, Winter 1991, pp. 45–76 (hereafter, referred to as "Stalin's Dialogue").

9. Archives of the President of the Russian Federation, folio 39, list 31, pp. 23–24, cited in Andrei Ledovsky, "Mikoyan's Secret Mission to China," *Far Eastern Affairs*, no. 2, 1995, p. 74.

10. Ibid., p. 75.

11. Ibid., pp. 76–77; also see Bo Yibo, *Ruogang zhongda jueze yu shijian de huigu* (Recollection on several important policies and events) (Beijing, 1991), pp. 36–37.

12. *Mao nianpu*, v. 3, p. 439.

13. Shi Zhe, *"peitong Maozhuxi fangsu"* (Accompanying Chairman Mao to visit the USSR), *Renwu* (People), 1988, V, pp. 5–21.

14. For instance, Salisbury suggests that "by early March 1948 he [Mao] had become convinced that he would have to go to Moscow for a showdown with Stalin." But Stalin refused to see him, and perceived a victorious Mao as a threat. (*New Emperors*, pp. 87–88.) Similarly, the authors of *Uncertain Partners* also believe that Mao's intention to visit the USSR was to make sure that Moscow would recognize the CCP's soon-to-be national government, and Stalin's polite rejection of Mao's visit "suggests the complexities that plagued the relations between the two leaders well before Mao's victory" (pp. 29–30).

15. See Memorandum of A. I. Mikoyan, Archives of the President of the Russian Federation, folio 3, list 65, file 606, pp. 1–17, printed in *Far Eastern Affairs*, no. 2, 1995, pp. 79–80.

16. Shi Zhe Memoirs, pp. 372–88; Shi Zhe, "Accompanying Mao"; Shi Zhi, "Mao Zedong zai Xibopo huijian Mikoyan" (Mao meets Mikoyan in Xibopo), *Dangde wenxian*, 1991, VI, pp. 34–41; *Zhou nianpu*, pp. 810–11.

17. Some scholars speculate that Mao was greatly concerned by the issue of whether or not Moscow would recognize the CCP government when it was proclaimed, and he intended to confront Stalin on this issue in person in 1948 and early 1949. (*Uncertain Partners*, p. 30.) I believe that this is only one case in which *Uncertain Partners* interprets what I call minor technical differences between Mao and Stalin, such as the timing for Mao's visit, as major indications of "complexities that plagued the relations between the two leaders."

18. Mikoyan's memo, op. cit., p. 86.

19. The article was in Lui Shaoqi's name, and we know now that it was a collective decision, and Mao approved it in person. For the content of it, see *Liu Shaoqi Xuanji*, Tokyo: Zhonghua wenhua fuwushe, 1967, pp. 227–55.

20. The CCP Central Committee, "Instruction on Circulating the Northeast Bureau's Resolution on Learning Lessons from the Problems Concerning the Yugoslavian Communist Party," 4 August 1948, interview; Jian Chen, *China's Road to the Korean War*, New York: Columbia University Press, 1994, p. 68. My translation is slightly different from Chen's.

21. "Stalin's Dialogue."

22. Ibid.

23. This and the following two paragraphs are based on seven telegrams of Mao and Stalin, available in *Bulletin*, Cold War International History Project, Woodrow Wilson International Center, Issue 6–7, Winter 1995/96, pp. 27–29; also in *Chinese Historians*, no. 7, Spring/Fall 1994, pp. 163–72.

24. For a recent example of this argument, see Brian Murray, Working Paper, no. 2, Wilson Center.

25. After 40 years, General Ye Fei finally admitted that he and General Yang Yong gave orders to the artillery units to attack the British gunboat, and then blamed the British for firing on the CCP first. See *Ye Fei Huiyilu* (Ye Fei Memoirs), Shanghai, 1988, pp. 272–76.

26. "Stalin's Dialogue."

27. For more details, see FRUS, 1944 and 1945, China. There are large sections of State Department documents referring to the Xinjiang situation.

28. "Stalin's Dialogue."

29. Deng Liqun, "Xinjiang heping jiefang qianhou—zhongsu guanxi zi yiye" (About the peaceful liberation of Xinjiang—a page on the Sino-Soviet relations), *Jindaishi yanjiu* (Studies of modern history), 1989, V, pp. 143–50. Salisbury claims that Mao "was not made more comfortable by the fact that the Russians were still trying to . . . detach China's western province of Xinjiang." (*New Emperors*, 85.) He, however, does not offer any reference for his judgment.

30. Ibid.

31. The Party Center to the Northeast Bureau, 1 November 1948, interview; also *Zhou nianpu*, p. 794.

32. *Xuanji*, v. 17, pp. 35–39.

33. FRUS, 1948, v. 7, pp. 829–33.

34. The "Ward Case" has been treated by this author in the article in *Modern Asian Studies*, v. 28, no. 3, pp. 475–502. Therefore, much of the details about the case will be omitted, and the emphasis will be on the CCP-Soviet cooperation and its importance in the making of Mao's radical diplomacy.

35. "Stalin's Dialogue."

36. "Zhonggong zhongyang gai dongbeiju de zhishi" (The Party Center's Directive to the Northeast Bureau), 10 November 1948, interview; also see *Zhou nianpu*, p. 796.

37. Ibid.

38. FRUS, 1948, v. 7, p. 840.

39. Ibid., pp. 834–37.

40. Gao Gang to Mao, 16 November 1948, interview; also see Yang Kuisong, "The Soviet Factor and the CCP's Policy," *Chinese Historians*, v. 5, no. 1, Spring 1992, pp. 22–25.

41. Mao to Gao Gang, 17 November 1948, interview; also see Yang Kuisong, ibid.

42. Mao to Gao Gang, 18 November 1948, interview. In public, however, the CCP charged the Americans with "espionage" to legitimize its actions against the U.S. consulate in Shenyang.

43. FRUS, 1949, v. 8, p. 952.

44. For Mao's telegrams, see *Jianguo yilai Mao Zedong wengao* (Collection of Mao's Writings after the Establishment of the PRC), Beijing: Zhongyang wenxian chubanshe, 1987–1992 (hereafter, *Wengao*), v. 1, pp. 219–43.

45. See FRUS, 1949, 9:474–75, 821–22. Also see E. Martin, pp. 4–7.

46. For speeches of Mao and Liu Shaoqi at the meeting, see *Dangde wenxian*, 1989, no. 5, pp. 3–11.

47. See Mao's telegram to the Party Center, January 3, 1950, *Wengao*, v. 1, p. 213. Emphasis is mine.

48. FRUS, 1949, v. 9, pp. 219–20.

49. SW, v. 4, p. 370.

50. *Zhou nianpu*, pp. 824–25.

51. Ibid.

52. FRUS, 1949, v. 9, pp. 219–20.

53. Ibid., 1949, v. 8, p. 175.

54. Ibid.

55. For the resolution, see *Junshi wenxuan*, pp. 326–32.

56. "Stalin's Dialogue."

57. *Xuanji*, v. 18, pp. 203–8.

58. Ibid., pp. 292–30.

59. Ibid., pp. 308–9.

60. *Junshi wenxuan*, pp. 333–36.

61. SW, v. 4, pp. 361–75, 401–3. These statements have been used by many scholars of the "lost chance" interpretation.

62. "Stalin's Dialogue."

63. FRUS, 1949, v. 8, pp. 746–48. Edward Martin has ably shown us that there were many aberrations in CCP behavior which suggested that the CCP's overture was not sincere. *Divided Counsel*, pp. 23–31. Huang Hua's recently published memoir squarely denies that his conversations with Stuart were designed to send signals for accommodation with Washington. See *Xinzhongguo waijiao fengyun* (New China's Diplomatic Events), Beijing, 1990, pp. 22–32.

64. The Party Center's Directive to Huang Hua, 10 May 1949, interview; also see Huang's memoir, ibid.

65. FRUS, 1949, v. 8, pp. 357–60. Since there is no "hard evidence" of the existence of the Zhou Demarche, some scholars tend to dismiss it as a possible fabrication by the Australian journalist. However, we should be more cautious in dismissing the case if we take note of the fact that the same type of information (or disinformation) about Zhou's liberal inclination and moderate policy position had been passed on to the Americans before and after the "Zhou Demarche."

66. See "Information Circular Airgram," March 30, Box 11, RG 84, WNRC (Washington National Record Center, in Suitland).

67. FRUS, 1949, v. 9, pp. 976–77.

68. Ibid., v. 8, p. 370.

69. Ibid., p. 373.

70. Ibid., p. 377.

71. The Central Military Committee of the CCP to the General Committee of the Front, 28 April 1949, *Dangde wenxian*, 1989, no. 4, p. 43. It is worth noting that this was also after Mao received the above-mentioned Stalin telegram in April 1949.

72. Interview with one of Huang's associates, 8 July 1992. This is in accordance with Huang's published recollection of the event; see *Waijiao fengyun*, pp. 22–32.

73. FRUS, 1949, pp. 373–77. For Acheson's signature, see "Information Circular Airgram," 30 March 1949, Box 11, RG 84, WNRC.

74. Nancy Tucker, *Patterns in the Dust*, New York, 1983, pp. 42–43.

75. See the CCP's "Manifesto of the Second National Congress," *Xuanji*, v. 1, pp. 99–118.

76. "Zhongyang tonggao disanhao" (The Party Center's Circular No. 3), 18 September 1928. Ibid., v. 4, pp. 590–603.

77. *Zhou nianpu*, p. 496.

78. SW, v. 4, pp. 370–71.

79. Ibid., pp. 368–69.

80. Ibid., pp. 369–70.

81. FRUS, 1949, v. 8, pp. 1184–86; see Martin, pp. 39–43.

82. See Martin, p. 42.

83. Judging from some of Zhou's telegrams to the CCP organizations in the GMD-controlled urban areas, it is obvious that the CCP Center encouraged, directed, and organized the anti-GMD, anti-American movements among students and other city dwellers in 1946–49. See *Zhou nianpu*, pp. 712–15, 767; Lu Qingliang, "Zhou Enlai yu diertiao zhanxian" (Zhou and the second front), *Xinhua ribao* (New China Daily), 3 March 1988.

Conclusion

1. For an interesting discussion on "nationless state nationalism," see John Fitzgerald, "The Nationless State: The Search for a Nation in Modern Chinese Nationalism," *Australian Journal of Chinese Affairs*, no. 33, January 1995, pp. 75–104. Although Fitzgerald points out that the concept of nation is fundamentally lacking in Chinese political culture, he still tries to put the modern history of the "nationless" country into the groundwork of "nationalism."

2. For more discussion on Confucianism and its sociopolitical implications in Chinese political culture, see T. de Bary, *The Trouble with Confucianism*, Harvard University Press, 1991; and the Roundtable Discussion on de Bary's book, *China Review International*, v. 1, no. 1, Spring 1994, pp. 9–47.

3. Li Rui, *Lushan huiyi shilu* (Historical Records of the Lushan Conference), Hunan renmin chubanshe, 1994, pp. 133–35; interview with Li Rui, June 1993.

4. Chen, Jian, *China's Road*, conclusion.

5. For more discussion on Mao's perception of the Korean situation and how it propelled him to send the Chinese Volunteers to Korea in 1950, see M. Sheng, "Beijing's Decision to Enter the Korean War: A Reappraisal and New Documentation," *Korea and World Affairs*, Summer 1995, pp. 294–313.

6. D. Macdonald, *International Security*, v. 20, no. 3, p. 185.

Select Bibliography

Chinese-Language Materials

Documents and Contemporaries' Writings

Jiefangjun zhengzhi xueyuan (Political College of the PLA), ed. *Zhonggong dangshi cankao ziliao* (Reference Materials on Party History), 10 vols. (n.p., n.d.).

Jiefangjun guofang daxue (Defence University of the PLA), ed. *Zhonggong dangsh. jiaoxue cankao ziliao* (Educational Reference Materials on Party History), Beijing: Guofang daxue chubanshe, 1985–86 (24 vols. internal circulation).

Jiefangshe (Liberation Press) ed., *Muqian xingshi he women de renwu* (Current Situation and Our Tasks), Dongbei shudian (The Northeast Bookstore), 1949.

Liu, Shaoqi, *Liu Shaoqi xuanji* (Selected Works of Liu Shaoqi), Beijing: renmin chubanshe, 1981.

———, *"Lun guoji zhuyi yu minzu zhuyi"* (On Internationalism and Nationalism), Liu Shaoqi xuanji, Tokyo: Zhonghua wenhua fuwushe, 1967, pp. 227–55.

Mao, Tse-tung (Zedong), *The Selected Works of Mao Tse-tung*, Peking: Foreign Languages Press, 1965–77. 5 vols.

Mao, Zedong, *Mao Zedong ji* (Collected Writings of Mao), ed. Takeuchi Minoru, Tokyo: Hokubosha, 1971–72, 10 vols.

———, *Mao Zedong ji bujuan* (Collected Writings of Mao, Additional Volumes), ed. Takeuchi Minoru, Tokyo: Hokubosha, 1980–83, 8 vols.

———, *Mao Zedong shuxin xuanji* (Collected Letters of Mao), Beijing: renmin chubanshe, 1985.

———, *Mao Zedong junshi wenxuan, neibuban* (Selected Military Writings of Mao Zedong, for internal circulation), ed. Zhongguo renmin jiefangjun junshi kexueyuan (Military Academy of the PLA), Beijing: Jiefangjun zhanshi chubanshe, 1981.

———, *Mao Zedong junshi wenji* (Collections of Military Writings of Mao Zedong), Beijing: Zhongyang wenxian chubanshe, 1993, 6 vols.

———, *Mao Zedong wenji* (The Collection of Mao Zedong's Writings), Beijing: Renmin chubanshe, 1993.

———, "Guanyu Wang Jiaxiang de pingjia" (Comments on Wang Jiaxiang), June 10, 1945, *Wenxian he yanjiu*, 1986, no. 4, pp. 32–33.

Nanfangju dangshi ziliao zhengji xiaozhu (The Collecting Group of the Materials of the South China Bureau of the CCP), ed. *Nanfangju dangshi ziliao—dashiji* (The Party Historical Materials on the South China Bureau—a Chronology), Chongqing: Chongqing chubanshe, 1986.

———, *Nanfangju dangshi ziliao—tongyi zhanxian gongzuo* (On the United Front Works), Chongqing: Chongqing chubanshe, 1990.

Qin, Xiaoyi, ed. *Zhonghua minguo zhongyao shiliao chubian, duiri kangzhan shiqi* (A Preliminary Collection of Important Materials on Republican China, the Period of the War of Resistance); part 5, "Zhonggong huodong zhenxiang" (The Truth About the CCP's Activities); part 7, "Zhanhou zhongguo" (Postwar China); (each part includes 4 vols.) Taiwan: Guomindang zhongyang weiyuanhui dangshi weiyuanhui (The Party History Committee of the GMD Central Committee), 1985.

Wang, Jiaxiang, "Wang Jiaxiang wengao sipian" (Four Pieces of Wang Jiaxiang's Writings), *Wenxian he yanjiu*, 1986, no. 4, pp. 27–31.

Wang, Ming (Chen Shaoyu), *Wang Ming xuanji* (Selected Works of Wang Ming), v. 4, Tokyo, 1974.

Wei, Hongyun, ed. *Zhongguo xiandaishi ziliao xuanbian* (Selected Materials on Chinese Contemporary History), Beijing: renmin chubanshe (People's Press), 1979, 5 vols.

Zhonggong zhongyang (The Party Center of the CCP), 'Guanyu Xi'an shibian de 34 feng wendian" (34 Telegrams Regarding the Xi'an Incident), Dec. 1936–Feb. 1937, *Wenxian he yanjiu*, 1986, no. 6, pp. 26–45.

———, "Guanyu hongjun beishang kangri fangzhen de 18 feng dianbao" (18 Telegrams Regarding the Red Army's Strategy in the Northern Expedition to Resist Japan, May–October 1936), *Wenxian he yanjiu*, 1986, no. 5, pp. 2–14.

Zhongguo dier lishi dang'anguan (The Second National Archives of China), "Kangzhan chuqi Yang Jie deng he sulian cuoshang yuanhua shixian mimi handian xuan" (The Selected Telegrams of Yang Jie et al. Regarding Discussions with the USSR for Assistance to China During the Early Period of the War of Resistance), *Minguo dang'an*, 1985, no. 1, pp. 44–56.

Zhongyang dang'anguan (The CCP Central Archives), ed. *Wannan shibian, ziliaoxuanji* (The NFA Incident, Selected Material), Beijing: Zhongyang dangxiao chubanshe, 1982.

Zhongyang dang'anguan, ed. *Zhonggong zhongyang wenjian xuanji* (Selected Materials of the Party Center of the CCP), Beijing: Zhongyang dangxiao chubanshe, 1989–1992, 18 vols.

Zhongyang dang'anguan, zhongyang tongzhanbu (The Department of The United Front of the Party Center), ed. *Zhonggong zhongyang jiefang zhanzheng shiqi tongyi zhanxian wenjian xuanbian* (Selected Documents of the Party Center on the United Front During the War of Liberation), Beijing: Dang'an chubanshe, 1988.

———, *Zhonggong zhongyang kangri zhanzheng shiqi tongyi zhanxian wenjian xuanbian* (Selected Documents of the Party Center on the United Front During the War of Resistance), Beijing: Dang'an chubanshe, 1984–85, 3 vols.

Zhongyang dangxiao dangshi jiaoyanshe (The Party History Office, the Party School of the Central Committee of the CCP), ed. *Zhonggong dangshi cankao ziliao* (Reference Materials on the Party History), Beijing: renmin chubanshe, 1979, 5 vols.

Zhongyang wenxian yanjiushe (Office of Document Studies of the Center of the CCP), ed. *Jianguo yilai Mao Zedong wengao* (Collections of Mao Zedong's Writings after the Establishment of the PRC), Beijing: Zhongyang wenxian chubanshe, 1987–1992, 8 vols.

Zhou Enlai, *Zhou Enlai xuanji* (Selected Works of Zhou Enlai), Beijing: renmin chubanshe, 1980.

———, *Zhou Enlai shuxinji* (Selected Letters of Zhou Enlai), Beijing: Zhongyang wenxian chubanshe, 1988.

Zhu, De, *Zhu De xuanji* (Selected Works of Zhu De), Beijing: renmin chubanshe, 1983.

Contemporary Newspapers

Jiefang (Liberation, a weekly), Yan'an, 1939–1941.
Jiefang ribao (Liberation Daily), Yan'an, 1941–1947.

Qunzhong (the Masses), Chongqing, Shanghai, Hong Kong, 1937–1949.

Renmin ribao (People's Daily), 1947–1949. (In this period, this was the official organ of the Jin-ji-lu-yu Liberated Area. After the fall of Yan'an in March 1947, this paper carried much of the news transmitted from northern Shaanxi where the Party Center and the New China News Agency were officially located.)

Xinhua ribao (New China Daily), Chongqing, Nanjing, 1938–1947.

Xinzhonghua (New China Semimonthly), Shanghai, Hong Kong, 1946–1947.

Zhengbao (Righteousness, a weekly), Shanghai, Hong Kong, 1946–1948.

Memoirs, Biographies, and Chronologies

Bo, Yibo, *Ruogang zhongda jueze yu shijian de huigu* (Recollection on Several Important Policies and Events), Beijing: Zhongyang wenxian chubanshe, 1991.

Cheng, Zihua, *Cheng Zihua huiyilu* (Cheng Zihua Memoirs), Beijing: Jiefangjun chubanshe, 1987.

Deng, Liqun, "Xinjiang heping jiefang qianhou—zhongsu guanxi zhi yiye" (The Peaceful Liberation of Xinjiang—A Page in the Sino-Soviet Relations), *Jindaishi yenjiu*, 1989, no. 5, pp. 143–150.

Ding, Xiaochun, *Dongbei jiefang zhanzheng dashiji* (The Chronology of the Liberation War in the Northeast), Beijing: Zhonggong dangshi ziliao chubanshe, 1987.

He, Changgong, *He Changgong huiyilu* (He Changgong Memoirs), Beijing: Jiefangjun chubanshe, 1987.

Hong, Xuezhi, *Kangmei yuanchao zhangzhen huiyi* (Recollections on the War of Resisting the U.S. and Assisting Korea), Beijing: Jiefangjun wenyi chubanshe, 1991.

Huang, Kecheng, "Cong subei dao dongbei" (From Northern Jiangsu to the Northeast), *Zhonggong dangshi ziliao*, vol. 16, Beijing: Zhonggong dangshi ziliao chubanshe, 1985, pp. 56–81.

Huang, Hua, "Nanjing jiefang chuqi wo tong Stuart de jici jiechu" (My Several Contacts with John L. Stuart after the Liberation of Nanjing), *Xinzhongguo waijiao fengyun* (Diplomatic Events of New China), ed. Foreign Ministry, Diplomatic History Office, Beijing: Shijie zishi chubanshe, 1990, pp. 22–31.

Jin, Cheng, "Yi zhongwai jizhe canguantuan fangwen Yan'an" (Recollection on the Visit of Chinese and Foreign Reporters to Yan'an), *Zhonggong dangshi ziliao* (Materials on CCP History), v. 27, Beijing: Zhonggong dangshi ziliao chubanshe, 1988, pp. 72–94.

Junshi kexueyuan (Military Academy), ed. *Zhongguo renmin jiefangjun dashiji, 1927–82* (The Chronology of the PLA, 1927–82), Beijing: Junshi kexue chubanshe, 1983.

Kang, Maozao, "Yingjian 'zishiying' hao shijian" (The "Amethyst Gunboat Incident"), *Xinzhongguo waijiao fengyunlu*, pp. 33–47.

Liu, Xiao, "Chushi sulian" (Mission to the Soviet Union), *Shijie zhishi* (The World Knowledge), 1987, nos. 3–18.

Lu, Zhengcao, *Lu Zhengcao huiyilu* (Lu's Memoirs), Beijing: Jiefangjun chubanshe, 1987.

Luo Ronghuan zhuan bianxiezhu (Editing Group of the Biography of Luo Ronghuan), "Luo Ronghuan tongzhi tan dongbei jiefang zhanzheng" (Luo Ronghuan Talks about the Liberation War in the Northeast), *Junshi shilin* (Military History Magazine), 1988, no. 4, pp. 22–26.

Nie, Rongzhen, *Nie Rongzhen huiyilu* (Nie Rongzhen's Memoirs), Beijing: Jiefangjun chubanshe, 1984.

Peng, Dehuai, "Kangri shiqi dihou zuozhan zhidao yuanze" (The Principles of Military Conduct Behind the Enemy Line During the War of Resistance, June 1963), *Wenxian he yanjiu*, 1987, no. 5, pp. 14–19.

———, *Peng Dehuai zishu* (Peng Dehuai's Memoirs), Beijing: renmin chubanshe, 1981.

Peng, Shilu, "zai dongbei kangri lianjun de yiduan huiyi: sulian beiyeying de wunian" (Recollections on the Manchurian Anti-Japanese Union Army: About the Five Years in the USSR's Northern Camp), *Junshi ziliao*, 1984, no. 2, pp. 60–91.

Shi, Zhe, "Peitong Mao zhuxi fangsu" (Accompanying Chairman Mao to Visit the Soviet Union), *Renwu*, 1988, no. 5, pp. 5–21.

———, "Mao Zedong zhuxi diyici fangwen sulian jingguo" (Chairman Mao's First Journey to the USSR), *Xinzhongguo waijiao fengyun* (New China's Diplomatic Events), ed. Diplomatic History Office, Foreign Ministry of the PRC, Beijing: Shijie zhishi chubanshe, 1990, pp. 3–9.

———, "Mao Zedong zai Xibopo huijian Mikoyan" (Mao Meets Mikoyan in Xibopo), *Dangde wenxian*, 1991, no. 6, pp. 34–41.

———, *Zai lishi juren shenbian: She Zhe huiyilu* (Besides the Historical Heroes: She Zhe Memoirs), Beijing: zhongyang wenxian chubanshe, 1991.

Waijiaobu, Waijiaoshi bianjishe (Foreign Ministry, Diplomatic History Office), ed. *Xinzhongguo waijiao fengyun* (Diplomatic Events of New China), Beijing: Shijie zhishi chubanshe, 1990.

———, *Yanjiu Zhou Enlai* (Study Zhou Enlai), Beijing: Shijie zhishi chubanshe, 1989.

Wang, Mingui, "Dongbei kanglian renyuan qu sulian zhengxun de jingli" (The Experience of the Northeast Resistance Alliance Members in the Soviet Union), *Junshi ziliao* (Military History Materials), 1985, no. 7, pp. 34–39.

Wu, Xiuquan, "Wo de waijiao shengya" (My Diplomatic Career), *Chunqiu* (Autumn and Spring, Wuhan), 1987, no. 3, pp. 4–9.

———, *Huiyi yu huainian* (Reflections and Remembrance), Beijing: 1991.

Xiao, Jingguang, *Xiao Jingguang huiyilu* (Xiao Jingguang's Memoirs), Beijing: Jiefangjun chubanshe (The PLA Publishers), 1987.

Xu, Xiangqian, *Lishi de huigu* (Historical Reminiscences), Beijing: Jiefangjun chubanshe, 1985.

Ye, Fei, *Ye Fei huiyilu* (Ye Fei Memoirs), Shanghai: Shanghai renmin chubanshe, 1988.

Zeng, Kelin, "Dadi chongguang: you guan jinjun dongbei de huiyi" (Recovery: Recollections of Marching into the Northeast), *Renwu*, 1984, no. 5, pp. 73–82.

Zhang, Guotao, *Wode huiyi* (My Recollections), Hong Kong: Mingbao cubanshe, 1971.

Zhang, Wenjin, "Zhou Enlai yu Marshall shihua" (Zhou Enlai and the Marshall Mission), *Zhou Enlai yanjiu xueshu taolunhui lunwenji* (Collection of Articles Presented at the Conference on Zhou Enlai Studies), Beijing: Zhongyang wenxian chubanshe, 1988, pp. 259–72.

Zhong, Xidong, "Boqu meijun de huapi" (Unmask the U.S. Troops), *Jiefang zhanzheng huiyilu* (Recollections on the Liberation War), Beijing: Qingnian chubanshe, 1961, pp. 43–54.

Zhonggong Shanghai Shiwei dangshi ziliao zhenji weiyuanhui (The CCP Shangahi

Municipal Committee, the Committee for Collecting Party History Materials), ed. *Zhonggong Shanghai dangshi dashiji* (The Chronology of the CCP in Shanghai, 1919–49), Shanghai: Zhishi chubanshe, 1988.

Zhonggong zhongyang dangshi ziliao zhenji weiyuanhui (The Committee on Collecting Party History Materials, the CCP Central Committee), "Huiyi dongbei jiefang zhanzheng qijian dongbeiju zhu beichaoxian banshichu" (Recollection on the Branch of the Northeast Bureau in North Korea During the Liberation War in the Northeast), *Zhonggong dangshi ziliao*, vol. 17, Beijing: Zhonggong dangshi ziliao chubanshe, 1986.

Zhonggong zhongyang wenxian yanjiushi (The Archival Research Office of the Central Committee of the CCP), *Zhou Enlai nianpu* (Chronology of Zhou Enlai), Beijing: renmin chubanshe, 1989.

———, *Mao Zedong nianpu* (Chronology of Mao Zedong), Beijing: Renmin chubanshe, 1993.

———, chief ed. Jin Chongji, *Zhou Enlai zhuan* (Biography of Zhou Enlai), Beijing: renmin chubanshe & Zhongyang wenxian chubanshe, 1989.

Zuo, Ling, *Huang Kecheng dajiang* (General Huang Kecheng), Henan: Haiyan chubanshe, 1987.

Books and Articles

Cao, Zhongbing, *Wang Ming Zhuan* (Biography of Wang Ming), Changchun: Wenshi chubanshe, 1991.

Chen, Guangxiang, "Po Gu yu nanfang hongjun youjidui de gaibian" (Po Gu and the Reorganization of the Red Army Guerrilla in the South), *Dangshi yanjiu yu jiaoxue*, 1990, no. 3, pp. 23–28.

Chen, Tiejian, "Lun xilujun" (On the Western Expedition Army), *Lishi yanjiu*, 1987, no. 2, pp. 3–15.

Deng, Lifeng, *Xinzhongguo junshi huodong jishi* (Historical Records on New China's Military Activities), Beijing: zhonggong dangshi ziliao chubanshe, 1989.

He, Di, "Kangri zhanzheng houqi meiguo duihua zhengce de yanbian" (The Evolution of U.S. China Policy in the Later Period of the War of Resistance), *Jindaishi yanjiu*, 1981, no. 4.

———, "1945–1949 nian zhongguo gongchandang duimei zhengce de yanbian" (The Evolution of the CCP's U.S. Policy in 1945–49), *Lishi yanjiu*, 1987, no. 3, pp. 15–23.

Hua, Jun, "Shilun sanwei yiti yu xi'an shibian" (The Trinity [of the Red Army, the Northeast Army, and the Northwest Army] in the Xi'an Incident), *Shehui kexue*, 1990, no. 1, pp. 84–87.

Huang, Qijun, "Zhonggong zhongyang zai 1935 zhi 1936 nianjian yu gongchan guoji huifu dianxun lianxi de jingguo" (The Process of Restoring Electronic Communication Between the Party Center and the Comintern, 1935–36), *Dangshi yanjiu*, 1987, no. 2.

———, "Wang Jiaxiang 1937 nian qu gongchan guoji de jianyao jingguo" (Brief Account on the Experience of Wang's Trip to the Comintern), *Dangshi yanjiu*, 1987, no. 6, pp. 97–98.

———, "Zhonggong zhu gongchan guoji daibiaotuan yu kangri minzu tongyi zhanxian de xingcheng" (The CCP Delegation to the Comintern and the Formation of the Anti-Japanese National United Front Policy), *Zhonggong dangshi yanjiu*, 1988, no. 3, pp. 3–10.

Huang Xiurong, *Gongchang guoji yu zhongguo gemingshi* (A History of the Comintern-CCP relations), Beijing: Zhongyang dangxiao chubanshe, 1989.

Jin, Yunfang, "Kangri zhanzheng shenglihou zai dongbei wentishang sanguo sifang de guanxi he douzheng" (The Relations and Conflict Among Three Countries [China, the U.S., the USSR] and Four Sides [the CCP, the GMD, the U.S., the USSR] Over the Northeast after the Victory of the War of Resistance), *Zhonggong dangshi ziliao*, vol. 28, 1988, Beijing: Dangshi ziliao chubanshe, 1988, pp. 150–79.

Junshi kexueyuan, junshi lishi yanjiubu (Military History Department), *Zhongguo renmin jiefangjun zhanshi* (A Military History of the PLA), Beijing: Junshi kexue chubanshe, 1987, 3 vols.

Li, Liangzhi, "Kangri minzu tongyi zhanxian xingcheng wenti yanjiu shuping" (Comments on the Question of the Formation of the Anti-Japanese National United Front), *Jiaoxue yu yanjiu* (Teaching and Research), 1986, no. 4, pp. 77–80.

———, "Guanyu Wang Ming dui jianli kangri minzu tongyi zhanxian de zuoyong" (On the Role of Wang Ming in the Establishment of the Anti-Japanese National United Front), *Shixue yuekan*, 1989, no. 2, pp. 64–72.

Liu, Chunkuan, "Yalta xieding yu 1945 nian zhongsu tiaoyue" (The Yalta Protocol and the Sino-Soviet Treaty of 1945), Conference on "Modern China and the World," unpublished manuscript, Beijing, 1990.

Ma, Zhisun, "Hurley laihua yu 1944 nian guogong tanpan" (Hurley's Mission to China and the GMD-CCP Negotiations in 1944), *Wenxian he yanjiu*, 1984, no. 1, pp. 21–27.

Miao, Chuhuang, *Tongyi zhanxian gongzuo* (The United Front Work), Chongqing: Chongqing chubanshe, 1990.

Niu, Jun, "Shilun taipingyang zhanzheng qijian zhongguo gongchandang de duimei zhengce" (The CCP's U.S. Policy During the Pacific War), *Zhongguo renmin jingguan daxue xuebao* (Journal of Chinese People's Police Officers' University), 1986, no. 1.

———, "Hurley yu 1945 nian qianhou de guogong tanpan" (Hurley and the GMD-CCP Negotiations in 1944–45), *Jindaishi yanjiu*, 1986, no. 1, pp. 188–206.

———, "Zhanhou chuqi meisu guogong zai zhongguo dongbei diqu de douzheng" (The Struggle Among the U.S., the USSR, the CCP, and the GMD in the Northeast During the Immediate Postwar Era), *Jindaishi yanjiu*, 1987, no. 1, pp. 217–43.

———, "Qianxi Chongqing tanpan de guoji beijing" (An Analysis of the International Background of the Chongqing Negotiations), *Lishi jiaoxue*, 1986, no. 6, pp. 16–19.

———, "Shilun taipingyang zhanzheng qijian zhongguo gongchandang de duimei zhengce" (On the CCP Policy Toward the U.S. During the Pacific War), *Zhongguo renmin jingguan daxue xuebao* (Journal of the Chinese Police Officers' University), 1986, no. 1, pp. 7–13.

———, "Marshall tiaochu yu dongbei neizhan" (The Marshall Mission and the Civil War in the Northeast), *Zhonggong dangshi yanjiu*, 1989, no. 1, pp. 34–44.

———, *Cong Yan'an zouxiang shijie* (From Yan'an toward the World), Fujian: remin chubanshe, 1992.

Qi, Xuede, "guanyu kangmei yuanchao zhanzheng zhanlue mubiao de tantao" (Analysis of the Strategic Goal of the War of Resistance to the U.S. and Assistance to Korea), *Zhonggong dangshi yanjiu*, 1989, no. 6, pp. 64–67.

Tai, Dong, "Feng Shaobai sijin Shanghai" (Feng Shaobai's Four Missions in Shanghai), *Renwu*, 1987, no. 6, pp. 41–48.

Tao, Wenzhao, "Lun jianguo qianhou zhonggong 'yibiandao' fangzhen de lishi biranxing" (On the Historical Inevitability of the CCP's "Lean-to-one-side" Policy on the Eve of the Proclamation of the PRC), Conference on "Modern China and the World," unpublished manuscript, Beijing, 1990.

———, "Dui 'Hurley jieshou zhonggong wudian jianyi xiyi' de shangque" (A Comment on the Article of "An Analysis of Hurley's Acceptance of the CCP's Five-Point Proposal"), *Jindaishi yanjiu*, 1989, no. 6, pp. 251–54.

Wang, Dinglei, *Tangdai zhongguo kongjun* (Modern Chinese Air Force), Beijing: Shehui kexue chubanshe, 1989.

Wang, Gongan and Mao Lei, *Guogong liangdang guanxishi* (A History of the CCP-GMD Relations), Wuhan: Wuhan chubanshe, 1988.

Wang, Hong, "Lun wannan shibian qianhou zhonggong zhongyang dui shiju de panduan" (The CCP Center's Analysis on the Situation Before and After the New Fourth Army Incident), *Jindaishi yanjiu*, 1990, no. 5, pp. 199–207.

Wang, Jianmin, *Zhongguo gongchandang shigao* (Draft History of the CCP), Hong Kong: Zhongwen tushu, 1974, 3 vols.

Wei, Xia, "Guanyu nanfangju jige wenti de bianxi" (Analysis of Several Issues Regarding the Southern Bureau of the CCP), *Zhonggong dangshi yanjiu*, 1990, no. 5, pp. 60–65.

Wen, Zhonghao, "Shixi xinzhongguo chengli qianhou zhonggong duimei zhengce" (On the CCP's Policy Toward the U.S. Before and After the Proclamation of the New China), Second Conference on Sino-American Relations, unpublished manuscript, Nanjing, 1988.

Wu, Jingping, "Meiguo yu 1945 nian de zhongsu huitan" (The U.S. and the Sino-Soviet Negotiations in 1945), *Lishi yanjiu*, 1990, no. 1, pp. 176–90.

Xiang-qing, *Gongchan guoji he zhongguo geming guanxi shigao* (A Draft History of Comintern-Chinese Relations), Beijing: Beijing daxue chubanshe (Beijing University Press), 1988.

Xie, Wen, "Lun zhongguo gongchandang zhengque chuli yu gongchan guoji guanxi de lishi jinyan" (On the Experience of the CCP's Correct Handling of Its Relations with the Comintern), *Jindaishi yanjiu*, 1988, no. 4, pp. 244–59.

Xu, Zehao, "Wang Jiaxiang dui liujie liuzhong quanhui de gongxian" (Wang Jiaxiang's Contribution to the Sixth Plenum of the Sixth Session), *Wenxian he yanjiu* (Archives and Research), 1986, no. 4. pp. 34–39.

Xu, Yan, "Kangri zhanzheng shengli qianxi zhi shenglihou wodang zhanlue fangzheng de zhuanbian" (The Shift of Our Party's Strategy Before and After the Victory of the War of Resistance), *Dangshi yanjiu ziliao*, v. 7, Sichuan: renmin chubanshe, 1987, pp. 231–49.

———, "Kangri zhanzheng zhong liangge zhanchang de xingcheng jiqi xianghu guanxi" (The Formation of the Two Theaters of War and Their Mutual Relations in the War of Resistance), *Jindaishi yanjiu*, 1986, no. 4, pp. 102–20.

———, "Zhanhou meisu duihua zhengce he zhongguo gongchandang jinjun dongbei fangzhen de bianhua" (The U.S. and the USSR Postwar Policies Toward China and the Changes in the CCP's Policy in the Northeast), *Lishi jiaoxue*, 1988, no. 12, pp. 21–24.

———, "'Rangkai dalu, zhanling liangxiang' shi jiefang quandongbei de biyu shilu" ("Retreat from the Major Path, Occupy Two Flanks" Is the Only Way to Liberate the Whole Northeast), *Wenxian he yanjiu*, 1987, no. 5, pp. 37–39.

———, "Chubing ruchao canzhan juce zuihou queding de quzhe guocheng" (The Tortuous Process toward the Final Decision to Enter the Korean War), *Dangshi yanjiu ziliao*, 1991, no. 4, pp. 7–13.

Yang, Kuisong, "Kangzhan shiqi gongchan guoji, sulian, yu zhongguo gongchandang guanxi zhongde jige wenti" (Issues in the Relations Between the Comintern, the USSR, and the CCP in the Period of the War of Resistance), *Dangshi yanjiu*, 1987, no. 6, pp. 132–49.

———, "Dierci guogong hezuo de xingcheng" (The Formation of the Second GMD-CCP Cooperation), *Jindaishi yanjiu*, 1985, no. 3, pp. 60–89.

———, "Sanshi niandai gongchan guoji, sulian he zhongguo geming guanxi ruogan shishi kaobian" (To Ascertain Some Historical Events Regarding Relations Among the Comintern, the USSR, and the Chinese Revolution), *Dangshi yanjiu*, 1987, no. 2.

———, "Kangri zhanzheng baofahou zhongguo gongchandang duiri junshi zhanlue fangzhen de yanbian" (The Evolution of the CCP Military Strategy After the Outbreak of the War of Resistance), *Jindaishi yanjiu*, 1988, no. 2, pp. 105–27.

———, "Wang Ming zai kangri minzu tongyi zhanxian celue fangzhen xingcheng guocheng zhongde zuoyong" (Wang Ming's Role in the Process of Formulating the Policy of the Anti-Japanese National United Front), *Jindaishi yanjiu*, 1989, no. 1, pp. 199–219.

———, "Guanyu gongchan guoji yu zhongguo gongchandang 'liang-Jiang kangri' fangzhen de guanxi wenti" (On the Relations of the Comintern and the CCP's Policy of United Front with Jiang to Resist Japan), *Zhonggong dangshi yanjiu*, 1989, no. 4, pp. 51–59.

———, "Guanyu 1936 nian guogong liangdang mimi jiechu jingguo de jige wenti" (Questions Regarding the GMD-CCP Secret Contacts in 1936), *Jindaishi yanjiu*, 1990, no.1, pp. 244–65.

———, "1946 nian guogong liangdang douzheng yu Marshall tiaochu" (The GMD-CCP Struggle and Marshall Mediation in 1946), *Lishi yanjiu*, 1990, no. 5, pp. 52–67.

———, "Zhongguo gongchangdang dequ dongbei de zhanlu yanbian yu sulian" (The Soviet Union and the Evolution of the CCP's Strategy of Seizing the Northeast), *Zhonggong dangshi yanjiu*, 1990, additional issue.

———, *Makesi zhuyi zhongguohua de lishi jingcheng* (The Historical Process of Sinicizing Marxism), Henan: Renmin chubanshe, 1994.

———, *Zhongjian dedai de geming* (Revolution in the Middle Zone), Beijing: Zhongyang dangxiao chubanshe, 1992.

———, "Sulian daguimo yuanzhu zhongguo hongjun de yici changshi" (The Soviet Attempt to Deliver Massive aid to the Chinese Red Army), *Jindaishi yanjiu*, 1995, no. 1, pp. 245–75.

———, and Yang Yunruo, *Gongchang guoji he zhongguo geming* (The Comintern and Chinese Revolution), Shanghai: Renmin chubanshe, 1988.

Yang, Kuoqing and Bai Run, *Luo Ronghuan zai dongbei jiefang zhanzheng zhong* (Luo

Ronghuan in the Liberation War in the Northeast), Beijing: Jiefangjun chubanshe, 1986.

Yang, Zhongmei, *Zunyi huiyi yu Yan'an zhengfeng* (The Zunyi Conference and the Yan'an Rectification), Hong Kong: Bengma chubanshe, 1989.

Yuan, Wei, *Zhongguo renmin jiefangjun wuda yezhan budui fazhan shilue* (A History of the Development of the Five Major Field Armies of the PLA), Beijing: Jiefangjun chubanshe, 1987.

Zhang, Baijia, "Yingxiang zhonggong duimei zhengce de sange yinsu, 1945–46" (Three Elements Influencing the Changing of the CCP Policy Toward the U.S., 1945–46), Conference on "Modern China and the World," unpublished manuscript, Beijing, 1990.

Zhang, Kuitang, "Zhonggong zhongyang heping jieju Xi'an shibian fangzhen de ziding" (The Formation of the CCP Center's Policy of Peaceful Solution to the Xi'an Incident), *Jindaishi yanjiu*, no. 2, 1991, pp. 243–55.

Zhang, Yimin, "Kangzhan shengli qianhou wodang zhanlue fangzheng de zhuanbian" (The Shift of Our Party's Strategy Before and After the Victory of the War of Resistance), *Dangshi yanjiu*, 1984, no. 1.

Zhao, Shude, "Zhonggong zhongyang guanyu kaipi wuling kangri minzhu gengjudi de zhanlue jueche de yanbian" (The Evolution of the Party Center's Strategy on Opening up the Wuling Base Area in the War of Resistance), *Dangshi yanjiu*, 1986, no. 4, pp. 49–56.

Zhonggong dangshi yanjiuhui (The CCP history research association), ed. *Kangri minzu tongyi zhanxian yu dierci guogong hezuo* (The Anti-Japanese National United Front and the Second GMD-CCP Cooperation), Beijing: Zhongguo wenshi chubanshe, 1987.

Zhongyang dang'anguan dangshi ziliao yanjiushe (The CCP Central Archives, Research Office of Party Historical Materials), "Yan'an zhengfeng zhongde Wang Ming" (Wang Ming in the Yan'an Rectification Movement), *Dangshi tongxun* (Newsletter on the Party History), 1984, no. 7, pp. 6–13.

Zhu, Peimin, "Xinjiang heping jiefang shimu" (The Peaceful Liberation of Xinjiang), *Kashi shifang xueyuan xuebao* (Journal of Kashi Teachers' College), 1989, no. 4, pp. 10–21.

Zhu, Yuanshi, "Liu Shaoqi yu kangzhan jieshuhou zhengduo dongbei de douzheng" (Liu Shaoqi and the Struggle Over the Northeast After the End of the War of Resistance), *Jindaishi yanjiu*, 1988, no. 5, pp. 124–45.

Russian Materials in Chinese or English

Borisov, O. B., *From the History of Soviet-Chinese Relations in the 1950s*, Moscow: Progress Publishers, 1982.

——, *The Soviet Union and the Manchurian Revolutionary Base, 1945–1949*, Moscow: Progress Publishers, 1975.

Borisov, O. B., and B. T. Koloskov, *Soviet-Chinese Relations, 1945–1970*, ed. Vladimir Petrov, Bloomington: Indiana University Press, 1975.

Communist International (Ma, Guifan, trans.), "Suliang xinfabiao de gongchan guoji youguan zhongguo geming de dang'an wenjian"(The Comintern Documents on the Chinese Revolution Newly Released in the Soviet Union), *Zhonggong dangshi yan-*

jiu, 1988, nos. 1, 2, 3. (There are 21 pieces of Comintern documents which are released for the first time in the USSR in 1986.)

Dimitrov, Georgii, "Dimitrov zhi Mao Zedong dian, 4 January 1941" (Dimitrov's Telegram to Mao), *Zhonggong dangshi yanjiu*, 1988, no. 3, pp. 87–88.

————, "Dimitrov gei Mao Zedong de xin, 15 June 1942" (Dimitrov's Letter to Mao), *Zhonggong dangshi yanjiu*, 1988, no. 3, p. 88.

————, "Dimitrov jiu zhonggong dangnei zhuangkuang gei Mao Zedong de xin, 22 December 1943" (Dimitrov's Letter to Mao on the Inner-party Situation of the CCP), *Zhonggong dangshi yanjiu*, 1988, no. 3, pp. 88, 61.

Fedorenko, N. T., "The Stalin-Mao Summit in Moscow," *Far Eastern Affairs* (Moscow), no. 2, 1989, pp. 134–48.

Goncharov, S. N., "Stalin's Dialogue with Mao Zedong, Interview with I. V. Kovalev," *Journal of Northeast Asian Studies*, Winter 1991, pp. 44–76.

Stalin, Josoph, "Stalin to Mao Zedong," 10, 11, 14, 15 January 1949, "Mao Zedong to Stalin," 13, 14 January 1949, Archives of the President of the Russian Federation, f.45, op.1, d. 330, pp. 95–105, *Bulletin*, Cold War International History Project, Woodrow Wilson Center, Issue 6–7, Winter 1995/96, pp. 27–29.

Vladimirov, Peter, *The Vladimirov Diaries, Yenan, China: 1942–1945*, New York: Doubleday, 1975.

Yudin, P. F., "Transcript of the Conversation with Comrade Mao, 31 May 1956," *Far Eastern Affairs*, no. 4–5, 1994, pp. 134–44.

English-Language Materials

Unpublished U.S. Archival Sources

Army Intelligence Document Files, RG 286, General Archives Division, Washington National Records Center (WNRC), Suitland, MD.

Dixie Mission Papers, Modern Military Records Division, National Archives, Washington, D.C.

Foreign Service Post Files, China, RG 84, General Archives Division, WNRC, Suitland, MD.

Office of Strategic Services (OSS) Research and Analysis Reports, Modern Military Records Division, National Archives, Washington, D.C.

OSS/State Department Reports, microfilm, National Archives, Washington, D.C.

State Department Records, Decimal File, RG 59, National Archives, Washington, D.C.

State Department, Records of the Office of Chinese Affairs, 1945–1950, RG 59, Lot 56D151, National Archives, Washington, D.C.

Published U.S. Government Documents

U.S. Congress, House, Committee on Foreign Affairs, *Hearings on Emergency Foreign Aid*, 80th Cong., 1st sess., 1947.

U.S. Congress, House, Committee on Foreign Affairs, *Hearings: Military Assistance Act of 1949*, 80th Cong., 1949.

U.S. Congress, Joint Committee on the Economic Cooperation Administration, *Report Concerning China*, 80th Cong., 2nd sess., December 1949.

U.S. Congress, Senate, Committee on Foreign Relations, *Economic Assistance to China and Korea: 1949–1950*, Washington, D.C.: Government Printing Office, 1947.

U.S. Congress, Senate, Committee on Foreign Relations, *Reviews of the World Situation: 1949–1950*, Hearings in Executive Session, 81st Cong., 1st, 2nd sess., Washington, D.C.: Government Printing Office, 1974.

U.S. Congress, Senate, Committee on Foreign Relations and Armed Services, *Hearings: Military Situation in the Far East*, 82nd Cong., 1st sess., 1951.

U.S. Congress, Senate, Committee on the Judiciary, *The Amerasia Papers: A Clue to the Catastrophe of China*, 91st Cong., 1st sess., Washington, D.C.: Government Printing Office, 1970.

U.S. Congress, Senate, *Hearing Before the Committee on Foreign Relations*, 92nd Cong., 1st sess., July 21, 1971, Washington, D.C.: Government Printing Office, 1972.

U.S. State Department, *The China White Paper, August 1949*, republished by Stanford University Press, 1969.

U.S. State Department, *Foreign Relations of the United States*, 1942, China; 1943, China; 1944, v. 6, The Far East: China; 1945, v. 7, The Far East: China; 1946, v. 9 & 10, The Far East: China; 1947, v. 7, The Far East: China; 1948, v. 7 & 8, The Far East: China; 1949, v. 8 & 9, the Far East: China; 1950, v. 6, East Asia and the Pacific; v. 7, Korea, Washington, D.C.: Government Printing Office, 1965–78.

U.S. State Department, *Transcript of the Round Table Discussion on American Policy Toward China*, 6, 7, 8 October 1949, Washington, D.C.: Government Printing Office, 1949.

U.S. War Department, *The Chinese Communist Movement: A Report of the United States War Department, July 1945*, ed. L. P. Van Slyke, Stanford: Stanford University Press, 1967.

Memoirs and Contemporaries' Writings

Acheson, Dean, *Present at the Creation: My Years in the State Department*, New York: W. W. Norton & Company, 1969.

———, "American Policy Toward China." *Department of State Bulletin*, 24:963–74.

———, "Crisis in Asia—An Examination of United States Policy." *Department of State Bulletin*, 22:111–18.

Esherick, Joseph W., ed., *Lost Chance in China: The World War II Despatches of John Service*, New York: Random House, 1974.

Mao, Tse-tung, *Selected Works of Mao Tse-tung*, Peking: Foreign Languages Press, 1966–68.

Schram, Stuart, ed., *Mao's Road to Power: Revolutionary Writings, 1912–1920*, New York: M. E. Sharpe, 1992.

Stuart, John Leighton, *Fifty Years in China*, New York: Random House, 1954.

Books and Articles

Armstrong, J. D., *Revolutionary Diplomacy: Chinese Foreign Policy and the United Front Doctrine*, Berkeley: California Univ. Press, 1977.

Ashley, Richard, "The Poverty of Neorealism," *International Organization*, v. 38, no. 2, 1984, pp. 225–86.

Barrett, David, *Dixie Mission: The United States Army Observer Group in Yenan, 1944*, Berkeley: University of California Press, 1970.

Beal, John Robinson, *Marshall in China*, Toronto: Doubleday & Company, 1970.

Benton, Gregor, "The 'Second Wang Ming Line,' 1935–1938," *China Quarterly*, v. 61, pp. 61–94.

Bloom, William, *Personal Identity, National Identity, and International Relations*, Cambridge: Cambridge University Press, 1990.

Borg, Dorothy, and Waldo Heinrichs, eds., *Uncertain Years: Chinese-American Relations, 1947–1950*, New York: Columbia University Press, 1980.

Chang, Gordon H., *Friends and Enemies: The United States, China, and the Soviet Union, 1948–1972*, Stanford: Stanford University Press, 1990.

Chang, Kia-ngau, *Last Chance in Manchuria: The Diary of Chang Kia-ngau*, trans. Dolores Zen, Stanford: Hoover Institution Press, 1989.

Chen, Jerome, "The Chinese Communist Movement to 1927," *Cambridge History of China*, v. 12, Cambridge University Press, 1983, pp. 505–26.

———, "The Communist Movement, 1927–1937," *Cambridge History of China*, v. 13, Cambridge University Press, 1986, pp. 168–229.

Chen, Jian, "China's Changing Aims During the Korean War, 1950–1951," *The Journal of American-East Asian Relations*, vol. 1, no. 1, pp. 8–41.

———, *China's Road to the Korean War: The Making of the Sino-American Confrontation*, New York: Columbia University Press, 1994.

Chen, Yung-fa, *Making Revolution: The Communist Movement in Eastern and Central China, 1937–1945*, Berkeley: University of California Press, 1986.

Chiang, Kai-shek, *Soviet Russia in China*, New York: Farrar, Straus & Giroux, 1965.

Chou En-lai, *Selected Works of Chou En-lai*, Peking: Foreign Languages Press, 1980.

Clubb, O. Edmund, "Chinese Communist Strategy in Foreign Relations," *Annals of the American Academy of Political and Social Science*, 1951, 277:156–66.

———, "Titoism and the Chinese Communist Regime: An American View," *The World Today*, 1952, 8:521–31.

———, *China and Russia: The Great Game*, New York: Columbia Univ. Press, 1971.

Cohen, Paul A., *Discovering History in China: American Historical Writing on the Recent Chinese Past*, New York: Columbia University Press, 1984.

Cohen, Warren, "American Observers and the Sino-Soviet Friendship Treaty of August, 1945," *Pacific Historical Review*, 1966, 35:347–49.

———, *America's Response to China: A History of Sino-American Relations*, 3rd ed., New York: Columbia University Press, 1990.

———, ed. *New Frontiers in American-East Asian Relations*, New York: Columbia University Press, 1983.

———, "The Development of Chinese Communist Policy Toward the United States, 1922–1933," *Orbis*, v. 11, pp. 219–37.

———, "The Development of Chinese Communist Policy Toward the United States, 1934–1945," *Orbis*, v. 11, pp. 551–69.

———, "Research Note, Conversation with Chinese Friends: Zhou Enlai's Associates Reflect on Chinese-American Relations in the 1940s and the Korean War," *Diplomatic History*, 1987, pp. 283–89.

Davies, John, *Dragon by the Tail: American, British, Japanese, and Russian Encounters with China and One Another*, New York: Norton, 1972.

Erikson, Erik H., *Identity, Youth, and Crisis*, London: W. W. Norton, 1968.

———, *The Life Cycle Completed*, London: W. W. Norton, 1982.

Fairbank, John King, "Introduction: Maritime and Continental in China's History," *Cambridge History of China*, Cambridge University Press, v. 12, pp. 1–27.

Feis, Herbert, *The China Tangle*, New Jersey: Princeton University Press, 1953.

Fitzgerald, C. P., "The Nationless State: The Search for a Nation in Modern Chinese Nationalism," *Australian Journal of Chinese Affairs*, no. 33, 1995, pp. 75–106.

Garver, John W., *Chinese-Soviet Relations, 1937–1945: The Diplomacy of Chinese Nationalism*, New York: Oxford University Press, 1988.

———, "The Origins of the Second United Front: The Comintern and the Chinese Communist Party," *China Quarterly*, v. 113, March 1988, pp. 29–59.

———, "The Soviet Union and the Xi'an Incident," *Australian Journal of Chinese Affairs*, no. 26, July 1991, pp. 145–75.

Gati, Charles, ed., *Caging the Bear: Containment and the Cold War*, Indianapolis: Bobbs-Merrill, 1974.

Gittings, John, "New Light on Mao: His View of the World," *China Quarterly*, no. 60 (1974).

———, *The World and China, 1922–1972*, London: Eyre Methuen, 1974.

Goncharov, Sergei, John Lewis, and Xue Litai, *Uncertain Partners: Stalin, Mao, and the Korean War*, Stanford: Stanford University Press, 1993.

Greenfeld, Liah, *Nationalism: Five Roads to Modernity*, Cambridge, Mass.: Harvard University Press, 1992.

Harding, Harry, and Yuan Ming, eds., *Sino-American Relations, 1945–1955: A Joint Reassessment of a Critical Decade*, Wilmington: Scholarly Resources Books, 1989.

Hsueh, Chun-tu, ed., *Dimensions of China's Foreign Relations*, New York: Praeger Publishers, 1977.

Hunt, Michael, *The Genesis of Chinese Communist Foreign Policy*, New York: Columbia University Press, 1996.

Hunt, Michael, and Odd A. Westad, "The Chinese Communist Party and International Affairs: A Field Report on New Historical Sources and Old Research Problems," *China Quarterly*, v. 122, June 1990, pp. 258–72.

Iriye, Akira, "Was There A Cold War in Asia?" John Chay, ed., *The Problems and Prospects of American-East Asian Relations*, Boulder, Colo.: Westview Press, 1978, pp. 3–26.

———, *Across the Pacific: An Inner History of American-East Asian Relations*, New York: Harcourt, Brace & World, 1967.

———, *China and Japan in the Global Setting*, Cambridge, Mass., Harvard University Press, 1992.

Israel, Jerry. "Mao's Mr. America: Edgar Snow's Images of China." *Pacific Historical Review*, Feb. 1978, 47:107–22.

Kataoka, Tetsuya, *Resistance and Revolution in China*, Berkeley: University of California Press, 1974.

Kedaurie, E., *Nationalism*, 4th ed., Oxford: Blackwell, 1993.

Keith, Robert, *The Diplomacy of Zhou Enlai*, Macmillan, 1989.

Kubek, Anthony, *How the Far East Was Lost: American Policy and the Creation of Communist China*, Chicago: Henry Regnery, 1963.

Levine, Steven, *Anvil of Victory: The Communist Revolution in Manchuria, 1945–1948*, New York: Columbia University Press, 1987.

Levine, Steven, "A New Look at American Mediation in the Chinese Civil War: The Marshall Mission and Manchuria," *Diplomatic History*, 1979, no. 3, pp. 349–75.

———, "If My Grandmother Had Wheels She'd Be a Trolley, or Reflections on the 'Lost Chance in China.'" *Contemporary China*, Dec. 1976, 1:31–32.

———, "On the Brink of Disaster: China and the United States in 1945," *Sino-American Relations, 1945–1955*, ed. Harry Harding and Yuan Ming, Wilmington: Scholarly Resources, 1989, pp. 3–13.

Macdonald, Douglas, "Communist Bloc Expansion in the Early Cold War," *International Security*, vol. 20, no. 3, pp. 152–88.

Mao Tse-tung, *Selected Works of Mao Tse-tung*, Peking: Foreign Languages Press, 1965–1977, 5 vols.

Martin, Edwin W., *Divided Counsel: The Anglo-American Response to Communist Victory in China*, Kentucky: The University Press of Kentucky, 1986.

———, "The Chou Demarche: Did the U.S. and Britain Miss a Chance to Change Postwar History in Asia?" *Foreign Service Journal*, November 1981, pp. 13–16.

May, Ernest R., and James C. Thomson, Jr., eds., *American-East Asian Relations: A Survey*, Cambridge: Harvard University Press, 1972.

McCagg, William O., Jr., *Stalin Embattled, 1943–1948*, Detroit: Wayne State University Press, 1978.

McLane, Charles B., *Soviet Policy and the Chinese Communists, 1931-1946*, New York: Columbia University Press, 1958.

McLean, David, "American Nationalism, the China Myth, and the Truman Doctrine: The Question of Accommodation with Peking, 1949–1950," *Diplomatic History*, v. 10, 1986, pp. 25–42.

Messer, Robert L., "Paths Not Taken: The United States Department of State and Alternatives to Containment, 1945–46," *Diplomatic History*, Fall 1977, 1:297–319.

Murray, Brian, "Stalin, the Cold War, and the Division of China," Working Paper no. 2, Cold War International History Project, The Woodrow Wilson Center.

Nagai, Yonosuke, and Akira Iriye, eds., *The Origins of the Cold War in Asia*, New York: Columbia University Press, 1977.

Ng-Quinn, Michael, "Ideology and the Origins of Mutual Hostility in U.S.-China Relations: The 1940s in Retrospect," *Asian Thought & Society*, v. 5, no. 30, November 1985, pp. 165–78.

North, Robert C., *Moscow and the Chinese Communists*, Stanford: Stanford University Press, 1965.

———, ed., *The Foreign Relations of China*, 3rd ed., North Scituate, Mass.: Duxbury Press, 1978.

———, *M.N. Roy's Mission to China*, Berkeley: University of California Press, 1963.

Oksenberg, Michael, and Robert Oxnam, eds., *Dragon and Eagle: United States-China Relations, Past and Future*, New York: Basic Books, 1978.

Paterson, Thomas G., "If Europe, Why Not China? The Containment Doctrine, 1947–1949," *Prologue*, Spring 1981, 13:19–38.

Pepper, Suzanne, "The Student Movement and the Chinese Civil War, 1945–1949," *China Quarterly*, no. 48 (1971), pp. 726–35.

———, *Civil War in China: The Political Struggle, 1945–1949*, University of California Press, 1978.

Pye, Lucian, "How China's Nationalism was Shanghaied," *Australian Journal of Chinese Affairs*, no. 29, January 1993, pp. 105–33.

Quested, R.K.I., *Sino-Russian Relations: A Short History*, Sydney: George Allen & Unwin, 1984.

Reardon-Anderson, James, *Yenan and the Great Powers: The Origins of Chinese Communist Foreign Policy, 1944–1946*, New York: Columbia University Press, 1980.

———, "The Case For the 'Lost Chance in China.'" *Contemporary China*, Dec. 1976, 1:33–34.

Salisbury, Harrison, *The New Emperors: China in the Era of Mao and Deng*, Boston: Little, Brown, 1992.

Schaller, Michael, *The U.S. Crusade in China, 1938–1945*, New York: Columbia University Press, 1979.

———, *The United States and China in the Twentieth Century*, 2nd ed., New York: Oxford University Press, 1990.

Schram, Stuart, "Mao Tse-tung's Thought to 1949," *Cambridge History of China*, v. 13, part 2, Cambridge University Press, 1986.

———, *The Political Thought of Mao Tse-tung*, New York: Praeger, 1969.

———, ed., *Chairman Mao Talks to the People: Talks and Letters, 1956–1971*, New York: Pantheon Books, 1974.

Schwartz, Benjamin I., *Communism and China: Ideology in Flux*, Cambridge, Mass.: Harvard University Press, 1968.

———, *Chinese Communism and the Rise of Mao*, Cambridge, Mass.: Harvard University Press, 1968.

Service, John, *The Amerasia Papers: Some Problems in the History of U.S.-China Relations*, Berkeley: University of California Press, 1971.

Sheng, Michael M., "Ideology and Foreign Policy: The Chinese Communist Party's Relations with the United States, 1942–1946," M.A. thesis, University of New Brunswick, 1988.

———, "Maoist Dualism and Chinese Communist Foreign Relations, 1935–1950," Ph.D. Dissertation, York University, 1992.

———, "Mao, Stalin, and the Formation of the Anti-Japanese United Front: 1935–1937," *China Quarterly*, no. 129, 1992, pp. 149–70.

———, "America's Lost Chance in China? A Reappraisal of Chinese Communist Policy toward the United States before 1945," *Australian Journal of Chinese Affairs*, no. 29, January 1993, pp. 135–57.

———, "Chinese Communist Policy toward the United States and the Myth of the 'Lost Chance,' 1948–50," *Modern Asian Studies*, vol. 28, no. 3, 1994, pp. 475–502.

———, "Beijing's Decision to Enter the Korean War: A Reappraisal and New Documentation," *Korea and World Affairs*, Summer 1995, pp. 294–313.

Shewmaker, Kenneth E., *Americans and Chinese Communists, 1927–1945*, Ithaca: Cornell University Press, 1971.

Shum, Kui-kwong, *The Chinese Communists' Road to Power: The Anti-Japanese National United Front, 1935–1945*, Hong Kong: Oxford University Press, 1988.

Snow, Edgar, *Red Star Over China*, London: Victor Gollancz Ltd., 1937.

Stuart, John L., *Fifty Years in China: The Memoirs of John Leighton Stuart, Missionary and Ambassador*, New York: Random House, 1954.

Thompson, E. P., *The Poverty of Theory and Other Essays*, New York: Monthly Review Press, 1978.

Tozer, Warren, "Last Bridge to China: The Shanghai Power Company, the Truman Administration and the Chinese Communists," *Diplomatic History* (Winter 1977), 1:64–78.

Tsou, Tang, *America's Failure in China, 1941–1950*, Chicago: University of Chicago Press, 1963.

Tuchman, Barbara W., *Stilwell and the American Experience in China, 1911–1945*, New York: Macmillan, 1972.

———, "If Mao Had Come to Washington," *Foreign Affairs*, v. 51, October 1972, pp. 44–64.

Tucker, Nancy B., "An Unlikely Peace: American Missionaries and the Chinese Communists, 1948–1950," *Pacific Historical Review* (Feb. 1976), no. 45, pp. 97–116.

———, *Patterns in the Dust: Chinese-American Relations and the Recognition Controversy, 1949–1950*, New York: Columbia University Press, 1983.

Van Slyke, Lyman P., *Enemies and Friends: The United Front in Chinese Communist History*, Stanford: Stanford University Press, 1967.

Waldron, Arthur, "Representing China: The Great Wall and Cultural Nationalism," *Cultural Nationalism in East Asia*, ed. H. Befu, Berkeley: Institute of East Asian Studies, 1993.

Wendt, Alexander, "The Agent-Structure Problem in International Relations Theory," *International Organization*, v. 41, no. 3, Summer 1987, pp. 337–70.

Westad, Odd Arne, *Cold War and Revolution*, New York: Columbia University Press, 1993.

Wilbur, Martin, "The Nationalist Revolution: From Canton to Nanking, 1923–1928," *Cambridge History of China*, v. 12, 1983, pp. 527–721.

Zagoria, Donald S., "Mao's Role in the Sino-Soviet Conflict," *Pacific Affairs* (Summer 1974), 47(2):145.

———, "Containment and China," *Caging the Bear*, ed. C. Gati, Indianapolis: Bobbs-Merrill, 1974, pp. 109–27.

Index

MICHAEL M. SHENG is Associate Professor of History at Southwest Missouri State University. He is the author of many articles in *China Quarterly, China Journal, Diplomatic History, Pacific Historical Review*, and *Modern Asian Studies*, on the subject of CCP-Moscow-Washington relations.